HISTORY OF EUROPE 1500-1848

Charles A. Endress

Professor of History
Angelo State University

BARNES & NOBLE BOOKS

A DIVISION OF HARPER & ROW, PUBLISHERS

New York, Evanston, San Francisco, London

To Ellen, Ginny, and Molly

First BARNES & NOBLE BOOKS edition published 1975

LIBRARY OF CONGRESS CATALOG CARD NUMBER: 74-24507

STANDARD BOOK NUMBER: 06-460152-8

75 76 77 3 2 1

Acknowledgments

I wish to express my gratitude and acknowledge my debt to all my teachers. In particular, I must single out Professor Hans A. Schmitt of the University of Virginia, Professors Charles F. Delzell and Alexander Marchant of Vanderbilt University, and the late Professor John L. Snell of the University of North Carolina. I thank my parents for a lifetime of encouragement.

I would also like to express my appreciation to Professor Ronald L. Hayworth for the time he took to read, listen, and make suggestions; to Jo White and Beverly Herndon for their painstaking typing of the manuscript; and to Nancy Cone, Libby Siegel, and Lynda Hobson of Barnes and Noble who helped turn the manuscript into a book.

Finally, I thank my wife Peggy whose suggestions brought clarity and whose support enabled me to write.

About the Author

Charles A. Endress received his B.A. degree from Vanderbilt University and his M.A. and Ph.D. degrees from Tulane University. He served in the United States Army as a military intelligence officer from 1965 to 1969. He has taught at Tulane, the United States Military Academy, and Angelo State University, where he is now Professor of History and Head of the History Department. He is also a member of the Curriculum Development Committee, the Committee on International Education, and the graduate faculty; he is a member of the consulting faculty of the U.S. Army Command and General Staff College.

Contents

Maps

1

The Medieval Heritage

The medieval civilization that emerged around A.D. 1000 was an amalgamation of Roman and so-called barbarian cultures. Woven from the most useful remnants of a diversified past, it developed a distinctive culture that forms the foundation of our own world. The term *Middle Ages* was often used by Renaissance and Enlightenment scholars in a derogatory sense to describe what they considered a stagnant era between the glories of the classical age and the accomplishments of the modern world. Such a view failed to note that medieval institutions, with the aid of slender resources, provided a solution for the problems of day-to-day existence in an insecure world. At the same time, the society evolved highly sophisticated intellectual, technological, and artistic traditions.

Land was the basis of power and wealth in the medieval world, and the political and economic institutions of the time reflect this fact. Unlike contemporary society, which is directed from urban industrial and administrative centers, medieval society was fragmented and decentralized. It revolved around the agricultural unit, which formed the nucleus of both political and economic life. Medieval society, however, did develop institutions that mitigated this parochialism. The medieval city emerged as a focal point for the collection and dissemination of goods and ideas that helped bind Europe together. Above all the Church drew society together under its mantle and provided the unifying force of Christendom for a European world so diverse in other respects. Although many of its institutions failed to function effectively after the crises of the fourteenth century, the medieval heritage nonetheless provided the soil from which the Renaissance world blossomed.

The Political Structure

Because of the constant danger of attack, the limited availability of bureaucratic skills, and a primitive economic base, early medieval Europe relied on a decentralized political system known as *feudalism*. It evolved from the warrior culture of the Germanic tribes into a complex military, judicial, and administrative system. The relationship of the warlord to his comrades-in-arms was at the heart of feudalism. As groups of armed men claimed dominion over large areas of land, the tribal organizations gave way to a political organization resting on a king and his nobilty. This relationship in turn rested on two related institutions, vassalage and fiefdom.

Vassalage. Vassalage constituted a personal bond between a warrior and his leader. The primary responsibility of the vassal was to support his lord in combat. His secondary obligations included providing shelter and other aid when required and attendance at court when called. Though he took on serious obligations with his oaths of homage and fealty, the vassal was in no way servile. The Germanic culture, unlike Roman society, held the warrior in high esteem. His lord was required to provide him with maintenance befitting his station, and his obligations as a vassal were strictly limited.

The Fief. The king gained the support of his armed retainers by supplying them with the only asset that he had in abundance—land. This grant of territory, called a fief or benefice, was made to enable the vassal to maintain himself in a constant state of military preparedness. The fief consisted of any number of organized agricultural communities called manors, which consisted of developed land and the peasants who worked it. An important vassal, such as a duke or count who was expected to provide a large military contingent, might be granted an entire province or county consisting of many villages and manors. He would, in turn, divide his fief (subinfeudate) among his own vassals. The smallest division, a knight's fee, was a single manor designed to support one mounted warrior. The lord of the manor, though the lowest person in the feudal structure, had absolute control of the peasants who lived on the estate.

Political Implications of Feudalism. The medieval monarch in this manner created a structure that enabled him to field a military force against an external enemy, while delegating his authority for the administration of the country at a time when he could not provide the bureaucracy for such a task. As a result the king was often no more than a figurehead at the mercy of vassals who controlled more land and therefore more military power than he did. The feudal nobility engaged in numerous devastating civil wars that the crown was powerless to prevent and that had a destructive impact on the rural economy and commerce.

Evolution of the Feudal Nobilty. As early as the twelfth century, important changes began to appear in the warrior society. The fiefs, though originally granted to individuals in return for military services, were slowly recognized as the hereditary property of the nobility. With the rise of a money economy, the monarch began accepting a cash payment (*scutage*) in lieu of personal knight's service. With this money and growing revenue from commercial activities, the monarch was able to purchase a more dependable military force and expand the scope of the royal bureaucracy. As a result, the nobility could not prevent the emergence of powerful dynastic states in the fifteenth and sixteenth centuries. Deprived of their function as an irresponsible warrior caste, the nobility evolved into a class of country gentlemen who lived from agricultural rents. By maintaining their social status in rigidly stratified societies, they played a leading role as royal officers in the emerging national states.

The Rural Economy

Agriculture provided the dominant element of the medieval economy. The production of food and fiber required the labor of as much as 90 percent of the population because despite endless toil productivity was low. Even in the best years the peasant could expect only a small yield to provide food, taxes, tithes, and seed grain for the following season. The specter of famine was a constant warning to the rural community to maintain its proven practices of cultivation and labor. The enforcement of these rules from generation to generation in the struggle to maintain the precarious balance between adequacy and deprivation did much to promote the conservativism of the Middle Ages. However, the changeless aspects of medieval life should not be overstressed. The population, and with it the economy, expanded continuously until the fourteenth century. New land was cleared in the most densely populated areas of western Europe, and the agricultural frontier steadily expanded to the east. Technological innovations, including the horseshoe, horse collar, and wheeled plow as well as improved agricultural techniques, produced an ever-increasing yield with which a new urban society and centralized states were slowly built. Throughout the following discussion of the organization of land and labor, it must be remembered that terrain, climate, and local custom created widely diversified approaches to the pattern of survival and growth.

Organization of Land. The pattern of agricultural production in the Middle Ages is called *manorialism*. The manor, an almost self-contained economic unit, was the nucleus of the system. It produced all its own food and clothing and had a few artisans, including perhaps a blacksmith, miller, and baker, who provided the most essential services. Though isolated, the manor was not cut off entirely from the community at large and obtained such essentials as salt and iron through purchase or barter.

THE VILLAGE. The built-up area of the manor contained only a few structures. By modern standards, the typical peasant home was often little more than a shed. Constructed of timber and sod and lacking windows or ventilation, it often provided shelter for both man and beast. The priest presided over a small church, but his home would probably differ little from those of his parishioners, for though he was their social superior, he was often their economic equal. The most imposing residence was the home of the lord of the manor, but it might be distinguished only by its stone construction and an additional floor. The manor house might also be a *motte and bailey* castle. Originally a relatively unimposing structure consisting of a mound (motte) upon which was built a single tower and a courtyard (bailey) surrounded by a wooden palisade, it slowly evolved into an imposing stone fortification that provided both defense and a home for the lord.

THE LAND. Though many different patterns of land use existed in the Middle Ages, one of the most widespread and effective techniques was the three-field system. The fields were rotated among spring planting, fall planting, and a season of fallowness. Each field contained numerous strips that were divided among the peasant households. The lord's land (*demesne*), comprising between one-sixth and one-third of the total acreage, was included in these open fields. Other subdivisions included the priest's allotment (*glebe*), the common pasture, and, often, a wooded area that provided game, fuel, and building material.

Division of Labor. The society of medieval Europe was highly stratified. The nobility, who formed the dominant social and political caste, also controlled the land and directly supervised agricultural production. At the beginning of the Middle Ages, the overwhelming majority of the population consisted of a servile class of peasant farmers called *serfs*. By the beginning of the fourteenth century, this peasant mass had rid themselves of the most oppressive practices of serfdom and had risen to the status of free peasant tenants.

SERFS. In theory a sharp distinction can be made between a serf (*villein*) and a slave (*thrall*), but in practice their life styles might vary only slightly. As the vassal held his land from his superior in return for political support, the serf held his land from the lord of the manor in return for economic obligations. The serf had two important rights: to cultivate the soil and to receive protection. In return for these, he undertook severe obligations. Although these were often clearly defined in law or custom, in fact the peasant was at the mercy of the lord of the manor, for there were no other legal authorities to whom he might appeal. The serf was bound to the soil and could not leave the estate without the permission of the lord. Although in theory he could not be sold off the land, in practice this custom was often violated. The serf could not marry or dispose of his property without authorization from the manor house. In addition to these claims on his person, the lord had a claim to the serf's labor. Besides tilling his own land, he worked on the lord's demesne two or three days a week and did boon, or extra, work during planting and harvesting.

The serfs were required to provide the lord with special products, such as honey, eggs, and fish, at specific times, and they were required to use services provided by the lord: for example, the bakery and grist mill, for which they also paid a fee (*banalité*). When a serf died, his household forfeited its best animal (*heriot*), and his heir paid a heavy inheritance tax (*relief*). Despite these onerous obligations, the serfs improved their condition until by the fifteenth century serfdom had virtually disappeared in western Europe.

FREEMEN. There were some freemen throughout the Middle Ages, and they emerged as the most numerous class after 1400. Although a freeman might be poorer than a serf, he was personally free to move about and marry whom he pleased, and he could not be forced to provide unpaid services. The rise of this free class of peasants resulted from increased agricultural production, which fostered a market economy and a greater flow of money. The nobility were willing to accept cash payments in compensation for the servile obligations, and thus the serfs emerged as tenant farmers who, despite heavy financial obligation, became freemen. The inflationary tendency of the fifteenth and sixteenth centuries further reduced their burden at the expense of the nobility.

The Urban Economy

Despite the chaos that resulted from the collapse of Roman authority, trade never disappeared in western Europe. However, cities emerged as a vital element in medieval life only after the reappearance of political stability and increased agricultural productivity in the eleventh century.

Trade in the Middle Ages. Trade rests in large measure on the ability to produce an agricultural surplus. Only after a community has provided for its subsistence does it have goods to sell or the ability to buy. Thus urban centers for local trade remained small until the rural sector had something to sell and until artisans could be freed from agricultural labor. However, throughout the early Middle Ages, some commercial centers continued to thrive, particularly in coastal areas.

BYZANTINE TRADE. Constantinople (Byzantium) was the greatest medieval city. With a population of half a million, it drew to itself like a magnet the meager goods, primarily cereals, hides, and timber, produced in the West. Italian cities, including Venice, Genoa, and Pisa, grew rich as intermediaries in this Mediterranean trade, particularly after the Crusades opened up new markets and customers.

NORTHERN TRADE. A second area of commerce developed along the North Sea and the Baltic Sea after Viking depredations subsided. In the west such Flemish cities as Bruges throve on the trade and manufacture of linen and wool, while farther to the east the Hansa towns, including Hamburg and Lübeck, flourished on timber, fur, and fish.

FAIRS. The northern trading areas were linked to the Mediterranean by traveling merchants who led their pack animals over rutted paths that passed for roads. By the twelfth century, these merchants had developed a circuit of fairs, the most important of which took place in the Champagne country of eastern France. The fairs evolved into traveling tent cities that followed a regular schedule. They were usually held under the auspices of a powerful lord or bishop for a period of four to six weeks. The merchants developed their own commercial rules and court system. These fairs provided rural Europe with their goods and maintained contact between isolated agricultural communities, which otherwise would have been lost.

The Medieval City. Although the wealthy and powerful trading centers played an increasingly important role in medieval economic life, they were far from being typical. Medieval cities were small by modern standards, for the economy could not support more than 10 percent of its population as urban dwellers. Cities did not blossom from sleepy hamlets on the basis of mere population growth but were singled out by political or religious leaders as centers for defense, administration, religion, or commerce, and thus they played a role far out of proportion to their size.

PHYSICAL STRUCTURE. The typical medieval city was small and compact. It was surrounded by a protective wall because its concentrated wealth made it an ideal target for attack.

The larger city's most important buildings, the castle, the cathedral, and the guild halls, emphasized the function of the urban center.

Because of the constraining fortifications, life was cramped. Streets were narrow, and buildings were packed side by side. Despite the lack of garbage disposal and sewage facilities and the catastrophes of fire and epidemic resulting from overcrowding, the medieval city's picture was not so dark as it is often painted. A strong sense of community pervaded the city, and the practice of living in or near the place of work created a vitality often missing in today's urban sprawl. It also should be remembered that the medieval city produced neither the mountains of trash and refuse, nor the smog, nor the deafening noise of its modern industrial counterpart.

SOCIAL STRUCTURE. The world of the bourgeoisie (that is, the city dwellers) required a social structure far different from that of the rural sector. The city depended on the skill and enterprise of each individual, and personal freedom was therefore absolutely necessary. But despite this personal freedom, neither political democracy nor real free enterprise existed. In many ways life in the city was as stratified and controlled as rural life.

ECONOMIC THEORY. The basic ideas of modern capitalism were unknown in the Middle Ages. Both the nobility and the Church suspected businessmen of an unchristian desire to accumulate wealth and a willingness to undertake fraudulent means to obtain it. The society rejected the profit motive as a valid principle for the operation of business and, generally speaking, merchants and artisans shared this view. The underlying premise of business activity was that the economy, like the rest of society, was static. Aggressive competition for the limited market was rejected in favor of strict controls designed to give every merchant and manufacturer a fair share with which to maintain himself in his station in life. They included restrictions on the volume of production (to prevent flooding of a limited market), price controls, and quality control of products.

ORGANIZATION OF LABOR. The organizations used to regulate urban production and distribution were called *guilds*. They not only controlled economic life but regulated social and very often political life as well.

The Merchant Guild. The merchant guild was the oldest form of urban guild. There was one merchant guild for each city, and its function was to protect the city's merchants from outsiders. It controlled the trading of all foreign goods within the city and set prices and standards for export goods. These controls were important, for the reputation of a city specializing in the production and sale of cheese, woolen cloth, or swords might suffer irreparable damage from the activities of a single unscrupulous or shoddy merchant. It was the general practice for the merchants of a city to be collectively responsible for the obligations of their colleagues who might default on a debt in another city.

The Craft Guild. The craft guilds were the organizations of specific occupations within a city, corresponding to the trade union locals of modern occupations such as carpenters, plumbers, and electricians. If he produced items of export, a craft guildsman might be a member of the merchant guild. The craft guild was controlled by the master craftsmen, who, because of their recognized skill, were allowed to operate their own shops. Journeymen or day laborers worked under the supervision of the master for many years while they perfected their skills. By the end of the Middle Ages, the majority of journeymen found it impossible to become masters, and the result was a breakdown of the system with attending social and political agitation.

At the bottom of this hierarchy was the apprentice, who was indentured to the master. In return for his services as a general helper and handyman, he was given room and board while he undertook the arduous task of learning his trade.

The Church

Medieval Christianity was the most important force in maintaining the unity of a basically decentralized society. As the spokesman for Christ on earth and the repository of his laws, the Church wielded immense prestige. Besides being the guardian of medieval ideology, the Church held vast economic and political power. This power increased its authority but at the same time often diverted the Church's attention from its role as a spiritual institution.

The Papacy. The Bishop of Rome emerged from the chaos of the early Middle Ages as the pope, the Vicar of Christ, and the undisputed leader of Western Christendom. The papacy reached the height of its influence under Pope Innocent III (1198–1216), who not only claimed spiritual authority but regarded the Holy Roman emperor and the other secular rulers as his subordinates. Despite his control of the papal states of central Italy and the vast ecclesiastical estates throughout Europe, the pope was never able to exert overt political control over the Continent. The Church's prestige and authority were derived, rather, from its spiritual monopoly as the keeper of Saint Peter's keys. In this role the pope acted as the chief arbiter amid the atomized political milieu and, through the papal government (*curia*) and the hierarchy of archbishops and bishops, administered the indispensable sacramental system.

Christian Belief and Popular Religion. Christianity supplied medieval civilization with a universal ideology that served as a standard for ethical conduct, a guide to eternal salvation, and an explanation for the nature of the physical universe. On the one hand, medieval philosophers elaborated a sophisticated theological structure to explain the relation of man to God, while on another level, the great masses of unlettered peasants found solace in simplified versions of man's struggle against evil and toward salvation.

BASIC DOGMA. The central theme of Christianity is the redemption of mankind from the sin of Adam through the life and death of Jesus Christ, the Son of God. Christ's supreme sacrifice of crucifixion made salvation possible for men who by their free will accepted the gift of grace and lived according to divine law, as interpreted by the Church. The seven sacraments were the most plentiful source of this life-giving grace. Three of these, baptism, confirmation, and extreme unction (the last rites), were received by every Christian to affirm his membership in Christendom. Penance and communion (the Lord's Supper) were received periodically to cleanse the soul and to participate spiritually in Christ's sacrifice. Matrimony confirmed the holy state of marriage, and holy orders (ordination) bestowed the powers of the priesthood. With the exception of baptism (under special circumstances), the sacraments could be administered only by a priest, and it was this control of the keys to heaven that gave the clergy its awesome social power. Anyone who opposed the authority of the Church could be excommunicated (deprived of the sacraments), and in extreme cases of royal defiance, an entire country could be placed under interdict, thus depriving the whole population of the sacraments.

POPULAR PIETY. The intricacies of Christian theology were lost upon the pious but illiterate masses, who followed a simple faith based upon obedience to their priests, observance of ritual, and prayer for intercession of kindly saints. The veneration of the Virgin Mary, in fact, developed into a cult that approached idolatry. Holy relics, the mortal remains of saints or their possessions, and artifacts supposedly related to Christ's Passion and death became the focus of pious veneration, and the shrines that housed them were objects of pilgrimage.

Intellectual Life. Medieval societies did not have a highly organized educational system. Education, even literacy, was limited to a small fraction of the population and was generally controlled by the Church. Its primary function was to teach bureaucratic skills and prepare men for religious vocations.

GRAMMAR SCHOOLS. Elementary education was usually provided by cathedral or monastery schools. The curriculum included the *trivium* (grammar, rhetoric, and logic) and the *quadrivium* (arithmetic, geometry, astronomy, and music). The main task of each student was to acquire fluency in Latin, a prerequisite for university studies and the official language of the government and the Church.

UNIVERSITIES. Medieval universities, which began to emerge in the twelfth century, were much less rigidly organized than their modern counterparts. They were often nothing more than communities of scholars and students. The usual pattern of instruction was for a lecturer to read the text of an ancient authority and provide explanatory commentary and interpretation (called *glosses*) while his audience took verbatim notes. At the conclusion of each course, the diligent student would have a handwritten textbook with the teacher's commentary. The greatest universities of southern Europe were located at Salerno, Pisa, and Bologna, while the most important centers of learning in the north were the universities of Paris, Oxford, and Cambridge.

SCHOLASTICISM. Theology was the dominant academic discipline, and the theologians who spent their lives in this pursuit of ultimate truth were known as *scholastics* or *schoolmen*. The greatest of these was Thomas Aquinas (1225?–1274), whose *Summa Theologica* was a brilliant attempt to integrate the truth of divine revelation, which Christians accepted on faith, with the reasoned arguments of the pagan philosophers of ancient Greece. Though Thomism provided the medieval world with a systematic synthesis of human knowledge based on both faith and reason, it did not go unchallenged. Duns Scotus (d. 1308) and William of Ockham (d. 1349) were the most prominent among many scholastics who denied the ability of finite reason to plumb the depths of infinite truth. Their opinions were very influential as the medieval epoch drew to a close, and reliance on faith was a key ingredient in the sixteenth-century Reformation.

Disintegration of the Medieval World

The medieval synthesis began to disintegrate in the fourteenth century. This collapse resulted from a number of interrelated conditions, including chronic warfare, economic depression, universal pestilence, social unrest, and a decline in the prestige and authority of the Church.

The Hundred Years' War. This was not one but many wars fought for more than a century from 1338 to 1453. Causes for the struggle included: (1) English fears that France would disrupt their valuable Flemish wool trade, (2) English claims to the French throne, (3) French desire to eliminate the English possessions in France, and (4) a deep-seated love of combat in the European nobility.

FIRST PHASE (1338–1360). England clearly dominated the early stages of the conflict. She held a decided edge in leadership and possessed a well-organized royal army to combat French feudal levies. English archers, wielding their deadly longbows, stood their ground at Crécy (1346) and Poitiers (1356) and won the day against the impetuous French knights. The first phase of the war ended with the Treaty of Bretigny (1360) that ceded Gascony and Guienne (southwestern France) to England.

SECOND PHASE (1369–1375). Charles V of France reorganized the government, levied new taxes, and created a royal army, which he placed under the command of Bertrand Du Guesclin. As a result the French regained the initiative and drove the English from all but a few coastal areas. Though no general peace resulted, the conflict subsided in sporadic raids between 1375 and 1415.

THIRD PHASE (1415–1453). In 1415 Henry V of England took advantage of French civil war and renewed hostilities. In the first few years, he swept all before him. After inflicting a stunning defeat on his more numerous adversaries at Agincourt (1415), he dictated the terms of the Treaty of Troyes (1420), which made him lord of northern France and heir to the French throne. But the legendary Joan of Arc rallied the dispirited Armagnac faction that still supported the disinherited dauphin. She led an army to the relief of Orléans and made possible the coronation of Charles VIII at Reims (1429). Though Joan was captured and burned as a witch by her enemies, the initiative had clearly passed to France. By 1453 the English held only the port of Calais.

RESULTS OF THE WAR. The decisive victory of French arms promoted both English and French nationalism at the expense of decentralized feudalism. The reemergence of the infantry as the dominant force on the battlefield decreased both the military and political importance of the mounted knight. The active phases of the war worked an enormous hardship on both nations, and the social disorganization wrought by the conflict was significant, particularly in France. The political repercussions of the war are discussed on p. 18 and p. 21.

The Fourteenth-Century Depression. The economic expansion of the early Middle Ages gave way to stagnation in the fourteenth century. All available land had already been brought under cultivation, and the standard of living began to fall as population outstripped agricultural production. Continual warfare added an additional dimension to economic decline.

The Great Dying. The Black Death (bubonic plague) swept across Europe from 1348 to 1350. Combined with the recurrence of other epidemic diseases, chronic malnutrition, and periodic famines, it killed between 20 and 30 percent of Europe's people. This demographic disaster not only accelerated economic decline but also cast a psychological pall over the survivors. In the long run, the ensuing labor shortage quickened the demise of serfdom and helped to destroy the guild system.

Social Unrest. The dislocations of the time caused intense suffering among the peasants and threatened the nobility with economic ruin. The resulting social tensions triggered numerous peasant revolts. Typical of these savage outbursts of despair were the French *Jacquerie* (1358) and Wat Tyler's Rebellion in England (1381). As is usually the case, the peasants' early victories were followed by savage suppression and few reforms.

Decline of the Church. As has already been noted, the Church was the most influential institution of medieval Europe and provided cohesion for an otherwise decentralized civilization. Its dominant position declined in the fourteenth century in the face of expanding national monarchies and from its own institutional failure to provide spiritual leadership.

THE BABYLONIAN CAPTIVITY. Pope Boniface VIII (1294–1303) attempted to expand the role in secular affairs that the papacy had played for centuries. He directly challenged the authority of England's Edward I and France's Philip the Fair in two papal bulls (formal papal pronouncements). *Clericis laicos* (1296) denied the right of civil authorities to tax Church property and *Unam sanctum* (1302) claimed absolute authority over all secular officials. In retaliation, Philip convened the nobility and clergy of France who condemned Boniface. The pope died in 1303 after being arrested by Philip's agents. Philip used his influence to force the election of a French cardinal as Clement V (1305). Clement moved his court to Avignon, on the southern border of France, and for the next seventy years he and his successors ruled the Church in the shadow of the French monarchy. During this period, known as the "Babylonian Captivity," it was generally believed that the French monarchy was using the papacy to further its own aims. This partiality undermined the Church's role as a universal arbiter and spiritual leader.

THE GREAT SCHISM. Pope Gregory XI returned the papal court to Rome in 1377, but his death the following year precipitated an even more serious crisis. The French-dominated College of Cardinals succumbed to Roman pressure and elected the Italian Urban VI. Urban's policies alienated the cardinals, who declared his election invalid and proceeded to elect a Frenchman, Clement VII. This dual election divided Christendom. England, Italy, the Holy Roman Empire, and eastern Europe remained loyal to Urban, while France, Spain, Scotland, and Naples supported Clement. The prestige of the papacy declined further in 1409 when a general council of the Church met at Pisa and compounded the problem by electing a third pope. The schism finally ended when the Council of Constance (1414–1418) deposed all three claimants and elected Martin V in 1417. The schism, like the Avignon period, thrust the papacy into the political arena as a mere pawn, thus further reducing its prestige.

HERETICAL MOVEMENTS. The political activism of the papacy and the widespread corruption in the Church aroused indignation and led to the demand for sweeping reform. Though individual critics were often silenced, a strong undercurrent of dissatisfaction continued throughout the century and laid the groundwork for the Reformation.

Wycliffe. John Wycliffe (1320?–1384) was a theologian and professor at Oxford. In 1375 he launched an attack on papal supremacy, clerical wealth, and the sacramental system. He based his arguments upon the Scriptures and demanded a return to simple Christianity. Though dismissed from his Oxford post and condemned as a heretic by Gregory XI, he remained safe under the protection of the English crown. His teachings spread throughout the island, and he remained a parish priest until his death. But his followers, known as Lollards, were brutally suppressed during the reign of Henry IV (1399–1413).

Huss. Wycliffe's teachings spread to central Europe, where they were taken up by John Huss (1369?–1415), a priest and professor at the University of Prague. Huss also stressed the authority of the Bible as the sole guide to salvation, and he won an enormous following among his Czech compatriots by demanding an end to papal and German domination. Huss was summoned to the Council of Constance in 1414 to answer charges of heresy. He was condemned and, though traveling under a safe-conduct issued by Emperor Sigismund, was burned at the stake. His martyrdom led to open warfare in Bohemia, where his countrymen were able to hold out and win concessions in the Hussite Wars (1420–1433).

2

The
Political Transformation
of Western Europe

The last half of the fifteenth century witnessed a marked acceleration in the transition of European political organization from weak, decentralized, feudal states to powerful, centralized, dynastic monarchies. This change did not take place so suddenly as to be revolutionary, nor did it occur in the same sequence or at a uniform rate throughout the Continent. In fact, some political entities failed to make the transformation and were destroyed.

England, France, and Spain led Europe in the transition from feudalism to centralization. Though they were all dynastic states during the fifteenth century, each built upon a foundation of nascent cultural nationalism. This tendency was abetted by the long medieval struggles that pitted the English against the French and the Spanish against the Moors and thus gave these peoples a stronger sense of national identity. Finally, the Atlantic states were much more deeply involved than eastern Europe in the commercial growth that followed the economic doldrums of the fourteenth century.

The Evolving State Structure

The central theme of this chapter is the beginning of the transition from the feudal state to the dynastic state at the end of the fifteenth century. In order to understand early modern politics, it must be remembered that neither type of government corresponds to the modern nation-state in either organization or operation.

The Feudal State. Feudalism was the most typical organization of medieval civilization. Although it took a unique form in each state, it evolved from common needs of societies beset by military attack but unable to support a strong centralized government with the meager resources of their rural economies. Monarchs lacking any assets except land traded this land for the military service of a warrior caste (that is, the nobility). The concept of sovereignty did not exist within this feudal relationship, for the king by giving up his land had alienated the source of his wealth and power and thus had neither the legal right to interfere within the fiefs of his vassals nor the military might to force them to obedience. The division of power among king, church, nobleman, and city created decentralized states vulnerable to external aggression and plagued by civil war.

The Centralized Dynastic State. The civil authority of all secular rulers was enhanced by the declining prestige of the papacy, and economic growth provided tax revenues that fatally weakened the ability of the insubordinate nobility to check the spread of royal power. As a result, a new type of state emerged in which the monarch, aided by an increasingly efficient bureaucracy and a professional army, subordinated all other factions to the interests of the state. During this Age of Kings, which reached its apogee in the seventeenth and eighteenth centuries, the interests of the state were thought to be synonymous with the well-being of the dynasty (the reigning royal family). The personal estates of the ruling family formed the nucleus of the state though they were often geographically separated from other parts of the realm and might be governed under a separate title and different constitutional practices. Territory could be acquired or alienated as a result of inheritance, marriage, war, or other reasons the ruler thought appropriate. The inhabitants of such states were thus *subjects* of the ruler rather than *citizens* of a nation and were bound together by political obedience rather than by ethnic or cultural affiliations.

England

Few reigns have so dramatically altered the fortunes of a country as that of Henry VII (1485–1509), the first Tudor king of England. The half century before his coming was a time of humiliating defeat abroad and universal disintegration at home. By the time of his death, the feudal structure had given way to a centralized government that commanded the respect of a well-ordered and prosperous nation. (A discussion of economic and cultural developments in England during this period will be found on page 41.)

Influence of Medieval Institutions. The task of consolidation was not so difficult in England as on the Continent because the Tudor monarchs drew upon a heritage of centralization that dated from the Norman Conquest (1066).

FEUDALISM. William the Conqueror (r. 1066–1087) made aristocratic insubordination and rebellion difficult by scattering the manorial

EUROPE: FRONTIERS ABOUT 1500

NORWAY

SW

Oslo

SCOTLAND

Edinburgh

IRELAND

Dublin

DENMARK

Copenhagen

ENGLAND

London

NETHERLANDS

Antwerp

Lübeck
Hamburg
Bremen

BRANDENBURG

Cologne

Le Havre
Rouen

Rheims

Paris

THE

Prague

Nuremberg

BOHEMIA

Blois

EMPIRE

FRANCE

Augsburg

Vienna
AUSTRIA

Tyrol

Styria

La Rochelle

2

1

3

Bordeaux

4

5

Milano

VENICE Venice

Corunna

Toulouse

Avignon

7

14 Genoa

8

9

Burgos

NAVARRE

Marseilles

13

Valladolid

Salamanca

6

10

11

Florence

PORTUGAL

CASTILE

Madrid

ARAGON

Barcelona

Corsica

12

PAPAL
STATES

Lisbon

Toledo

Rome

Seville

GRANADA

Granada

Balearic Is. (Aragon)

Sardinia (Aragon)

Naples

MEDITERRANEAN

Palermo

Sicily
(Aragon)

Messina

(From *Europe in the Sixteenth Century*, pp. 24–25, by H. G. Koenigsberger and George L. Mosse. Copyright © 1968 by H. G. Koenigsberger
and G. L. Mosse. Reprinted by permission of Holt, Rinehart and Winston,
Inc.)

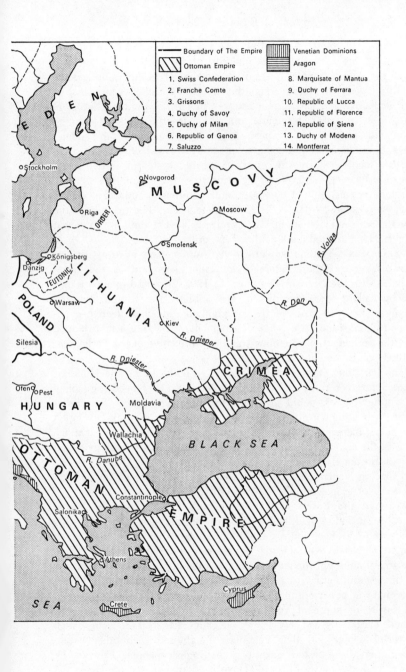

—— Boundary of The Empire	▨ Venetian Dominions	
▨ Ottoman Empire	▤ Aragon	
1. Swiss Confederation	8. Marquisate of Mantua	
2. Franche Comte	9. Duchy of Ferrara	
3. Grissons	10. Republic of Lucca	
4. Duchy of Savoy	11. Republic of Florence	
5. Duchy of Milan	12. Republic of Siena	
6. Republic of Genoa	13. Duchy of Modena	
7. Saluzzo	14. Montferrat	

SWEDEN

Stockholm

Novgorod

MUSCOVY

Riga

ORDER

Moscow

Smolensk

R. Volga

Königsberg

Danzig

TEUTONIC

LITHUANIA

Warsaw

R. Don

POLAND

Kiev

R. Dnieper

Silesia

R. Dniester

CRIMEA

Ofen Pest

HUNGARY

Moldavia

BLACK SEA

Wallachia

OTTOMAN

R. Danube

Constantinople

Salonika

EMPIRE

Athens

Cyprus

SEA

Crete

holdings of his most powerful vassals and commanding liege homage from even his subvassals. The inability of any single baron to challenge the king, except in times of extreme royal weakness, forced the nobility to act in unison when they felt their rights were violated. This collective action was demonstrated in 1215 at Runnymede where King John confirmed his feudal obligations in the Magna Carta.

COMMON LAW. Another important factor in the unification of England was the development of a common or universal law. Henry II (r. 1154–1189) issued the decrees necessary to create a system of justice at the Assize of Clarendon (1166). From this arose the custom of *case law*, in which judges applied the precedents of previous judicial decisions to cases presented to them by local grand juries. The prestige of the law rose to such heights in the decades following these reforms that even the king ignored it only at his own peril.

PARLIAMENT. The Parliament evolved from a group of royal advisers known as the Witan under Anglo-Saxon kings and as the Great Council after the Norman Conquest. In 1295 Edward I opened a new era by calling representatives of the nobility, the church, and the commons from all parts of the kingdom to provide collective council and maintenance (the Model Parliament). The king acknowledged that the authorization of money was the prerogative of the Parliament in the Confirmation of Charters (1297).

The Parliament emerged as a legislative body during the Hundred Years' War (see p. 10) when it exploited the king's need for money by voting temporary aid in return for increased rights. The Parliament, by holding a firm grip on England's purse strings, thus developed into a permanent and powerful legislature representing the "nation" (that is, the landed and monied interests of England). It even extended its constitutional prerogatives by deposing Richard II in 1399 and and placing Henry IV upon the throne. Parliamentary power reached its medieval apogee during the Wars of the Roses.

Wars of the Roses. In 1455 England's feudal monarchy lay in ruins. Military debacle had come fast on the heels of Henry V's conquest of France, and by the 1453 England held only the French seaport of Calais. At home the countryside festered in anarchy while the great families of the realm struggled to gain preference at the court of the intermittently insane Henry VI (r. 1422–1461; 1470–1471). The civil war between the reigning house of Lancaster (Red Rose) and the insurgent house of York (White Rose) consisted of a series of armed clashes spread over three decades (1455–1485), in which powerful nobles and their retainers slaughtered each other before the rather disinterested gaze of the English people. Edward IV (York, r. 1461–1470; 1471–1483) succeeded in deposing Henry VI

(Lancaster), but his own family was torn by dissension when he died in 1483. Richard III (York, r. 1483–1485) was an able administrator, but his Machiavellian cynicism, capped by the murder of Edward IV's small sons, repulsed even his staunchest supporters. Thus encouraged, the Lancasterians again took the field behind Henry Tudor, earl of Richmond, who defeated and slew Richard at Bosworth Field (August 1485). By this time, the English people were ready to support any man who had the power to restore law and order.

Reign of Henry VII (1485–1509). Henry Tudor's claim to the throne after Bosworth Field rested upon the right of conquest and a very tenuous line of descent from Edward III. He moved quickly to consolidate his position, first by having Parliament confirm his right to rule and then by marrying Elizabeth of York, the sole heir of that royal house.

PACIFICATION OF ENGLAND. Although the nobility had been decimated by the Wars of the Roses, powerful families still survived in baronial estates to challenge regal authority. They supported both Simnel (1487) and Warbeck (1496), who attempted to rekindle Yorkist pretentions through unsuccessful armed insurrection. Henry circumvented the nobility by calling into his council men of lower birth who had proven their loyalty and worth by past services. Besides functioning as advisors, the men of the council served in a judicial capacity as members of the Court of Star Chamber. Star Chamber stood above the common law courts and protected them from intimidation by enforcing the ban on livery and maintenance, a practice by which the nobility had illegally kept large private armies.

The old nobility were replaced by Tudor supporters raised to the peerage from the gentry, the gentle-born but nonnoble class of prosperous landowners. The gentry also supplied the unpaid servants of the crown who, as justices of the peace, enforced the king's writ in every parish of the kingdom.

FINANCIAL RECOVERY. The long civil wars and the disorder that accompanied them had emptied the royal treasury. Henry devoted his reign to filling it with income from his own estates, customs duties, and the expedients of forced loans (*benevolences*) from his friends and confiscations from his enemies. He was miserly in his expenditures and as a result, gained such independence of parliamentary control that Parliament declined in importance until its seventeenth-century resurgence. When Henry died he purportedly left the "richest treasury in Christendom."

FOREIGN AFFAIRS. England remained at peace throughout most of Henry's reign, though not without difficulty. Ireland bridled under English rule, and this hostility grew after the enactment of the Statute of Drogheda (Poynings's Laws) in 1494. Henceforth all Irish laws required the acquiescence of the English Parliament, while English law automatically went into effect in Ireland. Scotland, on the other hand, maintained its independence, and in order to regularize relations between the two countries, Henry gave the hand of his daughter Margaret to James IV of Scotland (1502). Their grandson, James VI, inherited the English throne in 1603 as James I. Another royal alliance that would ultimately have international repercussions was the marriage of Henry's infant son Arthur to Catherine of Aragon, daughter of Ferdinand and Isabella of Spain (1494). When Arthur died Catherine married her brother-in-law, the newly crowned Henry VIII.

France

The first three decades of the fifteenth century were a time of civil war, military defeat, and political humiliation in France. The enfeebled monarchy, caught in a vise between England's Henry V and Henry's Burgundian ally Philip, went so far as to renounce the dauphin, the heir to the throne, and to bequeath the kingdom to Henry. However, the appearance of Joan of Arc brought a sharp reversal of fortune; by the end of the century, England had been swept from the Continent, and the French monarchy, relying upon medieval institutions, had asserted itself as the dominant political element in France.

Medieval Institutions. The king was not the dominant political force in early medieval France. The territory under his direct control (the Île de France) consisted of small and scattered holdings in the vicinity of Paris. His vassals, though theoretically under his command, were in fact the independent rulers of vast feudal domains. Despite its political weakness, an aura of majesty and divine protection cloaked the Capetian dynasty, whose kings passed the crown from father to son in an unbroken line from 987 to 1328. During this interval the monarchy built an administrative apparatus within the royal domain that slowly expanded to encompass the entire realm.

ROYAL ADMINISTRATION. Under Philip II, "Augustus" (r. 1180–1223), the monarchy began relying on the skills of professional civil servants rather than on the spasmodic and lukewarm cooperation of its vassals. These professionals were rewarded in cash rather than in land, and their continued dependence upon the crown made them staunch supporters of royal prerogative. The first such appointees were bailiffs (*baillis* or *sénéchaux*), who supervised finance and justice within the royal domain. As its duties expanded, the civil service emerged as the *nobility of the robe,* a new class distinct from the old feudal *nobility of the sword.* Under Louis IX, "Saint Louis" (r. 1226–1270), the king's council (*Curia Regis*) underwent a transformation in which specialized groups of advisors emerged to administer finances (*chambre des comptes*) and justice (*parlement*). Louis began the practice of issuing decrees with the force of law throughout the kingdom and in this manner banned private warfare and instituted a common currency. The royal courts established by Louis throughout the realm were recognized as the most efficient means of obtaining justice.

ESTATES GENERAL. The clergy, the nobility, and the bourgeoisie, representing the estates of the feudal regime, assembled for the first time in 1302. Called by Philip IV, "the Fair" (r. 1285–1314) to strengthen the crown during a controversy with Pope Boniface VIII, this Estates General henceforth functioned as an instrument in the expansion of royal authority rather than as an independent legislative body comparable to the English Parliament. This failure resulted in part from the rigid class structure that precluded cooperation between the lower nobility and the bourgeoisie. The Estates General set a dangerous precedent in 1369 by granting Charles V (r. 1364–1380) the right to continue indefinitely the collection of taxes already voted.

Resurgence of France. The royal prerogatives built into the institutions of medieval France were worthless in the hands of a weak king. The dramatic improvement of French fortunes after 1429 brought with it the consolidation of royal authority and French territorial unification.

CHARLES VII, "THE WELL-SERVED" (r. 1422–1461). Paralyzed by indecision and defeat, Charles hardly seemed the man to lead France in a national crusade. He took the initiative after the appearance of Joan of Arc, who broke the English siege at Orléans (1428) and had him crowned king at Reims (1429). Though Joan was captured and burned as a witch, Charles continued the fight. He negotiated a settlement with Burgundy and took Paris (1436). Charles received from the Estates General the right to collect a permanent land tax (*taille*), which was the most important source of royal revenue from 1439 to 1789. His financial resources were also enhanced under the terms of the Pragmatic Sanction of Bourges (1438), which brought the French church and its resources under royal control. Charles used these funds to create a permanent army consisting of independent companies of cavalry, archers, and artillery. Not only had he forged the weapons with which the English were expelled from France (1461) but he had also gained financial independence and military protection for the crown.

LOUIS XI, "THE SPIDER," (r. 1461–1483). The end of the Hundred Years' War left Louis free to concentrate on domestic affairs. He perfected the machinery necessary for the collection of taxes voted to Charles VII. His orders were carried out by decree, for at their own request, the Estates General met only in times of national crises after 1469. Louis nearly completed the process of national unification. The incorporation of the Burgundian (1477) and Angevin (1480) dukedoms left only Brittany outside royal control. The marriage of Charles VIII (r. 1483–1498) to Anne of Brittany (1491) rounded out the kingdom and brought it under royal administrators.

The Renaissance Monarchy. Francis I (r. 1515–1547) and Henry II (r. 1547–1559) reaped the rewards of the long struggle waged during the preceding century. The monarch's self-assurance was reflected in the flowering of Renaissance arts and letters at Francis's court and in the circle of his sister, Margaret of Navarre. The kings of France, no longer cowering before their English brethren, pursued an aggressive foreign policy in Italy.

Despite the splendor of the French monarchy, there were two basic and ultimately fatal flaws in its institutional structure. First, the nobility, though temporarily subdued, maintained its landed economic power and social status within the rigidly stratified class structure. It struggled to maintain its tax-exempt position and political independence even to the detriment of state interests. Second, the concentration of executive and legislative power in the hands of a hereditary monarch demanded a succession of competent kings, which the Valois dynasty did not produce. The accidental death of Henry in 1559 left his three small sons in the care of his widow, Catherine de Medici. The regency of Francis III opened a new era of aristocratic infighting, compounded by the religious controversies of the age that divided France in bloody civil war for the remainder of the century.

Spain

The marriage of Isabella of Castile to Ferdinand of Aragon produced a dynastic union of their kingdoms and laid the foundation of a united Spain that, building upon Aragon's European experience and Castile's Iberian culture, became the dominant Atlantic power by the middle of the sixteenth century.

Medieval Influences. The unique character of Spanish culture is partially explained by the confrontation of European and Middle Eastern civilization in the physical isolation of the Iberian peninsula from 711 to 1492. There were three significant consequences of this contact.

MOORISH CULTURE. Despite their animosity toward the Moors, the more backward Spanish unconsciously drew from the reservoir of classical and Eastern learning brought by the Moors from the eastern Mediterranean. The greatest transfer of knowledge came in philosophy, science, and architecture.

CATHOLICISM. Catholicism was the psychological weapon used to rally the divided Spaniards against the Islamic invaders. As a result, Christian orthodoxy became the test of patriotism, and the two ideas were fused in Spanish consciousness. Though this served as a force for national unification, it also bred religious intolerance.

THE RECONQUISTA. This counterattack to drive the Moors from the peninsula raged for centuries and produced a political system much different from the feudalism in the north. The nobility retained its role as a warrior caste far longer than its northern counterparts. In return for their military service, nobles received grants of land rather than estates bound by feudal tenure. Their long military service and their economic independence made them virtually independent of royal control.

The Kingdoms of Spain. By the middle of the twelfth century, four Christian kingdoms existed in Spain: Navarre, Portugal, Aragon, and Castile.

NAVARRE. Though one of the first states to regain its independence from the Moors, Navarre gained no territorial advantage from the reconquest because it was cut off by Castile and Aragon from expansion to the south. It was ruled by Frenchmen from 1234 until 1513, when its Spanish provinces were annexed by Ferdinand of Aragon.

PORTUGAL. Portugal was liberated from the Moors and granted to Henry of Burgundy by the king of Castile (1093). It continued to participate in the military crusade and took part in the decisive defeat of the resurgent Moors at the battle of Rio Salado (1340). Henceforth the greatest danger to Portuguese independence came from Castile. By right of descent, the crown of Portugal should have passed to Castile upon the death of Ferdinand I in 1383, but the Portuguese retained their independence through force of arms at Aljubarrota (1385). Portugal's greatest contribution to Iberian grandeur and European expansion came during the fifteenth century (see p. 42).

ARAGON. During the early Middle Ages, Aragon was part of a heterogeneous state that stretched along the Mediterranean coast of what is today northeastern Spain and southern France. Although James I (r. 1213–1276) abandoned his French possessions, he drove the Moors from Valencia (1245) and at the same time developed Barcelona into a trade rival of Genoa and Pisa. Through statecraft and conquest, the Aragonese carved out a Mediterranean empire that at its full expanse included the Balearic Islands, Corsica, Sardinia, Sicily, and Naples. The nobility and bourgeoisie balked at bearing the expense arising from these new obligations, and, they maintained their privileges through the cortes (assembled estates). Chronic depression and diplomatic reversals during the fifteenth century led John II to link the fortunes of Aragon to Castile through the marriage of his son Ferdinand to Isabella.

CASTILE. Castile encompassed the heartland of Spain. Its union with Léon (1230) made it by far the most powerful state on the peninsula. The Castilians took the lead in the reconquista. The forces of Ferdinand III drove the Moors from Cordova (1236) and Seville (1248), thus confining them to the enclave of Granada. Although the monarchy had ended the Moorish menace, it had created a powerful and uncontrollable nobility in the process. Through the *Mesta*, an association of sheep raisers with vast holdings, the grandees dominated the rural economy, and with their martial experience, they posed a political threat.

The crown was able to maintain its position only with the assistance of the towns, which preferred royal dominance to aristocratic anarchy. The towns provided their support in two ways. (1) As the third estate in the Castilian cortes, they were much more willing to grant revenues than either the Church or the nobility. In this manner the sales tax (*alcabala*) was introduced under Alfonso XI (r. 1312–1349). (2) Urban brotherhoods (*hermandades*), first organized in the thirteenth century, provided the king with militia to back him in confrontations with the nobility. Under Henry IV (r. 1454–1474) the monarchy nearly dissolved in a protracted struggle for the throne. Queen Isabella won the crown (1474) and set Spain on the road to European dominance.

Unification of Spain. Ferdinand and Isabella married secretly in 1469. Ferdinand raised an army to back Isabella's claim to Castile in 1474, and he became king of Aragon in 1479. Throughout their reigns the kingdoms were united only by virtue of this dynastic marriage and were ruled as separate political units. The Catholic Kings were not united in their views. Isabella's outlook was primarily Castilian: She was determined to rebuild royal power, complete the reconquest, and establish rigid Catholic orthodoxy. Ferdinand was a

Renaissance prince, reared in the more cosmopolitan court of Aragon and vitally interested in European power politics. The combination of these two views in a single household provided the catalyst for Spanish predominance in the sixteenth century.

ESTABLISHMENT OF ROYAL ABSOLUTISM. Ferdinand and Isabella proceeded warily against their entrenched opposition. Because Aragon had a long tradition of local rights that the Crown could not usurp, the work of consolidation proceeded mainly in Castile. The towns played a vital role in this task. The *Santa Hermandad,* a confederation of towns, was organized to resist aristocratic threats. Through their representative in the cortes, the cities provided crown revenue, which was collected by royal officials (*corregidores*) who also enforced the law. Sources of royal revenue were also expanded to include confiscations from recalcitrant nobles, the treasures of religious knightly orders, and "contributions" from the Church and the Mesta. The crown also received huge sums from the empire after the first decades of the sixteenth century and used this money to consolidate its position and expand its influence in Europe.

CHRISTIAN ORTHODOXY. Since Christianity supplied the basic values of Western civilization, orthodox religious views were considered a prerequisite for a stable political body. Nowhere was the equation of nonbelief with treason carried further than in Spain. Isabella was determined to enforce orthodoxy. The Inquisition was established in 1478 to track down deviationists, and under the terms of the Concordat of 1482, control of the Spanish church passed to the crown. The queen accompanied her army in the destruction of the last Islamic stronghold of Granada (1492). The expulsion of an estimated two hundred thousand Jews in 1492, followed in 1502 by expulsion of Moors who refused to abandon their religion, was a high price to pay for religious conformity. Those non-Christians were the backbone of Spanish commercial life, and many historians trace modern Spain's economic backwardness to their departure.

FOREIGN AFFAIRS. The reordering of Spain's domestic life left Ferdinand and Isabella free to pursue dynastic interests outside the peninsula. They entered an arena in which the internal anarchy of the late Middle Ages had given way to the international anarchy of expansionist dynasties. Friction with France over rival claims in Italy led Ferdinand into war that continued intermittently for half a century after his death. (For the international relations of this era, see p. 76.) Isabella had taken a slight interest in an enterprise that proved to be far more rewarding. Columbus's voyages of discovery opened the possibility of vast overseas empires. Isabella's only child,

Juana, married Philip of Hapsburg, archduke of Austria. Juana became incurably insane, and upon Ferdinand's death (1515) the entire Spanish inheritance passed directly to their grandson, Charles I (r. 1515–1556). In his lifetime Charles would hold title to a continental and overseas empire larger than that of the Roman caesars (see p. 74).

3

The States of Central
and Eastern Europe

The process of consolidation begun in England, France, and Spain in the fifteenth century was far less pronounced in central and eastern Europe. Germany and Italy were mere geographical expressions, totally lacking in political unity. Farther to the east the boundaries of the feudal states did not correspond to modern boundaries, and only in Russia did a centralized monarchy emerge with a structure to rival the western states.

The Holy Roman Empire

The Holy Roman Empire, despite its grandiose name, was a loose confederation of German and Italian states under the theoretical suzerainty of the Holy Roman emperor. It is a good example of a feudal state in which many diversified interests were able to prevent the consolidation of a centralized monarchy. The roots of this decentralization that bordered on anarchy were buried deep in the early Middle Ages.

The Imperial Myth. The memory of Roman glory and power lingered for centuries in northern Europe. The Frankish empire of Charlemagne and the Roman empire of the German nation forged by Otto the Great (r. 936–973) were both attempts to reunite Europe under the temporal and spiritual guidance of one leader. This dream was challenged by two serious rivals: the papacy, which claimed for itself the role of universal arbiter of European affairs, and the hundreds of lesser princes who, though their own families were not powerful enough to claim the imperial dignity, could band together to protect their independence.

Imperial Structure. The emperor reigned over but did not rule a motley assortment of over two hundred independent states, including secular and ecclesiastical principalities and imperial (that is, independent) cities. In addition, the emperor was the nominal overlord of nearly two thousand imperial knights who owed allegiance to no other man. When danger threatened, the emperor convened the diet, which consisted of three estates representing the electors, the nonelectoral principalities (excluding the knights), and the cities. The diet's main function was to provide a forum for the formulation of an imperial policy, since it had neither the will nor the machinery to act as a regular legislature.

Imperial-Papal Rivalry. Before 1000 the emperors had protected the papacy from military attack and at the same time had controlled the Church. After external aggressors were defeated, the papacy bridled at the continued domination by the emperor. An overt struggle arose from Otto's attempt to maintain his dominance in the Germanies against other powerful families, for although he was stronger than any other single rival, they posed a collective threat. The emperor adopted the practice of appointing ecclesiastical princes as military vassals and imperial advisers. These clerics provided invaluable administrative services and could be counted on to support the emperor against the nobility. Although clerical vows of celibacy precluded the creation of new family dynasties, the ecclesiastical fiefdoms were henceforth Church property. In this manner vast areas of the empire passed into the hands of the Church. It was imperative that the emperor maintain the right to invest all high-ranking clerics since their role was as much political as it was religious. The papacy challenged the right of secular rulers to appoint bishops and further inflamed the situation by claims of temporal authority. The struggle continued throughout the Middle Ages and reached epic proportions in the contest of Emperor Henry IV (r. 1056–1106) and Pope Gregory VII (1073–1085) over investiture. Neither the imperial forces (known as Ghibellines) nor papal supporters (called Guelphs) could win a victory for their universalist pretensions. The real victors were the supporters of particularism on both sides who hoped to maintain their independence.

Imperial-Princely Rivalry. The reign of Emperor Frederick II (r. 1211–1250) ended the hopes of imperial dominance. He freed the ecclesiastical principalities from imperial control under terms of the Confederation with the Ecclesiastical Princes and extended this agreement to refrain from maintaining fortifications or imperial officials within the secular principalities in the Statute in Favor of the Princes (1232).

The German princes continued the ritual of electing the emperor but were determined to turn him into a mere figurehead. They accomplished this in 1356 by the promulgation of the Golden Bull (so-called because of its golden seal). This edict confirmed the practice of imperial election. The electoral college consisted of four secular rulers (the king of Bohemia, the duke of Saxony, the count palatine of the Rhine, and the margrave of Brandenburg) and three ecclesiastical princes (the archbishops of Trier, Cologne, and Mainz). These men, though not necessarily the most powerful in the Germanies, took on added prestige, and within their realms the emperor had no authority. The bull, by its choice of electors and its exclusion of the pope, confirmed the shift of the imperial center of gravity from Italy to Germany. Henceforth the electors attempted to choose the weakest among them for the imperial dignity. It was in this way that a Hapsburg was first elected in 1273. After 1438 the title remained in this family until the Holy Roman Empire disappeared with scarcely a ripple in 1806.

States within the Empire

Although a unified German state failed to develop along the lines followed by Spain, France, or England, strong states did emerge within the empire.

The Hapsburg State. By the middle of the fifteenth century, the German emperors had long since given up hope of turning their imperial dignity into a powerful office. However, the Hapsburg family had used its position to create the strongest dynastic state in central Europe. Through a succession of marriages, the Hapsburgs had emerged as the most powerful family in Germany. Emperor Maximilian I (r. 1493–1519) bequeathed to his nephew Charles V the family domains within the empire, including the archduchy of Austria and his wife's Burgundian inheritance of the Netherlands, Luxemburg, and the Free County. The Netherlands were the commercial center of northern Europe and, as such, one of Charles's most valuable territories. To these Charles added his own inheritance, including the united kingdoms of Spain (where he ruled as Charles I), the kingdom of the Naples, and the Spanish Empire in the New World. In addition, Charles's brother Ferdinand was king of Bohemia and had the dubious honor of being elected king of Hungary at a time when it was threatened by the Turks.

Saxony. Electoral Saxony was one of the richest states of Germany. The Wittin dynasty ruled the territory after 1423, and their lands encompassed the most industrialized area of central Europe.

Brandenburg. The electorate of Brandenburg was a poor state that spread across the Oder and Elbe rivers. In 1415 it passed into the hands of Frederick Hohenzollern as a gift from Emperor Sigismund.

Despite the land's unpromising appearance and lack of resources, the Hohenzollerns developed a powerful dynastic state that ultimately effected the unification of Germany in the nineteenth century.

The Swiss Confederation. The Swiss Confederation was formed in 1291 by the forest cantons (districts) of Schwyz, Uri, and Unterwalden in order to provide for their common defense. Additions to this original group, including the important city cantons of Lucerne, Zurich, and Bern, continued throughout the Middle Ages. Each district maintained its local independence, but a federal diet was created in 1391 to formulate a common foreign policy. The chief threats to Swiss independence were the expansionist designs of the archduke of Austria and, later, of the dukes of Burgundy. The intermittent struggle reached a climax in the last quarter of the fifteenth century. The Burgundian threat ended, after a three-year war, at Nancy (1477) where Charles the Bold was killed and his army routed. Emperor Maximilian in turn met defeat at the hands of Swiss pikemen at Dornach, and in the subsequent Treaty of Basel (1499), he gave de facto recognition to Swiss independence. Though social unrest continued to disturb the cantons, the martial prowess of their infantry discouraged further aggression and made the Swiss the most sought-after mercenaries on the Continent.

Italy. In 1500 only the geography of the Italian boot gave the peninsula an illusion of unity. Three major areas of political development stand out amidst the diversity.

DUCHIES AND REPUBLICS. Northern Italy had maintained its urban culture throughout the Middle Ages, and the wealth of these financial, commercial, and manufacturing centers gave them an importance far beyond their limited size. These states owed only nominal allegiance to the Holy Roman emperor. The duchies had generally fallen under the control of despots who maintained themselves with the aid of mercenaries (*condottieri*). Francesco Sforza, himself a soldier of fortune, ruled (1450–1466) the powerful duchy of Milan, which controlled the Alpine passes above the fertile Lombard plain. The republics survived in the leading commercial centers where the wealthy merchants maintained themselves as a tight oligarchy. The most powerful republics were Venice, which gained its wealth as a middleman in European trade, and Florence, which thrived as a center of woolen cloth manufacture and finance.

PAPAL STATES. The pope ruled as an elected monarch over a wide band of territory from the mouth of the Tiber in the south to Ravenna and Bologna in the north. Despite their theoretical function as spiritual leaders, the popes of the fifteenth century held court and pursued politics in the same manner as the other secular rulers of the peninsula. It was through diplomacy and war that the independent nobility of the Papal States were reduced to obedience under the strong arm of Cesare Borgia, son of Pope Alexander VI (1492–1503), and his successor Julius II (1503–1513), the warrior pope. The Papal States remained the political adjunct of the Catholic church until the unification of Italy (1866–1870).

KINGDOM OF NAPLES. All the territory south of the Papal States, including the island of Sicily, was the domain of the king of Naples. Although the countryside barely maintained the poorest peasantry in Italy, the city of Naples served as the center of a Mediterranean commerical empire after Alfonso of Aragon (r. 1435–1458) added it to his Spanish domains. Like other Italian rulers of his age, Alfonso patronized the arts, and he transformed Naples into a brilliant cultural center.

The States of Eastern Europe

Eastern Europe did not experience the development of centralized states so prevalent in the West during the fifteenth and sixteenth centuries. Although strong states sometimes did emerge, their strength reflected the skill of a few dynamic leaders rather than the emergence of institutions and customs that could guarantee long-term security and prosperity. This pattern resulted from the dominance of semi-independent landed magnates who sustained their position over the lesser gentry and maintained a system of oppressive serfdom through the election of weak kings. Thus the vast territorial expanses of Hungary, Poland, and Lithuania belied their internal weakness.

Hungary. The election of Matthias Corvinus (r. 1458–1490) began an era of strong monarchial government in Hungary. In alliance with the lesser nobility, Matthias temporarily broke the power of the great landowners. By raising new taxes with a rationalized administration, he created a standing army unsurpassed in Europe. He expanded his area of dominance with the conquest of Bohemia, where he became king in 1470, and the occupation of Silesia and Moravia. He made Vienna his capital after seizing it in 1485. When he died in 1490, he left Hungary the dominant state in central Europe. His work of consolidation disintegrated during the reigns of Ladislas II (r. 1490–1516) and Louis II (r. 1516–1526) when the magnates reasserted their autonomy. In this weakened situation, Hungary was unable to withstand the Turkish onslaught beginning in 1521. At the battle of Mohács (August 1526), Louis was slain and his feudal army destroyed, leaving the country open to conquest. The Turks eventually seized all of the kingdom except a narrow strip of territory on the Austrian frontiers.

Poland. The history of Poland during the fifteenth and sixteenth centuries closely resembles the Hungarian pattern. Casimir IV (r. 1447–1492) allied himself to the gentry (*szlachta*) in order to curb the powerful magnates. The monarchy paid a high price for its support, however, for henceforth the gentry gained the right to veto legislation. John Albert (r. 1492–1501) continued this policy and the Statute of Piotrkow (1496) confirmed the rights of the nobility to control land and peasants. Alexander I (r. 1501–1506) completed the transformation of Poland into an aristocratic ogligarchy. Under the terms of the Constitution of Radom (1505), an aristocratically elected diet became the sole legislative organ. Such a step might have led to the development of a parliamentary system similar to England's, but the irresponsible Polish nobility concerned only with short-term class interests such as the formal establishment of serfdom in 1511, turned the diet into a totally negative instrument incapable of formulating coherent national policy. The same failure can be noted in the system of elective monarchy which, after the extinction of the Jagellon dynasty with the death of Sigismund II (1572), brought increasing instability and foreign intervention. The Union of Lublin (1569), unifying Poland and Lithuania, temporarily strengthened the state in its struggle with Russia, but in the long run, Poland remained too disorganized to face the challenges of more efficient states.

Russia. Russia stands apart in the history of Europe. Its contact with the West was continual but limited. Russia absorbed much of its culture from Byzantium while hardly being affected by either the Renaissance or the Reformation. Under Czars Ivan III and Ivan IV, it evolved an autocratic government, built upon the service of the nobility and the servitude of peasant masses, that lasted until the twentieth century.

RUSSIA'S MEDIEVAL ORIGINS. No unified Russian state existed during the early Middle Ages. The Russians were an assortment of principalities, the most important being the Kievan state. The Rus, a Scandinavian people related to the marauding Vikings of the west, ruled this commercial state from their capital on the banks of the Dnieper River. Kiev controlled the trade route that throughout the tenth and eleventh centuries linked the Baltic region to Constantinople, the great metropolis of the medieval world. Kiev declined during the twelfth century and was destroyed by the Mongols in 1240, but by that time Russia had been indelibly imprinted by Byzantine culture. The Mongol invaders, known as the Golden Horde, settled in south-central Russia and collected tribute from the Russian states that continued to exist by their sufferance.

The largest Russian state to survive the conquest was the northern principality of Novgorod. Prince Alexander Nevski (r. 1238–1263) successfully defended the western frontiers of Novgorod against the Swedes (1240) and the Teutonic Knights (1242), while at the same time restraining the hot bloods whose desire to throw off Mongol hegemony would have led to annihilation. After Nevski's death in 1263, complex rules of succession triggered intermittent civil war that debilitated the Russian states. Despite the early leadership of Novgorod, Muscovy (the principality of Moscow) emerged to lead the struggle against the Mongols. A Muscovite army led by Dmitri Donskoi destroyed the myth of Mongol invincibility at the battle of Kulikovo (1380), and during the reign of Vasili II (r. 1425–1462) the Metropolitan of Moscow (roughly equivalent to a Western archbishop) became the focus of a Russian national church.

REIGN OF IVAN III, "THE GREAT" (1462–1505). The history of modern Russia dates from the accession of Ivan III, Prince of Moscow, for it was through his conquests, marriage, and diplomacy that Russia emerged as a significant European state.

Territorial Expansion. Ivan conquered Novgorod (1478), annexed its vast northern domains, and subdued Moscow's southern rival, Tver (1485). The Mongols, wracked by internal disorder, could not maintain their suzerainty over Moscow after 1480, and the khan of the Crimea allied himself with Ivan during the Russian conquest of eastern Lithuania (1501–1503).

The Byzantine Dowry. In 1472 Ivan married Sophia Palaeologus, niece and only heir of Constantine XI, the last Byzantine emperor. Constantine had died when the Turks stormed his capital in 1453, and under Ivan's direction Moscow became the "third Rome" as the successor to the imperial heritage. It was Ivan who began to use the title *Czar* (caesar) and instituted the practice of autocracy that became the dominant element of Russian state development. Russia also became the repository of Byzantine culture and ultimately the leader of Orthodox Christianity. Working under the direction of Sophia, Italian architects and artists converted the Kremlin from a medieval fortress into a royal palace and administrative center. Sophia also replaced the informality of the Muscovite court with the etiquette and ritual befitting the seat of imperial power.

Political Consolidation. Among the rulers of eastern Europe, the Russian autocrats alone succeeded in destroying the independence of the great landowners (*boyars*) by reducing them to subservience. This transformation began slowly during the reigns of Ivan III and his son Vasili III (r. 1505–1533). Unlike the Western warrior class, the boyars traditionally held personal estates unencumbered by military obligations and were free to shift their allegiance from one prince to another. But Ivan's conquests greatly reduced their range of choice, and he began the practice of granting estates (*pomestie*) that carried with them obligations of service to the state. Slowly the difference between free and service estates disappeared, and the nobility (*dvorianstvo*) became totally dependent upon the czar. A major consequence of this subjugation was the reduction of the Russian peasantry to a condition of servitude bordering on slavery. This was allowed in order to provide support for the service nobility. Thus, while serfdom virtually disappeared in the West, it was imposed in Russia and remained a dominant feature of the social structure until 1861.

REIGN OF IVAN IV, "THE DREAD" (1533–1584). Ivan IV completed the centralization begun by his predecessors. Though his influence is unquestioned, it is difficult to determine which of his actions were motivated by the cool rationalism of a power politician raised in an age of intrigue and sudden death and which were the acts of a paranoid who felt beset by traitors.

Early Life. Ivan ascended the throne at the age of three. He was fortunate to survive his minority, as boyar families struggled to reassert their authority. In 1547 he became the first ruler to take formally the title *Czar of all the Russias*, and he moved quickly thereafter to extend his authority and to destroy boyar independence.

Territorial Expansion. Ivan followed the expansionist trail blazed by his father. His conquest of Kazan (1552) and Astrakhan (1556) brought the entire Volga River and the shore of the Caspian Sea under Muscovite control, while expansion to the east brought a tenuous hold over western Siberia. In the West the protracted Livonian War (1558–1583), fought in an attempt to gain the Baltic providences of Lithuania, won no long-term gains. Contact with the West was obtained, however, through the English merchants of the Muscovy Company, who carried out extensive trade from their White Sea outposts after initial contact in 1553.

Centralization of Government. Instead of using the boyar council (*Duma*), Ivan relied on a select council of lower-ranking men and created a consultative assembly (*zemski sobor*), which, though little used, was designed to provide the government with information from a relatively large cross section of appointed advisers. He also created administrative offices (*prikazy*) to provide bureaucratic support for the expanding empire. Local councils (*zemstva*) were created to enforce government decisions and collect taxes.

The Oprichnina (1564). Ivan lost confidence in most of his intimate advisers after 1560. His belief that his wife had been murdered triggered a deep depression marked by growing suspicion of a treasonous conspiracy against him. In 1564 he abruptly renounced the throne and withdrew from Moscow. He agreed to resume his authority only on the conditions that many of the leading boyars be executed and that he be granted a vast royal estate (*oprichnina*) that he could rule without reference to regular administrative structure.

During the subsequent reign of terror, thousands of boyars were slaughtered and their lands within the oprichnina distributed as service estates of Ivan's supporters. Although this was a calculated technique of definitely eliminating challengers to czarist authority, the sadistic tortures of his captured opponents can be attributed only to the work of a deranged mind.

The Byzantine and Ottoman Empires

The Eastern Byzantine Empire maintained itself against the barbarian onslaught that engulfed the Roman West in the fifth and sixth centuries. Constantinople served as the commercial hub of the Western world at the peak of its power in the ninth and tenth centuries, but by the eleventh century a decline set in. The city was sacked by Christian crusaders in 1204, and the empire never regained its political or economic equilibrium. Faced wth Venetian trade rivalry and Turkish aggression, the empire slowly contracted while its dwindling resources were consumed in continual civil war. Despite the decline of its material fortunes, the empire experienced an intellectual revival based on hellenic classicism that shone throughout the fourteenth and fifteenth centuries only to be snuffed out by the Turkish conquest in 1453.

Although the Ottoman Turks had maintained pressure in Anatolia for several centuries, they first entered Europe by invitation to help defend the empire against the Serbs. They proved to be dangerous allies, for after first settling in Gallipoli (1354), they made Adrianople their capital (1366) and proceeded to conquer Macedonia (1371) and Bulgaria (1372). They laid seige to Constantinople (1391) but were forced to abandon the attack when their own territory was overrun by Timur's Mongols. Constantinople, however, had only a short reprieve, for the Turks regrouped and, behind Sultan Mohammed II, "the Conqueror" (r. 1451–1481), stormed the city (1453). Led by Suleiman I, "the Magnificent" (r. 1520–1566), the Turkish tide swept over Hungary, whose feudal army was annihilated at Mohács (1526) in a vain attempt to save the country. The flood was stemmed by the Europeans first at the gates of Vienna (1529) and then at Lepanto (1571), the greatest naval battle since antiquity. The Turks nevertheless retained their hold on the eastern Mediterranean and southeastern Europe and remained a serious threat until the end of the seventeenth century.

4

Economic and Social Patterns in the Sixteenth Century

Europe experienced a sharp acceleration in economic growth about 1450, after a century of dislocation and depression. The rapid expansion of financial, industrial, and mercantile activity in turn triggered important alterations of the social structure. The prime mover of this revival was merchant capitalism. *Capitalism* can be described as the production and exchange of goods and services through private initiative for private profit. It is characterized by the consolidation of the means of production in the hands of entrepreneurs who acquire the raw materials, provide the necessary tools or machinery, pay cash wages for the manufacture of the goods, and market the finished product over a wide area. Such activity also presupposes elaborate credit facilities. Capitalism existed throughout the Middle Ages, but it operated on a limited scale because of the ideological constraints of medieval Christianity and the economic limitations of a predominantly agricultural environment. Capitalism became the dominant type of economic organization during the early modern period as the result of the complex interaction of a number of forces.

Causes of Economic Revival

No single factor can explain the resurgence of the European economy. Each of the following developments combined to produce change.

Population Growth. The European population grew rapidly between 1450 and 1700. Although precise demographic statistics are not available, economic historians estimate that the population rose from about fifty million to seventy million, with the greatest increase coming after 1450. Urban development clearly supports this view, as do contemporary accounts of the hardships caused by population pressure. Such growth required a greater production of food, clothing, and housing. Although the additional manpower drove wages down, it stimulated business by lowering costs.

Political Stability. The political consolidation discussed in chapters 2 and 3 provided greater security for the rural population and thus increased agricultural production. It also provided a secure area of operation for merchants. In addition, the monarchs themselves stimulated economic growth by increased expenditures and the granting of valuable trading monopolies.

Development of Business Techniques. In order to expand their operations as business opportunities increased, merchants added to the techniques developed during the Middle Ages to facilitate more complex transactions. The elaboration of the credit system to provide for the exchange of commercial paper by brokers and banks played a greater role in the development of capitalism in this era than did technological innovations.

Overseas Expansion. The growth and transformation of the European economy began independently of the overseas expansion of the fifteenth century. However, the discovery of new trade routes and the New World had an immediate and profound effect on every facet of economic life. The importation of precious metal and agricultural products changed the role of the merchants and affected the political fortunes of every major political power. Ultimately the discoveries shifted the balance of economic and political power from the Mediterranean to the Atlantic.

Merchant Capitalism

The merchant capitalist was the driving force of the commercial expansion. He combined the roles of financier, industrialist, and merchant within a single firm, and by infusing the old techniques with vibrant capitalist spirit, he helped transform European life.

Business Techniques. The key to large-scale capitalism was accurate accounting and extended credit facilities. Double-entry bookkeeping (begun in the fourteenth century) provided the entrepreneur with an accurate and current record of all his transactions and enabled him to determine his financial situation from day to day. Bills of exchange (begun in the twelfth century) enabled merchants to do business without the immediate transfer of goods or cash. The bill of exchange and the draft (begun in the fourteenth century), which were similar to the modern bank check, permitted complicated and widespread transactions without the cumbersome exchange of coin or bullion. The *bourse* (exchange) provided a centralized financial facility. Merchants from all over Europe gathered at London, Antwerp,

Lyons, and other centers to settle accounts, make purchases, and buy insurance. Banks received deposits for safekeeping, acted as clearinghouses, and loaned money at interest. Private bankers had operated in the Middle Ages, but in the fifteenth century, the danger of bankruptcy resulting from defaulted loans led to the creation of public banks of deposits.

Types of Business Organization. There were three basic types of business organization in common usage during the early modern period. The partnership and the regulated company were survivals from the medieval period. The joint-stock company was a new kind of organization designed to fit changing business needs.

PARTNERSHIP. Partnership was the most common type of business organization throughout the early modern period. It was a very flexible arrangement that might consist of two men and a single shop or a mammoth consortium with branches in every financial center of Europe. Partnerships could be formed for a lifetime or for the duration of a single venture. The major drawback of this type of combination was that it could be easily disrupted by the death of one member.

REGULATED COMPANY. The regulated company was chartered by the government and given a trade monopoly over a single area or product. The directors of the company determined general trading rules for all the members, but each merchant was individually responsible for his own clients and accounts.

JOINT-STOCK COMPANY. This type of company was similar to the modern corporation. The company received a charter and was governed by directors elected by the shareholders. The company sold shares to accumulate capital for operating expenses. The joint-stock company differed from the partnership in that it was a permanent association of capital rather than a temporary federation of men. It differed from the regulated company by engaging in business ventures in the name of the company and then dividing the profits in the form of dividends. This form of association had the advantage of accumulating large amounts of permanent capital, and some of them, such as the Dutch East India Company (founded in 1602), returned enormous profits for over a century. The limited need for such vast reservoirs of capital and the loss of confidence after the collapse of some ventures as a result of stock manipulation created public mistrust that was not overcome until the nineteenth century.

Centers of Capitalism. Although Europe remained predominantly rural and agricultural throughout the fifteenth and sixteenth centuries, urban commercial activity expanded enormously in Germany, the Netherlands, and England. Industrial capitalism also developed, at the expense of the guild system. Unlike modern industrialism, however, sixteenth-century production was often carried out by dispersed craftsmen working in a rural setting. This was particularly true of the textile industry in Holland and England. It should also be remembered that despite the economic potential of overseas discoveries, most economic activity was between Europeans who bought and sold European products.

ITALY. The city-states of northern Italy had been the most important commercial centers of medieval Europe. Florence shared economic control of Italy with Venice. It was no accident that the apogee of Florentine brilliance and wealth coincided with the activities of her greatest merchants, Cosimo de Medici (1389–1464) and his grandson Lorenzo, "the Magnificent," who ruled Florence from 1478 to 1492. Their principal activities were banking and trade, and they maintained branch offices in every major capital of western Europe. In addition they had interests in the manufacture of woolen textiles, for which Florence was famous, and the mining of alum, an indispensable mineral used to fix dyes in cloth. Though the Medici were the most powerful merchant financiers in Italy and supplied the Church with two popes (Leo X and Clement VII) and France with two queens (Catherine and Marie), their activities were typical of the kind of men who made their fortunes in the counting house.

SOUTHERN GERMANY. Augsburg became the commercial center of central Europe early in the sixteenth century. It owed its prominence to its geographical position on the major north-south trade route, the discovery of silver in the Tirol and Hungary, and its success in developing more advanced business practices than those of many of its neighbors (such as Nuremberg, which had evolved a rigid guild system during the Middle Ages). Within Augsburg there were a number of powerful family firms, including the Welsers, who were prominent in financing activities in the New World; the Hochstetters, who grew rich from the spice trade; and the Fuggers, who amassed their fortune in mining and metallurgy.

The Fuggers had flourished in the textile trade during the early fifteenth century. They emerged as the most powerful merchant family in the sixteenth century through the efforts of Jakob II (1459–1525) and his nephew Anton (1493–1560), who controlled the newly exploited silver, copper, and lead deposits in Hungary and the Tirol. These mines and the foundries associated with them are important examples of early industrial capitalism. Although by modern standards they operated on a limited scale, they required a large initial outlay of capital, and their operations concentrated many wage laborers in a single establishment. The Fuggers accumulated so much wealth from their widespread financial empire that they became the primary bankers of the Hapsburgs during the reign of Emperor Charles V.

THE NETHERLANDS. By the middle of the fifteenth century, the Netherlands had displaced not only the Italians but also its Flemish and Hanseatic rivals and emerged as the financial and commercial center of Europe. Between the 1440s and the 1560s, Antwerp was the nerve center of this activity. It became the hub of northern Europe, acting as the entrepôt for the East Indian spice trade, as Spain's northern outlet for the American trade, as the agent for English wool exports, and as the distribution point for Baltic ship stores. To handle these transactions, the city operated two bourses, one for commodities and one for financial operations. Besides being the financial capital of Europe, Antwerp developed important industries, including the finishing and dyeing of English cloth, sugar refining, and the manufacture of glass and fine earthenware.

ENGLAND. Wool was the most important item in England's commerce, and throughout the Middle Ages, it bound her economy to the Flemish textile industry. In order to extract the largest possible revenue from its most valuable natural resource, the English crown bestowed an export monopoly upon a regulated company known as the Merchant Staplers (1313). By restricting the trade to a single group of merchants and limiting the traffic to designated Flemish cities, the treasury was assured a steady income. The merchants in turn received handsome profits from their exclusive rights.

As a result of trade restrictions, continental weavers paid higher prices for wool than Englishmen did. This in turn stimulated the production of English cloth, which by the middle of the fifteenth century had replaced raw wool as the major export.

English cloth was generally produced in rural areas away from the guild regulations by the *putting-out system*. Under this method a wool merchant purchased the raw material, which he then placed in the hands of artisans. Carders, spinners, weavers, and fullers, each in a different shop, performed their tasks at piece rates while the wool remained the merchant's property. The cloth merchants formed a regulated company (ca. 1400), known as the Merchant Adventurers, which, like the Merchant Staplers, directed a lucrative monopoly from London. The putting-out system was also employed on the Continent, where industrial production was concentrated in the cities. Wherever these new techniques were employed, merchant capitalists grew wealthy while the artisans' standard of living generally declined. The result was simmering discontent that often erupted in peasant revolts and urban riots.

The Voyages of Discovery

The explorations of the fifteenth and sixteenth centuries gave impetus to the commercial expansion that had already begun, dramatically changed the political power structure of Europe, drastically altered the dimensions of the known world, and had an incalculable psychological impact on European civilization.

Early Portuguese Explorations. Portugal took the lead in oceanic exploration under the leadership of Prince Henry, "the Navigator" (1394–1460). Henry earned his reputation as the royal patron and organizer of a systematic program of exploration rather than as an actual participant. He was motivated by a scholarly interest in the unknown, his obligations as a Christian prince in crusades against the North African Moslems, and hopes for trading opportunities. The Portuguese settled the Madeiras (1418), the Azores (1430–1450), and the Cape Verde Islands (1456). By the time Henry died, his captains had also explored the northern third of the African coast and opened trading posts. Although exploration subsequently lagged for a generation, it was renewed by John II (r. 1481–1495), who dispatched Pedro de Covilhão to India by way of the Mediterranean to examine trading possibilities and ordered Bartholomeu Dias to sail for India by circumnavigating Africa. Dias failed to complete the journey but rounded the southern tip of Africa, subsequently known as the Cape of Good Hope. The glory of landing in India fell to Vasco da Gama, who reached the western coast and returned with a valuable cargo of spices in 1498.

Early Spanish Explorations. While Portugal concentrated on the eastern passage of the Indies, the Spanish struck out to the west. The Genoese explorer Christopher Columbus, sailing under the banner of Castile, made four voyages (1492–1504) that resulted in the discovery of Santo Domingo, Puerto Rico, and Jamaica, which he believed formed part of the Japanese archipelago. However, the voyages of Pinzon (1499), Vespucci (1499), and the Portuguese Cabral (1500) made it obvious that a hitherto unknown landmass blocked the westward passage to the East Indies. The disappointment disappeared with Cortes's discovery and conquest (1519) of the Aztec Empire (see p. 44). The full extent of the discoveries emerged with the voyage of Ferdinand Magellan, who left Spain (1519) in search of a southern passage around the American continent. Having passed through the straits that now bear his name, he crossed the Pacific to the Philippines, where he was killed by natives. Sebastian del Cano brought the survivors back to Spain (1522) and thus became the first captain to circumnavigate the globe.

Treaty of Tordesillas. Spain and Portugal realized the importance of their discoveries almost immediately. To avoid conflict, they enlisted the arbitration of Pope Alexander VI, who formulated the Treaty of Tordesillas (1494). The treaty's main feature was a line of demarcation dividing the world into spheres of influence. The Spanish received all the territory to the west of the line including the Americas except Brazil, while the Portuguese laid claim to Africa and India. Using its own geographical information, each side assumed that its hemisphere would include the Indies. The right of two countries to divide the world was, of course, challenged by all the other powers.

Other Voyages of Exploration. England and France sent expeditions into the Atlantic in hopes of finding a northern passage to the Indies. The Venetian John Cabot sailed from England and discovered Cape Breton Island, Newfoundland, and Labrador (1497–1498). Richard Chancellor failed to reach the East via the White Sea but made contact with the Russians at Archangel (1553). Giovanni da Verrazano, in the service of France, skirted the North American shore from South Carolina to Newfoundland, and Jacques Cartier explored the mouth of the Saint Lawrence River (1535).

The Portuguese Empire. Da Gama's voyage (1499) clearly demonstrated the economic rewards available if Portugal could force its way into the Indies trading area. Almeida, the first viceroy of the Indies (1505–1509), destroyed the Arab monopoly by defeating an Egyptian fleet at Diu (1509). His successor, Alfonso Albuquerque (1509–1515), captured strategic points all along the trade routes, and his conquest of Goa (1510), Ceylon (1511), and Malacca (1511) put the spice-producing areas in Portuguese hands. The Portuguese made no attempt to colonize but relied on fortified trading points and sea power to insure their fortune. Despite their initial success, they were not able to prevent Dutch incursions and were finally overpowered in the seventeenth century. They had a far greater long-range impact in Brazil, though initially they had ignored this Western possession. The first colony was organized in 1532, and later a feudal structure based on black slaves from Portuguese Angola provided valuable agricultural products, including sugar and brazilwood.

Spanish Conquest of the Americas. Having established a foothold in Cuba and Hispanola, the Spanish began an armed reconnaissance of the mainland in search of treasure. These expeditions were led by *conquistadores*, usually drawn from the lower nobility, who often held personal honors and private gain above Spanish interests. The greatest of these was Hernando Cortes (1485–1547), who landed on the coast of Mexico in 1519. Although his force contained barely five hundred men, his horses and cannon gave him a distinct psychological edge over his opponents. With the aid of Indian allies, he broke the power of the Aztec Empire in barely two years. From Panama Francisco Pizarro (1470?–1541) launched the conquest of the Peruvian Inca Empire (1531–1535), but a falling-out among his lieutenants prevented rapid exploitation of the area. Further to the north, scores of expeditions attempted to track down rumors of even greater wealth. Although the mythical empires alluded them, the explorers discovered the extent of the North American continent. The expedition of Hernando de Soto sailed from Havana and landed near Tampa Bay in May 1539. De Soto wandered as far north as Tennessee and turned west to central Texas. Though he died on the banks of the Mississippi River, which he discovered, the remainder of his party reached Mexico in September 1543. In 1540 Francisco Coronado marched north from Mexico in search of the Seven Cities of Gold, and during his two-year trek, he explored the region from Arizona to Kansas. (A discussion of the organization of the Spanish Empire will be found on page 86.)

Impact of Overseas Discovery. It is impossible to separate the effects of overseas expansion from preexisting developments in Europe, but it is clear that, whatever the mix, the effect was a rapid acceleration of commercial activity accompanied by profound social and political adjustments.

THE PRICE REVOLUTION. There was a sharp rise in European prices resulting from population growth, the opening of new mines in central Europe, and the influx of bullion from overseas. Inflation hurt those unable to adjust their income to rising costs. Initially, it struck landowners who were bound to honor long-term leases at low rents. Although some of the nobility caught in this vise lost their lands, most eventually renegotiated short-term leases and began to produce commercial goods for cash. Merchant capitalists probably gained most, for they were able to adjust prices to cost, and their business transactions were aided by the increased circulation of money. The working class lost most in this transformation. Small cultivators had to leave their lands to make way for large-scale farming or, at best, see their small profits eaten by higher rents. The wages of artisans failed to keep pace with the rising cost of living, and their living standard actually declined throughout the sixteenth and seventeenth centuries.

INTERNATIONAL TRADE. The opening of new trade routes that relied on longer but cheaper sea lanes to the East and easy access to the New World precipitated a gradual but significant shift in the focus of economic activity from the Mediterranean and south Europe to the Atlantic seaboard. Cadiz, Lisbon, Antwerp, and London were among the cities that took advantage of their geographic location to become major European entrepôts.

SHIFT IN THE BALANCE OF POWER. Although the sources of political power are difficult to gauge, it is obvious that the European balance of power adjusted to the new economic realities. Those states most able to take advantage of the new resources, whether developed at home or imported from abroad, rose to preeminence. Spain and Portugal were the first to profit by new opportunities in the sixteenth century, but they were displaced by the more productive and better-organized French, Dutch, and English in the seventeenth century.

Technology

Technological developments in the fifteenth and sixteenth centuries were generally limited to improvements on medieval innovations. The voyages of discovery were made possible by improvements in the compass and the astrolabe (used to determine latitude). New rigging techniques made ships more maneuverable and better able to sail off the wind. The waterwheel was adapted from its traditional role as a gristmill into a power source for the textile industry and paper manufacturing, while the windmill became a valuable water pump. Although these adaptations played an important role in European life, they did not have the dramatic impact of three new discoveries: gunpowder, printing, and paper.

Gunpowder. Gunpowder, an explosive mixture of saltpeter, sulfur, and charcoal, was a Chinese invention introduced into Europe by the Arabs. Although it was known during the Middle Ages, it had a significant impact only in the fifteenth century when the development of the cannon and the handgun revolutionized warfare.

The expense of artillery pieces limited them for all but the most powerful princes. Though too unmaneuverable for the battlefield, the cannon could breach the previously impregnable fortifications of insubordinate vassals, and in pitched battle the armored knights, whose forefathers had dominated the medieval battlefield, were no match for the musketeer. The production of these weapons also stimulated the metallurgical industry, which developed the casting of bronze and iron cannon into a fine art.

Printing and Paper. Printing, like gunpowder, arrived in a rudimentary form from the East by way of the Arabs. Impressions were originally lifted from woodcuts, which, while satisfactory for pictures, were hardly adaptable to written copy. A breakthrough came around 1440 with the invention of movable type in the German city of Mainz. Although this invention is usually ascribed to Johann Gutenberg (1400?–1468), he was only one of a community of printers who developed the type, ink, and presses necessary for their trade. At approximately the same time, ragpaper, developed in the fourteenth century, began to replace parchment and vellum as writing material. This inexpensive medium made large-scale printing practical.

It is difficult to overstate the importance of printing to European civilization. Relatively economical and accurate copies of every type of book, from the Bible to business ledgers, became available throughout Europe in great quantities. Widespread access to the accumulated knowledge of centuries, which had previously been much restricted, spurred scholarly humanistic studies and raised the educational level, particularly among the bourgeoisie. The circulation at the beginning of the Reformation of hundreds of thousands of copies of Martin Luther's pamphlets attacking the papacy is only one example of the dramatic impact of this new medium. Wholesale censorship and the banning of books also date from this era.

5

The Renaissance

The term *Renaissance* (French, "rebirth") is used by historians to denote the transitional period from the fourteenth through the sixteenth centuries that witnessed the disintegration of the medieval world and the emergence of so-called modern values and institutions. The political and economic origins of this transition have been discussed in chapters 2, 3, and 4. This chapter will outline the intellectual aspects of this evolution.

The origins, nature, impact, and even the existence of the Renaissance have formed the topic of a long and unresolved scholarly debate, but several general tendencies can be noted. Renaissance scholars and artists perceived the crumbling of the medieval synthesis and felt themselves to be participants in a new historical epoch. They were contemptuous of what they derisively called the "Middle Ages" and hoped to build a new society, using the remnants of the ancient Roman and Greek civilizations as their blueprint. Their rejection of the medieval preoccupation with metaphysics and their concentration upon human fulfillment account for the brilliant flowering of arts and letters. The break with the past, however, was neither so abrupt nor complete as they imagined, and the values of the Renaissance remained essentially Christian.

The Italian Phase

The Renaissance found its earliest and clearest expression among the city-states of northern Italy. The commercial ethos of this region fostered a cosmopolitan outlook that encouraged individualism and new ideas. Vast profits from manufacturing, trade, and finance created a class of wealthy merchants and urban noblemen with both the leisure time and the funds to beautify their surroundings and enrich their minds. Thus the Medici of Florence, the Sforzas of Milan, the Estes of Ferrara, and the papacy itself, to name only a few examples, became the patrons of a flourishing intellectual and artistic community. Throughout the study of the Renaissance, it should be remembered that only a fraction of the population participated in or savored the cultural achievements and that the city-states were not a quiet haven for scholars and artists. On the contrary, the Italian peninsula was continually wracked by conspiratorial coups, foreign invasions, economic dislocation, and social unrest.

Humanism. Humanism was a scholarly movement devoted to the study of Latin and Greek literature dealing with the proper method of expression and the rules of human conduct. The humanities included grammar, rhetoric, poetry, history, and ethics. Although the humanists concentrated initially on the rediscovery and imitation of the pure style of classical Latin and Greek, which had been corrupted or lost during the Middle Ages, the movement broadened into an appreciation of human potential and a striving to fulfill it.

The humanist movement stimulated the spirit of inquiry, sharpened the techniques of scholarly investigation, and promoted the use of proper literary form. At the same time, it must be noted that the humanist often stressed form over content, imitation over creativity, and Latin and Greek over the vernacular. This last development probably retarded the literary use of the living languages, particularly Italian, which had come alive in the *Divine Comedy* through the brilliance of Dante Alighieri (1265–1321), Petrarch, and Boccaccio.

Early Humanists. Francesco Petrarch (1304–1374) is considered the father of Italian humanism. Educated at the papal court in Avignon, he abandoned the study of law to pursue his passion for classical literature. He devoted his life to the study of Latin and the collection of Greek manuscripts, which he treasured but could not read. Despite his highly developed Latin style, his greatest contributions to literature were his sonnets to Laura, which he wrote in Italian.

His student Giovanni Boccaccio (1313–1375) followed in his footsteps. Boccaccio brought humanism to Florence and added Greek to his accomplishments but wrote his masterpiece, the *Decameron*, in Italian. This tale of aristocratic courtiers entertaining themselves while fleeing from the plague demonstrates the vitality and joy for life typical of the Renaissance. It is also typical of the age that Boccaccio was later ashamed of both his use of Italian and his ribald stories.

THE FLOWERING OF HUMANISM. Medieval scholars were familiar with the writings of Virgil, Ovid, Seneca, and Cicero, among other Roman writers, and the Aristotelian philosophy formed an integral part of Thomist philosophy. Many of the priceless manuscripts were "discovered" by humanist treasure hunters in monasteries, where they had been preserved through the long "Dark Ages." Although new writers and manuscripts were discovered, the most significant element of new Greek and Latin studies was the examination of classical writings within the context of the pagan societies that created them. Attempts were made, however, particularly by Platonists, to reconcile the ancient philosophy to Christian values. The many facets of humanism can be seen throughout the work and interests of its most prominent representatives.

Bruni. Leonardo Bruni (1369–1444) was one of a new breed of historians who rejected the view of history as a chronicle illustrating the unfolding of a divine plan for mankind. His *History of Florence* set the tone for secular history by tracing the development of the city's institutions to the Roman Republic. History became the study of man and a guide to human action rather than an adjunct to theology.

Valla. The great contribution of Lorenzo Valla (1406–1457) was the development of *philology*, the critical examination of texts to ascertain their authenticity and to study the evolution of language and ideas. In the course of his studies, he was able to prove that the *Donation of Constantine*, under whose terms the emperor who died in 337 supposedly bequeathed his temporal power to the pope, was an eighth-century forgery. Further studies of Greek manuscripts uncovered significant errors in Saint Jerome's Latin translation of the Bible.

Ficino. With Medici support, Marsilio Ficino (1433–1499) gathered about him a group of Florentine scholars dedicated to the study of Plato. Neoplatonism stressed the dignity of man and the ideals of beauty, harmony, and love which though imperfect in the physical world, were reflections of ideas in the mind of God. Neoplatonism had a powerful impact on art, sculpture, and architecture.

Pico della Mirandola. Pico della Mirandola (1463–1494) absorbed the skills of his teacher Ficino and then blazed new trails. During his short life, he shone as the greatest linguist of his age and the most skilled non-Jewish Hebraic scholar in the West. His *Oration of the Dignity of Man* extolled the flexibility and potentiality of the greatest of God's creations.

THE RENAISSANCE MAN. A new vision of humanity emerged from the intense study of the pagan classics, and it reinforced the secular culture of urban Italy. Life was no longer regarded simply as the preparation for a Christian death. Renaissance writers stressed the dignity of man and the importance of the fulfillment of human potentiality. The Renaissance hero possessed *virtù*, a quality of manliness that not only included the masculine skills of war and statecraft but presupposed virtuosity in arts and letters as well. He was expected to take an active part in civic life, hone his individual skills, and bear himself with style and grace.

Castiglione. The most popular guide to the attainment of virtù was *The Courtier*, published by Baldassare Castiglione (1478–1529) in 1528 and translated into every major European language. It stressed the value of humanist education and served as a handbook for courtly etiquette.

Machiavelli. The life and work of Niccolò Machiavelli (1469–1527) embody much that is typical of the Renaissance. He served as secretary of state for republican Florence from 1498 until the re-establishment of the Medici despotism in 1512. Besides being a dedicated civil servant, he was a versatile humanist scholar. He wrote two major historical works: a *History of Florence* and *Discourses on the First Ten Books of Livy*, an analysis of the Roman Republic. He also wrote prose fiction, poetry, and several plays, including *Mandragola*, a biting satire of Florentine life that is one of the best comedies in the Italian language.

Machiavelli's greatest accomplishments were as a political theorist, and he is best remembered as the author of *The Prince* (1513), the first purely secular political treatise of modern times. Medieval theorists had viewed politics as one aspect of the divine order, in which God's earthly representatives, including the emperor and the pope, were given authority to facilitate the salvation of mankind. Political action was thus theoretically based on Christian morality. Machiavelli lived in an age in which this theoretical model bore no resemblance to reality. *The Prince* is an empirical examination of politics as a human activity whose sole function is the seizure and retention of power. In it, Machiavelli warns prospective rulers that all men are guided by self-interest and will employ cunning, deceit, and force to gratify their appetites. The "Machiavellian" ruler can maintain himself in office and protect his state only by ignoring the constraints of personal morality and adopting the same stratagems as his enemies. Machiavelli has often been condemned by idealists for his amorality, but he gave Western man an astute appraisal of the nature of politics and the functioning of the state.

The Arts. Few eras have known such a flowering of artistic genius as the Italian Renaissance. Although artists drew heavily upon the medieval and Byzantine heritage, they approached their subjects from a new perspective. They perceived man as a noble and beautiful creature who gloried in life and ruled the world. Art came to reflect the classical precepts of balance, symmetry, and harmony. The artist, usually competent in more than one medium, rose to an honored position, and his talent was sought by princes and popes.

PAINTING. Painting reflected the secularization of Renaissance interests. Though religious themes continued to predominate, they were challenged by an interest in secular subjects, particularly portraits and mythological scenes. Artists developed new techniques to create the illusion of three-dimensional reality. These included: (1) linear perspective, which creates a sense of depth by decreasing the size of objects receding to the vanishing point; (2) aerial perspective, in which the sense of depth is enhanced by diminishing detail and sharpness; and (3) *chiaroscuro*, which creates solidity and form through the interplay of light and shadow. Renaissance artists also developed oil painting as a new medium to complement *tempera*, which employed a water-soluble base to bind pigments, and *fresco*, a technique in which paint is applied on wet plaster to decorate walls. Only a few of the greatest artists can be mentioned here.

Giotto. The work of Giotto di Bondone (1266?–1337) binds medieval art to the Renaissance. His religious frescoes, particularly his decoration for the chapel at Padua, exhibit solidity of form that was an inspiration to fifteenth-century Florentine artists.

Masaccio. The frescoes of Masaccio (Tommaso Guidi, 1401–1428) in the Florentine Brancacci Chapel set the standard for early Renaissance artists. Their dramatic effect is derived from the expert use of perspective and chiaroscuro coupled with Masaccio's ability to portray emotion.

Botticelli. The influence of Neoplatonism is clearly evident in the work of Sandro Botticelli (1444?–1510). The *Primavera* (ca. 1478) and the *Birth of Venus* (ca. 1485) use mythological themes to convey a Platonic statement of idealized beauty.

Leonardo da Vinci. Leonardo da Vinci (1452–1519) must be considered the epitome of the ideal Renaissance man. His wide-ranging genius included painting, sculpture, engineering, and science. Though there remain barely a dozen of his paintings, they comprise some of the greatest examples of Western art. The *Last Supper* (1497) and the *Mona Lisa* (ca. 1503) not only display his mastery of all the artist's technical skills but also convey a sense of emotional drama.

Raphael. Raphael Santi (1483–1520) embodied in his work the main currents of Renaissance art and philosophy. The Neoplatonic search for idealized beauty received harmonious and tender treatment in his madonnas, while his impressive Vatican frescoes, particularly the *School of Athens* and *Disputa* (1509–1511), demonstrate a desire to reconcile the body of pagan philosophy with Christian values.

Michelangelo. Michelangelo Buonarroti (1475–1564) is best remembered as a sculptor, but his fresco decoration of the Sistine Chapel (1508–1512) is a masterpiece that testifies to the artist's total dedication to his work. Hundreds of figures span the ceiling to tell the biblical story of Genesis. The powerful nude figures illustrate both the artist's background as a sculptor and his feeling of mankind's link with God. This mural is a marked contrast to the *Last Judgment* (1541), which rises above the main altar. Completed during the spiritual agony of the Reformation, it is a brooding statement of human mortality and the wages of sin.

Titian. Tiziano Vecelli (1477–1576), known as Titian, was the great master of the Venetian school and the capstone of the High Renaissance. His work is typified by a highly refined sense of color, particularly flesh tones. His most notable works include portraits, mythological tales, and female nudes.

SCULPTURE. Renaissance sculptors were not content to provide merely the architectural ornamentation that typified medieval sculpture. Though continuing to apply their skill to the adornment of religious buildings, they revived the classical art form by creating freestanding masterpieces that were independent artistic statements.

Ghiberti. Lorenzo Ghiberti's (1378–1455) masterpiece was the set of doors for the baptistry of the Florence cathedral. Consisting of ten bronze panels of exquisite design and execution, they were esteemed to be fit as the *Gates of Paradise*.

Donatello. Donatello's (1386?–1466) bronze *David* exemplifies the adaptation of classical models to biblical themes so typical of the Renaissance. This work, commissioned by Cosimo de Medici, was the first freestanding nude created since antiquity.

Verrocchio. Andrea Del Verrocchio's (1435–1488) monumental equestrian statue of the military commander Colleoni clearly demonstrates the virtuosity of Renaissance sculpture. It combines the scientific knowledge of anatomy and newly developed bronze-casting techniques with a realistic portrayal of horseflesh and the psychological portrait of a self-possessed warlord.

Michelangelo. Michelangelo (see p. 51) was the incomparable master of Renaissance sculpture, and he has few peers in any age. His marble *David* almost abandons the biblical theme in favor of the Platonic idealization of an Olympian athlete, while the deeply moving *Pietà* combines a central event in Christian theology with the universal statement of maternal grief for a dead son.

ARCHITECTURE. Renaissance architecture followed the trend of classical revival by stressing geometrical symmetry and mathematical proportion. This style was applied to ecclesiastical buildings and the palatial residences of merchants and princes. The most striking innovation was the massive dome, designed not only to enclose interior space but also to present a monumental exterior. Brunelleschi (1377?–1446) capped the Florence cathedral with a magnificent dome. It served as a model for the crown of Saint Peter's in Rome, which combined the designs of Bramante (1444–1514) and Michelangelo.

The Renaissance outside Italy

Though Renaissance culture spread from Italy into the rest of Europe, creative genius was not the exclusive province of Italian scholars and artists. Northern and western Europeans were not mere imitators but made their own distinct contribution to the Renaissance. Of particular importance is the fact that outside Italy secularization had not generally advanced so far. As a result, arts and letters still remained predominantly media for the expression of Christian values.

Germany and the Netherlands. Germany and the Netherlands were divided into many political units, but they were drawn together by a common intellectual heritage and commercial ties.

CHRISTIAN HUMANISM. Humanism in northern Europe received its impetus and direction from a group of devout Christian scholars, and thus the tone of the movement was much different from the secular orientation of Italian humanism.

Groote. Gerard Groote (1340–1384) founded the Brethren of the Common Life, a Dutch brotherhood dedicated to piety and learning. The Brethren's many schools set a standard for excellence that combined grammar, biblical and classical studies, and a devotion to Christian ethics. Humanists who received training in this atmosphere directed their studies to classical sources that shed light on early Christianity.

Reuchlin. Johann Reuchlin (1455–1522) was the greatest non-Jewish Hebraic scholar in the north. His Hebrew grammar and dictionary (1506) was an important aid to fellow students of early Christianity. Though his studies brought him under the suspicion of more conservative Christian theologians, other humanists rallied to his defense.

Melanchthon. Philip Melachthon (1497–1560) became Martin Luther's close associate during the Reformation, but he was a biblical scholar in his own right and pursued his studies through the earliest available sources.

Erasmus. Desiderius Erasmus (1466?–1536) of Rotterdam was the embodiment of Christian humanism and the most respected scholar of his day. He received his early training in a school of the Brethren and pursued his education in European centers of learning for the remainder of his life. Like many of his colleagues, he studied the New Testament from the earliest Greek sources, and he made a new Latin translation that served as a guide for further study. Though a devout Catholic, he joined the chorus of critics who demanded thoroughgoing Church reform. His *Praise of Folly* (1511) mocked earthly pretensions and corruption wherever he found them, but he saved his most scathing attacks for clerical abuses. Erasmus broke sharply with the idea of amorality in public life advocated by Machiavelli. His *Handbook of a Christian Knight* (1503) and *On the Education of a Christian Prince* (1516) both argued that not only could a man of affairs live a life of Christian morality but that a prince could rule his state on the basis of the same principles.

FLEMISH AND GERMAN ARTISTS. The Netherlands was the center of fiifteenth-century art in northern Europe. The art of the Flemish school is typified by the brilliant use of color and naturalism obtained through attention to minute detail. Flemish artists continued to give primary attention to such religious work as altarpieces and manuscript illumination, but their art also reflected the secular interests of such patrons as the dukes of Burgundy and wealthy merchants. Jan van Eyck (1370?–?1440), to whom is usually attributed the development of oil painting, and Rogier van der Weyden (1399?–1464) were the greatest masters of this movement. Hieronymus Bosch (1450?–1516) drew upon the techniques of his predecessors, but his surrealistic landscapes in which realistic detail intermingled with psychological fantasy had no counterpart among his contemporaries. The work of Pieter Brueghel the Elder (1520?–1569) has a greater vitality, and his concentration upon the detailed portrayal of peasant life provides a wealth of information for social historians.

The unrivaled leader of fifteenth-century German art was Albrecht Dürer (1471–1528), who was not only a master craftsman but also a profound student of the human condition. His greatest contributions to art were woodcuts and copper engravings used to illustrate books pouring off the German presses. His mastery of this medium is seen in *The Knight, Death, and the Devil* (1513), *St. Jerome in His Study* (1514), and *Melancholia* (1514). The art of Matthias Grünewald (1485–1530) clearly reflects the deep religious preoccupation of the German people. His *Isenheim Altarpiece* (ca. 1515) focuses on the Crucifixion with a combination of brutal realism and mystical pietism. Hans Holbein the Younger (1497?–1543), on the other hand, is best known for his highly finished portraits of great Renaissance personages, including Erasmus, Luther, Columbus, and Henry VIII.

France. As France emerged from the political disorder of the Hundred Years' War (1340–1453), its cultural life also took on a new vitality. The development was reinforced by both Burgundian and Italian influences. Italian artists, architects, and teachers were welcomed in France, and this trend accelerated after Charles VIII's invasion of Italy (1494).

HUMANISM. Humanist scholarship thrived under the patronage of the Renaissance King Francis I (r. 1515–1547) and at the court of his gifted sister Marguerite of Angoulême. It continued under Henry II (r. 1547–1559).

Budé. Guillaume Budé (1468–1540) was the best-known and most versatile French humanist scholar. His Latin studies included an annotated analysis of Roman law and a treatise on Roman coinage. In addition, his *Commentaries on the Greek Language* spread his reputation throughout Europe. He directed studies at the newly founded *Collège de France* and promoted the study of Latin, Greek, and Hebrew against the opposition of conservative Sorbonne scholastics.

Lefèvre. Lefèvre d'Étaples (1450?–1537) was the most eminent scholar in the circle that gathered at Meaux under the patronage of Bishop Briçonnet. There he devoted himself to the study of early Christian writings. Although his *Commentaries on the Pauline Epistles* (1512) demonstrates a belief similar to Martin Luther's, in salvation by faith, he remained loyal to the tradition and discipline of the Catholic church.

Calvin. John Calvin (1509–1564) received a humanist education, and while studying law he came into contact with the leading scholars of his day. His early work, including commentaries on Seneca's *De clementia* (1532) were typical of the age, but after 1533 he broke with religious authorities on theological issues and fled from France. His role in the Reformation is discussed on page 63.

LITERATURE. French literature was marked by brilliant contributions to stylistic development in the novel, poetry, and the essay.

Rabelais. France has produced few literary figures whose genius surpasses that of François Rabelais (1494?–1553). His masterpiece, *Gargantua and Pantagruel,* an enormous work published in parts between 1533 and 1553, relates the adventures of Gargantua and his son Pantagruel as a backdrop for Rabelais's commentary on the human condition. From his storytelling ability and ribald humor, the author emerges as a dedicated humanist appalled by what he considered the cultural degeneracy of the day. His most bitter attacks are directed against pedantic scholastic philosophers and worldly clerics. More important than this negativism, however, is the constant reaffirmation of life.

Ronsard. A small circle of poets, known as *La Pléiade,* dedicated themselves to rebirth of French verse through the incorporation of classical images and style. The lyric poetry of Pierre de Ronsard (1524–1585) is a beautiful example of this successful fusion.

Montaigne. The modern essay is the creation of Michel de Montaigne (1533–1592). Ranging over a wide variety of subjects from cannibalism to elementary education, he combined an incomparable prose style with the ability to examine his own society through the eyes of a detached observer.

ARCHITECTURE. French sixteenth-century architecture demonstrates the gradual influence of new tastes on old forms that typifies cultural development. The medieval preoccupation with churches and fortresses gave way to the construction of immense public buildings and private palaces. The section of the Louvre constructed under the direction of Pierre Lescot between 1546 and 1576 shows the displacement of the vertical lines typical of Gothic design by the horizontal symmetry in keeping with Renaissance tastes. In the provinces the châteaus of the Loire Valley, while maintaining many structural elements of medieval fortifications, received external ornamentation and internal decoration in keeping with their new role as elegant country retreats.

England. England's relative isolation, military involvement, and civil disorder partly account for the slow arrival of the Rennaissance. The prosaic reign of Henry VII (r. 1485–1509), however, provided a sound foundation for the sparkling court life of his son Henry VIII (r. 1509–1547) and granddaughter Queen Elizabeth (r. 1558–1603). Under Tudor patronage humanist scholarship flourished, and English literature, particularly poetry and drama, experienced a golden age.

HUMANISM. English humanism, like its counterparts across the channel, combined classical scholarship with a deep religious commitment. Thomas Linacre (1460?–1524) and William Grocyn (1446?–1519) studied in Italy and returned to Oxford University, where they fostered the study of Greek and Latin sources. Their teaching inspired other English scholars, including John Colet and Thomas More.

Colet. John Colet's (1467?–1519) lectures at Oxford on the Pauline Epistles clearly demonstrate the humanistic abandonment of scholastic speculation for philological examination and common sense. Though not a great academician, Colet wielded wide influence as Dean of Saint Paul's Cathedral, where he preached for Church reform, and he founded Saint Paul's grammar school, which under the direction of William Lily became the model for the combination of Christian education and classical studies.

More. Thomas More (1478–1535) was the most versatile English humanist. He combined a warm personality, a scholarly mind, a career of public service, and a resolute religious faith. The incompatibility of his obligations as lord chancellor for Henry VIII and his religious beliefs led to his execution (see page 66), and he was later canonized by the Catholic church. More's greatest literary work was *Utopia,* written in Latin and published in 1516. Utopia was an ideal society built upon tolerance, justice, and cooperation. It compared very favorably with contemporary England, where More felt the law worked to the advantage only of the rich, and justice, tolerance, and fundamental Christianity itself had practically vanished. The book has remained one of the most influential calls of modern times for social and economic justice.

LITERATURE. The greatest achievement of the English Renaissance was literary. Besides More's *Utopia,* the outstanding works of the first half of the sixteenth century were English translations of the Bible by Miles Coverdale and William Tyndale and Thomas Cranmer's *Book of Common Prayer* (1552). Secular prose writers emerged after the midcentury; they included historians Raphael Holinshed, renowned for his *Chronicles* (1578), and Richard Hakluyt, whose *English Voyages* (1589) contributes to our knowledge of the age of discovery. Less mundane were the works of England's poets and playwrights.

Sidney. Sir Philip Sidney (1554–1586) exemplifies the Renaissance model of a soldier poet. He exercised an important influence on his contemporaries though his major works were published posthumously. He experimented with the adaptation of classical structure to English verse and wrote a series of beautiful sonnets entitled *Astrophel and Stella* (1591). His *Apologie for Poetrie* (1595), a critical examination of poetic principles, was the first of its kind in English. He was mortally wounded at Zutphen during a military expedition against Spain.

Spenser. Edmund Spenser (1552–1599) was also a public servant and played an active role in the governing of Ireland. His masterwork *The Faerie Queene* (1596) is an epic poem extolling virtue and glorifying Queen Elizabeth. The poem's basic element is a nine-line stanza (Spenserian stanza), which was used by later poets, including Keats, Shelley, and Byron.

Shakespeare and other playwrights. The crowning glory of Elizabethan literature was the drama that began to appear on the London stage in the 1590s. The most illustrious playwrights were Thomas Kyd (1557?–1595), Christopher Marlowe (1564–1593), Benjamin Jonson (1573?–1637), and William Shakespeare (1564–1616), the incomparable master.

Shakespeare wrote to entertain the audiences that flocked to the open-air theaters, and he satisfied them with comedy, tragedy, romance, and bloody adventure. His work has endured because of his ability to dramatize human passion in all its forms and to illustrate the unique and lonely struggle involved in each human life. A partial list of his many plays must include: *The Merchant of Venice, Twelfth Night,* and *The Tempest* (comedies); *Hamlet, Macbeth, King Lear,* and *Othello* (tragedies); and *Richard II, Richard III,* and *Henry IV* (historical). Shakespeare's sonnets also place him in the first rank among English poets.

Spain. Spain was to a great extent culturally isolated from her European neighbors. As Rennaissance influences filtered through the Pyrenees or touched ashore at the Mediterranean entrepôts, they acquired a particularly Spanish flavor. In this setting throve four of the greatest Renaissance figures.

JIMÉNEZ DE CISNEROS. Cardinal Jiménez de Cisneros (1437–1517) was Spain's greatest humanist scholar. He reformed the University of Alcalá and used it as the center for clerical education in the humanities. His best-known scholarly work, the *Complutensian Polygot,* included juxtaposed versions of the Latin New Testament. His role as Spain's primate and grand inquisitor is discussed on page 68.

EL GRECO. Dominico Theotokopoulos (1548–1614) was known as El Greco because of his birth on the Greek island of Crete. After studying at Venice and Rome, he adopted Spain and settled at Toledo. He created vibrant and emotional pictures by setting angular and often elongated figures amid sharply divided colors. By his own account, his masterpiece is *The Burial of Count Orgaz.* His *Portrait of Cardinal Guevara* demonstrates his unique virtuosity.

CERVANTES. The well-deserved reputation of Miguel de Cervantes (1547–1616) as one of Europe's greatest prose writers rests upon a single literary masterpiece, *Don Quixote de la Mancha.* This novel, published in 1605, tells the story of Don Quixote, an eccentric nobleman whose fantasies lead him in search of adventure, and Sancho Panza, his faithful and down-to-earth servant. Cervantes demonstrates that while the chivalric past is dead, quixotic fantasies are often as valuable as common sense in dealing with an incomprehensible world.

LOPE DE VEGA. Spain's most accomplished dramatist was Lope de Vega (1562–1635). He wrote romances, and his prodigious output for the Madrid stage included over fifteen hundred *comedias.* Although his purpose was light entertainment following a prescribed format, he covered the whole range of human emotions and set society laughing at its own overblown sense of importance.

6

The Reformation

The Reformation wrought one of the most significant cultural trans-
formations in the history of Western civilization. The movement began
in the hearts of pious laymen and priests who sought a more rewarding spiritual life and an end to clerical abuses. Although at first few
of the reformers had any intention of breaking with Rome, as the
debate intensified, many of them, including Luther, Zwingli, and
Calvin, concluded that the established Church had drifted so far from
Christ's teaching that a completely fresh start was warranted. Many
others felt that the abuses were superficial and that no structural or
doctrinal changes were required. In the end the Christian church,
which had provided Europe with a unifying ideology for centuries,
was torn asunder.

The German Reformation

It is difficult to explain why the spiritual revolution began in Germany and why it met with such instantaneous success. As in the case
of all cultural phenomena of this magnitude, its origins were complex.
A pervading sense of spiritual revivalism coincided with a deep-seated
contempt for clerical wealth and corruption. These conditions were
particularly strong in Germany, where powerful ecclesiastical princes
ruled a church that seemed organized solely for the economic benefit
of an Italian pope. Once the movement began, many groups and individuals took advantage of the disorganized political situation to amelio-
rate their personal difficulties. Despite these other characteristics, the
Reformation was essentially a religious upheaval and was given its
direction by the religious reformers who led it.

Luther. Martin Luther (1483–1546) was the son of a moderately
prosperous mine operator who had risen from the ranks of the peasantry. Though driven by his father to raise the family name even

higher, he suddenly abandoned the study of law in 1505 and entered an Augustinian monastery. This decision rested upon his deep-seated sense of guilt and helplessness before the judgment of a just and all-powerful God. He was ordained a priest in 1508, and after receiving a doctorate, he became a professor of theology at Wittenberg University in the electorate of Saxony. Despite his new vocation, he could not shake his dread of impending damnation. It was only around 1515 that he found in the Scriptures the key to his salvation.

THEOLOGY. Luther reached the conclusion that man, being naturally corrupt, was unable to win salvation on his own merits. From his studies, particularly in the writings of Saint Augustine, he had concluded that each individual is predestined from eternity for paradise or damnation. He regained hope in his own destiny from Saint Paul's Epistle to the Romans, which affirmed that "the just shall live by faith." Luther interpreted this to mean that those elected for salvation (that is, justified) would be given faith as a sign of their deliverance. Justification by faith became the central theme of his theology, and the belief in predestination, the focal point of Calvin's theology, receded into the background. Luther's long journey out of despair had ended. He settled into his scholarly chores unaware that events would drive him into a direct confrontation with the pope and the Holy Roman emperor.

The Indulgence Controversy. It was the teaching of the Church that even after confession, sinners faced purifying punishment in Purgatory before they could enter Paradise. Since the era of the Crusades, the Church had issued indulgences, which were the remission of punishment in Purgatory, to believers who performed good works or supported them through donations to the Church. In 1517 a particularly flagrant abuse of this practice resulted from the sale of indulgences to raise funds for the building of Saint Peter's in Rome. Luther objected on two grounds. He believed that not only did the ignorant often contribute with the mistaken belief that they were buying salvation but also that even indulgences rigorously administered were worthless as a means to salvation. He challenged the practice by posting the Ninety-five Theses that he proposed to defend in open debate (31 October 1517). His mounting criticism spread far beyond the range of his voice, for through an effective use of the printing press, he flooded Germany with hundreds of thousands of pamphlets. As he attracted supporters, he also drew the attention of the papacy. What had begun as an inquiry on indulgences spread to a rejection of the entire Church structure. Luther's ideas had slowly led him to the conclusion that the only vital elements in the drama of redemption were God, the human sinner, and the Scriptures, which formed the vital link between them. The sacramental system and the church hierarchy that administered it were thus irrelevant. Luther had thus inadvertently become a full-blown heretic and might have been quickly suppressed save for the patronage of the elector of Saxony and the unsettled political conditions resulting from the death of Emperor Maximilian I (1519), which prevented Pope Leo X from excommunicating him until 1520.

DIET OF WORMS. The newly crowned emperor Charles V summoned Luther to appear before the imperial diet meeting at Worms in 1521. Threatened by the combined power of the empire and the Church, Luther stood by his beliefs. He left Worms under a safe-conduct, and though subsequently declared a heretic and an outlaw, he gained sanctuary under Frederick of Saxony. During his year of seclusion, he translated the Bible into German. This literary masterpiece enhanced his position as a religious leader and theologian.

LUTHERAN CHURCH. Luther returned to Wittenberg in 1522 and began to organize his church. The clergy was divested of its mystical power, and the monasteries were dissolved. All practices designed to dispense grace through good works, including fasts, pilgrimages, and the veneration of relics, were abolished. However, many traditional practices were retained, including the sacraments of Baptism and the Lord's Supper. Administratively the Church came under control of the state.

Social and Political Consequences of Lutheranism. Luther had stirred the hearts and minds of the German nation, and the resulting upheaval was not limited to spiritual affairs.

KNIGHTS' WAR (1521). One major consequence of the Reformation was an armed assault on the vast landholdings of the Catholic church. The first major attack came when an army of imperial knights led by Franz von Sickingen and Ulrich von Hutten attempted to seize the estates of the archbishop of Trier. Though the invasion failed and the revolt disintegrated after the death of the ringleaders, vast amounts of Church land, with the political and economic power that went with it, passed into secular hands throughout the sixteenth century.

PEASANTS' WAR (1524–1526). Although Lutheranism did not cause this massive revolt of the German peasantry, its major theme of spiritual freedom clearly served as a rallying point as men who bore the burdens of serfdom rose up demanding an end to personal bondage. The nobility, perched at the top of the tottering social structure, lashed back in terror and in the process slaughtered an estimated one hundred thousand leaderless and poorly armed serfs. Luther condoned the massacre in the name of law and order, a point on which he was sensitive since he had been declared an outlaw. As might have been expected, the lower classes drifted away from Luther in large numbers. Lutheranism became associated with the landed aristocracy, and as a result of this brush with anarchy, it became a primary support of the emerging absolutist states of north Germany. In Denmark Christian III (r. 1534–1559) completed the consolidation of a Lutheran state church that he then imposed on his Norwegian domains. After the conversion of Sweden to Lutheranism, a state church emerged under Gustavus Vasa (r. 1523–1560), and the same was true of Brandenburg during the reign of Joachim II (1535–1571).

The Anabaptists. The fatal flaw in Luther's logic was that having denied the right of the Catholic Church to dictate to his conscience, he nevertheless attempted to enforce his own beliefs on others. Out of the debacle of the Peasants' War arose numerous sects that denied the authority of both the state and the church and, in some cases, even the Scriptures. The largest of these groups was known as the Anabaptists, from their practice of requiring the rebaptism of adults. Although some resorted to armed terrorism to prepare the world for the Second Coming of Christ, most Anabaptists practiced a primitive Christianity that stressed a life of piety and brotherhood. Their insistence on a direct personal relationship with God, repudiation of interference from outside the congregation, and tolerance of other religions made them a target for persecution. The Anabaptists were virtually eradicated in Germany after an allied army of Catholics and Lutherans overpowered their community in Munster (1535). Their spiritual descendants thrived, however, and formed the nucleus of later Baptist and Mennonite churches. For a continuation of events in the German Reformation, see p. 80.

The Swiss Reformation

The second major center of religious reform was Switzerland where, under the guidance of Huldreich Zwingli at Zurich and John Calvin at Geneva, a brand of Protestantism emerged that had its greatest impact in western Europe. The churches that followed the pattern of the Swiss Reformation are known as *reformed* churches.

zwingli. Huldreich Zwingli (1484–1531) was ordained a priest in 1509, and after serving as an army chaplain with Swiss mercenaries in the Italian wars, he took up pastoral duties in Zurich. Under the influence of a humanist education and the horrors of the Italian wars, he arrived independently at many of the same conclusions as Martin Luther. His popular sermons condemned church abuses and extolled Swiss patriotism.

When his views were challenged by the bishop of Constance, the populace of Zurich supported their zealous priest. By 1525 he had created a Reformed church. Like Luther, Zwingli rejected the sacramental system of the Catholic church as well as indulgences, fasts, pilgrimages, and the veneration of saints and relics. Mass was abolished and the church trappings became more austere. Both Zwingli and Luther closed the monasteries and sanctioned marriage for the clergy.

Despite these similarities, Luther and Zwingli disagreed on several important points. Zwingli, though agreeing with Luther on justification by faith, stressed man's freedom to accept or reject salvation. Zwingli created a church-dominated state to supervise a Christian community. Luther, on the other hand, viewed religious commitment as an intensely personal relationship between God and each individual and left to the state the problem of ordering day-to-day life. The major point of dispute between Zwingli and Luther concerned the Lord's Supper. Both men rejected the Catholic belief that through a miracle the bread and wine of the Mass were changed into the body and blood of Christ (*transubstantiation*). Luther did believe that though no such miracle took place, Christ was actually present (*consubstantiation*). Zwingli, on the other hand, regarded the Communion ceremony as solely a remembrance of Christ. Zwingli and Luther met in 1529 to iron out their differences, which were causing many princes acute political problems. But no accommodation could be reached on the Communion issue, which continued to be a major point of contention throughout the Reformation.

Zurich's religious activity and military power frightened neighboring cities, and the city drifted into war with the Catholic cantons. When Zwingli was killed in battle in 1531, many of his followers joined Calvin, but Zwinglianism remained an influence in Switzerland and had a strong impact on the English Reformation.

CALVIN. John Calvin (Jean Chauvin, 1509–1564) was the dominant Protestant theologian and organizer outside of northern Germany and Scandinavia. In many respects his early life was similar to Luther's. Encouraged by his uneducated but prosperous father, he studied theology at the University of Paris and then pursued his education in law. Though he did not suffer from Luther's spiritual insecurity, he was a critic of Church abuse. He moved freely among the French humanists who were patronized by such important figures as Margaret of Navarre the king's sister. Francis I, although personally tolerant, began to enforce Catholic orthodoxy for political reasons, and Calvin fled the country in 1533. He settled in Geneva, Switzerland, where except for one brief interlude he spent the remainder of his life.

THEOLOGY. The evolution of Calvin's theology was elaborated in his major work, *Institutes of the Christian Religion,* which appeared in many editions between 1539 and 1559. The central theme of his belief was man's relationship to God in the working out of a divine plan preordained from all eternity. Although Luther shared this belief in *predestination,* for Calvin it was the key to all man's activities. The idea that some were predestined for salvation while others would be consigned to damnation despite anything they might do was not conceived by Calvin as an excuse for a life of either stoic resignation or riotous living in the face of the inevitable. Although man could not work for salvation, God worked through men to carry out his design. It was the task of the elect to surrender themselves to the will of God and work for its fulfillment. As a corollary of this belief, the nonelect were not allowed to do anything that would mar the glory of God's creation. Though the need for constant action in the struggle with Satan might seem superfluous in a scheme based on predestination, the doctrine nevertheless had a significant impact on the development of western European culture.

THE CHRISTIAN COMMUNITY. Geneva was an important banking center ruled by a small and wealthy oligarchy. By the time Calvin arrived in 1536, it had already established itself as an independent Protestant city-state. Here Calvin attempted to materialize his vision of Christian community, an ordered society free from the anarchy that would otherwise rise from man's inherent corruption. After a long struggle, the Calvinist church emerged. Organized along lines set down by the *Ecclesiastical Ordinances* (1541), it was controlled by a consistory composed of ministers and lay elders elected by the congregations. It had absolute authority on religious matters, being thus independent of the government. Calvin's insistence on this independence and equality with the state was much closer to Catholicism's perception of the proper relationship than either Lutheranism (state control of church) or Zwinglianism (church control of state). Because of its theology and organization, it was the Catholic church's most deadly opponent.

IMPACT OF CALVINISM. Calvin gave to Protestantism a well-ordered theology and church organization that served as a model for other reformers. By the time the Reformation ended, Calvinist majorities existed in the Netherlands and Scotland, and significant minorities spread in an unbroken chain from England and France through Switzerland, Austria, and Bohemia to Hungary and Poland. In the following century, Calvinist emigrants became the first and most influential colonists in English North America. In addition, Calvin, like Luther before him, stressed the necessity of civil obedience and justified revolution only when led by civil magistrates. Calvinists, however, saw the creation of Christian society as an obligation and were rarely willing to allow Catholic monarchs to thwart their goal.

The English Reformation

While the Reformation in the Germanies and Switzerland was triggered by charismatic religious reformers, the English Reformation was initiated by King Henry VIII for political reasons. It nevertheless struck a responsive chord among a large portion of the Catholic clergy and the mass of Englishmen. The Church of England that emerged amalgamated the ideas of Luther and Zwingli with the Catholicism of their forefathers and cast the new church in a particularly English mold.

Pre-Reformation England. The Catholic church in England suffered from many of the same abuses already noted on the Continent. Concerned with their large holdings and the affairs of state, many prelates totally ignored their religious duties. Monasteries were probably not so corrupt as vocal critics of the age would have us believe, but it is fair to say that most were economically parasitic and made scant contribution to the spiritual life of the society. Ecclesiastical courts were criticized for their violation of the system of common law, and the attempts of the Church to extract funds were a constant source of complaint. Although the fourteenth-century teachings of John Wycliffe were little more than history, a new group of reformers had begun to emerge. The Christian humanists at Oxford, including John Colet and Thomas More, made strong appeals for Church reform, while the Lutheran influence among a small group of Cambridge dons became so strong that their meeting place at the White Horse Inn became known as Little Germany.

Henry VIII (r. 1509–1547). Henry VIII was a dedicated Catholic upon whom the pope had bestowed the title Defender of the Faith for his denunciation of Martin Luther. Despite his personal convictions, dynastic politics led Henry to challenge the spiritual authority of the pope and ultimately to create an independent state church.

ANNULMENT CONTROVERSY. The crisis arose in 1527 over the legitimacy of Henry's marriage to Catherine of Aragon, daughter of Ferdinand and Isabella. Catherine was the widow of Henry's brother, but biblical prohibitions against such a marriage had been overridden by papal dispensation. The union seemed cursed, for of Catherine's six children, only the princess Mary had survived. England was but a generation removed from civil war, and Henry was determined to provide for the continued order and security through a male heir to the Tudor line. Through Cardinal Wolsey, the lord chancellor, Henry petitioned Pope Clement VII to denounce the original dispensation as a papal error and grant an annulment. Clement was reluctant to contradict his predecessor and in addition feared military reprisals from the emperor Charles V, Catherine's nephew.

The negotiations dragged on. Henry's determination to end the interminable negotiations, take the government into his own hands, and marry Anne Boleyn brought the controversy to a head. Wolsey, who had virtually controlled the government since 1515, retired in disgrace and was replaced by Sir Thomas More (see p. 57).

REFORMATION PARLIAMENT (1529–1536). Henry carried through his reformation by using the landed gentry of England as his parliamentary allies. By reinforcing his decisions with legal and popular sanctions, he emerged from the struggle with unprecedented royal power. In the long run, however, he also strengthened the Parliament by tacitly confirming its right to participate in important constitutional issues. The Act of Annates (1532), the first parliamentary challenge to papal authority, transferred payment of the first year's income from church property from the pope to the king. The Act of Appeals (1533) prohibited the appeal of cases to papal courts, thus strengthening the hand of the government in ecclesiastical matters. The statute cleared the way for Henry's divorce, which was granted by the newly appointed archbishop of Canterbury, Thomas Cranmer. Henry's marriage to Anne Boleyn and the birth of their only child proved a political disappointment. Henry could not foresee that the newborn Princess Elizabeth would later reign as one of England's most respected and powerful monarchs.

The decisive moment for the English Reformation was the passage of the Act of Supremacy (1534), which created the Church of England (Anglican church) with the king rather than the pope as its supreme administrative and spiritual officer. Every Englishman was required to take an "oath of supremacy," recognizing this decision. Sir Thomas More, though for years an ardent Church critic, refused to endorse this rejection of papal authority and died on the scaffold with Bishop Fisher of Rochester.

ANGLICAN SETTLEMENT. The political, rather than religious, nature of Henry's reformation can be clearly seen in the events of 1539.

The dronelike existence of English monasteries made them a vulnerable target for religious reformer and administrator alike. Under the supervision of Thomas Cromwell, the king's chief adviser since the execution of More, the monasteries were dissolved and their property seized. Although the royal treasury profited little from the sale of these lands, the transaction further committed the aristocratic purchasers of the land to Henry's break with Rome.

Through all the decade's shifting currents, Henry remained committed to Catholic theology if not papal authority. The growth of Protestant sentiment in England led him to confirm publicly Anglican belief against Protestant heresy. The Six Articles reaffirmed belief in the Mass, transubstantiation, confession, celibacy, and the vows of chastity.

HENRY'S LAST YEARS. Henry had carried out a reformation that recognized the national aspirations of Englishmen without violating their religious sensibilities. In the process he had increased royal prerogatives until in the last years of his reign he became an egotistical tyrant. He renewed the inclusive wars with his French rival Francis I to no effect. Of all his friends, only Cranmer escaped disgrace or the executioner's ax. Though married six times, he sired only one son, the sickly Prince Edward, who succeeded to the throne when Henry died in 1547.

Edward VI (r. 1547–1553). Edward was a boy of nine when he became king, and the burdens of government fell upon two Protestant regents, the duke of Somerset (r. 1547–1549) and the duke of Northumberland (r. 1549–1553). The most important aspect of the short reign was a sharp shift toward Protestant theology within the Anglican church. Archbishop Cranmer produced the inspirational English ritual in the *Book of Common Prayer* (1549). An English translation of the Bible came into general use. The Six Articles were repealed and the Forty-two Articles, which carried the heavy influence of Zwinglian thought, came into force.

Mary Tudor (r. 1553–1558). Queen Mary, Henry's daughter by Catherine of Aragon, was determined to redeem her mother's name and religion. Had she been willing to enforce Catholic theology under the emblem of a national church as her father had done, the English nation might have followed her, but her determination to wipe out Protestantism and reinstate the authority of the pope infuriated her subjects. Her marriage to the Catholic king of Spain, Phillip II, widened the breach between crown and commons. Any hopes of a reconciliation between Catholicism and England ended with Mary's fanatical persecution of Protestants.

Although the number of people sent to the stake was small by sixteenth-century standards, the choice of her victims was enough to win for the queen the epithet Bloody Mary. Foxe's *Book of Martyrs*, relating the execution of Archbishop Cranmer and Bishop Latimer of London and Bishop Ridley of Rochester, along with hundreds of common folk, took its place beside the Bible in many English homes. Mary's disastrous reign might have confirmed his father's opinion of daughters had she not been followed to the throne by her half sister Elizabeth.

Elizabeth I (r. 1558–1603). As the daughter of Anne Boleyn, Elizabeth was as committed to Protestantism by fate as Mary had been to Catholicism. Acceptance of Catholicism would mean a rejection of her mother and of the legitimacy of her own birth. Despite her Protestantism, she had no interest in prolonging the unrest generated by her Catholic sister. Elizabeth wanted to create a church so comprehensive that a large majority of her subjects could maintain their political loyalty without violating their religious consciences. Like her father, she called upon Parliament to ratify her decisions. The Act of Supremacy, which had lapsed during Mary's reign, was reintroduced (1558), along with the Act of Uniformity that prescribed the use of Cranmer's revised *Book of Common Prayer*. The doctrinal settlement was reached in 1563 by the adoption of moderate Protestantism with the Thirty-nine Articles. Those excluded from the settlement were Catholics who continued to acknowledge the supremacy of the pope and Puritans who felt that Cranmer's liturgy had not cleansed Christianity of its Catholic ritual.

Elizabeth's greatest achievement was her ability to draw Englishmen together through a half century that on the Continent witnessed the fratricidal slaughter of hundreds of thousands of men, women, and children in the name of Christ. (See p. 91 for a discussion of other aspects of Elizabeth's reign.)

The Catholic Reformation

The Catholic Reformation was the movement that attempted to regenerate the spiritual life of Europe within the framework of the traditional Church. It took two major forms. The first movement predated Luther, and after the Protestant breach it continued to work for reform within the traditional framework. The second emerged in the mid-sixteenth century and was directed at the eradication of what Catholic reformers regarded as a full-blown Protestant heresy.

The Pre-Lutheran Reformers. Luther was not the first to see the abuses that had crept into the medieval Church over the centuries. The reform of the Church was well on its way, though it certainly lacked papal support or guidance by the time Luther posted the Ninety-five Theses.

CARDINAL JIMÉNEZ DE CISNEROS AND SPANISH REFORM. Unlike many other states of western Europe, Spain had a large non-Christian population of Moors and Jews throughout the Middle Ages. The task of creating a homogeneous body of orthodox Christians in the emerging Spanish states fell to Cardinal Jiménez (1437–1517), who as archbishop of Toledo and grand inquisitor ranked in power below only King Ferdinand and Queen Isabella. Jiménez, a humanist scholar, created the University of Alcalá (1498) to train an enlightened corps of clergy. He closed monasteries and removed corrupt bishops at will. By the time the Reformation crisis began in central Europe the abuses that had weakened the Church for centuries had practically vanished in Spain. As was the case with most reformers of his age, his dedication and self-righteousness led to a brutal suppression of his opponents. The Inquisition was established in Spain (1478) to question those suspected of religious deviation and commit to the fire those guilty of heresy.

ORATORY OF DIVINE LOVE. The Oratory of Divine Love was founded in 1516 by a group of humanists, prelates, and Catholic laymen. Its members, including Bishop Caraffa (later Pope Paul IV), stressed the importance of personal sanctity and Christian good works. The example of Christian piety set by these men had an important effect on the spiritual life of Italy.

Papal Reform. As has already been noted, the papacy at the turn of the century was more the center of political intrigue, international finance, and cultural effervescence than of spiritual leadership. Pope Julius II (1503–1513) and Leo X (1513–1521), though shepherds of the Church, had more in common with the wolves than with the flock and were too preoccupied with pleasure or personal interests to bestir themselves in the name of spiritual matters. The brief reign of Adrian VI (1522–1523) marked the first major attack on the corruption within the Roman curia, but his untimely death ended reform for a decade.

POPE PAUL III (1534–1549). Though often regarded as the last of the Renaissance popes, Paul was a man of intelligence and vision. He was the first of a succession of competent and dedicated pontiffs who began the arduous task of Catholic reform.

Paul began where Adrian VI had ended. His appointment of reform-minded cardinals and bishops resulted in a thorough rehabilitation of the Roman curia. He appointed the Commission of Nine (1536) to investigate the current state of the Church. Its scathing indictment of Church abuses served as the basis for reform.

Paul's first inclination was to seek an accommodation with the Protestants. This attempt failed, however, at the Diet of Regensburg (Ratisbon) in 1541. Though temporary agreement was reached concerning the relation of faith to good works, the meeting broke up over the crucial issue of transubstantiation and the power of Church councils. It was becoming evident that the gulf of years was too wide to span.

ROMAN INQUISITION (CONGREGATION OF THE HOLY OFFICE). The Roman Inquisition was a slightly milder version of the Spanish Inquisition. It was formed in 1542 to perform general surveillance, to investigate suspected heretics (using whatever means were necessary to obtain information), and to dispose of the guilty. Though less brutal than its Spanish couterpart, it was no less thorough.

THE INDEX (CONGREGATION OF THE INDEX). The advent of the printing press had opened up new communication networks that were increasingly used by Church critics to air their opinions. In 1559 the pope created a permanent Committee of Cardinals to meet this threat. The Congregation of the Index maintained a close surveillance on all publications and banned all books that contradicted Catholic opinion concerning faith or morals.

Jesuit Order. The Jesuits, as members of the Society of Jesus were called, were universally despised by Protestants as the most fanatic representatives of the Catholic counterattack. They proved to be one of the most effective instruments of the Catholic Reformation and a pervasive influence in the molding of modern Catholicism.

IGNATIUS LOYOLA. As a member of the Spanish nobility, Ignatius Loyola (1491–1556) was destined by birth to be a soldier, but his military career was ended by a crippling wound in 1521. While convalescing, he experienced a spiritual awakening reminiscent of Luther's. Loyola, however, arrived at a diametrically opposed theological position. He became totally committed to the Catholic belief in the existence of free will, the importance of good works, the efficacy of the sacramental system, and the necessity of total submission to the spiritual guidance of the Church.

SOCIETY OF JESUS. The profession of arms had left Loyola poorly equipped for his new calling, and he spent over a decade in an educational pilgrimage that finally brought him to the University of Paris. There in 1534 he united a group of friends who dedicated their lives to God through service to the papacy. The Society of Jesus was formally sanctioned by the pope in 1540.

Loyola gave the society its final form in *The Constitutions* (1550), which were marked by the military organization and jargon Loyola had known in the past. Each member took the traditional vows of poverty, chastity, and obedience, while the generals of the society took the additional vow of total and unflinching obedience to the pope that gave the order its unique character. In addition each Jesuit followed Loyola's *Spiritual Exercises*, designed to bring him a mystical union with Christ that would enable him to bear the trials of selfless service in defense of Christ's vicar, the pope.

The Jesuits labored under adverse conditions; not only did their enemies despise them but also their total dedication to the papacy made them suspect to Catholic monarchs and bishops who pursued their own national interests. Because of their religious education, however, they became sought after as advisers and confessors by the Catholic monarchs, and their colleges soon gained a virtual monopoly over Catholic education. The Society of Jesus was largely responsible for stemming the tide of Calvinist expansion in southern Germany and keeping Poland and Hungary in the Catholic fold from which they had nearly strayed.

Council of Trent. The Holy Roman emperor had long desired a general council of the Church in the hopes that political turmoil could be ended by religious compromise. The papacy, however, feared the power of such councils and the danger of negotiation with heretics. When Pope Paul III finally convened the bishops in 1545, he was determined to maintain a firm control of the proceedings. His goal was not negotiations with the Protestants but a clear statement of the Church's doctrinal tenets and an administrative reorganization that would strengthen Catholicism for the struggle. In the council's three sessions (1545–1547, 1551–1552, 1562–1564), a power struggle also developed between those who favored papal authority, mainly Italians, and those who supported autonomy of each national segment of the Catholic church, predominantly Frenchmen and Spaniards.

CATHOLIC DOCTRINE. The church fathers took great care to define and clarify the traditional position of the Church on every major point of contention with the Protestants. The council confirmed the following beliefs: (1) Mankind had been marred but not irredeemably corrupted by Original Sin; (2) grace was a gift from God that men were free to accept or reject; (3) both faith and good works (including pilgrimages and the veneration of saints and relics) were necessary for salvation; (4) the Church administered grace through the seven sacraments; (5) the Mass, as a daily reaffirmation of the Redemption, included the miracle of transubstantiation; and (6) the body of Christian truth included the Scriptures and the traditional teachings of the divinely inspired Church.

ADMINISTATIVE REFORM. Despite the decision to adhere carefully to the body of traditional belief without compromise, the prelates clearly understood that corruption and poor administration had hampered Church operation. The council moved to end clerical abuses. Pluralism, simony, and nepotism were condemned and suppressed. Bishops, abbots, and other benefice holders were enjoined to take an

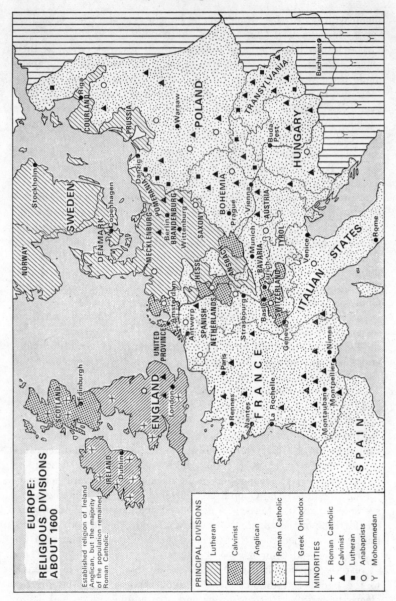

EUROPE:
RELIGIOUS DIVISIONS
ABOUT 1600

Established religion of Ireland
Anglican, but the majority
of the population remained
Roman Catholic.

PRINCIPAL DIVISIONS

Lutheran
Calvinist
Anglican
Roman Catholic

Greek Orthodox

MINORITIES

+ Roman Catholic
◀ Calvinist
■ Lutheran
○ Anabaptists
Y Mohommedan

(From *Europe in the Sixteenth Century*, p. 273, by H. G. Koenigsberger and George
L. Mosse. Copyright © 1968 by H. G. Koenigsberger and G. L. Mosse. Reprinted by
permission of Holt, Rinehart and Winston, Inc.)

active part in the administration of their holdings. The council recommended the establishment of seminaries in every diocese to end the justifiable criticism of clerical incompetence. Enforcement of clerical celibacy and the rigid supervision of the regular clergy ended another constant source of complaint.

RESULTS OF THE COUNCIL OF TRENT. Though the council's decision ended what faint hopes remained for reconciliation between Protestants and Catholics, the Catholic church emerged more self-confident and sure of its direction than at any time since the thirteenth century. The work of the council and other reforms of the Catholic Reformation remolded the Church and assured its survival.

7

Dynastic Politics during the Reformation

The preceding chapter dealt with the religious upheaval that shook Europe during the first half of the sixteenth century. Although the Reformation received its impetus from the spiritual challenge to the dominance of the Roman church, the splintering of Western Christendom resulted in large measure from the political rivalries of the most powerful dynastic states.

The period from 1519 to 1556 is often referred to as the Age of Charles V. As a result of war and shrewd dynastic marriages, Charles inherited a vast domain that stretched from the New World to central Europe. His realm did not, however, comprise a single constitutional unit. It consisted of diverse states and provinces, each with its own form of government, its own interest, and its unique problems.

Charles faced three separate and concurrent challenges during his long reign. His rivals were the French monarchy, the Turks, and the Lutheran princes. Though the following discussion will treat each threat separately, Charles had to deal with them simultaneously. It is this fact that explains why Charles, despite his competence, energy, and vast resources, met with such little success.

The Hapsburg Empire

The following genealogical chart is provided to demonstrate the process by which Charles came into the vast inheritance bequeathed to him by his four grandparents. Because his holdings were so diverse he divided them for administrative purposes among his relatives, although he maintained titular control. When he abdicated in 1556, the Hapsburg lands were divided, and henceforth it is necessary to refer to the Spanish Hapsburgs and the Austrian Hapsburgs.

The Netherlands. Charles grew up in the Netherlands, where his personality was shaped by the splendor of the Burgundian court,

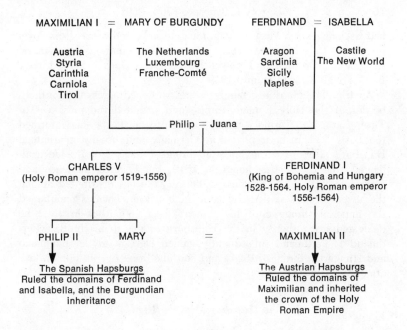

MAXIMILIAN I = MARY OF BURGUNDY   FERDINAND = ISABELLA

Austria	The Netherlands	Aragon	Castile
Styria	Luxembourg	Sardinia	The New World
Carinthia	Franche-Comté	Sicily	
Carniola		Naples	
Tirol			

Philip = Juana

CHARLES V
(Holy Roman emperor 1519-1556)

FERDINAND I
(King of Bohemia and Hungary
1528-1564. Holy Roman emperor
1556-1564)

PHILIP II   MARY   =   MAXIMILIAN II

The Spanish Hapsburgs
Ruled the domains of Ferdinand
and Isabella, and the Burgundian
inheritance

The Austrian Hapsburgs
Ruled the domains of
Maximilian and inherited
the crown of the Holy
Roman Empire

which maintained its chivalric life style at the close of the Middle
Ages. He always considered himself a Christian knight, duty bound
to defend the faith against both heretics and infidels. He inherited
the diverse Burgundian territories from his father in 1506. Throughout his reign he delegated his authority to a succession of regents
who, while levying heavy taxes, maintained Flemish loyalties by a
respect for local law and custom.

Spain. Charles inherited the Spanish throne in 1516 from Ferdinand
of Aragon, his maternal grandfather. In time it became the center
of his far-flung political activities, and he came to consider himself
a Spaniard. Initially, however, he angered his Spanish subjects by his
reliance on Flemish advisers, his demands for money, and his ab-
senteeism while campaigning for imperial election in Germany. The
result was the outbreak of widespread revolt in 1520 among the
burghers of Castile (*comuneros*) and the peasants of Valencia, who
formed themselves into brotherhoods (*germanias*). The revolts were
suppressed in 1521, and as a result Charles completed the centralization of Castile begun by Ferdinand and Isabella. At the same time, he
became sensitive to the Spanish attitudes and interests, and Aragon
continued to maintain many of its traditional liberties.

Italy. Charles had no personal interest in Sardinia, Sicily, and Naples,
nor in the duchy of Milan, which he acquired in 1540. He was satis-

fied as long as his viceroys continued to collect revenue from loyal taxpayers. Italy, however, served as a battleground in the dynastic struggle for prestige and power between the Hapsburgs and their French rivals from 1494 until 1559.

Austria. The Hapsburg family estates stretched across the southern border of the Holy Roman Empire and included the provinces of Tirol, Carinthia, Carniola, Styria, and Austria. These lands formed the basis of Hapsburg power in Germany and usually guaranteed Hapsburg election to the imperial throne. Francis I of France challenged Charles for this honor in 1519, but Charles' influence and eight hundred and fifty thousand florins in bribes distributed among the seven electors settled the issue in his favor. Charles maintained the imperial throne until his abdication in 1556, but in 1522 he delegated his authority in the Hapsburg estates to his brother Ferdinand I. Ferdinand subsequently gained election to the Bohemian and Hungarian thrones (1524) and bore the brunt of constant Turkish attacks for several decades.

The Hapsburg-Valois Rivalry

The rivalry of two great dynasties dominated the power politics of western Europe from 1494 to 1559. The imperial pretensions of the Hapsburgs were challenged by two equally aggressive representatives of the French house of Valois, Francis I and Henry II. Intricate diplomacy and continual warfare were pursued to promote the personal prestige and power of these rivals. They gave no thought to a higher "national" interest, because the nation-state as we know it did not exist. The aphorism "I am the state," attributed to the seventeenth-century monarch Louis XIV, best expresses the very personal nature of the political units that existed during the sixteenth century.

At stake in this conflict were valuable territories to which each dynasty laid claim. In the north on the frontier between France and the Holy Roman Empire were the disputed areas of Flanders, Artois, and the duchy of Burgundy. On the border between France and Spain lay the kingdom of Navarre. Finally, in the Italian peninsula were the wealthy and strategically located duchy of Milan and kingdom of Naples. All these areas were ravaged by war, but the heaviest fighting occurred first in Italy and then on the eastern frontier of France.

Italian Wars. Italy's geographic position made the peninsula a valuable prize in terms of both Mediterranean trade in the south and the link between western and central Europe in the north. To this

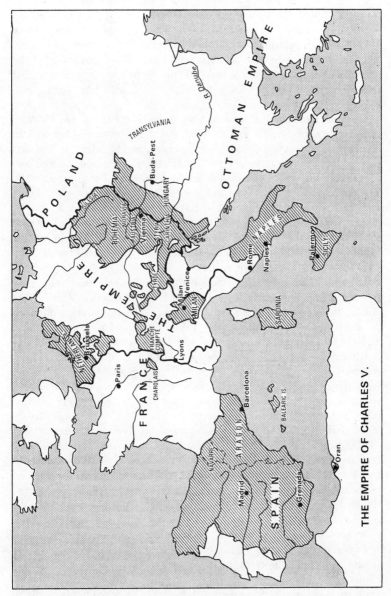

(From *Europe in the Sixteenth Century*, p. 177, by H. G. Koenigsberger and George
L. Mosse. Copyright © 1968 by H. G. Koenigsberger and G. L. Mosse. Reprinted by
permission of Holt, Rinehart and Winston, Inc.)

must be added the concentration of urban wealth in the relatively weak and quarreling principalities. Throughout the wars these Italian states, including the papacy, attempted to protect their independence and prevent the dominance of the peninsula by either of the great powers. This explains in part the sequence of alliances that turned friend to foe and back again to friend with bewildering regularity.

The war began in 1494 when Charles VIII of France laid claim to the kingdom of Naples and invaded Italy. The invasion turned into a triumphal procession down the Italian boot, and Charles VIII wrested Naples from the Aragonese in 1495. However, as happened so often, a coalition emerged to challenge foreign dominance of the peninsula. The papacy, Milan, Florence, and Venice allied themselves with Aragon and the Holy Roman emperor and forced Charles to withdraw (1498). The struggle was renewed by Charles's successor, Louis XII, whose intricate diplomacy divided his enemies and enabled him to occupy Milan. He in turn, however, was forced by the anti-French Holy League (1511) to retreat from Italy.

Hapsburg-Valois Wars. Although the war in Italy continued after the accessions of Francis I (r. 1515–1547) and Charles V (r. 1516–1556), the scope of the conflict broadened. The Hapsburg lands consolidated in the hands of Charles V formed a cordon around France, and the struggle became a contest for hegemony in western Europe.

Francis I invaded Italy and with a victory at Maringnano (1515) regained the contested duchy of Milan. Charles rallied his forces and with the support of his Italian allies, including the pope, inflicted a stunning defeat on the French at Pavia (1525), where Francis was taken prisoner. Francis relinquished his claims to Italy in the Treaty of Madrid (1526), but when he regained his freedom, he repudiated the agreement and reopened hostilities. Charles's overwhelming victory had frightened his Italian allies, who switched their allegiance to Francis. The pope paid dearly for his decision, as Charles's army of unpaid German mercenaries turned their wrath on Rome and looted the city with unprecedented ferocity (1527). Pope Clement VII thus became a veritable hostage of the emperor, and his lack of independence played a decisive part in his failure to prevent the Protestant Reformation in England (see p. 66). Francis once more sued for peace, and under the terms of the Treaty of Cambrai (1529), he was allowed to retain Burgundy in return for a third renunciation of Italy as well as the cession of Artois and Flanders on his northern frontiers.

Despite his reverses in Italy, Francis was not prepared to concede defeat. He conspired with Protestant princes in Germany to weaken Charles in the empire and allied himself to Sultan Suleiman, "the Magnificent," who was threatening Christendom's eastern frontiers (see p. 35). The death of the duke of Milan in 1535 brought a renewal of hostilities in Italy without decisive results (1536–1538), and hostilities also recurred again in the Netherlands and Roussillon, on the Spanish frontier, from 1542 to 1544. In neither case was Francis able to dislodge his tenacious adversary. The struggle continued after the death of Francis I (1547) under the guidance of his successor, Henry II (r. 1547–1559). Henry captured the imperial cities of Verdun, Metz, and Toul when fighting resumed (1552–1557), but he failed in his attempt to seize Naples.

TREATY OF CATEAU-CAMBRÉSIS (1559). This treaty ended the long Hapsburg-Valois struggle. Under the terms of the agreement, France retained the bishoprics of Verdun, Toul, and Metz on the east bank of the Meuse River, as well as several fortress cities on the Italian slopes of the Alps. The Hapsburgs retained their control of the Italian peninsula. The death of Henry II (1559) temporarily ended French expansionism. When the country emerged four decades later from its domestic turmoil, its efforts were directed toward the Rhine Valley rather than the Mediterranean. Finally, the treaty marked the emergence of Spain as the dominant power in western Europe, a position it maintained for almost a century.

The Turkish Threat

The aggressive expansion of the Ottoman Empire posed a second major threat to Charles V. These Moslems had conquered Constantinople in 1453 and now threatened to break into Europe itself.

Ottoman Expansion. By 1481 the Ottoman Empire included western Anatolia (modern Turkey) and the Balkan peninsula as far north as Bosnia, Serbia, and Wallachia. Under Sultan Selim I (r. 1481–1520), an internecine war was fought among Islamic sects for control of the Moslem world. The conflict resulted in Ottoman expansion into Egypt, the western coast of the Arabian peninsula (including the holy cities of Medina and Mecca), Palestine, Syria, and northwestern Mesopotamia. With the eastern Mediterranean firmly in their grasp, the Turks again turned their attention toward the Christian territories on their northwestern frontiers.

Suleiman I (r. 1520–1566) launched the attacks against the frontiers of Christendom that continued throughout the century. He first seized Belgrade (1521) and then Rhodes (1522), the island gateway to the Aegean Sea. His armies struck terror into the hearts of western Europeans when they killed Louis II of Hungary and annihilated his army on the field of Mohács (30 August 1526).

Hapsburg Resistance. The obligation to defend Christendom fell to Charles, whose own territory was directly threatened and who was the only political ruler with universal prestige in the West.

THE STRUGGLE FOR HUNGARY. The death of Louis II opened a struggle for the Hungarian throne. Those noblemen who saw the Hapsburgs as the only possible bulwark against Ottoman expansion elected Ferdinand I, brother of Charles V, as their new king. A nationalist faction opposed to the absorption of their kingdom into the Hapsburg domains elected John Zápolya. In the ensuing civil war (1526–1528), Zápolya was defeated and appealed to the Turks for assistance. Suleiman led a counterattack that not only overran Hungary but also forced Ferdinand to withstand a two-month siege at Vienna (September–October 1529). Despite the successful defense of his capital, Ferdinand was unable to regain more than a small portion of western Hungary in the decades of warfare that followed.

WAR AT SEA. While their armies clashed in the Balkans, the adversaries also struggled for control of the Mediterranean. Khair ed-Din, commander of the Turkish squadron, seized both Algiers (1529) and Tunis (1534). Although an armada sent by Charles V and commanded by Andrea Doria recaptured Tunis in 1535, it proved to be but a brief respite. By the end of Charles V's reign (1556), the North African coast was firmly in Turkish hands.

Political-Religious Struggle in Germany

As Holy Roman emperor, Charles V felt a deep moral responsibility to protect the universal Church. Despite his political differences with the papacy, particularly Clement VII, he was bound by his conscience as a Christian prince to maintain the religious solidarity of Europe against both infidels and heretics. He recognized that abuses existed and was willing to support reforms that did not alter the basic Catholic dogma. However, when conciliation failed he attempted to crush heresy with all the power at his disposal.

The period from the beginning of the German Reformation through the Peasants' War (1526) has been discussed in chapter 6. The peasant uprising frightened the political authorities in the German states, and most princes were prepared to reach an accommodation with both the emperor and the pope if three general conditions were fulfilled: (1) an end to flagrant corruption and violations of canon

law, (2) a redefinition of Christian beliefs and ritual that would
fulfill the spiritual needs of the German people, and (3) the formulation of an imperial policy designed to promote German interests.

Speyer Resolution. The imperial diet convened in the city of
Speyer in August 1526. Charles V realized that a resolution of theological issues could be reached only in a general council of the Church.
He was also reluctant to antagonize Lutheran princes; at that time
he needed the support of all Germans in order to meet the threat of
Francis I, who was recovering from his defeat at Pavia (1525), and
to blunt the Turkish expansion into Hungary. The diet therefore
adopted a resolution suspending enforcement of the Edict of Worms,
which had condemned Luther (see p. 61), until the convocation
of a general council. This resolution, designed as a temporary ex-
pedient, strengthened the Lutherans. Pope Clement refused to call
a general council because he feared that a conciliatory settlement would
weaken his authority. In addition, Charles was deeply involved in
Italian affairs, in which a military confrontation with the pope culminated in the sack of Rome (see p. 78).

Protestation of Speyer. By 1529 Charles had his enemies in check
and had resolved his differences with the papacy. Therefore he returned to Germany with the intention of suppressing Lutheranism. The
imperial diet reconvened at Speyer and revoked the Resolution of
1526. The Lutheran princes responded with a Protestation, which
denied the right of the diet to enforce religious conformity. (It is
from this protest that the term *Protestant* is derived.) Although they
claimed the right of individuals to answer to their own conscience,
they were referring to the rights of sovereign princes, not the rights
of individual peasants.

Confession of Augsburg. The imperial diet convoked at Augsburg
resulted in a clear division of the opposing forces. Philip Melanchthon,
Luther's highly esteemed colleague, presented a reasoned defense of
the Lutheran position in the hope of reconciliation. Though rejected
by the Catholics, the Augsburg Confession (1530) became the most
authoritative statement of Lutheran belief. The Catholic majority responded with a total denunciation of all the Protestant sects and
demanded strict enforcement of the Edict of Worms. Thus the battle
lines were clearly drawn.

Armed Standoff to 1546. Faced with the determination of Charles
to suppress them, the Protestant princes formed an alliance known
as the League of Schmalkalden (1531). Once again, however,
Charles was distracted by the Turks. In an effort to protect his German
territories, he declared an armistice, known as the Nuremberg Stand-

still (1532), which once more postponed the resolution of the German conflict. Between 1532 and 1545, his constant distraction by other problems kept Charles occupied outside of Germany. In this long interval, the growth of Protestantism in Germany continued until only the Hapsburg domains, Bavaria, and a few ecclesiastical principalities remained in the Catholic fold.

Schmalkaldic War and Its Aftermath. The armed conflict that had threatened Germany for decades broke out in 1546. The Protestant leaders, including John Frederick of Saxony and Philip of Hesse, let their initial advantage slip away through irresolution and inaction. Charles seized the initiative and decisively defeated the Protestants at the battle of Mühlberg (1547). After years of diplomatic maneuvering, Charles seemed to have had his enemies at his mercy, but his victory proved short-lived.

Lutheranism might easily have been suppressed with a decisive stroke in 1517, but Charles's attempt to reinstate Catholicism in 1548 was clearly unenforceable and led to deep resentment. German patriots also denounced his use of Spanish troops during the war and his favoritism toward his Spanish son Philip at the expense of his brother Ferdinand, who had served Germany faithfully since 1522. Finally, the German princes feared that the emperor would now move to enhance his own power at the expense of their liberties. Included in this group were Maurice of Saxony, who deserted Charles and allied himself with Henry II of France. War ensued (1552–1556), and at the outset Charles was forced to flee to Italy. Although Charles attempted to restore the situation, he was approaching the end of his physical and spiritual endurance.

Peace of Augsburg. In 1554 Charles decided to abdicate, and he called upon Frederick to negotiate a settlement within the empire. The diet met at Augsburg and drafted the treaty that ended forty years of religious and political strife. The major stipulations of the Peace of Augsburg (1555) follow. Lutheranism was officially recognized within the empire, and each prince was allowed to determine the religion of his own territory. This precept of *cuius regio, eius religio* did not extend freedom of conscience to individuals, nor did it recognize any Protestant religion other than Lutheranism. Any ecclesiastical prince who henceforth abandoned Catholicism for Lutheranism would be obliged to surrender his holdings. All Church property seized before 1552 was the lawful property of those in current possession.

Abdication of Charles V. Charles had defended his dynastic inheritance for four decades against the French, the Turks, and the princes of the Germanic empire. Exhausted by his efforts, an old man at fifty-eight, he abdicated his political offices (1555–1556). To his son Philip II, he bequeathed Spain and the colonial empire, Naples, Milan, the Netherlands, and the Franche-Comté. To his brother Ferdinand went the Hapsburg domains and the imperial title. Charles withdrew to a Spanish monastery, where he died in 1558. With him died the medieval dream of a universal empire.

8

Western Europe, 1550-1600

The latter half of the sixteenth century witnessed a continuation of the religious and dynastic struggles that marked its opening decades. The scene of this conflict shifted decisively to the West, where Spain emerged as the most powerful standard-bearer of the resurgent Catholic church (see p. 68). Calvinism posed the greatest ideological threat to Catholic orthodoxy, and Philip II attempted to crush its adherents in France, the Netherlands, and England with military force. Although France played an active role in international affairs, it was wracked by religious controversy and political infighting and could pose no serious threat to Spanish pretensions. Thus England and the United Netherlands emerged as Spain's most formidable Protestant opponents. Through the effective use of their maritime power, they were able to thwart Philip's Catholic crusade and his dynastic ambitions.

Though we may be appalled by the degree of religious intolerance displayed by both sides and by the atrocities they committed in the name of God, we can draw a close parallel to the ideological conflicts of the twentieth century, in which every belligerent has predicted universal catastrophe as the fruits of his opponent's victory.

Spain

During the last half of the sixteenth century, Spain experienced a golden age. The domains inherited by Philip II from his father Charles V included the Iberian kingdoms of Navarre, Castile, and Aragon plus the Netherlands and the Italian territories of Milan and Naples. The Spanish Empire in the New World produced such enormous wealth that Philip became the envy of every monarch in Europe. He used part of his income to finance a standing army that dominated European battlefields for almost a century. At the same time, Spanish arts and letters produced such masters as Velázquez, Cervantes, and Lope de Vega (see p. 58). However, beneath this brilliant display, Spain suffered from chronic maladies that sapped her strength and ultimately reduced her to a position of second rank among European powers.

Philip II (r. 1556–1598). Philip placed the imprint of his personality upon the period. He was one of the most conscientious rulers Europe has ever known. Despite his enormous wealth, he made himself a virtual prisoner in the palace of the Escorial, where he toiled in solitude night and day. Notwithstanding his good intentions, this dedicated and religious monarch had a tragic flaw that brought most of his projects to ruin. His sense of personal responsibility made it psychologically impossible for him to delegate authority. Thus the only man with the authority to make vital decisions strangled on the minutiae of daily administration that should have been left to clerks. His schemes were grandiose but often poorly executed. His reign may justly be characterized as a "brilliant failure."

The Iberian Peninsula. While Philip ruled Aragon, Castile, and Navarre as separate kingdoms in the manner of his predecessors, he carried the process of centralization still farther. The cortes (parliamentary bodies) continued to atrophy, and Philip ruled his domains by executive decree. Each political unit was supervised by a council, among which the most important were those for Castile, Aragon, Italy, Portugal (after 1580), the Indies (for the empire), and the Privy Council (the Netherlands). In addition, the Council of State advised on foreign-policy questions, the *Suprema* directed the Inquisition, and the *Casa de Contratación* supervised the imperial economy (see p. 87). Despite the talented advisers at his disposal, Philip maintained tight personal control and often followed his own council.

ECONOMIC AND SOCIAL SYSTEM. Spain, like most of Europe, maintained a rigid caste system. The peasantry, including the majority of the country's eight million inhabitants, were among the poorest and least productive in western Europe. The nobility were exempt from the crushing burden of taxation, and their vast estates encompassed the most valuable land in the realm. On these estates were raised the merino sheep whose fine wool comprised Spain's primary export. The clergy, though they certainly provided spiritual solace for Spain's peasantry, were inordinately numerous and economically parasitic, further increasing the burden of their spiritual wards.

Thus Philip ruled one of the most backward commercial and industrial areas in western Europe. He raised monies from those least able to pay, while enormous wealth remained untouched and unproductive in the hands of the privileged classes. Though this situation was certainly not unique, Philip did nothing to vitalize Spain's fatally weak economy.

THE INQUISITION. The function of the Inquisition in maintaining Catholic orthodoxy has already been discussed (see p. 70). Philip was a religious zealot, and the extermination of Protestants and infidels became his guiding principle. He supported the Inquisition even when its gruesome manhunt conflicted with Spain's economic and political interests.

REVOLT OF THE MORISCOS. The Moriscos were those Moors who had renounced Islam for Christianity after the reconquista. Although they were loyal and productive subjects, Philip suspected them of harboring their former beliefs. He therefore turned the full force of the Inquisition upon them and sought to eradicate every remnant of their Moorish culture. His actions triggered a revolt that ended with the defeat of the Moriscos after a three-year bloodbath (1568–1571). Those who survived Philip's fury were expelled from Spain ten years after his death (1609). The extermination of this community demonstrated not only Philip's fanaticism but the intolerance of an age that equated religious deviation with treason.

INCORPORATION OF PORTUGAL. The king of Portugal died in 1580 without an heir. Of the rival claimants to the vacant throne, Philip II was by far the most powerful, and he seized the throne without serious difficulty. In one stroke the Spanish crown thus acquired not only the Atlantic port of Lisbon and its agricultural hinterland but also the far-flung Portuguese Empire, which included the East Indian Spice Islands, the African slaving stations, and Brazil. Although these new territories temporarily enhanced Spain's power and prestige, in the long run, they proved too difficult either to exploit or to protect. In the protracted maritime war that accompanied the revolt in the Netherlands, the Dutch Sea Beggars conquered the East Indies. The Portuguese had not objected violently at first, but discontent mounted as their interests were sacrificed. They revolted in 1640 and regained their independence.

The Spanish Empire. During the sixteenth and seventeenth centuries, the Spanish pursued a mercantilist policy—an economic program designed to enhance the state's political power. A key element in this policy was the exploitation of the empire for the benefit of the Spanish crown to the exclusion not only of foreigners but of non-Castilian Spaniards as well. The political and economic bureaucracies appointed to this task were closely intertwined.

ADMINISTRATION. The colonial empire was the personal property of the king and was administered through a complex bureaucracy. The Council of the Indies, created in 1524, advised the king and supervised every facet of colonial administration, although it was not always able to enforce its decisions. The empire itself was originally divided into two viceroyalties: New Spain (1535), which included the West Indies, Mexico, and all land to the north and was governed from Mexico City; and Peru (1544), which encompassed the remainder of the Americas and was ruled from Lima. The viceroys were the king's chief colonial officers. They had wide-ranging executive, legislative, and judicial powers, but checks were developed to limit their independence. Each viceroyalty was divided into judicial districts called *audiencias*, which were administered by a council of the same name. The primary audiencias presided in Mexico City and Lima and functioned as high courts and viceregal advisers. The isolated provincial audiencias exercised executive and legislative prerogatives. Their right to communicate directly with the crown provided a check on the viceroy that was often welcomed by both colonists and crown.

ECONOMIC STRUCTURE. The function of the colonies was to provide wealth for the crown. The *Casa de Contratación* (Board of Trade), founded in 1503, supervised the imperial economy, which operated through a Castilian monopoly. All trade was funneled through the port of Cadiz, where it could be closely supervised. Royal tax collectors garnered one-fifth of the mineral wealth (the *Quinto*) and levied additional taxes on all forms of property and business transactions. The treasure of Montezuma II provided the first trickle of what proved to be a torrent of Mexican and Peruvian gold and silver. At the height of production, from 1591 to 1600, over three thousand tons of silver and twenty tons of gold were transported by armed convoys that sailed annually from Vera Cruz (the *flota*) and Cartegena (the *galleons*). The colonies also provided agricultural products including sugar, hides, cochineal (a rose dye) and indigo (a blue dye). All this wealth was extracted with the labor of Indians and black slaves. The crown perpetuated European feudalism by making grants that included both land and the Indians who lived on it. Under the *encomienda* system, the grantee received the right to Indian labor or tribute, while the *mita* provided labor for the mines. Although the crown explicitly demanded Christian treatment and religious education for the Indians under the New Laws (1542), they were often reduced to the same brutalizing regime that was imposed on black slaves.

STRUCTURAL WEAKNESSES OF THE EMPIRE. The empire suffered from two inherent weaknesses. First, Spain's backward economy could not supply the country with the goods it needed; thus most of the wealth that flowed into Cadiz left the country to purchase foreign goods. Second, the colonies could not obtain manufactured goods from Spain in return for the treasure and agricultural items they exported. So despite the regulations, they engaged in contraband trade with Spain's mercantile enemies. Impossible as it may seem, Spain's treasure did not prevent a steady decline in her economic life, nor did it relieve the chronic bankruptcy resulting from Philip's costly foreign policy.

The Mediterranean War

Philip won his greatest victory in the Mediterranean. His lifelong preoccupation with the area was derived from two factors—the commercial interest of his Aragonese possessions and his crusading spirit. Both these instincts were aroused by Turkish expansionism. When he became king, only a few Spanish outposts were left in North Africa, while the remaining coastline provided bases for Barbary pirates who preyed upon European shipping. The Knights of Saint John were able to defend the naval stronghold at Malta against a determined Turkish attack (1565), but Cyprus fell into Moslem hands in 1570.

The Holy League. One reason for Turkish success in the Mediterranean had been the uncoordinated efforts of the major Christian maritime powers, particularly Venice and Spain. Under papal auspices a Holy League was created in 1571, and the allied fleet of over two hundred ships was assembled under the command of Don John of Austria, Philip's half brother.

Battle of Lepanto. Both the Christian and Turkish flotillas included warships that had changed little from ancient times. The ships, called *galleys*, were propelled by banks of oars and lateen sails. Tactical doctrine had also changed little, and the two basic maneuvers consisted of either ramming the adversary or drawing alongside so that infantry could board the enemy.

The greatest naval battle since Actium (sixteen hundred years earlier) took place off Lepanto in the Gulf of Corinth on 7 October 1571. The numerically superior Turkish fleet was virtually wiped out. The forces of Christendom had a momentary advantage that might have proved decisive, but Don John allowed this opportunity to slip away, and within a year the Turks made up their losses. Although the Spanish could henceforth hold their own against the Turkish menace, an ironic consequence of the battle was to lull Spain into a false sense of naval superiority that proved disastrous in its war with England.

War in the Netherlands

In 1566 the Netherlands consisted of seventeen independent provinces, which today comprise the countries of the Netherlands (Holland), Belgium, and Luxembourg. They were held together only by their common allegiance to the dukes of Burgundy, whose inheritance ultimately passed through Charles V to Philip II. Together they comprised the wealthiest area in Europe. In the county of Flanders, the cities of Bruges, Ghent, and Antwerp had been renowned textile centers since the Middle Ages. By midcentury, Antwerp was the financial and commercial capital of Europe, and as such it served as the northern terminus for Spanish trade. Further to the north, the fisherman of the counties of Holland and Zeeland controlled the North Atlantic herring industry. It was across this prosperous region that one of the most bitterly contested wars in European history raged from 1566 to 1648.

Dutch Revolt. In the past the Netherlands had been obedient subjects of any prince who protected their interests and respected their privileges. Emperor Charles V had derived much of his strength from the financial resources of the counties by following such a policy. The Netherlanders were less inclined to support Philip II. He was a foreigner who disliked their country and whose government seemed interested only in the taxes it could extract from them. In addition the growing influx of Protestants, mainly Calvinists, infuriated Philip. But the Inquisition was unable to "purify" his territory, and Philip's direct interference with the administration of the Catholic church enraged his coreligionists.

The leaders of the nobility, including William of Orange and the counts of Egmont and Horn, advised Philip to moderate his rule by taking them into his confidence if he hoped to avoid further resentment, but they were rebuffed. When two hundred of the lesser nobility subsequently petitioned the regent, Margaret of Parma, for a redress of grievances, they were contemptuously dismissed as "beggars." The result was an outbreak of anti-Catholic rioting and iconoclasm that led Philip to declare marital law.

The duke of Alva, the new regent, arrived in the Netherlands with ten thousand troops and a group of advisers that soon earned the nickname the Council of Blood. From 1567 to 1572, a reign of terror gripped the country. The rebels were no match for the Spanish infantry. The Inquisition methodically executed those recalcitrants who fell into its hands, including Egmont and Horn. The leadership of the rebellion fell to William ("the Silent") of Orange, whose chief qualification was a total devotion to the cause and its adherents.

Though defeated on land, the rebels held their own at sea, where they flaunted the name Sea Beggars. They harried Spanish commerce and challenged Philip's men-of-war. In 1572 they gained a foothold on the islands of Zeeland and the coast of Holland. Their victories brought the remainder of the two counties over to the rebellion. William of Orange was elected *stadtholder* (chief magistrate), and henceforth the area was the center of Dutch resistance.

As the Meuse and Rhine rivers turn westward and empty into the sea, they form a military obstacle to attack from the south. This prevented Alva from crushing the pocket of rebellion. Even when they could force a bridgehead, the Spaniards were reluctant to operate in areas where the dikes could be opened to flood the low-lying countryside. Holland became a sanctuary for the rebels. The Protestants, who had originally been concentrated in the south, slowly emigrated northward. As a result, the Netherlands eventually evolved into two distinct areas, with the Dutch-speaking Protestants in the seven northern counties and the French-speaking Catholics in the ten southern counties.

Pacification of Ghent. In the 1570s the division of the Netherlands had only begun, and the southern counties had not been reconciled to Spanish rule. The sack of Antwerp by unpaid Spanish troops in 1576 led the southerners to disregard religious differences, and in the agreement known as the Pacification of Ghent (1576), they joined the north in a determined effort to expel the Spaniards. Philip averted the loss of the Netherlands by appointing Alessandro Farnese, duke of Parma, as the Spanish governor. Parma was not only a competent general but also a skilled diplomat. He was able to convince the southerners that their interests would be better served by Spanish rule than by the anarchy of Calvinist mobs. In this way he detached the south from their previous alliance and drew them into the League of Arras (1579), whose stated purpose was the defense of Catholicism.

Creation of the United Netherlands. The northern provinces responded with an alliance of their own, the Union of Utrecht (1579), which sealed the division of the counties into two political units. This breach was formalized in 1581, when the allies renounced Philip and declared the existence of the sovereign United Netherlands (Dutch Republic). Despite this act of bravado, the outlook was bleak. William of Orange was struck down by an assassin (1584), and the leadership fell to his young son William of Nassau. Parma's troops appeared invincible, and the capture of Antwerp (1584) seemed to signal a final offensive that would drive the rebels into the sea. Elizabeth of England provided enough assistance to ward off disaster, but the Dutch were saved ultimately by Philip's attempt to force a decision at sea. The defeat of the Spanish Armada in 1588 (see p. 93) and growing Dutch maritime power ended Philip's hopes of reconquering the United Provinces. In 1609 a twelve-year truce was negotiated that virtually ended the conflict, but it was not until 1648, under the terms of the Treaty of Westphalia, that Spain formally recognized Dutch independence.

Elizabethan England

Many must have predicted a bleak future for England when the twenty-four-year-old princess Elizabeth succeeded her half sister Mary Tudor to the throne. The government was in disarray, and the treasury was empty. The circumstances of Elizabeth's birth to Henry VIII and Anne Boleyn had placed her in the center of controversy between Catholics and Protestants who threatened at any moment to take up arms in the defense of their beliefs. Ambitious men lurked in every corner to take advantage of Elizabeth's precarious hold on the throne.

Despite this inauspicious beginning, Elizabeth's reign is one of the most cherished memories of England's long history. Two important aspects of her reign, the religious settlement and the outpouring of literary masterpieces, have already been discussed (pp. 57, 68). This section will deal primarily with England's development as a major maritime power.

Elizabeth I (r. 1558–1603). Much of the credit for England's success during the last half of the century must go directly to her greatest queen. Elizabeth was a handsome woman with a humanist education, a quick mind, and a strong will. Her approach to politics was decidedly Machiavellian. Although she ruled with a firm hand, she was known as Good Queen Bess to her subjects. Elizabeth never married. Her failure to provide an heir posed a serious threat for an England only two generations removed from civil war. On the other hand, her maidenhood was a valuable asset in diplomacy. What England could not gain by force or persuasion it often gained from men who sought Elizabeth's hand and her dowry of the English realm.

ELIZABETHAN GOVERNMENT. Interesting contrasts can be drawn between the government of the strong-willed monarchs of England and Spain. Like Philip, Elizabeth maintained a firm hold on every facet of government and relied on her own instincts to arrive at crucial decisions. While both maintained glittering courts to impress their subjects and foreign dignitaries, neither succumbed to the empty vanities of courtly life. On the other hand, Elizabeth displayed several virtues that Philip lacked. She had the ability to choose shrewd and loyal advisers and the wisdom to place upon them the heavy responsibilities of administration. Of these advisers the most important were William Cecil, later Lord Burghley, who served her for forty years, and the younger Francis Walsingham. Finally, in the age of religious fanatics, Elizabeth was a political realist more concerned with order, obedience, and power than with orthodoxy.

THE ENGLISH PARLIAMENT. The Parliament, a legislative body representing the interests of the landed gentry, posed a unique problem for the queen. She was determined to control the government without directly challenging the prerogatives of her most powerful subjects. She closely supervised Parliament and directed its work toward goals she desired, thus maintaining a working relationship without sacrificing her power. The conciliatory religious settlement that allowed the great majority of Englishmen to remain loyal subjects without violating their religious scruples is a good example of both Elizabeth's wisdom and her ability to enforce her will on the Parliament.

Mary, Queen of Scots. In the sixteenth century, Scotland was a poor backward kingdom. Its greatest nobles still lived as autonomous warlords, often beyond the king's control. Constant political factionalism led to sporadic civil war, which was aggravated by the struggle between England and France for control of the Scottish crown.

As an infant Mary Stuart (1542–1587) became a pawn in the Anglo-French power struggle. She grew up in France and at the age of seventeen became the queen consort of Francis II, who died after reigning only fifteen months. When in 1561 Mary returned to assume the throne of Scotland, she was a Frenchwoman in all respects but birth.

Mary had a short and tragic reign. She disliked Scotland and longed for the glitter of the French court. Her disdain was returned by John Knox, leader of the Scottish Reformation. Knox disapproved of Mary's sex, her Catholicism, her politics, and her private life. She was certainly open to criticism on the last two counts. She was a notorious flirt, and though a poor politician, she developed into a chronic intriguer. Many believed her to be implicated in the murder of her husband, Lord Darnley, and her precipitate marriage to the earl of Bothwell, his suspected killer, led to open rebellion. Mary abdicated in favor of her son James (1567) and fled to England (1568).

Mary spent the last nineteen years of her life in English exile. She was an unwelcome guest there, for she posed a serious threat to Elizabeth. As a great-granddaughter of Henry VII, she was next in line of succession to the English throne. In fact among Catholics, who regarded Elizabeth as an illegitimate child, Mary had a prior claim to the crown. During the two decades of semicaptivity, she became the center of conspiracies supported by Philip II, who sought to place her on the throne. Despite warnings from her advisers, Elizabeth was reluctant to act against her Scottish cousin until the revelation of Babington's plot (1586), a conspiracy to assassinate Elizabeth and place Mary on the throne. As a result, Mary, Queen of Scots, fell beneath the executioner's blade (1587).

Anglo-Spanish Conflict. After 1559 Spain replaced France as the main threat to English security. Philip II hoped to return England to Catholic orthodoxy and to manipulate her foreign policy to his own interests. For this reason he had married Queen Mary Tudor. After her death he had to deal with the less tractable Elizabeth. The relations between England and Spain deteriorated over three issues: (1) their religious differences, (2) England's support of the Dutch rebellion, and (3) the armed incursion of English mariners into the Spanish Empire.

THE SEA DOGS. The wealth of Spain's empire lured adventurers who ran high risks in the hope of great returns. Elizabeth unofficially supported these Sea Dogs while avoiding an open conflict with Spain. Incursions into the Spanish main took several forms. Beginning in 1562, John Hawkins illegally traded African slaves to Spanish colonists. His ventures were lucrative until 1568 when a Spanish squadron practically destroyed his small fleet in the harbor of Vera Cruz. Francis Drake was far less subtle than Hawkins. In 1572 he plundered the Panamanian coast, and in 1577 he attacked the Pacific sea-lanes of Central America. To avoid capture he sailed the treasure-laden *Golden Hind* westward and returned home as the first English captain to circumnavigate the globe.

DEFEAT OF THE SPANISH ARMADA. Philip's policies in England and the Netherlands seemed stalled. The Dutch rebels could not be dislodged from their stronghold north of the Rhine. The Sea Dogs continued their depredations, and Mary, Queen of Scots, had been executed. In an attempt to end his frustrations with one decisive stroke, Philip assembled an armada of 130 ships and thirty thousand men, most of whom were infantry troops. The plan called for the fleet to rendezvous with Parma's army in the Netherlands and to invade England. After a series of delays occasioned by poor administration and English harassment, the armada sailed in July 1588.

The enterprise was doomed from the start. A running fight up the English Channel demonstrated that the large, slow Spanish ships were no match for the English, who boasted a superiority in maneuverability and firepower. There was no opportunity to link up with Parma, and the destruction begun by the English was finished by high winds and heavy seas. The remainder of the shattered armada limped back to Spain in defeat.

Spain remained the most powerful state in Europe well into the next century, but the defeat of the armada ended Spanish hopes of reconquering the United Netherlands. It also gave a psychological boost to the Protestant forces.

French Wars of Religion

The Treaty of Cateau-Cambrésis (1559) suspended the Hapsburg-Valois struggle for dominance in western Europe. France receded into the background of international affairs, while Philip II's Spain emerged as the most powerful state in Europe. During this period, spanning the last four decades of the century, France was wracked by religious dissent and political factionalism that led to continual civil wars.

France at the Death of Henry II. There is probably no better example of monarchy's need for a mature and well-balanced king than that supplied by the events following the accidental death of Henry II in 1559. He left France in the hands of his widow, Catherine de Médicis (1519–1589), and three small sons, who lived to reign as Francis II (1559–1560), Charles IX (1560–1574), and Henry III (1574–1589). All were incapacitated by physical or psychological defects. The task of preserving Valois interests fell to Catherine de Médicis. As the power behind the throne, she faced two major problems.

RELIGIOUS CONTROVERSY. During the reign of Francis I (1515–1547), Calvinism had begun to challenge Catholicism's spiritual monopoly. In the following decades, the French peasantry remained overwhelmingly loyal to the mother church, but a large portion of the intellectuals, the skilled artisans, the bourgeoisie, and nearly one-half of the nobility adopted Calvinism. The Huguenots (French Calvinists), by demanding religious toleration and local autonomy, began to pose a political threat to the crown.

POLITICAL FACTIONALISM. The French nobility took the opportunity provided by weak royal leadership to reassert their political rights. The Guise, Montmorency, and Bourbon families each represented a political faction that hoped to expand its own influence at the expense of the crown. François, duke of Guise, was the most influential Catholic nobleman immediately after Henry II's death. His most formidable adversaries in the contest for control of the government were Henry of Navarre and the prince of Condé (Bourbons) and Admiral Coligny (a nephew of Montmorency). Their conversion to Calvinism intensified the struggle and brought the country to the brink of civil war.

Wars of Religion to 1572. Catherine attempted to arbitrate a settlement with the houses of Guise and Bourbon. A conference, known as the Colloquy of Poissy, failed to produce agreement. The subsequent massacre of Huguenots at Vassy (1562) by Guise troops ignited civil war. Though the Catholics won most of the battles in the intermittent warfare that followed, Huguenot influence continued to grow. A truce signed in 1570 granted the Protestants religious toleration.

Saint Bartholomew's Day Massacre. The emergence of Admiral Coligny as Charles IX's chief minister and the marriage of Henry of Navarre to Margaret of Valois, the king's sister, threatened to eclipse both Catherine de Médicis and the duke of Guise. The two therefore conspired to wipe out the Huguenot leadership in a single stroke. They carried out their plan on Saint Bartholomew's Day, 24 August 1572. Three thousand Protestants, including Admiral Coligny, were slain in Paris, and thousands more were murdered in the provinces. Henry of Navarre escaped.

Continuation of the Wars to 1589. During the reign of Henry III (1574–1589), the political and religious struggle reached its climax. Henry's attempts to reach a political compromise on the religious issues cost him supporters among both Catholic and Protestant fanatics, and his notorious homosexuality discredited the tottering Valois dynasty.

CATHOLIC LEAGUE. Henry Guise, who had succeeded his murdered father (1563), formed and led the Catholic League (1576). Its avowed purpose was to destroy the Huguenots and to place Henry Guise on the throne. The Catholic League was strengthened by Philip II (Spain), who hoped to use France in his struggle with the Dutch and the English.

HUGUENOT STRONGHOLDS. Despite the Saint Bartholomew's Day slaughter, Henry of Navarre rallied many supporters to his cause. The Huguenots were particularly strong in the west and south, where their fortified towns escaped the king's control.

THE POLITIQUES. Jean Bodin (1530–1596), one of the most brilliant political theorists of the sixteenth century, was the spokesman for an emerging third faction. The *politiques* realized that a continuation of the religious warfare would destroy the state. Bodin argued in *The Six Books of the Republic* (1576) that only powerful centralized monarchy with sovereign powers to control factionalism could bring an end to anarchy and a return to law, order, and prosperity.

WAR OF THE THREE HENRYS. The final struggle among the Henrys of Valois, Guise, and Bourbon wound to a grisly end in a series of coups and countercoups. Henry of Guise, coordinating his efforts with the projected sailing of the armada, seized Paris and Henry III (December 1587). Henry III escaped to Blois, where he first made Guise his chief minister and then had him assassinated. The king then allied himself with Henry of Navarre to destroy the Catholic League. Henry III was assassinated in turn by a monk (July 1589). The Valois dynasty thus ended, and the crown passed to Henry of Navarre, a direct descendant of Louix IX.

Religious Settlement of Henry IV. Henry of Navarre founded the Bourbon dynasty, which ruled France continuously until 1789, but his right to rule as Henry IV (1589–1610) did not go uncontested.

Dissident Catholics and Philip II continued the war and prevented Henry from entering Paris. Henry realized that the politiques were correct; no Huguenot king could ever hope to rule in tranquility. He therefore renounced Calvinism and became a Catholic (1593). Paris, which could not be stormed by Huguenot troops, opened her gates to a Catholic king (1594).

Having placated the Catholics, Henry was also determined to conciliate the Huguenots. The Edict of Nantes (1598), by granting toleration to a religious minority, was a milestone in European history. The most significant concessions made to the Huguenots were: (1) freedom of conscience, (2) a wide-ranging, though not unlimited, freedom of public worship, and (3) complete civil rights. Their rights were guaranteed by the maintenance of one hundred fortified towns whose Huguenot garrisons were paid by the state. With this political solution to a religious problem, Henry IV followed the path trod by England's Elizabeth. In this way he set France on the road to political and economic recovery. (Other aspects of Henry's reign will be discussed on page 111.)

9

The Emergence
of Parliamentary Power
in England

The primary significance of seventeenth-century English history lies in the development of parliamentary government based on the rule of law. During the reign of the Stuart dynasty from 1603 to 1714, the English Parliament, through persuasion, stubborn confrontation, and open rebellion on two occasions, asserted itself as the sovereign power and the arbiter of public policy.

The Realm in 1603

At the beginning of the seventeenth century, English society exhibited several characteristics that set it apart from most continental states. England was relatively small and poor by great-power standards, but the adaptability of her social, economic, and political institutions proved a source of strength.

Economy and the Social Structure. England had a healthy economic base in the seventeenth century. Though relatively productive, the agricultural sector still demanded the toil of 80 percent of the population. It did, however, produce enough wool to supply the textile industry with the raw material for England's most precious export. London in 1603 was a teeming seaport and commercial center of two hundred thousand, and during the century England's merchant fleet became the largest in the world.

The most significant characteristic of England's social structure was the comparatively wide latitude for individual advancement and the lack of sharply defined class lines compared with the other states of Europe. The absence of social stratification allowed modernization to proceed much more rapidly than in any other European society. However, for purposes of study, English society can be divided into four broad and overlapping groups.

NOBILITY. Through its landed wealth and legal status, the nobility stood at the top of the social structure. But it did not form a caste because the younger sons of noblemen were by law commoners, and the industrious merchant might buy land and patents of nobility.

GENTRY. The gentry consisted of landowning squires, who formed the backbone of the agricultural society. Increasing numbers of successful merchants and professional men joined the group. The gentry took an active part in politics and served the crown as justices of the peace, the most important local judicial and administrative post.

YEOMAN AND TENANT FARMERS. This group of farmers stood below the gentry but were able to rise in wealth and status. The yeoman differed from the tenant farmer, not in wealth, but by virtue of his forty-shilling freehold, which marked him as an independent man and permitted him to vote in county elections.

COMMON PEOPLE. The great mass of commoners comprised at least 75 percent of the population. Throughout the seventeenth century, although some skilled artisans lived relatively comfortable lives, the vast majority of rural cottagers and unskilled town laborers eked out a bare existence.

The Monarchy. In 1603 the monarchy stood at the pinnacle of its power and prestige. It had been strengthened by three forceful Tudor monarchs: Henry VII (r. 1485–1509), who destroyed the military power of the nobility; Henry VIII (r. 1509–1547), who brought the Church under royal control; and Elizabeth I (r. 1558–1603), whose program of religious conciliation and vigorous foreign policy won the love and respect of the English people. Although these monarchs claimed total executive authority, England did not develop the absolutist government so common in the rest of Europe.

Parliament. Royal power was checked by the Parliament, which had emerged in recognizable form as early as the reign of Edward I (1272–1307). Although the Tudors carefully supervised its activities, the Parliament steadily increased in authority, particularly after Henry VIII and Elizabeth used it to sanction the Reformation settlement. By 1603 its members claimed the right to enact new laws, vote taxes, and debate matters of state. The Parliament consisted of two bodies.

HOUSE OF LORDS. The upper house of Parliament contained eighty-two peers of the realm and twenty-six bishops of the Anglican church. Although it remained an influential legislative body until early in the twentieth century, it played a secondary role in the constitutional struggle of the seventeenth century.

HOUSE OF COMMONS. The lower house of Parliament represented, in theory, the entire nation, but its members were selected by a small number of voters, generally property owners. There were two types of constituencies: the counties, which returned a total of ninety-two representatives known as knights of the shire, and boroughs (that is, towns), which elected approximately four hundred members. This apparent dominance of the towns conceals the fact that with the exception of the largest cities, most borough representatives were chosen from the ranks of the landed gentry.

Confrontation of Crown and Commons

The first two Stuart kings, James I and Charles I, lacked the political ability and tact of their Tudor predecessors. Instead of manipulating Parliament and avoiding constitutional issues, they opened three major areas of controversy: (1) the content of Anglican theology and ritual, (2) the right to raise revenues, and (3) the control of foreign policy. Eventually the direct confrontation over these issues raised the ultimate question of who wielded sovereign power in the state.

James I (r. 1603–1625). King James (Stuart) of Scotland ascended the English throne in 1603 when the death of his royal cousin Queen Elizabeth ended the Tudor dynasty. Although an able scholar and adequate politician, James failed to adjust completely to English custom and law. His habit of surrounding himself with incompetent Scottish advisers alienated his most powerful English subjects.

RELIGIOUS CONTROVERSY. Religion and politics were tightly intertwined in the seventeenth century, and as a result embittered political opponents refused to compromise. In his personal beliefs, James was a Calvinist, but he hated the Scottish Presbyterians, who had driven his mother, the Catholic Mary, Queen of Scots, from the throne.

At the beginning of his reign (1604), a delegation of Puritan clergymen of the Anglican church presented James with the Millenary Petition, requesting a simplified church service and a more Calvinist theology. Many of the Puritans also wanted to abandon the episcopal structure, based on control by bishops, for a presbyterian organization controlled by congregationally elected elders. The king's angry rebuttal, "no bishop, no king," was an affirmation of his belief that the Anglican church as then structured was a primary ingredient of his political power. Many Puritans left England for the Netherlands and after 1620 for North America. More significantly, however, Puritanism continued to gain influence among the Anglican clergy and the landed gentry who remained in England.

Some extreme Catholics were also disappointed with the king's religious outlook. In 1605 a small group conspired unsuccessfully to blow up the Parliament (the Gunpowder Plot). This only confirmed the belief among many Protestants that all Catholics were traitors.

CONSTITUTIONAL STRUGGLE. The powers of crown and Parliament were not clearly defined or separated when James became king. Though never questioning the monarch's right to rule, the House of Commons reacted sharply to his overbearing stress on the concept of divine-right monarchy. Its most powerful weapon was the right to withhold tax revenues. James tried to avoid this constraint by collecting custom duties, which he controlled, and by raising forced loans. He was able to rule without parliamentary funds from 1611 to 1621, but his extremely wasteful spending and an international crisis forced him to reconvene the legislature.

FOREIGN POLICY. The foreign-policy crisis resulting from the outbreak of what would be the Thirty Years' War brought to a head all the controversial issues of the reign. James had provided for the well-being of his people by maintaining peace since 1604. When the Austrians drove his son-in-law Frederick from the throne of Bohemia and the Spaniards seized the Rhenish territory he held as the elector palatine, James summoned Parliament to prepare a counterstroke. Although a maritime war against the detested Catholic monarch would have brought James immense popular support, he seemed intent on negotiating a settlement. Following the advice of the royal favorite George Villiers, duke of Buckingham, and Gondomar, the Spanish ambassador, he even attempted to arrange a marriage between Prince Charles and the Spanish Infanta. The Commons vehemently repudiated the policy, and when ordered by James to cease debate on an issue outside its jurisdiction, it replied with the Great Protestation (1621), claiming the right to debate all matters of state. Thus the king's right to conduct foreign policy was directly challenged by the Commons's demand for a voice in state affairs. Prince Charles and Buckingham nonetheless continued to pursue the Spanish match. In 1624 Charles traveled to Spain in an effort to complete the marriage, and though rejected as a suitable bridegroom for a Catholic princess, he was greeted as a hero by the English people, who were happy to see their prince return an unmarried Protestant. Accepting this adulation, Charles and Buckingham turned to the anti-Spanish policy desired by Parliament and the people. James, having raised issues that had not been resolved, drifted toward death. He left the government in the hands of Prince Charles and the inept Buckingham.

Charles I. When Charles came to power in 1625, the areas of disagreement between crown and Commons were sharply defined, but neither side had pressed its claim to the point of open confrontation.

Determined to rule without constraint, Charles failed to realize that the Parliament was no longer willing to submit to the personal whims of an irresponsible monarch.

FOREIGN POLICY. Charles's popular support suffered a severe check when an army sent to fight for Protestantism under the command of Count Mansfeld, a German soldier of fortune, disintegrated in the Netherlands from poor leadership, hunger, and disease without engaging the Spanish. In 1625, the king compromised himself further by marrying Henrietta Maria, the Catholic sister of King Louis XIII of France. Anything Charles might have gained from his French marriage alliance, forged at the expense of the goodwill of his subjects, was lost by the inept diplomacy of Buckingham. From 1625 to 1628, England found itself at war with Spain and France. Both his raid on the Spanish port of Cadiz (1625) and the expedition designed to relieve the besieged Huguenot garrison of La Rochelle (1627) ended in disaster. In 1628, when Charles finally called upon Parliament to provide funds for his expensive expeditions, he found it in an angry mood.

KING AND PARLIAMENT. The House of Commons demanded a redress of grievances before it was willing to authorize new taxes. Specifically, it wanted Charles to stop the illegal practices he had used throughout the war. The Petition of Right (1628) called for an end to four abusive measures: (1) forced loans or other arbitrary taxation, (2) imprisonment without due process, (3) the billeting of troops in private homes, and (4) martial law. The king's acceptance of the petition was a milestone in English constitutional law. Like the Magna Carta, it affirmed that the monarch was not above the law. Charles failed to live up to his agreement, however, and continued to collect customs duties without parliamentary approval.

The apprehension among Puritans that Charles's chief adviser, William Laud, archbishop of Canterbury, was reintroducing Catholicism into the Church of England increased the growing antagonism toward the crown. The Parliament was determined to deal with these issues when it convened in 1629. When King Charles attempted to dissolve Parliament rather than face its wrath, members barred the doors and passed three resolutions that (1) condemned papist innovations in religion, (2) declared illegal the collection of customs duties, and (3) denounced as a traitor anyone who paid the duties. After this act of defiance, the Commons immediately adjourned.

THE ELEVEN-YEAR TYRANNY. Charles ruled without Parliament until 1640. Though free from its criticism, he was also deprived of its financial support. He ended active participation in the Thirty Years' War, but this economy was insufficient. He then resorted to the collection of long-forgotten feudal dues and fines. The country enjoyed general prosperity throughout the period, but these levies caused widespread resentment. The greatest outcry resulted from the collection of *ship money*, a tax traditionally paid by the seaports to maintain the fleet but now raised in every inland county.

All the grievances of the reign were brought to a head in 1637 when Laud attempted to enforce the use of the new, reputedly papist prayerbook in Scotland. The angry Scots refused it and pledged in the National Covenant (1637) to use only the liturgy authorized by the elders of the Presbyterian church (the Kirk). Charles marched north with a ragtag army to subdue his rebellious subjects, but this First Bishop's War (1639) ended in a truce without bloodshed. The Short Parliament, called to provide funds needed to field a respectable force, refused to vote a farthing without a redress of grievances and was dissolved within weeks. Determined to secure their right, the Scots invaded England in August 1640. This Second Bishop's War forced Charles to reconvene Parliament. He now had to account for his arbitrary rule, for without funds he could not resist the Scots, who controlled all of northern England from their stronghold at Durham.

Civil War and the Commonwealth

The Parliament reconvened in 1640, but by 1642 the constitutional debate had reached an impasse. Charles based his claim to rule without restraint on the theory of divine right of kings, while the Parliament insisted on the rule of law based on the ancient liberties of Englishmen. The flames of political hostilities were fanned by religious intolerance. All hopes of compromise finally vanished, and issues of state were resolved on the executioner's block and on the battlefield.

The Long Parliament. The Parliament summoned in November 1640 met in various forms with a steadily diminishing membership until March 1660.

POLITICAL AND RELIGIOUS FACTIONS. For the purpose of analysis, those struggling for power in the years from 1640 to 1660 may be divided into at least five separate groups. Anglicans generally supported the political and religious prerogatives of the monarch and desired an episcopal state church. Their stress on ritual and acceptance of the belief in free will placed them closer to Catholicism than any other Protestant group of the time. The moderate Puritans demanded that the king respect lawful parliamentary prerogatives but at the same time were willing to support an episcopal church purified of its most blatant papist tendencies. The radical Puritans, led by John Pym, had lost faith in both Charles and Archbishop Laud. Although initially monarchists, they wished the Parliament to wield the sovereign power of the state and to control a state church cleansed of its episcopal structure. The Presbyterians had some influence among English theologians, but, generally speaking, they consisted of Scots who wished to enforce orthodoxy through a general assembly that supervised local congregations. Politically the Presbyterians tended to side with whatever factions would agree to endorse their strict Calvinist code. The Sectarians (or Independents) grew stronger as the conflict deepened. They supported Parliament to the point of republicanism, and their religious beliefs favored congregationalism. Their most renowned leader was Oliver Cromwell.

PARLIAMENTARY STRUGGLE. Holding the power of the purse, the Commons moved to consolidate its political position. Lord Strafford and Archbishop Laud, the two men thought most responsible for the king's arrogant policies, were imprisoned in the Tower of London. Strafford was condemned by a bill of attainder (a legislative act having the force of a court decision) and executed in May 1641. Laud followed him to the scaffold in 1645. The Parliament proceeded to outlaw collection of unauthorized revenues, such as knights' fees and ship money. It also abolished Star Chamber and other royal prerogative courts, which had been used by the Stuarts to circumvent the common law courts. Charles also agreed not to abolish the Long Parliament without its consent and to authorize sessions at least once every three years. A large majority supported these reforms, but the Root and Branch Bill, designed to abolish episcopacy, badly divided the Commons. The outbreak of the Catholic rebellion in Ireland (October 1641), followed by the massacre of thousands of Protestants in Ulster, further divided England. Though determined to crush the Catholics, Parliament refused to allow King Charles to exercise his constitutional prerogatives as commander of the army for fear that he might use it to supress Protestant parliamentarians instead of Catholic rebels.

The Parliament passed and published the Grand Remonstrance (December 1641). It contained a summary of the grievances of the reign and called for royal ministers who held the confidence of Parliament. The king in turn attempted to seize five leaders in the House of Commons by force (January 1642). When this failed King Charles withdrew from the capital and began to raise an army. The Parliament made a final bid for reconciliation on its own terms by submitting the Nineteen Proposals, which would have greatly extended the scope of parliamentary power in matters of state and religion. The king refused to sanction this infringement and signaled the recourse to arms by raising the royal standard at Nottingham (August 1642).

Civil War. The first phase of the Civil War was fought from 1642 to 1646 and the second phase during 1648. The war ended with the total defeat of the royalist cause.

THE BELLIGERENTS. It is impossible to divide the belligerents along clear-cut economic, social, religious, or political lines. Families were torn apart, and many men were forced to choose between their religious beliefs and their political convictions. Generally speaking, the upper and middle classes fought the war. Most of the people remained bystanders unless they were drafted into one of the armies. The Cavaliers (royalists)tended to dominate northern and western England and drew support from the Anglican gentry and peasantry of those areas. The Roundheads (parliamentarians) were strongest in the more prosperous eastern and southeastern counties, and though they drew a large measure of support from the Puritan gentry and commercial interests of these areas, they also had the support of some of England's most powerful noble families.

CAMPAIGNS. The decisive element of seventeenth-century warfare was cavalry, and at the outset the royalists fielded superior mounted troops. However, Oliver Cromwell's Ironsides, drawn from the counties of the Eastern Association, soon proved a match for any mounted force. The first major engagement was fought to a draw at Edgehill (October 1642), and though the royalists held the advantage during the next two years, they were unable to deliver a decisive stroke. The Parliament attempted to enhance its position by signing the Solemn League and Covenant (September 1643), a pledge to establish a reformed (Presbyterian) state church in England in return for Scottish military support. The turning point of the war came at the battle of Marston Moor (July 1644) when Cromwell's Ironsides won control of northern England by defeating the royalist army of Charles's nephew, Prince Rupert. A year later with the New Model Army organized on the pattern of the Ironsides, Cromwell inflicted a decisive defeat on Charles at Naseby (June 1645).

PEACE NEGOTIATIONS. Though Charles had been defeated militarily, hope revived when his enemies began quarreling among themselves. The Presbyterian majority in Parliament wanted to enforce Puritan orthodoxy, while the Independents in the army wanted freedom of conscience. Charles played these factions against each other and was prepared to support any group willing to return him to power. Charles finally allied himself with the Scots, but his cause suffered a second reversal at the hands of Cromwell at Prestonpans (August 1648). When the Parliament insisted on renewing negotiations over the objections of the army, Cromwell ordered Colonel Pride to exclude Presbyterian members from parliamentary sessions (Pride's Purge, December 1649). The Rump Parliament, ignoring the objections of the House of Lords, ordered Charles to stand trial for treason. Charles was convicted and executed (January 1649).

The Commonwealth. The personality of Oliver Cromwell (1599–1658) dominated the interregnum (1649–1660). Having won immortality as the leader of the Ironsides, this austere puritan attempted to steer a course of political and religious moderation. Ironically his victory failed to produce the representative government he desired. Beset by royalist and puritan fanatics and ruling a populace still devoted to monarchy, Cromwell resorted to military repression.

IRISH REBELLION. The Irish Catholics rose in the name of the Stuart heir, whom they proclaimed Charles II. Cromwell's expeditionary force ruthlessly suppressed the rebellion in a campaign typified by the massacre of the inhabitants of Drogheda and Wexford (1649). The land settlement, which lasted almost intact until the twentieth century, left English Protestant landlords in control of three-quarters of the country.

SCOTTISH REBELLION. In 1650 Charles II personally led an attempt to regain the throne of his dead father. Cromwell defeated Charles's Scottish army at Worcester (September 1650) and Charles fled to the Continent.

AGGRESSIVE FOREIGN POLICY. Having secured the country from his domestic enemies, Cromwell reestablished England's maritime position. The Navigation Act (1651) outlawed the Dutch carrying trade to English ports and precipitated the First Dutch War (1652–1654). He then turned English naval power against Spain and in the war that followed (1656–1659) seized Jamaica.

THE PROTECTORATE. Despite his military success, Cromwell's regime became increasingly unpopular. The parliamentary system functioned poorly, and Cromwell assumed extended powers as lord protector under the Instrument of Government (1653), England's only experience with a written constitution. He ruled the country briefly with twelve military governors (the major generals), and by the time of his death in 1658, the regime had instituted a severely puritanical legal code.

The Restoration and the Glorious Revolution

The Restoration era (1660–1702) represents the second major phase of English constitutional development in the seventeenth century. Charles II temporarily reasserted monarchial authority, but James

II was driven from the throne. Under William and Mary, the Parliament consolidated and confirmed its position as the dominant force in English political life.

Restoration. The death of Oliver Cromwell (1658) left England without stable government. Cromwell's son Richard, the new lord protector, did not provide effective leadership; thus England hung between anarchy and military dictatorship. In February 1660 General Monck marched south from Scotland and assumed control of the government. Under his protection the freely elected Convention Parliament invited Charles II to reclaim his throne (May 1660).

Charles II (r. 1660–1685). At the outset Charles II was an extremely popular monarch. Englishmen had tired of the restrictive moral code enforced by the puritans. During the Restoration such public amusements as dancing, sports, and the theater came back into vogue. Charles used his popularity to reassert his royal authority. He abandoned Charles I's practice of direct confrontation with the Commons and reverted to the technique of parliamentary manipulation developed by the Tudor despots.

CLARENDON CODE. This series of laws (1661–1665), enacted under the lord chancellorship of Edward Hyde, earl of Clarendon, enforced uniformity within the Anglican church and banned the religious observance of nonconforming Protestants. The laws also had the effect of reestablishing the Anglican landed gentry as the dominant political class.

YEARS OF DISASTER (1665–1667). England had barely recovered from the ravages of civil war when she was struck by a series of calamities. During the latter half of 1665, London was swept by the plague, and in September 1666 a vast fire destroyed the heart of the city. To these natural disasters must be added the government's inept handling of the Second Dutch War (1665–1667), which, like the first, arose from commercial rivalry. A panic swept London in June 1667 when the Dutch fleet sailed into the Thames estuary and sank a large portion of the English fleet as it lay at anchor. Despite this victory, the Dutch were forced to cede New York, Delaware, and New Jersey under the terms of the Treaty of Breda (1667) that ended the war.

SECOND STUART DESPOTISM. Though determined to rule England without parliamentary interference, Charles was too intelligent to attempt a direct attack. He ruled through a group of advisers known as the Cabal (1670–1673) and controlled Parliament by bribes and personal influence. To limit his financial dependence on Parliament, he signed the secret Treaty of Dover (1670) with France. Under its terms Charles pledged to go to war with Holland, which he did in the Third Dutch War (1672–1674), and to proclaim publicly his adherence to Catholicism. In return Charles received an allowance of three hundred thousand pounds.

Test Act. Charles had failed to gauge the animosity toward Catholicism even among his own supporters. James, duke of York and the future James II, openly professed Catholicism. The Parliament responded by passing the Test Act (1673), which precluded from public office anyone who did not take communion in the Anglican church. Charles continued to maintain his personal beliefs but now renounced Catholic politics in return for political support from Anglican churchmen and the landed gentry. The factions that tended to support royal prerogatives at the expense of Parliament were called Tories and over the next two centuries slowly evolved into the Conservative party.

The Popish Plot. In opposition to the Tories were a collection of nonconforming Protestants, merchants, and some of the most powerful noble families. Known as Whigs, they fought the resurgence of royal power. They gained power briefly (1678–1681) after announcing the discovery of the Popish Plot, an alleged Catholic conspiracy to seize the government. While avowedly protecting Charles from assassination, they attacked his Tory supporters. The only positive accomplishment from this period of political infighting was the Habeas Corpus Act (1679), a bulwark of Anglo-Saxon jurisprudence that prevents arbitrary imprisonment.

Though on the defensive for several years, Charles did prevent the exclusion of his Catholic brother from succession to the throne. Fearing a renewal of the Civil War, public opinion rallied behind Charles, and in the last years of his life, he drove the Whig leaders into exile.

James II (r. 1685–1688). James failed to understand that Charles II, despite his personal Catholicism, had based his political program on the support of the Anglican Tories. James attempted to turn his private religion into public Catholicism, which few Englishmen would accept. His continual attempts to circumvent the anti-Catholic law by issuing wholesale pardons alienated Tories and Whigs alike. The birth of his son in 1688 promised to ensure yet another Catholic monarch oblivious to parliamentary rights. The aristocratic factions forgot their political differences and rose in revolt.

The Glorious Revolution. The English people regard the Glorious Revolution (1688) as one of the greatest and most significant events in their history. In the span of a few months and with little bloodshed, England's political leaders solved the major constitutional issues of the century and reached a settlement that forms the foundation of Britain's system of government.

OVERTHROW OF JAMES II. Had James's second wife remained childless, upon his death the crown would have passed to his Protestant
daughter Mary. Faced with the birth of a Catholic heir apparent, the
Whig and Tory leadership conspired to bring Mary to the throne.
Her husband, William of Orange, stadholder of Holland, wishing to
use England in his war with France, demanded equal status. Finally,
the conspirators offered William and Mary the throne as cosovereigns,
an arrangement unique in English history. William landed his army
in southwestern England in November 1688, but a civil war was
avoided when John Churchill, commander of the English forces, defected to William and James fled the country.

DECLARATION OF RIGHTS. After James's flight the Parliament declared the throne vacant. Before receiving their crowns, William and
Mary ratified the parliamentary Declaration of Rights, which denounced the crimes of the Stuart dynasty, including illegal taxation,
royal suspension of laws, and illegal imprisonment. It also confirmed
the prerogatives of Parliament. By accepting the declaration, William
and Mary publicly confirmed that their right to rule rested on parliamentary sovereignty rather than divine commission.

William and Mary (1689–1702). The concurrent reigns of King
William III (1689–1702) and Queen Mary (1689–1694) mark a significant turning point in English constitutional history. The Revolution
Settlement put into legislative form the victory of the rule of law
over the forces of monarchial absolutism. As the century-long domestic
struggle ended, the stage was set for an international conflict that
would pit England and France in a struggle for world empire throughout the eighteenth century.

THE REVOLUTION SETTLEMENT. The Revolution Settlement was a
series of parliamentary acts that together form the basis of English
constitutional government.

The Bill of Rights (1689) was the parliamentary enactment of the
Declaration of Rights. It included provisions for parliamentary prerogatives and civil rights, excluded Catholics from the throne, and
stipulated the succession to the crown after the deaths of William
and Mary. The Bill of Rights clearly confirmed the dominance of
Parliament over royalty.

The Mutiny Act (1689) permitted the raising of an army and the
trial of soldiers by courts martial for a period first of six months and
later of one year. This ensured the annual meeting of Parliament, for
without its renewal the government could not maintain discipline in
the armed forces.

The Triennial Act (1694) required the election of Parliament at least every three years. Since its passage Parliament has been elected at fairly regular intervals.

The Act of Settlement (1701) reconfirmed the right of Parliament to select the monarch. Neither William nor his sister-in-law Anne, who succeeded him, had any surviving children. To preclude the return of James, "the Old Pretender" (the Catholic son of James II), the Parliament bestowed the crown on Anne's nearest Protestant relative, Sophia of Hanover, the mother of the future King George I. In addition the act made royal ministers responsible for the king's acts and freed judges from the threat of arbitrary dismissal.

Succession to English Throne

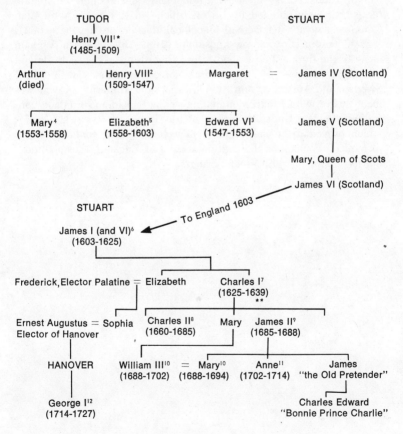

*Superscripts indicate order of succession.
**Commonwealth intervened between reigns of Charles I and Charles II.

IRISH REBELLION. William and Mary had hardly settled onto their thrones when their right to rule was challenged by James II, who landed in Ireland in March 1689, acclaimed by the Catholic populace. He was defeated at the battle of the Boyne (July 1690) and fled to France. Although William promised lenient terms to James's Catholic supporters, the Protestant-controlled Irish Parliament enacted a series of severely anti-Catholic laws that remained in force for over a century.

SCOTTISH UPRISING. In May 1689 the Highland clans loyal to James rose in rebellion. Led by Claverhouse, Viscount Dundee, they defeated William's army at Killiecrankie (July). At the moment of victory, "Bonnie Dundee" was mortally wounded, and the uprising died for lack of leadership. As in the Irish Rebellion, William offered moderate terms that were nullified by his own men—in this instance by Clan Campbell's savage massacre of MacDonald leaders at Glencoe (1692).

WAR OF THE LEAGUE OF AUGSBURG (1689–1697). When William came to the throne, he planned to use English naval power to defend his native Holland. He immediately joined in alliance with Spain, Sweden, and Austria to stop French expansion. Militarily the war was inconclusive, with France dominating the battlefield and England controlling the sea. Under the terms of the Treaty of Ryswick (1697), which proved to be only a truce in a century-long conflict, France recognized William as the legitimate ruler of England, thus abandoning its support of the Catholic Stuarts.

10

Absolute Monarchy in France and the Thirty Years' War

Four decades of civil war and maladministration in France ended with the accession of Henry IV (1589). The Bourbon kings, aided by astute advisers, reversed the disastrous disintegration of the kingdom. The fruits of this labor were seen during the reign of Louis XIV when the Grand Monarchy stood without peer in Europe.

While this consolidation was taking place in France, the Holy Roman Empire became the scene of the brutal Thirty Years' War (1618–1648). The conflict began as a limited religious and dynastic struggle and ended as a general European war. French intervention in the German conflict signaled its reappearance as an international power, and its subsequent drive for European hegemony precipitated a series of conflicts in the last decades of the century.

France 1589–1661

The French potential for greatness was realized during the seventeenth century. The monarchy consolidated its power until the king towered above the realm as an absolute monarch. At the same time, France successfully reasserted itself as a dominant international power. The credit for this revitalization must go in large measure to three ministers whose names have became inseparable with the kings they so ably served: Henry IV and Sully, Louis XIII and Richelieu, and Louis XIV and Mazarin.

Henry IV (r. 1589–1610) and Sully. Henry IV demonstrated his wisdom in the compromise solution to the religious conflict. By maintaining the Catholic monarchy and instituting toleration for the Huguenots, he resolved the most divisive issue in France. His political wisdom extended to his choice of Maximilien de Béthune, duc de Sully, as his chief administrator. Sully was not able to carry out a thorough restructuring of the administrative apparatus, but he did push through significant reforms.

Sully's main task was to increase royal revenues. Since the clergy and the nobility were exempt from taxation, the burden fell upon the common people. Taxes were collected under a corrupt and inefficient system known as *tax farming*. The *farmer* was a private individual who collected taxes under contract. The taxpayer ended by paying more than was due and the government by receiving less. It is estimated that 70 percent of the taxes went to dishonest middlemen. Sully did not change the system, but he was able to end the wholesale corruption and thereby supply the crown with adequate resources. He also promoted agricultural redevelopment, land reclamation, and the building of roads and bridges. It was at the insistence of Henry IV himself that the silk industry was introduced into France. More than anything else, Henry IV gave France a decade of peace with which to heal its wounds. Henry was assassinated (1610) while preparing to depart for war in Germany.

Regency of Marie de Médicis (1610–1624). The government of France passed into the hands of Henry's widow, Marie de Médicis, who served as regent for the nine-year-old Louis XIII. The extravagance, incompetence, corruption, and infighting that Henry and Sully had sought to eliminate all returned. The country seemed headed for a renewal of the long and bitter civil war as the Catholic nobility and the Huguenots squared off. From the midst of this turmoil emerged Armand Jean Du Plessis, Cardinal Richelieu.

Louis XIII (r. 1610–1643) and Richelieu. Although Louis XIII's reign began in 1610, his effective control of the government dates only from 1624, when he placed power in the hands of Richelieu. Louis had two qualities essential for a successful reign. He had the ability to pick a brilliant adviser and the resolve to support him. Richelieu virtually ruled the country from 1624 until 1642. During that period he had two basic goals: the supremacy of the king in France and the supremacy of France in Europe.

DOMESTIC POLICY. Richelieu faced three major obstacles that blocked the path to royal absolutism: (1) the military power of the Huguenots, (2) the political ambitions of both the princes of the blood (members of the royal family) and the nobility, and (3) the inefficient administrative system, which hampered the execution of royal desires.

Revolt of the Huguenots. Richelieu goaded the Huguenots into open revolt by making it clear that he would no longer tolerate their status of a "state within a state." The fighting that broke out in 1625 focused on the siege of La Rochelle, the Huguenots' seaport stronghold on the Bay of Biscay. The Protestants resisted for fourteen months (1627–1628) but capitulated after the failure of two English relief expeditions. The Peace of Alais (1629) stripped the Huguenots of their rights to bear arms and maintain fortifications but confirmed their religious rights. Richelieu thus enhanced the power of the crown while guaranteeing the loyalty of its Protestant subjects.

Shackling the Nobility. Richelieu faced a constant threat from the great nobles who fought to maintain their local and political influence. His chief adversaries in this contest were the queen mother, Marie de Médicis, and the king's brother, Gaston d'Orléans.

The cardinal was never able to eliminate their threat completely, but he successfully thwarted every conspiracy and armed revolt that challenged his rule. He began his campaign by ordering the destruction of every fortification not required for the defense of France. He then suppressed a revolt led by Orléans (1626), and an attempt by Marie de Médicis to have him removed from office (1630) failed due to the king's loyal support. The last serious insurrection (1632), again led by Orléans, also failed. As a result of this uprising, the duke of Montmorency, one of the greatest names in France and the virtual sovereign of Languedoc, was executed for treason. The nobility, though still capable of armed resistance, came to realize that Richelieu would be without mercy in his quest to extend the power of the king.

Administrative Reforms. Although the king had power to make law by fiat, there were institutions and customs that hampered the exercise of the royal will. Unlike the English Parliament, the Estates General failed to evolve into a legislative counterweight to the monarch. Called and dismissed in 1614, the representatives of the three estates did not gather again until 1789. The *parlements* (superior courts), particularly the great Parlement of Paris, posed a threat to the crown. The justices held that no decree was legally binding until registered by the court. This gave them the power to delay governmental action and in the case of a weak king actually to veto it.

The greatest embarrassment to the king was his inability to control his own civil servants. During the Middle Ages, the crown had begun the practice of selling public offices for cash. The purchaser thus obtained a property right to his post and could sell it or deed it to his heir. It became virtually impossible to impose an unpopular program upon such administrators. To relieve this problem, Richelieu created a new category of royal officials known as *intendants*, who slowly supplanted the governors as the chief royal officials in the provinces. They could be counted on to support the government, for they held their posts at the pleasure of the king and were thoroughly hated by the provincial nobility. In this manner Richelieu created an instrument for the effective implementation of the king's power.

FOREIGN POLICY. The goal of Richelieu's foreign policy was to place France in the forefront of European affairs. To accomplish this he did everything in his power to weaken the Austrian Hapsburgs in the persons of Emperor Ferdinand II and his Spanish cousin Philip IV. In the course of the Thirty Years' War (see p. 115), Richelieu supported Gustavus Adolphus, king of Sweden, with cash subsidies against the Hapsburgs and their allies. When Gustavus was killed and the Protestant cause seemed doomed, Richelieu intervened with arms to prevent a Hapsburg victory. Though Richelieu died in 1642 before a peace settlement was reached, he was certainly the architect of the French victory that was formalized at the Peace of Westphalia (1648).

Louis XIV (r. 1643–1715) and Mazarin. Mazarin had been groomed to succeed Richelieu, and he took the reins of government when his mentor died in 1642. Only months later Louis XIII was succeeded by his five-year-old son Louis XIV. The queen mother, Anne of Austria, served as regent and retained Mazarin in office. During his ministry, which lasted until his death in 1661, he ruled France in the same manner as Richelieu. He finally crushed the armed resistance of the nobility and brought the war with Spain to a successful conclusion in this period.

THE FRONDE. The simmering hostility to the growing power of the monarchy burst open in three insurrections (1648–1653), known collectively as the *Fronde*. The rebels might have posed a real threat to absolutism, but they were not united in their goals. The *parlementaries* represented the interests of the adminstrative nobility (*noblesse de la robe*) and the wealthy businessmen (*grandes bourgeoise*). They hoped to force the king to accept a rule of law. The center of their resistance was the *Parlement* (court) of Paris. The court nobility (*noblesse de l'épée*) wished to reassert its prerogatives as a political and economic oligarchy. The two factions therefore posed as great a threat to each other as they did to the crown. Mazarin was able to defeat the rebels piecemeal. The failure of the Fronde ended all hopes of checking the expanding power of the crown.

WAR WITH SPAIN. The policy of Richelieu and Mazarin to expand French influence in the Netherlands, Italy, and the Germanies led to a renewal of the hostilities with Spain that had typified the sixteenth century. This conflict was a phase of the Thirty Years' War. Spain was no longer a match for France in a war of attrition. The Treaty of Pyrenees (1659) confirmed the decline of Spain and the ascendancy of France in Europe. Under its terms France obtained territory on all its frontiers, and Louis XIV married Marie Thérèse, the infanta of Spain.

The Thirty Years' War

The Thirty Years' War (1618–1648) stands as a stark example of the price civilians pay for the irresponsibility of sovereigns. Although contemporary accounts exaggerated the catastrophic decline in population, there are few epochs in European history in which a densely populated region was subjected to such sustained devastation and atrocity. Rival armies, which seldom met in combat, crisscrossed the Germanies. They looted and burned as they went, not bothering to distinguish between friend and foe among the raped, slaughtered, and disinherited victims.

Background of the Conflict. Two basic factors lay at the root of the thirty-year bloodbath. The first was a deep religious division within the empire. Fanatics on both sides whipped their supporters into a spiritual frenzy. This ideological aspect remained a primary consideration among the common people throughout the conflict, and it extended to some princes, including Emperor Ferdinand II and King Gustavus Adolphus.

The second level of the war was a struggle for dynastic aggrandizement among all the belligerents. In its simplest form, this pitted the princes of Germany, whether Protestant or Catholic, against the emperor. One reason for the continuation of the conflict was the fact that the more victories the Hapsburgs won for Catholicism, thus increasing the power of their own dynasty, the more their erstwhile Catholic allies sided with the Protestants to check imperial power.

Bohemian Phase (1618–1623). Bohemia was an elective monarchy within the Holy Roman Empire. Its long tradition of religious freedom and local autonomy had been confirmed by Matthias, Holy Roman emperor and king of Bohemia, in the Letter of Majesty (1609). In 1617 the Protestant majority in the Bohemian estates elected Ferdinand of Styria (Hapsburg) to succeed to the crown upon the death of the childless Matthias. They soon regretted the choice. Ferdinand was determined to impose his sovereign will on the kingdom and to eradicate Protestantism. Negotiation failed to resolve the differences, and the Bohemian estates deposed Ferdinand (August 1618) and elected Frederick, the Lutheran elector palatine, in his place.

The deposed king was elected Ferdinand II, Holy Roman emperor (August 1619) and moved to regain his Bohemian realm. Frederick was unprepared for the onslaught and fled from the kingdom after the defeat of his forces at the battle of White Mountain (8 November 1620). Bohemia was absorbed into the Hapsburg Empire and did not regain its independence until 1918. The emperor also deprived

Frederick of his electoral estates, which he bestowed upon Maximilian of Bavaria. By this act he guaranteed the continuation of the war because many Protestant princes who had not supported Frederick in his bid for the Bohemian crown refused to accept the emperor's arbitrary distribution of German territory.

Danish Phase (1623–1629). The Protestants did not receive the support they expected from James I of England, Frederick's Protestant father-in-law. However, Denmark's Christian IV (r. 1588–1648) saw the possibility of enlarging his Baltic kingdom and entered the war. By 1626 the emperor had at his disposal two excellent armies, an imperial force led by Tilly and a mercenary army led by the soldier of fortune Albrecht von Wallenstein. They inflicted a series of defeats upon the Protestants, the most significant of which occurred at Dessau (April 1626) and Lutter am Barenberge (August 1626). Wallenstein drove into northern Germany, and Christian agreed to withdraw from German affairs under terms of the Peace of Lübeck (May 1629).

At this juncture Ferdinand again misplayed his hand. He issued the Edict of Restitution (March 1629), which required the return of all church lands secularized since 1552 and outlawed all Protestants, except Lutherans, within the empire. The emperor's determination to return to the letter of the Peace of Augsburg galvanized Protestant armed resistance as nothing else had. Though a renewal of hostilities was obviously imminent, Frederick no longer trusted the ambitious Wallenstein and dismissed him from imperial service.

Swedish Phase (1630–1635). The dominant figure in the third phase of the war was the king of Sweden, Gustavus II ("Gustavus Adolphus") (r. 1611–1632), one of the great generals of the seventeenth century. During the first years of his reign, he fought for control of the Baltic with Denmark (1611–1613), Russia (1611–1617), and Poland (1617–1618, 1621–1629). He also carried out significant governmental, economic, and military reforms with the aid of Axel Oxenstierna, his able chancellor.

The Lion of the North, as Gustavus Adolphus was known, intervened in the Thirty Years' War in 1630 when the Protestant cause seemed doomed. He landed in Germany with a thirst for glory, a deep personal commitment to the Lutheran cause, and a small army that would revolutionize European warfare. Conventional tactics of the day called for overwhelming the enemy with a massed formation of lumbering pikemen. For these he substituted small mobile units of musketeers in support of pikemen and cavalry. In addition he inaugurated the use of light maneuverable field artillery. The force was composed of Swedes, Germans, and Scots; after 1631 it was subsidized by French gold.

Though his intervention did not come soon enough to prevent the massacre of the twenty thousand troops and noncombatants in the Protestant stronghold at Magdeburg (May 1631), he soon won control of northern Germany. He then marched into Saxony, where he destroyed Tilly's army at Breitenfeld (17 September 1631), conquered the Rhineland, and then threatened Vienna itself (winter 1631–1632). The desperate emperor recalled Wallenstein. He sparred with Gustavus Adolphus until November 1632, when they finally met on the field at Lützen. The Swedes were victorious, but Gustavus Adolphus perished.

Wallenstein survived his adversary little more than a year. Emperor Ferdinand, fearful of political intriguers, had his ablest commander assassinated (February 1634). Although the Catholic forces were able to inflict a stunning defeat on the Swedes at Nördlingen (September 1634), neither side could hope to win a decisive victory in the stalemated conflict. Ferdinand finally agreed, under terms of the Peace of Prague (1635), to abrogate the Edict of Restitution. This provided a brief respite by conciliating the Lutheran princes and helping to restore the emperor's prestige in Germany.

French Phase (1635–1648). Although the exhausted Germans were ready for peace, Richelieu was not. He was determined to end the threat of Hapsburg encirclement permanently. With no Protestant allies left to carry the fight, France declared war on both Spain and Austria (1635). The German states were once more drawn into the bloodletting. In the war of maneuver that followed, the short-run advantage lay with the more experienced Spaniards. However, the weight of French resources slowly began to tell. The one significant battle of this period was fought at Rocroi (1643), near the Dutch frontier. The French, led by the duc d'Enghien (later known as the Great Condé), completely overwhelmed the Spanish force and thus ended the Spanish dominance of the European battlefield.

Peace of Westphalia. Animosities engendered by the long war ran deep, and the problems created by it were complex. Negotiations that culminated in a series of treaties known collectively as the Peace of Westphalia were begun informally in 1641 and ratified in 1648.

TERRITORIAL PROVISIONS. Among the most significant territorial provisions were the following: (1) France received confirmation of her rights to Verdun, Toul, and Metz and ambiguous rights in Alsace that were a source of later conflict. (2) Sweden emerged with a firm hold on the Baltic. Her acquisition of West Pomerania, Bremen,

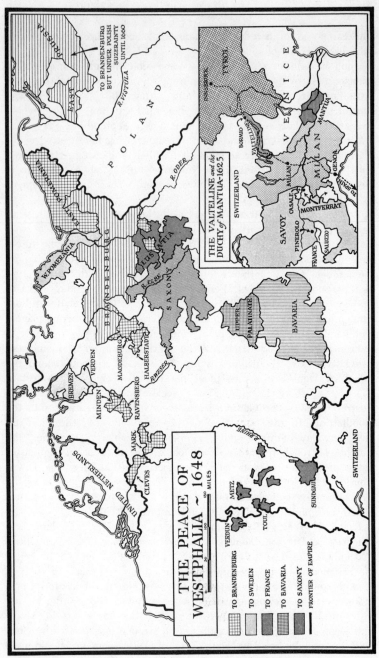

THE PEACE OF WESTPHALIA ~ 1648

MILES
50   100   150

TO BRANDENBURG
TO SWEDEN
TO FRANCE
TO BAVARIA
TO SAXONY
FRONTIER OF EMPIRE

THE VALTELLINE and the DUCHY of MANTUA—1625

PRUSSIA

EAST

TO BRANDENBURG BUT UNDER POLISH SUZERAINTY UNTIL 1660

R. VISTULA

POLAND

R. ODER

HINTERPOMMERN

W. POMERANIA

BRANDENBURG

LUSATIA

R. ELBE

SAXONY

UPPER PALATINATE

BAVARIA

VERDEN

MAGDEBURG

HALBERSTADT

R. WESER

BREMEN

MINDEN

RAVENSBERG

MARK

CLEVES

NETHERLANDS

UNITED

R. RHINE

METZ

VERDUN

TOUL.

SUNDGAU

SWITZERLAND

INNSBRUCK

TYROL

VENICE

BORMIO

VALTELLINE

MANTUA

MILAN

SWITZERLAND

SAVOY

CASALE

MILAN

MONTFERRAT

GENOA

TO SPAIN

PINEROLO

SALUZZO

FRANCE

and Verden gave her control of the Weser, Elbe, and Oder estuaries. (3) Brandenburg obtained western Pomerania and rights to East Prussia (full sovereignty in 1660). In the west Brandenburg obtained Magdeburg, Halberstadt, Minden, Ravenburg, and confirmation of her rights to Cleves and Mark. Although in some cases the acquisitions were small, they formed a series of bridgeheads from the Rhine to the Vistula and set the stage for later expansion. (4) Saxony received Lusatia. (5) Bavaria acquired the Upper Palatinate.

CONSTITUTIONAL PROVISIONS. The structure of the empire was also drastically changed by the settlement. The United Netherlands and Switzerland were both released from the empire and recognized as sovereign states. The sovereignty of the states remaining within the empire was also recognized. The result of the proviso was to guarantee the continued division of the Germanies into three hundred independent states, the most important of which were Brandenburg, Saxony, Bavaria, and the Hapsburg Empire.

RELIGIOUS PROVISIONS. The guarantees that had been afforded Lutherans under the Peace of Augsburg (1555) were extended to include Calvinists. The princes' rights to regulate public worship were confirmed, but freedom of conscience was also recognized. It is significant that papal denunciations of the settlement were completely ignored by European rulers.

France Under Louis XIV

Known to his contemporaries as the Sun King and the Great Monarch, Louis XIV set the style for monarchial government in the latter half of the seventeenth century. His reign of seventy-two years (1643–1715) was the longest in European history, and during his personal rule of fifty-four years, he fashioned an absolutist government worthy of Thomas Hobbes's *Leviathan*. However, despite the centralizing influence of Louis's reign, France remained a nation of paradox. In contrast to the splendor of Versailles, the peasantry struggled to maintain itself under the heavy burdens of taxation, disease, and recurrent famine. The inequitable and inefficient fiscal structure and overlapping provincial authorities were in marked contrast to the organized royal bureaucracy in the capital.

French Society at Midcentury. France was the largest and most populous state in western Europe. The population approached twenty million, and the vast majority was engaged in agriculture. Despite the rural dominance, Paris, with five hundred thousand inhabitants, ranked second to London among the cities of Europe. Socially France was divided into three broad groups called *estates*. This division of clergy, nobility, and commons conferred legal status upon each order, but these orders did not constitute economic classes. Although the separation inhibited social mobility, it did not preclude it.

CLERGY (FIRST ESTATE). The clergy held its privileged position because of its holy function. Numbering about one hundred and twenty-five thousand, its membership was drawn from all levels of society. The cardinals, bishops, and abbots were often the younger sons of noblemen who aspired to their offices for financial gain and paid little attention to their religious duties. The village priests (curés), on the other hand, were usually drawn from the lower ranks of society and often shared the poverty of their parishioners. They generally paid serious attention to their pastoral duties. Because of their exalted role, neither the clergy nor Church property was taxed, although a substantial free gift to the crown was made every five years.

NOBILITY (SECOND ESTATE). The nobility included approximately two hundred and fifty thousand members whose prestige, power, and wealth varied enormously. The nobility of the sword were members of the old landed aristocracy who traced their lineage into France's distant past. The greatest of these held large estates from which they received large incomes. Those holding the highest titles were required to live at court in order to enhance the splendor of the monarchy and to destroy their own political independence. Most of the landed nobility lived a much less ostentatious life on their provincial estates. They often sustained themselves on meager rents and dues and harbored a deep resentment toward the court nobility. The nobility of the robe were drawn from the wealthy bourgeoisie and attained their status by purchasing administrative offices that carried with them titles of nobility. This system of ennoblement provided upward social mobility for wealthy commoners and supplied the crown with revenue and able administrators. These men were held in contempt by the landed nobility, but after several generations, a family became fully integrated into their new social station.

Though secure in their social status, the nobility had little political power during the reign of Louis XIV. Furthermore, the aristocracy found it difficult to enhance their financial position. A nobleman who engaged in business activity could be punished with the loss of his noble status (dérogeance).

COMMONS (THIRD ESTATE). The greatest political, social, and economic divisions separated the members of the vast third estate. The wealthiest among them controlled French commercial life and were called into the highest councils of the government, from which the nobility were excluded. Their ambition was to obtain the social privileges of the Second Estate to complement their political power.

The less wealthy bourgeoisie formed the backbone of commerce, industry, and the professions.

At the bottom of the social and economic ladder were the great masses of the populace (*le menu peuple*) who comprised the French peasantry plus some urban artisans and common laborers. Only a small portion continued to live in personal servitude, but as a class they bore the greatest burdens of the society. Funds to build the palace at Versailles and to finance Louis's grandiose foreign policy were extracted through a myriad of direct and indirect taxes levied on this poorest of classes. To this affliction must be added recurrent famine, particularly in the 1660s and 1690s. Possibly many peasants concealed their relative prosperity to avoid the tax collector, but the recurrence of savage peasant revolts (*jacqueries*), the increase in sharecropping, and the abandonment of farms point to a desperate struggle for subsistence among a large portion of the population.

The Personal Rule of Louis XIV. Louis XIV was born in 1638 and became king at the age of five. His youth was spent under the regency of his mother, Anne of Austria, and the government remained in the able hands of Cardinal Mazarin. When Mazarin died in 1661, Louis took the government into his own hands. Although he had several able ministers, they never exercised the power of Richelieu and Mazarin. The king left no doubt that he reigned and ruled.

COURT. Louis XIV was the most powerful monarch in Europe, and he played the part. The life at court, first at the Louvre and after 1682 in the grandiose château of Versailles, consisted of an elaborate ritual from morning until night, the whole procedure being designed to enhance the glory of the Sun King. Although portraits of Louis XIV make him appear ridiculous to modern eyes, he was a well-coordinated athlete with a gargantuan zest for life. Though courteous in trivial matters, he could be ruthless without compunction. An endless round of hunts, gambling, and parties was maintained to relieve the boredom of the thousands of unemployed nobility whom the king required to live at Versailles.

COLBERT AND THE CIVIL ADMINISTRATION. Jean Baptiste Colbert served as Louis's chief minister for fiscal and civil affairs from 1661 to 1683. Colbert never had the liberty of action granted to Richelieu or Mazarin, but his achievements were impressive. His first task was to reorder the decrepit tax structure. Although he was able to increase receipts by tightening collections and accounting, the inherent weaknesses of a system that exempted the rich and taxed the poor utimately defeated all his efforts to maintain revenues at a level equal to Louis's enormous expenditures.

Colbert also took an interest in fostering French commerce and industry. He was one of the chief exponents of mercantilism. The major tenets of this theory were that national powers rested on economic power and that the economic gain of one country must ultimately result from the economic loss of another. Colbert worked to increase exports and reduce imports, thereby fostering economic self-sufficiency and building gold reserves from a favorable balance of trade. He promoted domestic trade by eliminating some internal tariffs and by financing road and canal construction. To foster exports and strengthen industry, he employed a number of techniques, including grants of monopoly, tax exemptions, and outright subsidies. Colbert also attempted to increase financial benefits derived from the overseas empire by chartering merchant companies, but they proved unsuccessful. Although hampered by special interests and traditional attitudes, Colbert made significant contributions to the economic development of France.

LOUVOIS AND THE FRENCH ARMY. The transformation of the French army from an ill-equipped, poorly trained, and insubordinate rabble into a superb fighting force of two hundred thousand men was the lifework of Louvois, who succeeded his father as minister of war in 1666 and held the post until 1691. Louvois devoted his entire career to fashioning a military instrument responsive to the royal will, able to fight foreign wars and maintain domestic order. He reformed the officer corps by eliminating graft and providing for the advancement of competent officers from every social class. New equipment, including the bayonet and the flintlock, was introduced, and training manuals came into use. Martinet and Fourilles, the inspectors of infantry and cavalry, ensured that Louvois's orders were carried out. Perhaps his greatest accomplishment was the creation of the most efficient military supply system of its day. Turenne and Prince Condé, two of the most brilliant commanders of the age, led the revitalized army during the first of Louis's many wars. After 1678 the military engineer Vauban became the king's chief military adviser. Vauban's expertise in siege warfare led to the belief that any position he held was safe and any fortress he attacked was doomed.

REVOCATION OF THE EDICT OF NANTES (1685). Louis XIV's decision to revoke the special dispensation granted to the Huguenots by Henry IV (1598) clearly illustrates both his desire to bring religious affairs under his control and the regime's financial embarrassment. The Assembly of the Clergy met every five years to grant the crown a financial subsidy. In the 1650s the Convocation began demanding that greater restrictions be placed upon the Protestants in return for this "free gift." The king, desperate for funds and chided by some for permitting Protestantism within his realm, slowly gave in to this pressure. In 1685 he formally revoked the Edict of Nantes, thus totally abrogating the rights of religious dissenters. This decision not only engendered hostility among the Protestant states of Europe but also deprived France of several hundred thousand of its most industrious citizens who migrated to England, Holland, and the German states. France paid a high price for absolutism.

The Wars of Louis XIV

Louis XIV was at war for thirty of his fifty-five years of personal rule. On the surface the cause of these conflicts was French legal claim to territories along her serpentine frontier. In reality the fundamental reason for interminable warfare was Louis XIV's egotistical drive for glory and territorial aggrandizement. In response he met a succession of coalitions determined to maintain a balance of power and thwart French aggression. The overseas phase of these conflicts, which developed after 1689, is discussed on page 147.

War of Devolution. Louis XIV's first attempt to gain territory came with his claims to the Spanish Netherlands in the name of his Spanish wife Marie Thérèse. He maintained that under Brabant law the territory "devolved" upon the eldest female of a first marriage (Marie Thérèse) before sons of a second marriage (Charles II of Spain). Spain rejected the claims, and in 1667 France invaded both the Spanish Netherlands and the Franche-Comté.

The English and Dutch, who had been at war (1665–1667), made peace and formed an alliance to meet the threat and were soon joined by Sweden. Faced with this triple alliance, Louis negotiated the Treaty of Aix-la-Chapelle (1668). Under its terms France restored the Franche-Comté to Spain but retained twelve fortresses within the Spanish Netherlands. All the belligerents realized that the settlement was a mere truce.

Dutch War. The War of Devolution had blunted Louis's territorial aims and bruised his ego. From 1668 to 1672, he plotted the destruction of Holland. He first bribed England's Charles II in the secret Treaty of Dover (1670); the same tactic succeeded with Sweden. After his preparation he fell upon the Dutch and routed the armies of Holland. In panic the Dutch breached their dikes to block the route to Amsterdam. They also overthrew the republican government, which the mob blamed for the disaster, and reinstated the house of Orange in the person of William III (1672–1702). Louis's reconquest of the Franche-Comté and invasion of the Palatinate demonstrated his insatiable greed and triggered the creation of a new anti-French coalition. Ranged against him were Holland, Denmark,

Brandenburg, Austria, and Spain. Stalemated again, he signed the Treaty of Nijmegen (1679). Fortresses along the frontiers again changed hands. France retained the Franche-Comté, but the Spanish Netherlands still eluded Louis. What he had not been able to gain by war he now sought to obtain through legal chicanery. His chambers of reunion sat in judgment on French claims to territory on the eastern frontier, and as regularly as they decided in his favor, each small enclave was occupied by French troops.

War of the League of Augsburg. Louis's claims to the Palatinate after the death of the elector (1685) and his interference with the succession of the archbishopric of Cologne signaled his determination to renew the conflict. The states of the Holy Roman Empire responded with the formation of the League of Augsburg (1686), comprising the emperor, the Palatinate, Bavaria, Saxony, Sweden, Spain, and Savoy (1687). In addition Louis's harsh treatment of the Huguenots, culminating in the revocation of the Edict of Nantes (1685) angered the Protestant powers. In 1688 England's Glorious Revolution (see p. 107) placed William III, prince of Orange and stadholder of Holland, on the English throne. William brought both England and Holland into the league. The war began in 1689 and raged for eight years. The armies of France, led by Marshal Luxembourg, inflicted defeat after defeat on the allies, but none were decisive. France could not hope to bring so many opponents to bay, although Savoy withdrew from the alliance in 1696. A compromise was finally reached with the Treaty of Ryswick (1697). Under its most important terms, (1) France gained Alsace and Strasbourg but renounced the territories taken by the reunions from 1680 to 1683 and disavowed claims within the Holy Roman Empire; (2) Holland regained all lost territory and obtained the right to garrison a series of "barrier forts" inside the Spanish Netherlands as a guarantee against a renewal of French aggression; (3) Louis renounced support of James II and recognized William III as the rightful king of England.

War of the Spanish Succession. The realization that the imbecilic and sickly Charles II of Spain would die without an heir led to Louis XIV's last and most protracted war (1701–1714).

SPANISH SUCCESSION. The complexity of the Spanish succession is seen in the following genealogical chart.
Louis XIV claimed the Spanish throne for his grandson by right of descent through both Anne and Marie Thérèse, the eldest children of Philip III and Philip IV. However, at the time of their marriages, both of these women had renounced their rights. Leopold I of Austria could make the same claims for both his son and grandson, who were descendants of younger daughters of the same two Spanish kings.

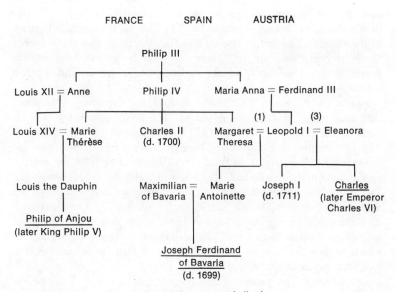

FRANCE   SPAIN   AUSTRIA

Philip III

Louis XII = Anne   Philip IV   Maria Anna = Ferdinand III

(1)   (3)

Louis XIV = Marie   Charles II   Margaret = Leopold I = Eleanora
Thérèse   (d. 1700)   Theresa

Louis the Dauphin   Maximilian = Marie   Joseph I   Charles
of Bavaria   Antoinette   (d. 1711)   (later Emperor
Charles VI)

Philip of Anjou
(later King Philip V)

Joseph Ferdinand
of Bavaria
(d. 1699)

Note: The three claimants to the Spanish throne are underlined.

Neither of these daughters had given up her rights. The other powers of Europe generally desired a partition of the Spanish inheritance or a settlement that would place the territories in the hands of a prince unlikely to succeed to the throne of either France or Austria. For this reason France's old enemies supported the claims of Archduke Charles after the death of the Bavarian prince (1699) and Charles II (1700). Knowing full well that his action would begin a new round of war, in 1701 Louis broke off the long negotiations and recognized his grandson as Philip V, heir to all the Spanish lands. He was supported by the Spanish nobility, who wanted to keep the realm intact. The Grand Alliance, which included England, Holland, Prussia, Austria, and Savoy, rallied to Archduke Charles.

COURSE OF THE WAR (1702–1713). Age and constant warfare had sapped Louis's energy and resources. The marshals who had led France to victory in his youth were dead. The greatest generals of the war were among his enemies. John Churchill, duke of Marlborough, and Eugene of Savoy inflicted a series of defeats on France at Blenheim (1704), Ramillies (1706), Oudenarde (1708), and Malplaquet (1709). Despite these victories, the allies were not able to turn the war to their political advantage. English casualties at Malplaquet were used as an excuse by Marlborough's political enemies in the new English government to secure his dismissal (1709). The untimely death of Emperor Joseph I (1711) brought Archduke Charles to the throne as Emperor Charles VI. The possibility that the emperor would reconstitute Hapsburg hegemony over both Spain and Austria posed as great a threat to the balance of power as did French aspirations.

PEACE OF UTRECHT. The war ended in a compromise settlement that maintained a balance of power. The most significant stipulations of the treaties of Utrecht (1713) and Rastatt (1714) included: (1) recognition of Philip V as king of Spain, contingent upon his renunciation of all rights to the French throne as well as the cession to England of Gibraltar and Minorca and rights to sell slaves within the Spanish Empire (the *asiento*); (2) Austrian acquisition of the Spanish Netherlands, Milan, Naples, and Sardinia; (3) French cession of Newfoundland, Nova Scotia, and Hudson Bay territory to England as well as recognition of the English house of Hanover; (4) recognition of Brandenburg as a kingdom; (5) recognition of Savoy as a kingdom and its acquisition of Sardinia.

CONCLUSION. The peace settlement put a definitive end to the expansionism of Louis XIV. His reign had been an age of power and glory and had witnessed a flowering of French literature (see p. 162). At the same time, he left the government in bankruptcy, and news of his death (1715) brought cheers and dancing in the streets throughout France.

11

The Development
of Absolutism
in Eastern Europe

A clearly defined and relatively stable state system existed in western Europe by 1648. In contrast, the states of central and eastern Europe had not formed a coherent or stable pattern. Significant territorial changes, including the creation and destruction of whole states, have continued into the twentieth century. In the middle of the seventeenth century, there were six states whose actions shaped the destiny of this area. They were Brandenburg-Prussia, Sweden, Poland, Russia, the Austrian Empire, and the Ottoman Empire. The monarchs of Brandenburg-Prussia, Austria, and Russia consolidated their positions against domestic opponents and mobilized sufficient resources to obtain positions as international powers. On the other hand, Sweden, Poland, and the Ottoman Empire receded into the background.

The Vanquished

The failure of Sweden, Poland, and the Ottoman Empire to retain their status as great powers arose from a variety of causes unique to each state. Except for the brief sketches presented below, these states will be discussed within the context of the emergence of the more powerful eastern European monarchies.

Sweden. The Vasa dynasty produced several outstanding monarchs equally at home in the councils of government and on the battlefield. From the reign of Gustavus I (1523–1560) to the reign of Charles XII (1697–1718), the kings of Sweden forged a well-administered and wealthy Baltic empire whose potential for future greatness certainly equaled Brandenburg-Prussia's in 1700. The failure to consolidate this position and Sweden's ultimate ruin resulted from the grandiose foreign policy pursued by Charles XII. Though a brilliant general, Charles lacked political wisdom. His defeat in the Great

Northern War (1700–1721) was the first in a series of disasters that stripped Sweden of her empire and reduced her to second-rate status.

Poland. The source of Polish weakness lay in a poorly developed sense of national unity among the self-willed aristocracy. They exhibited their irresponsibility in the exercise of the *librum veto* (the prerogative of any nobleman to block action in the diet) and in the election of kings too weak to challenge their authority. Throughout the seventeenth century, Poland engaged in a series of wars against Sweden, Russia, and Turkey that drained her resources and secured no real advantages. Even John III Sobieski (r. 1674–1696), whose armies helped relieve the beleaguered garrison of Vienna (1683) and drive the Turks from Hungary, could do nothing to prevent the disintegration of the kingdom. As the War of the Polish Succession (1733–1735) demonstrated, Poland had become a mere pawn in international power politics. In 1795 Poland disappeared from the map of Europe (see p. 186).

The Ottoman Empire. Although the Ottoman Turks had posed a cultural and military threat to Europe since the fifteenth century, the threat had lain dormant after the Turkish defeat in the great Mediterranean war with Spain that ended in 1585. The Turks continued sporadic warfare in the eastern Mediterranean, particularly against the Venetians (1645–1664), but during this period the empire deteriorated under the rule of a succession of weak sultans. They were unable to curb insubordination among the Janissaries (elite military forces) and failed to stop Persian incursions on the eastern frontier.

This disintegration was checked during the ascendancy of the Kuprili family, whose members served as grand viziers during the reign of Sultan Mohammed IV (1648–1687). Mohammed Kuprili (1656–1661) carried out a thorough housecleaning. He brought the Janissaries under control, ended harem influence, and raised revenues.

Having executed these domestic reforms, the Ottomans confidently resumed expansion on their European frontiers. In the 1660s wars ensued with Austria, Poland, and Russia that continued intermittently for a century and a half. The Ottomans were as strong as they had been in the sixteenth century, but their enemies were now much stronger. The Hapsburgs defended Vienna in a two-month seige (1683) and then went on the offensive. The Turks were defeated at the second battle of Mohács (1687) and never regained the initiative. The Peace of Karlowitz (1699) restored Hungary, Croatia, and Transylvania to the Hapsburgs. The Turks fared no better against the Russians, who finally seized Azov, at the mouth of the Don River. This event signaled the beginning of Russian expansion on the shores of the Black Sea, which had previously been a Turkish lake.

Brandenburg-Prussia

Of all the states that aspired to greatness in the seventeenth century, the most unlikely candidate was Brandenburg-Prussia. Emperor Sigismund had bestowed the electorate of Brandenburg upon Frederick Hohenzollern in 1415. To this nucleus the elector added Jülich and Cleves in the Rhineland (1609) and the duchy of East Prussia (1618), which he held as a fief of the Polish crown until 1660. Although these scattered and often unproductive lands harbored fewer than a million inhabitants in 1648, Brandenburg-Prussia surpassed both Saxony and Bavaria and emerged with Russia and Austria as one of the great monarchies of eastern Europe. Two Hohenzollern rulers, Frederick William and his grandson King Frederick William I, were the driving forces behind this growth.

Reign of Frederick William (1640–1688). Frederick William, known as "the Great Elector," laid the foundation for Prussian power. His primary concern was the creation of a permanent military force that could protect his widely separated territories. Like other rulers of his age, he was challenged in his efforts by parochial interests that sought to maintain their autonomy.

CONSTITUTIONAL CENTRALIZATION. In the attempt to create administrative centralization, Frederick William faced resistance from the provincial estates. These bodies, representing the time-honored prerogatives of the towns and the nobility (*Junkers*), fought to maintain local independence. The elector slowly reduced their political influence and extended his power to levy taxes on the towns and peasantry without their authorization. He compensated the nobility for this loss of political power by granting them tax exemption and absolute legal and economic control over the peasantry. Having exerted his right to collect revenue, he created the Military Commissariat (1674) to ensure the collection of the war taxes and provide the army with supplies. The military commissioners slowly extended royal power to every facet of local administration.

ARMY. Brandenburg-Prussia's limited financial and human resources prevented Frederick William from transforming his kingdom into a major military power, but he regularized recruitment, and under his supervision the regiments were brought under royal control. He slowly expanded the army from a force of about eight thousand men during the Thirty Years' War to a maximum strength of approximately forty thousand. Thus the army was adequate for the extension and maintenance of his domestic control, but it was a puny force compared to those fielded by the French and the Austrians.

ECONOMIC POLICY. Frederick William strengthened the economy

with a mercantilist policy. He erected protective tariffs and issued decrees for the regulation of industry. To reinvigorate the country's agriculture, which had been disrupted by the Thirty Years' War, he gave tax rebates to peasants who would bring land back under the plow. He improved transportation by financing construction of the Frederick William Canal, which joined the Oder and the Elbe by their tributaries. Perhaps his most important contribution to Brandenburg-Prussia's economic life was his settlement policy. By guaranteeing religious toleration to groups persecuted in other states, he ensured a steady flow of immigrants. An estimated one hundred and fifty thousand Huguenots, for example, emigrated from France after the revocation of the Edict of Nantes.

FOREIGN POLICY. Frederick William moved warily among the giants of international power politics. The Peace of Westphalia extended his domains, but Sweden and Poland still posed a serious threat on his eastern frontiers. Frederick William played off these adversaries during the First Northern War (1655–1660), and under the terms of the Treaty of Oliva (1660), he obtained full sovereignty in the duchy of Prussia. He also enhanced his prestige when he stopped the Swedish invasion of Brandenburg at the battle of Fehrbellin (1675). When the Great Elector died in 1688, Brandenburg-Prussia had not achieved great-power status, but he had created the machinery for its future development. In 1701 Frederick William's son was recognized as king of Prussia.

Reign of Frederick William I (1713–1740). Frederick William I followed in the footsteps of his grandfather the Great Elector. Abandoning the frivolity and extravagance of his father, Frederick I (r. 1688–1713), he completed the transformation of Brandenburg-Prussia into a great power whose strength rested upon a militarized society. The provincial assemblies and town corporations that had hindered the Great Elector were completely submerged under the regime of Frederick William I. He stood alone as absolute sovereign. Beneath him were two rigidly disciplined bureaucracies that carried out his will.

ARMY. Despite the pacifism of his foreign policy, Frederick William I directed all his energies to the development of his army. During his reign it became one of the best-drilled and -administered forces in Europe. In a population of only 2.5 million, the army counted nearly eighty thousand troops. Its officers were drawn from the Junker class, whose members were taught to regard their commissions as their greatest honor and most serious obligation.

CIVIL SERVICE. The king transformed the civil administration into a military force without weapons whose function was to provide financial and administrative support for the army. There was no cabinet in the parliamentary sense of the word, for each bureau chief reported directly to and received his orders directly from the monarch. Frederick William I unified the fiscal structure under the control of the General Directory, which supervised the royal tax collectors in the towns and rural districts. These local *counselors* were not only fiscal officers but served as the arm of the monarchy at the local level. With the landed aristocrats, they ensured the loyal obedience of the populace to the Prussian state.

The Hapsburg Empire

The Holy Roman Empire bore the brunt of the long ideological struggle set off by the Lutheran Reformation (1517). Only a shadow of its former glory and power remained after the Peace of Westphalia (1648) recognized the sovereignty of the German states. However, the debacle did not encompass the Hapsburg domains. In the century that followed, the Hapsburg emperors fashioned a new federal state of diverse and far-flung peoples that was able to retain its status as a great power until it was swept away in the holocaust of World War I (1918). This reorganization and expansion was directed by Ferdinand II, Leopold I, and Charles I.

Reign of Ferdinand II (1619–1637). The reorganization of the Hapsburg domains into a Danubian kingdom began in the midst of the Thirty Years' War (see p. 115). The war had begun among the rebellious nobility of Bohemia and Moravia, and Ferdinand acted with ruthless dispatch to force these areas into total submission. The Bohemian nobility was stripped of their titles and lands, which were distributed among Hapsburg loyalists. Protestantism, which had been a root cause of Bohemian resistance, was crushed and Catholicism restored. The final humiliation for the elective kingdom was its absorption as a hereditary possession of the Hapsburg dynasty (1627). With these acts Ferdinand created a more cosmopolitan nobility. Though they continued to control local government and the peasantry, the aristocracy no longer cherished local "liberties" but, rather, looked to Vienna for favor and advancement. With this nucleus tightly under its control, the dynasty could afford to be flexible with more distant parts of their realm.

Reign of Leopold I (1658–1705). Leopold devoted his attention to a reorganization of the central administration, the integration of Hungary, and the threat of Louis XIV.

ADMINISTRATIVE REFORMS. Leopold used a central bureaucracy to rule his lands. His closest advisers sat on the Privy Council and handled all important issues. The War Council directed military affairs, and the Court Chamber controlled finances. The Chancellery was slowly divided into several bureaus that administered Austria proper, Bohemia, Hungary, and Transylvania separately.

Because of the diversity of his many lands, the emperor made no effort to control every facet of local administration. The privileged estates of each area were represented in diets (*landtage*), which retained their rights to collect direct taxes, raise and quarter troops, and resolve purely local issues. However, overall supervision was the responsibility of a royal governor.

RECONQUEST OF HUNGARY. When Leopold took the throne, he claimed all of Hungary but controlled only a long slender portion including Croatia and Slovakia. In the area of Turkish occupation, the Hungarian magnates remained overlords in their districts and retained a voice in the administration of Hapsburg Hungary. They proved to be disruptive subjects of both the sultan and the emperor.

The imperial forces successfully blunted a Turkish attack in 1663 and obtained a twenty-year truce with the sultan in the Treaty of Vasvar (1664). In 1682 the Turks renewed the war in support of Imri Thököly's claim to the Hungarian throne. They succeeded in reaching the gates of Vienna but after a two-month seige (July–September 1683) were beaten off by a relief force led by John III Sobieski, king of Poland. The Austrians subsequently delivered a stunning blow at the second battle of Mohács (1687), but involvement in the War of the League of Augsburg against Louis XIV forced a curtailment of their operations (see p. 124). A settlement was finally reached with the Treaty of Karlowitz (1699), which restored Hungary to the Hapsburgs.

Even before the final settlement with Turkey had been reached, Leopold began to reassert his control. In 1687 the Hungarian Diet renounced its right to elect the king, and the crown became a hereditary possession of the Hapsburg dynasty. The nobility retained their lands, titles, control of local government, and toleration for their Protestant beliefs, but important policy decisions were transferred to the Hungarian section of the Chancellery in Vienna. Despite these formal steps, the nobility still posed a serious threat to centralized control. The long tradition of defending their autonomy with rebellion was renewed by Francis II Rákóczy, who led an abortive uprising from 1703 to 1711. Notwithstanding such occasional outbursts, Hungary was slowly integrated into the Danubian kingdom.

Reign of Charles VI (1711–1740). Charles VI succeeded to the imperial throne after the brief reign of his brother Joseph I (1705–1711). His accession in Austria ended hopes of realizing his claims to the Spanish throne. The Grand Alliance had thoroughly beaten

France in the War of the Spanish Succession, but Charles's allies had no interest in continuing a conflict that would result in a reunification of Austria and Spain. Charles refused to sanction this loss in the Peace of Utrecht (see p. 126) but had to abide by its terms.

TERRITORIAL CHANGES. Charles continued the practice of territorial aggrandizement with mixed results. Milan (1713), Parma (1735), Piacenza (1735), and Tuscany (1737) were all absorbed by the Hapsburgs as they extended their dominance over northern Italy. The kingdom of Naples, acquired in the Peace of Utrecht (1713), was lost in the War of the Polish Succession (1738). Serbia, Bosnia, and Wallachia were conquered in 1718 but returned to the Ottomans under terms of the Treaty of Belgrade (1739).

THE PRAGMATIC SANCTION (1720). The Hapsburg emperors had traditionally divided their inheritance among their sons. Charles wanted to ensure that his domains, accumulated with such difficulty, would pass undivided to a single heir. His effort was made more difficult by the fact that his only children were daughters, who were legally excluded from the throne. The Pragmatic Sanction, published in 1720, amended the traditional rules by stipulating that the entire Hapsburg inheritance would henceforth pass undivided to the ruler's eldest child. By the time he died in 1740, Charles had obtained consent for this change from all the estates of the realm and from most foreign governments, and his daughter Maria Theresa succeeded him. The continuation of the Austrian Empire as a great power was thus guaranteed.

AUSTRIAN EMPIRE IN 1740. The structure of the Austrian Empire in 1740 set it apart from the other great states of Europe. Despite the centralizing efforts, reflected in the Viennese bureaucracy, the empire resembled a confereracy more closely than an absolute monarchy. Its geographic expanse, coupled with its ethnic and cultural diversity, made absolute control impossible. Despite these drawbacks, the Hapsburgs maintained a remarkable influence from the Baltic to the Mediterranean and from the Rhine to the Carpathians.

Russia in the Seventeenth Century

At the beginning of the seventeenth century, the principality of Muscovy, consolidated and expanded under the direction of Ivan III ("the Great") and Ivan IV ("the Dread") stood on the brink of disintegration. The ensuing century witnessed the development of Russia under a new dynasty into an empire that linked Asia and Europe.

The Time of Troubles (1584–1613). The death of Ivan IV sent a sigh of relief throughout Muscovy but also created a power vacuum.

His successors, Fëdor (r. 1584–1598) and Boris Godunov (r. 1598–1605), were unable to cope with the resulting unrest. The great boyar families arrogantly demanded a return of their old liberties, and the peasant masses seethed in discontent. Sigismund III, king of Poland, awaited the opportunity to take advantage of Russian weakness.

A period of anarchy began in 1603 with the appearance of a pretended who claimed to be the dead son of Ivan IV. This "false Dimitri" gained the throne in 1605 but was assassinated in 1606. In the resulting turmoil, boyars, cossacks, peasants, and Poles struggled to win control of the slowly disintegrating prize of Muscovy. The factions destroyed successive governments but could not restore stability. A settlement was finally reached in 1613 when a *zemskii sobor* (national assembly), called to elect a czar, chose Michael Romanov, a compromise candidate whose chief recommendation was his political obscurity.

The Early Romanovs. Michael Romanov (r. 1613–1645) was the first czar of the dynasty that ruled Russia until 1917. He was a mediocrity, but his thirty-year reign and the successive reigns of his son Alexis (1645–1676) and grandson Fëdor (1676–1682) reestablished royal authority in Russia.

FOREIGN AFFAIRS. The unstable state structure of eastern Europe resulted in interminable warfare among Poland, Russia, and Turkey throughout the century. Besides their external enemies, the czars had to deal with the independent cossack communities along their frontier. The most significant result of this warfare was the incorporation of the Ukraine in 1654.

RELIGIOUS SCHISM. The Greek Orthodox church served as a primary support to Russia's traditional culture. However, its prestige and authority were badly shaken by a schism that developed during the tenure of Patriarch Nikon (1652–1666). A bitter controversy arose not over dogma but about minor changes made by Nikon in long-established rituals. The faithful were divided between reformers and Old Believers. The latter have maintained their beliefs down to the present, despite bloody persecution by both church and state.

PEASANT UNREST. The burden of Russian society rested squarely upon the backs of the Russian peasantry, who as a result of the legal code of 1649 were reduced to a position of serfdom approaching chattel slavery. Famine, taxes, and war were all root causes in the successive revolts that mark the era. The greatest revolt began in 1667 under the leadership of cossack Stenka Razin. As is usually the case in such uprisings, the target of peasant hatred was not the czar but the boyars and gentry who controlled the land. After early successes, the poorly organized force was scattered by czarist troops, and Razin was executed. Since the government made no attempt to relieve the intolerable burden, peasant uprisings remained a standard feature of Russian life.

Peter the Great (r. 1682–1725). In many respects the reign of Peter the Great is a test case for examining the role of the great man in history. Possessing boundless energy and vision, Peter attempted, virtually alone, to transform Russia into a modern European state. His greatest obstacle was not political opposition but the lethargic inertia of a traditional society.

EARLY YEARS OF PETER'S REIGN. Peter was lucky to survive the early years of his dual reign with his half brother Ivan V (1682–1689). During this period the country was governed by his ruthless half sister Sophia in alliance with the *Streltsy*, the arrogant palace guard.

He began his personal rule in 1689, and it was soon evident that he would not be bound by tradition. Two early events in his reign demonstrate the complexity of his character. In 1697 he undertook a grand tour of western Europe, where he concentrated on observing the skilled craftsmen of that more advanced area. Considering his background, his receptivity to new ideas was truly remarkable. A darker side of his nature was revealed when the Streltsy, taking advantage of his absence, rose in revolt (1698). The rebellion had been crushed by the time he arrived in Moscow, but he took great satisfaction in personally beheading many of the one thousand conspirators who were executed.

THE GREAT NORTHERN WAR. Peter was at war during virtually his entire reign. His greatest antagonist was Sweden's Charles XII, with whom he struggled for control of the eastern Baltic. At the beginning of the conflict, Charles proved himself one of the most brilliant tacticians of the period in a lightning campaign against the allied states of Denmark, Poland, and Russia. His eight-thousand-man army capped the campaign by inflicting a humiliating defeat on forty thousand Russians at Narva (30 November 1700). But Charles's strategic insights did not measure up to his tactical brilliance. His involvement in a long struggle for the Polish throne gave Russia time to recuperate. Peter used this respite to reorganize his army and build a fleet. When Charles renewed the Russian conflict in 1708, he confronted a formidable opponent. Peter's forces met the Swedes in the Ukraine and defeated Charles in the decisive battle of Poltava (8 July 1709). With his army destroyed, Charles fled to Turkey, where he remained until 1714, attempting to organize an alliance against Russia. Peter suffered a momentary setback in a war with Turkey (1710–1711), but in the Baltic provinces, he had clearly gained the advantage. Hopes for Swedish recovery died with Charles in 1718, and the war ended with the Treaty of Nystadt (1721). Under its terms Russia became a Baltic power with the acquisition of Livonia, Estonia, Ingira, and southern Karelia.

PETER'S ATTEMPTS TO WESTERNIZE RUSSIA. Many of the ideas adopted by Peter in his attempt to Westernize Russia were borrowed from his adversary Charles XII. He formed ten *colleges* or commissions, each of which handled a particular area of governmental planning and administration. In theory the boards were intended to work as committees, but the chairmen, responsible for such important matters as finance and the army, came to dominate the proceedings. Coordination among the colleges was obtained through the *senate*, a privy council created in 1711, which advised Peter and ruled in his absence. To ensure the orderly execution of his decisions, the country was divided into twelve regions (*gubernii*), which were subdivided into provinces. This bureaucracy was staffed by royal officers who were assisted by the aristocracy.

Peter also removed the church and the nobility as obstacles to his absolutism. When the Patriarch Adrian died in 1700, he did not appoint a successor. In 1721 he abolished the office and created a spiritual commission known as the Holy Synod, which after 1722 was controlled by the procurator, a layman. Peter also extended the obligation of state service to the entire nobility and established a Table of Ranks (1722), which defined the duties and rewards of every aristocratic officeholder.

Peter's reforms went far beyond governmental reorganization. He built Saint Petersburg, a Western capital for his new Russia. Noblemen were browbeaten and taxed into shaving their beards and adopting Western dress; women were brought out into society. The great weakness behind all of Peter's efforts was that his subjects were coerced rather than convinced, and thus many of his reforms died with him. Even if the Russian people had willingly followed his lead, the total reorientation of a culture is the work of generations, not a lifetime. Peter did not remake his empire in the image of Western society, but he opened Russia's windows on the West and thus began the long and difficult task of modernization.

12

Imperialism in the Seventeenth and Eighteenth Centuries

The overseas exploration of the late fifteenth and early sixteenth centuries had opened a new epoch in European civilization. The discovery of new worlds, accompanied by tales of strange peoples possessing enormous wealth, had a profound psychological and cultural impact. The effect was compounded by Portuguese exploitation of the Spice Islands and Spanish importation of bullion from New Spain (see pp. 42, 87). With their new holdings, the Portuguese and the Spanish were the dominant imperial powers during the 1500s, but their monopoly was soon challenged.

Throughout the sixteenth century, French, English, and Dutch raiders harassed Iberian shipping, and daring captains even attacked Spanish and Portuguese settlements. By the beginning of the 1600s, France, England, and Holland had become imperial powers themselves and the economic emphasis shifted from bullion to the more mundane, though equally lucrative, production of sugar, tobacco, spices, and dyes. The great struggle for empire reached its climax in the 1760s when England asserted itself as the dominant commercial and naval power.

Decline of Portugal and Spain

Although Portugal and Spain are neighbors on the Iberian peninsula, their domestic and imperial developments have often diverged. From 1580 to 1640, however, their destinies were united under the Spanish Hapsburgs, and together they suffered from the aggressive expansion of their North Atlantic rivals.

The Portuguese Empire. Portugal's empire comprised a series of commercial outposts and naval bases that perched precariously on the coasts of South America, Africa, India, and Asia and dotted the South Seas. Of its far-flung possessions, the most valuable were the

Moluccas, popularly known as the Spice Islands. Portugal achieved a monopoly of the spice trade through force of arms early in the 1500s, but it was destined to maintain its valuable trade only so long as it could maintain naval supremacy in the Indian Ocean.

Two events ultimately destroyed their control. In 1580 Philip II of Spain claimed and seized the Portuguese crown. The dynastic unification of the Iberian peninsula lasted until 1640. Philip pledged to protect the interests of his Portuguese subjects, but his preoccupations with European affairs and his own empire in New Spain overshadowed Portuguese interests. Secondly, the outbreak of revolt in the Spanish Netherlands (1586) closed Antwerp as a northern center for Portuguese exports. Excluded from the Lisbon trade, the Dutch and English obtained spices by preying upon Portuguese shipping and then, in the 1590s, by interloping in the Spice Islands. Portugal's tenuous imperial lifeline, which was maintained by a series of undermanned outposts separated by thousands of nautical miles, snapped. Although its most valuable possessions fell into the hands of the Dutch, Portugal maintained commercial enclaves at Goa, Macao, and Angola into the twentieth century and bequeathed its cultural heritage to Brazil, one of the largest states in the world.

The Decline of Spain. The apogee of Spanish power and the beginning of its decline occurred during the reign of Philip II (1556–1598). He worked to reinstate universal Roman Catholicism and maintain Hapsburg supremacy. His overambitious goals resulted in constant warfare that exhausted Spain's economy at the very time when imports of silver and gold from New Spain reached their highest level.

Philip II's successors, Philip III (r. 1598–1621), Philip IV (r. 1621–1665), and Charles II (r. 1665–1700), had neither his strength of character nor his dedication to affairs of state. The able ministry of Olivares (1621–1643) during the reign of Philip IV provided only a brief respite in the decline of Spain's continental and imperial interests.

The decline of Spain and the emergence of new imperial powers (which will be treated in the remainder of this chapter) must be kept in perspective. Despite the continual attacks of Holland, France, and England over a period of three centuries, Spain maintained its possessions intact, with the exceptions of Jamaica, which was captured by England in 1655, and Gibraltar, ceded to England in 1704. Spain's naval power declined, and the colonial economy stagnated from overcentralization and inefficient administration, but in the long run, its culture prevailed throughout South and Central America and the Caribbean islands.

Holland's Golden Age

The expansion of trade and the importance of commerce in seventeenth-century Europe is best reflected in the wealth and power of the United Netherlands. The Dutch people, numbering barely 1.5 million, thrived behind the earthen walls that protected their small country from the North Sea. The Netherlands had been a manufacturing center since the Middle Ages, and in the middle of the sixteenth century, Antwerp served as the commercial hub of northern Europe. The revolt against Spanish control that broke out in 1568 (see p. 89) cast a pall over the provinces and threatened to end their prosperity. Agriculture declined as the countryside became a battlefield; when the Dutch rebels blockaded the Scheldt River, grass grew in Antwerp's deserted streets. The United Netherlands, a federation of the seven northern provinces, emerged from the crucible of revolution stronger than ever before and maintained its position as Europe's greatest maritime nation throughout the seventeenth century.

Basis of Dutch Prosperity. Though threatened by savage storms that crashed against its dikes, Holland owed everything it had to the sea. Dutchmen dominated the fishing industry, braving the North Atlantic and Arctic oceans in search of herring, cod, and whale. Holland's merchant fleet, which totaled more ships than the rest of Europe combined, not only monopolized Europe's coastal trade but also predominated in the commercial routes of the seven seas. Its shipyards provided the ships for its own merchants and those of its rivals as well. Dutch merchants were also the preeminent wholesalers of Europe. Amsterdam served as the nerve center of this activity. Its bank, chartered in 1602, became the primary bank of deposit and the financial center for merchants from all over the continent. The Amsterdam stock exchange, reorganized in 1611, operated as a clearinghouse for stocks, commodities, and loans.

The Dutch Empire. The emergence of Holland as an imperial power coincided with the revolt against Spain (1568–1609). The Dutch armies were no match for the Spanish pikemen, but the Sea Beggars formed the nucleus of a growing navy that stymied Spanish attacks. Although the fleet began as a defensive force, Dutch men-of-war soon took the fight to their enemies and in the process carved out an empire.

DUTCH EAST INDIA COMPANY. The Dutch served as agents for the Portuguese spice trade until the 1590s, when Philip II excluded them from Iberian ports. Unable to function as middlemen, the Dutch went to the source of supply. In the last years of the century, several expeditions sailed to the East Indies. Despite heavy losses they returned with profitable cargoes. In order to organize these expeditions, the Estates General issued a charter authorizing formation of the Dutch East India Company (1602). It proved to be the most successful joint-stock venture of the age. The charter granted the company exclusive rights to trade under the Dutch flag in the Far East. Its prerogatives included the right to erect trading posts, administer justice, enter into commercial agreements with native governments, and even to make war and peace. Capital for the enterprise was raised by the public sale of stock. Real control of the company remained in the hands of seventeen directors, who were the leading merchants of the United Provinces. By controlling the company, the bank, the stock exchange, and the Estates General, they formed the ruling oligarchy of the United Netherlands.

CONQUEST OF THE EAST INDIES. Having obtained a monopoly of Dutch trade, the East India Company began a concerted effort to seize Portugal's eastern empire. The conquest was largely achieved during the administration of Governor-general Jan Pieterszoon Coen, who founded a Dutch capital at Batavia (1619) on the island of Java and systematically drove the Portuguese from every outpost in the Malay Archipelago. He also planted a colony on Formosa, which was maintained from 1624 to 1661, and promoted trade with the Japanese. Coen's successors captured Malacca (1641) and Ceylon (1658) and founded Cape Colony, on the southern tip of Africa, as a refitting station (1651).

In the first decades of conflict with Portugal, the Dutch and English traded and fought side by side. But as Portuguese resistance crumbled, the Dutch were determined to exert their monopoly. English traders were driven from the Spice Islands by 1623, and thereafter India became the primary area of England's Far Eastern trade.

THE DUTCH IN THE WESTERN HEMISPHERE. The Spanish and Portuguese possessions in the Western Hemisphere were not immune from Dutch incursions. The Dutch West India Company was chartered in 1621 on the same lines as its eastern counterpart. Its agents attacked Brazil in 1624 and brought most of the coast under its control until 1645, when a revolt forced them to relinquish all of the territory except Surinam. At the same time, West India Company fleets preyed upon Spanish commerce in the Caribbean, and in 1628 Piet Heyn, the company's most illustrious captain, captured the entire Spanish treasure fleet. Although such acts of piracy brought occasional bonanzas to stockholders in Holland, the daily routine of trade was more profitable in the long run. The West India Company seized Tobago, Curaçao, and Saint Eustatius in the 1630s and from these bases dominated carrying trade in the Caribbean. Further north, the Dutch founded a colony at the mouth of the Hudson River in 1615. New Netherland eventually extended from the site of modern Albany southward into Long Island and into New Jersey. The area was ceded to the English in 1664 and renamed New York.

DECLINE OF THE NETHERLANDS. The commercial interests of France and England clashed with the monopolistic pretensions of the Dutch. In the latter half of the seventeenth century, Holland was drawn into a series of wars with its imperial rivals, which will be discussed on page 146. Its large merchant marine was a vulnerable and lucrative target and suffered heavy losses during these conflicts. However, the ultimate cause of its decline lay in the fact that during the eighteenth century both the French and the English could mobilize far greater resources for the overseas enterprises.

The French Empire

During the 1600s the French monarchy was preoccupied with European power politics and took little interest in imperial affairs. However, the royal ministers Richelieu and Colbert believed that overseas territories could enhance the power and prestige of the crown and thus support the king's Continental ambitions. Since the impetus for colonial development came from the government rather than from merchants, as was the case in Holland and England, the French Empire reflected the tendency toward political centralization and stringent economic control current in France. The main areas of French empire building were the West Indies, North America, and India.

The Corsairs. French privateers (corsairs) were among the first to challenge the Spanish monopoly in the New World. Their attacks coincided with Valois attempts to prevent Hapsburg dominance on the Continent during the 1500s. The most notorious corsair, "Peg Leg" François Le Clerc, captured and looted Havanna in 1556. This and other French depredations led the Spanish to adopt the convoy system, initiate constant naval patrols in the Caribbean, and construct imposing fortifications at their major outposts.

West Indian Settlements. In 1565 the Spanish demonstrated their determination to protect their mainland monopoly by wiping out the French settlement of Fort Caroline in northern Florida. When the French renewed their efforts to colonize in the Caribbean, they limited their activities to the Lesser Antilles, where the Spanish had no interest. In this chain of islands that forms the eastern boundary of the Caribbean, the French planted a series of colonies, beginning in the 1620s on Saint Christopher (Saint Kitts) and expanding to include Martinique, Guadeloupe, and finally Haiti (the western half of Hispanolia). Economic development of these colonies languished under the administration of a series of chartered companies that failed to attract the financial support of French merchants despite the backing of Richelieu and later Colbert. It was only after the introduction of sugar cultivation during the 1640s that the islands began to thrive. A plantation system employing black slaves transformed the islands into France's most valuable imperial asset.

North America. Samuel de Champlain laid the foundation for a French empire in North America. The settlement of Quebec (1608) on the Saint Lawrence River served as the headquarters for administration, trade, and the further exploration of the continent. The Great Lakes were explored by French trappers and traders whose beaver pelts soon became the mainstay of the Canadian economy. While English colonists still hugged the Atlantic coast, Louis Jolliet traced the Mississippi River to its confluence with the Arkansas (1673) before abandoning hope that it would take him to the Pacific. He was followed by La Salle, who explored the river to its mouth (1682). His successors, Bienville and d'Iberville, placed the first French settlements in Louisiana (1699). The founding of New Orleans followed in 1718.

By the beginning of the eighteenth century, the French claimed and had posted themselves in a wide arc that encompassed the continent from the mouth of the Mississippi up its wide basin to the Great Lakes and eastward to the Atlantic. Despite the wide expanse of these holdings, the French Empire was flawed by fundamental weaknesses that contributed to its ultimate ruin. The government had granted large tracts and seigneurial rights to wealthy proprietors. The resulting lord-tenant relationship hampered the growth of a class of independent freeholders of the type that became the backbone of the English colonies. Another potential group of settlers was excluded by the ban on Protestant immigration. New France thus developed into a tightly controlled and sparsely populated royal colony designed primarily to exploit the fur trade and to prevent the expansion of the agriculturally minded and far more populous English settlements.

The French in Africa and India. French imperialism also extended into Africa and India. A slaving station was maintained in Senegal after 1645, and in 1642 the islands of Mauritius and Réunion were garrisoned to provide outposts for the Indian trade. French interests in India were strictly commercial. The establishment of trading points at Pondicherry (1674), on the southeastern coast, and Chandernagore (1690), in the delta of the Ganges, brought the French into direct commercial competition with England. As a result, India became a theater of military operations during the eighteenth century.

The English Empire

England was the most successful imperial power of modern times. Despite the domestic turmoil that wracked the country during the seventeenth century, it entered the fierce, worldwide struggle for wealth and influence. Its ultimate success in this competition rested upon two basic factors that were in marked contrast to the French experience. First, the English Empire was promoted by businessmen and, thus, was pieced together upon a foundation of solid commercial activity. The French Empire, on the other hand, was a government creation that often lacked the active interest and support of French merchants. Second, England, alone among the imperial powers, sent out not only a corps of colonial administrators but also great numbers of settlers. The English colonists formed stable agricultural and commercial communities that were political and economic assets rather than liabilities.

Early Settlements in North America. England was no more successful than France in its first effort to found colonies in North America. Sir Humphrey Gilbert perished at sea while attempting to place fisheries in Newfoundland (1584). Sir Walter Raleigh realized that settlements would prove more lucrative than piracy, but none of his colonies on the coast of North Carolina (1585–1587) survived.

England's first permanent colonies were commercial ventures promoted by joint-stock companies that funded expeditions through the public sale of stock. The directors hoped to profit from the commercial monopolies granted in their royal charter, while the colonists generally sought land and freedom of religious expression. Colonists sent out by the Virginia Company of London settled at Jamestown in 1607. After a decade of hardship, the colony finally developed tobacco as a commercial crop, which after 1619 was cultivated with the labor of black slaves. But despite this success, the company went bankrupt, and its charter was revoked (1624). Virginia became a royal colony with a governor and council appointed by the crown. These royal appointees shared their authority with the House of Burgesses, a representative assembly that spoke for local interests.

New England provided a second area of colonization. Plymouth, Massachusetts, was settled by Puritan dissenters in 1620 but was soon overshadowed by a larger colony planted at Salem under the auspices of the Massachusetts Bay Company in 1629. Continual religious unrest in England provided a stream of Puritan immigrants to

New England; by 1640 the colony had over sixteen thousand inhabitants. Since the company's directors had migrated to the colony with their charter, the Massachusetts Bay colony remained virtually a sovereign state throughout most of the seventeenth century.

Colonization was also fostered in North America through the proprietary grant. Under this system the king granted large tracts of land to individuals or syndicates who in turn bore the expense of colonization and administration. Maryland (1632), New Hampshire (1635), Carolina (1663), New York and New Jersey (1664), Pennsylvania (1681), and Georgia (1732) were proprietary colonies.

Settlement in the West Indies. English colonization in the Caribbean coincided with the first French settlements. Saint Christopher Island, barely twenty-three miles long, was occupied by both countries in 1625. Barbados was settled as a proprietary grant in 1624, and it soon attracted more settlers than New England. However, many of the colonists were forced to leave the island after 1640 when sugar plantations worked by slaves replaced tobacco farms cultivated by freemen and indentured servants. Jamaica was taken from the Spanish in 1655 and became the most valuable of England's chain of sugar islands in the West Indies.

The English in India. After being driven from the Spice Islands by the Dutch in 1623, the English East India Company concentrated their Far Eastern activities on the Indian subcontinent. At first powerful native rulers prevented the acquisition of territory, but valuable factories (trading posts) were established at Surat (1616), Madras (1639), Bombay (1665), and Calcutta (1686).

India was a poor market for English goods, but the East India Company produced a handsome profit from the export of cotton textiles. In the eighteenth century, English merchants expanded their activities, and China tea soon surpassed calicoes and muslins as the most valuable commodity.

Imperial Confrontation of England, Holland, and France

England, Holland, and France were imperial powers by the middle of the seventeenth century. Though all three pursued mercantilist policies, the English and the Dutch perceived the relationship between economic prosperity and national well-being most clearly. Their commercial rivalry soon led to open warfare. France joined the attacks on the Netherlands, but during the seventeenth century its main interest was the traditional goal of territorial aggrandizement on the Continent. Holland could not maintain its position against such formidable adversaries and was soon eclipsed. Following Holland's decline, the eighteenth century witnessed a climactic struggle between France and England for imperial dominance.

English Mercantilism. Mercantilism is a policy designed to enhance the power of a state by the regulation of its economic activity. England provides a good seventeenth-century example of this theory in action. Through a series of legislative acts, England excluded foreigners from its sphere of commercial influence and exploited its colonies for its economic benefit.

NAVIGATION ACT OF 1651. The first Navigation Act was designed to curb the Dutch carrying trade. It required that goods imported to England be carried either in English ships that were manned by English crews or by ships of the country of origin. This threat to the Dutch merchant marine, the mainstay of Holland's economy, triggered a commercial war (see p. 146).

NAVIGATION ACT OF 1660. The second Navigation Act provided that all goods moving between England and her colonies must be carried in English or colonial ships and further stipulated that certain enumerated items, including sugar, tobacco, and other major colonial products, could be exported only to England or an English colony.

STAPLES ACT OF 1663. To exclude foreign ships further, the Staples Act required that the shipment of all goods bound for an English colony must debark from an English port.

PLANTATIONS DUTIES ACT OF 1673. This act placed a duty on enumerated goods shipped from one English colony to another. Its purpose was to make England the focal point of all imperial trade and to prevent colonial merchants from violating the navigation acts by shipping goods outside the empire under the pretext of shipping to another colony.

IMPACT OF THE ACTS OF TRADE. This mercantilist program unquestionably enhanced England's economy and political power. The English merchant marine virtually monopolized its North Atlantic commerce, and colonial ships controlled the intercoastal trade of North America. English merchants benefited from the reexport trade of colonial and European goods. England's navy, essential for the enforcement of mercantilism, soon surpassed its rivals.

Notwithstanding these advantages, England could not maintain an airtight system, and its attempts to do so caused animosity both in the colonies and in Europe. The colonials, who despite their imperial status paid English customs duties, continued to trade illegally with Spain and France. (Molasses from the French West Indies, for example, was cheaper than its English counterpart because the French mercantile system prohibited the importation of rum in order to protect the domestic brandy industry.) New Englanders used the rum distilled from French molasses as a major item in the "triangular trade," which sent rum and other products to Africa, slaves to the Caribbean, and cash to New England. England's attempts to control this illegal traffic, so beneficial to its colonial subjects, embittered relations in the decades preceding the American Revolution (see p. 204). In addition, England's policy resulted in a prolonged dispute with Holland, whose carrying trade was badly damaged by English mercantilism.

The Dutch Wars. Holland had played a vital role in the long struggle to prevent Spanish dominance in western Europe. However, by mid-century with Spain in decline, Holland posed a commercial threat to England and a military threat to French expansion. The result was a series of wars that ended Holland's status as a great power.

FIRST DUTCH WAR (1652–1654). The first Anglo-Dutch conflict was a direct result of England's 1651 Navigation Act. The English fleet, led by admirals Blake and Monk, met the Dutch squadrons of Tromp and Ruyter in a series of sharp though indecisive engagements in the English Channel. The war was ruinous to Dutch commerce, however, and Holland sued for peace. Under the terms of the Treaty of Westminster (1654), the Navigation Act remained in force, and Holland agreed to pay an indemnity.

SECOND DUTCH WAR (1665–1667). English aggressiveness continued to manifest itself by the seizure of Dutch trading stations in Africa and the conquest of New Netherland, which they renamed New York (1664). These acts led to a renewal of the war, in which the English found themselves in conflict with an alliance of Holland, Denmark, and France. Again, the war at sea proved indecisive, but London was ravaged meanwhile by both plague (1665) and fire (1666). In June 1667 the English fleet was destroyed by the Dutch as it lay in anchor in the Medway. Despite these reversals, the terms of the Treaty of Breda (1667) were generally favorable to England. It retained New York in return for Surinam, while the Navigation Acts were amended to allow Holland to ship to England goods the Dutch had transported down the Rhine River. The French ceded Saint Kitts, Monserrat, and Antigua in the West Indies to England in return for Acadia (Nova Scotia).

THIRD DUTCH WAR (1672–1678). Under terms of the secret Treaty of Dover (1670), Charles II of England agreed to ally himself with France in a war against Holland in return for a cash subsidy. When the assault against Holland by land and sea came in 1672, only the resolute defiance of reinstated Stadholder William III of Orange saved the country from ultimate ruin. After two years England agreed to the second Treaty of Westminster (1674), which restored the status quo ante bellum. France continued the conflict until 1678 when the Treaty of Nijmegen halted the fighting. Throughout these wars the Dutch had held their own militarily and had managed to negotiate favorable treaties, but Holland could not stop the growth of English maritime power, nor could it single-handedly thwart French expansionism.

Anglo-French Colonial Wars. With the elimination of Holland as a contender for great-power status, England and France squared off in the contest for imperial dominance. The ensuing warfare continued intermittently from 1689 to 1763 and may be properly referred to as a world war. Although the stakes were high, the colonial wars were often only peripheral phases of European conflicts. Often months of effort by colonial troops in the North American hinterland or the Ganges delta was undone by a stroke of the pen.

KING WILLIAM'S WAR (1689–1697). King William's War was the North American phase of the War of the League of Augsburg, fought by a European alliance to prevent French expansion into the Rhineland (see p. 124). In the New World, France sent its Indian allies on deep forays into New England, while English troops captured Port Royal, the French stronghold in Acadia (Nova Scotia). Neither side could force a decision, and under the terms of the Treaty of Ryswick (1697), Port Royal was returned to France and North America reverted to the status quo ante bellum.

QUEEN ANNE'S WAR (1702–1713). With the renewal of European hostilities in the War of the Spanish Succession (see p. 124), war again spread to the colonies. The conflict was embittered by the French and Indian alliance, which again resulted in attacks on English settlers. The English again captured Port Royal but for a second time were unable to seize either Montreal or Quebec.

The Peace of Utrecht (1713), which definitively halted Louis XIV's aggression in Europe, also provided important gains for England in North America and the Caribbean. France ceded Nova Scotia, Newfoundland, and Hudson Bay to England. From Spain the English also received the *asiento*, a thirty-year monopoly to sell slaves within the Spanish Empire, and the right to send one trading ship annually to Panama. Finally, England obtained Gibraltar, the stone sentinel that guards the mouth of the Mediterranean.

ARMED TRUCE (1713–1739). Though at peace, the colonial rivals maintained a watchful eye on each other. The French hoped to make up for their deficiency in settlers by reinforcing their chain of military outposts along the internal waterways that provided the primary traces through the wilderness. The eastern anchor of these fortifications was the fortress of Louisburg, constructed, beginning in 1720, on Cape Breton Island to guard the Gulf of Saint Lawrence. Forts Frontenac (1679), Niagara (1679), and Detroit (1701), among many others, guarded the Great Lakes. A series of stockades were added on the modern sites of Miami (Ohio), Vincennes, Natchez, and Mobile to protect the river routes.

WAR OF JENKIN'S EAR (1739–1742). The quarter century of peace that followed the Utrecht settlement ended with the outbreak of war between England and Spain. English merchants had continually exceeded the limited trading rights that Spain had granted within its empire, but Spanish protests fell upon deaf ears. England was feeling aggressive, and Captain Jenkin's report to Parliament that his ear had been cut off by a Spanish coastguardsman was the only excuse needed for a declaration of war. An expeditionary force sent into the Caribbean scored some early victories, but yellow fever soon swept through the English squadron, sparing barely enough men to bring the ships home. The war soon merged with the general conflict that had engulfed Europe.

KING GEORGE'S WAR (1743–1748). The War of the Austrian Succession (1740–1748) involved all the major powers of Europe for the first time since the Peace of Utrecht (see p. 175). Its colonial phase was known as King George's War. In America the conflict was more intense than in preceding wars. Massachusetts militiamen invaded Canada and stormed the mighty French fortress of Louisburg (1745), thus removing the threat to English fisheries and opening the gateway to French Canada. The French fared better in India, where François Dupleix succeeded in capturing the English trade center of Madras. The Treaty of Aix-la-Chapelle (1748), which terminated the hostilities, negated these imperial gains for the sake of European interests. Although Louisburg and Madras were returned to their original owners, both sides realized that Aix-la-Chapelle constituted a truce rather than a peace.

SEVEN YEARS' WAR (1756–1763). The Seven Years' War that ravaged central Europe (see p. 176) also proved to be the climactic struggle in the Anglo-French competition for empire.

French and Indian War. In North America blood was spilled long before the formal declaration of hostilities. English fears of French expansion into the Ohio Valley led the English to begin construction of fortifications at the strategic point where the confluence of the Allegheny and Monongahela forms the Ohio River. The French seized the site (1753) and constructed Fort Duquesne. George Washington failed to recover the fort with a small force, and a subsequent expedition under the command of General Braddock was ambushed and virtually annihilated (1755). After William Pitt took over

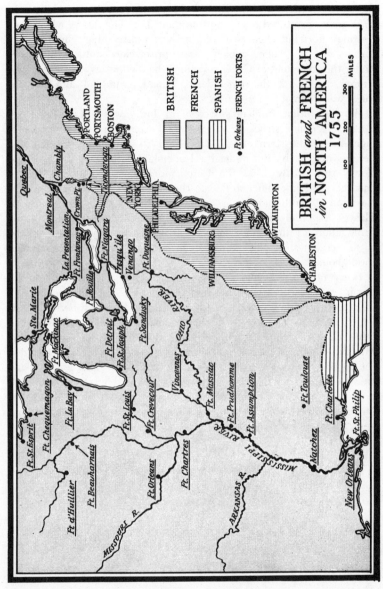

BRITISH *and* FRENCH
in NORTH AMERICA
1755

BRITISH
FRENCH
SPANISH
• Ft. Orleans FRENCH FORTS

0   100   200   300 MILES

Quebec
Chambly
Montreal
Portland
Portsmouth
Boston
La Presentation
Crown Pt.
Ticonderoga
NEW YORK
Ft. Frontenac
Ft. Niagara
Ft. Rouille
Presqu'ile
Venango
Ft. Duquesne
PHILADELPHIA
Ste. Marie
Ft. MacKinac
Ft. Detroit
Ft. St. Joseph
Ft. Sandusky
WILLIAMSBURG
WILMINGTON
CHARLESTON
Ft. Chequamegon
Ft. La Bay
Vincennes
OHIO RIVER
Ft. Massiac
Ft. Prudhomme
Ft. Charlotte
Ft. St. Esprit
Ft. St. Louis
Ft. Crevecour
Ft. Assumption
Ft. Toulouse
Ft. St. Philip
Ft. d'Huillier
Ft. Beauharnais
Ft. Orleans
Ft. Chartres
ARCANSAS R.
MISSISSIPPI RIVER
Natchez
New Orleans
MISSOURI R.

(From *Europe 1450 to 1815*, p. 449, by Ernest John Knapton. Copyright © 1961 by
Charles Scribner's Sons. Reprinted by permission of Charles Scribner's Sons.)

direction of the war, the English began to recoup their losses. In 1758 they recaptured both Louisburg and Fort Duquesne, which they renamed Fort Pitt. The greatest prize was the seemingly impregnable fortress city of Quebec, which was surprised and captured by troops under the command of General Wolfe, who died in his hour of victory. French defenses in the remainder of Canada crumbled, and the conquest was complete.

War in India. England's victory in India was equally decisive. François Dupleix struck alliances with the native rulers of the Coromandel (southeastern) coast, and by 1751 England's position had deteriorated badly. But under the leadership of Robert Clive, the tide slowly turned. By 1753 the Coromandel coast, including Madras, was secure. The conflict shifted to the north, where in 1757 Clive recaptured Calcutta and won control of Bengal with his victory at Plassey. Not only had the French been decisively beaten, but the subjugation of the native prince of Bengal set the stage for the British conquest of the entire Indian subcontinent, which continued throughout the next century.

Peace of Paris. England's decisive victory in the competition for empire was formalized in the Treaty of Paris (1763). It received all of French Canada with the exception of a few French fisheries. Spain, which had entered the war in time to share the defeat of its French ally, ceded Florida in return for the Louisiana territory west of the Mississippi. France retained its trading posts in India but forfeited the right to garrison troops or build fortifications. This left England free to expand its interests in India unmolested by European competitors. Thus England emerged as mistress of the seas and the greatest imperial power, a position it maintained until the twentieth century.

13

The Century of Genius

The seventeenth century witnessed a vast expansion of Western intellectual horizons. The key to this development was a growing confidence in the power of the human intellect to unravel mysteries that previously had been accepted on the basis of tradition and faith. This chapter will concentrate on the examination of two aspects of this development: the scientific revolution and the baroque consciousness.

The Scientific Revolution

The term *scientific revolution* refers to the relatively rapid development of a new cosmology based upon both theoretical and empirical science. This achievement generated a completely new frame of reference, which forms the intellectual foundation of twentieth-century industrial societies.

Medieval Background. The idea of revolutionary development might give the erroneous impression that medieval scholars had neither the interest nor the capacity to study natural phenomena. On the contrary, they constructed an elaborate system to explain the universe. Some distinctive aspects of their approach did, however, limit their ability to expand scientific knowledge.

Medieval science was an auxiliary of theology. Its purpose was to demonstrate the magnificence of Creation and to provide rational proof of what was already known through Christian faith. Speculation concerning the universe thus centered on the question "Why do things happen?", whereas modern science concentrates on the question "How do things happen?" In their attempt to relate natural phenomena to prime causes, medieval scholars developed a tightly reasoned deductive technique. The result was to inhibit the development of experimentation, which forms the basis of modern science.

Since knowledge of the physical world was of secondary importance and was based upon reason rather than faith, medieval scholars
felt no compunction in relying upon the work of ancient pagan authorities. Despite the wide diversity of ancient opinion, the medieval
world formulated a coherent amalgamation of knowledge based upon
Aristotle's physics and Ptolemy's astronomy. At the center of the universe was the earth, the corrupt abode of man. All earthly substances were thought to be compounds of the four elements: earth,
water, fire, and air. Terrestrial motion was explained as the natural
attempt of displaced bodies containing mixtures of these elements
to regain their natural state. The less perfect earth and water were
drawn down by their gravity, while fire and air rose to their more
exalted levels through levity.

The incorruptible heavens surrounding the earth operated with a
different set of laws. Celestial movement was not the result of un-
fortunate displacement but the work of God, and thus the movement
of the moon, sun, and planets incorporated the perfection of uniform
circular orbits. Although the hypothesis was erroneous, Ptolemy was
able to save appearances (that is, fit his data within the accepted
theory) by postulating the existence of eighty epicycles—that is,
complex variations of circular orbits moving along imaginary circular
paths to explain the seemingly erratic, and therefore unacceptable,
wandering of the planets.

This system was intellectually satisfying to the medieval world, but
by the fifteenth century, scholars were confronted with a growing
array of terrestrial and celestial observations that could neither be
ignored nor forced within the traditional mold. The declining prestige
of scholastic theology, a growing tendency to question ancient authorities, and an increase in empiricism opened the way to the scientific revolution.

The New Astronomy. The first major scientific breakthroughs of the
sixteenth century were in astronomy. The work of several brilliant
astronomers not only destroyed Ptolemy's cosmology but ultimately
raised crucial questions regarding the nature of the universe and mankind's place in it.

COPERNICUS. Nicolaus Copernicus (1473–1543) was born in Poland
and educated at the University of Padua, the medieval center of scientific learning. His studies and observations left him dissatisfied with
the Ptolemaic system, which despite its complexity failed to account
for observed planetary movement. Relying primarily on Ptolemy's
own observations, the medieval belief in the perfection of circular
orbits, and a suggestive fragment from the ancient Greek astronomer

Aristarchus, Copernicus formulated a heliocentric (sun-centered) theory of the universe.

Copernicus reduced the number of Ptolemaic epicycles from eighty to forty-eight by postulating the solar system, but his inability to conceive of noncircular planetary orbits prevented him from fitting all known data within his theory. His ideas were published in *On the Revolution of Celestial Spheres* (1543). Although his theory was only partially correct, it constituted a significant breakthrough. The full implications of his complex ideas did not become fully understood for over a generation. He had called into question not only the cosmology of Ptolemy but also Aristotle's teaching of the nature and functioning of the universe upon which man had based his conception of physical reality.

BRAHE. Tycho Brahe (1546–1601) of Denmark was a stargazer rather than a theoretician. From his observatory he spent a lifetime mapping the heavens without the aid of a telescope. The object of his painstaking labor was the acquisition of precise data with which he cast horoscopes. Brahe rejected the Copernican theory, but his own modified version of the Ptolemaic system made no contribution to theoretical astronomy. However, his tables of planetary movement were the most accurate of the day and provided essential data needed for the theoretical work of his brilliant assistant, Johannes Kepler.

KEPLER. The genius of German astronomer Johannes Kepler (1571–1630) lay in his ability to break away from traditional patterns of thought and to perceive new ways of organizing information. He struggled to formulate a mathematical theory of planetary motion consistent both with Brahe's observations and with his own Pythagorean beliefs that all of divine creation would adhere to the simplest mathematical relationships needed for its operation. He crossed the threshold of discovery when he accepted the possibility of elliptical planetary orbits. He was then able to formulate three laws of celestial motion that satisfied his own demand for an integrated solar system whose operation corresponded with Brahe's observations. His laws stated that: (1) the planets move around the sun, which is situated at one focus of their elliptical paths; (2) a planet's velocity is inversely proportional to its distance from the sun, and its orbital arc sweeps out equal areas (pie slices) in equal times; (3) there is a direct relationship between the average distance from the sun and the time of one planetary orbit. The third law tied all the planets together in a unified system. Kepler's work did not have an immediate impact. His mystical beliefs in the mathematical relationship of all creation and his complex computations restricted his work to a very narrow audience. It was Isaac Newton who first appreciated the full signifi-cance of Kepler's work (see p. 157).

GALILEO. The Italian astronomer Galileo Galilei (1564–1642) but-tressed the work of the theoreticians with the first practical application of the telescope, which he handcrafted in 1610. He discovered the mountains of the moon and sunspots, neither of which were thought possible within the framework of the Aristotelian universe. His ob-servation of the phases of Venus, Jupiter's moons, and Saturn's rings, seemed to confirm the Copernican hypothesis. These findings, which he published in the *Starry Messenger* (1610), helped popularize scientific study but also aroused the authorities to the dangers of scientific inquiry. Galileo's contributions to mechanics are discussed on page 156.

Development of the Scientific Method. The discoveries of the fifteenth century raised doubts concerning the whole body of accepted scientific truth. Amid this uncertainty, philosophers began to formu-late postulates for systematic scientific inquiry. The most significant of these methodologists were the Englishman Francis Bacon and the Frenchman René Descartes.

BACON. Francis Bacon (1561–1626) was not a great scientist, but he made a significant contribution to the popularization of science and the formulation of scientific method. In *The New Organon* (1620) and *The Advancement of Learning* (1605), he criticized scholasticism's reliance on the arid logic and unverified teachings of ancient authori-ties. He argued that preconceptions and prejudice should be replaced by the careful collection of data through experimentation and ob-servation. By the *inductive method,* such specific knowledge could then be employed to form general hypotheses that in turn could be confirmed by further experimentation. Bacon explained his belief that science would open the way to utopia in the *New Atlantis* (1626). His greatest weaknesses lay in his inability to recognize the importance of preliminary "hunches" or hypotheses that would give direction to experimentation and in his failure to recognize the importance of mathematics in the quest for scientific truth.

DESCARTES. The skepticism of René Descartes (1596–1650), like that of Bacon, served as a solvent for conventional beliefs and opened new channels of inquiry. Unlike Bacon, however, Descartes doubted the accuracy of sense impressions and therefore rejected empiricism as a technique capable of supplying ultimate truth. He relied instead on the analytical capacity of the mind, which he believed was totally detached from material reality.

Descartes explained his approach to problem solving in his *Dis-course on Method* (1637). It contained four basic axioms: (1) accept only the self-evident as true, (2) divide every problem into its basic components, (3) proceed from the simple to the complex, (4) review continually to avoid error. Thus Cartesianism employed the *deductive method* of the scholastics. Deduction begins with the formulation of principles and through a logical process arrives at a knowledge of the particular. Beginning with his own universal doubt and his ability to contemplate perfection, Descartes arrived at the self-evident proof of his own existence ("I think; therefore, I am") and the existence of God. He continued this logical process by employing mathematics, which he believed provided the precise language necessary to unravel the mystery of a rational universe. In the process he formulated analytic geometry, which enabled him to express geometric forms with algebraic notation. Descartes's great weakness lay in his predilection to spin out theoretical hypotheses based on rather shaky premises without experimental verification.

Together Bacon and Descartes enhanced the belief in man's rational capacity and also demonstrated that the inductive and deductive methods must be integrated in the search for scientific knowledge.

Scientific Societies. The growing interest in science during the seventeenth century was reflected in the creation of scientific societies that drew together the greatest minds of the age. The royal patronage often extended to these organizations reflects the increased respectability of scientific inquiry. The *Accademia dei Lincei* was founded in Rome in 1611. The Royal Society of London for Improving Natural Knowledge received its charter from Charles II in 1662. Its French counterpart, the *Académie Royale des Sciences,* was granted a charter by Louis XIV in 1666. The great reputations of these societies grew as their illustrious members pooled their intellects to solve practical problems and expand the frontier of theoretical knowledge.

Empirical Science. Experimental science made impressive and continual gains after 1450. Empiricism was aided by the invention of many instruments that added precision to laboratory calculation. They included the pendulum clock, the telescope, the microscope, the barometer, the thermometer, and the air (vacuum) pump.

VESALIUS. Andreas Vesalius (1514–1564) was the founder of modern anatomy and the precursor of biology. His studies while professor of surgery and medicine at the University of Padua led to the publication of *On the Structure of the Human Body* (1543). *De Fabrica,* as it is generally known, was the most significant treatise on human anatomy since antiquity. Its precise anatomical drawings and nomenclature provided the foundation for all subsequent anatomical study.

GALILEO. Galileo's telescopic observations convinced him of the validity of the Copernican hypothesis (see p. 152). His defense of Copernicus opened a controversy with Church authorities, and the publication of his *Dialogue concerning the Two World Systems, the Ptolemaic and the Copernican* (1632) led to his condemnation by the Roman Inquisition. The *Dialogue* was placed on the Index; Galileo recanted his astronomical theories; and he was placed under permanent house arrest. It was during his last years that he performed his greatest service to science. Galileo, like Descartes, was convinced that mathematical laws controlled the universe. Combining the inductive technique of controlled experimentation with the deduction of mathematical abstractions, he disproved Aristotle's theories of motion. In his *Dialogue and Mathematical Discourses concerning the Two New Sciences* (1638), he formulated the laws of inertia and acceleration. This work provided the foundation for the field of study known as *dynamics*.

BOYLE. Robert Boyle (1627–1691) is often referred to as the father of modern chemistry. With the aid of Robert Hooke, he improved the vacuum pump, with which he made several significant discoveries. He formulated Boyle's Law (pressure × volume = a constant), and he studied the function of air in the propagation of sound. His chemical experiments led him to the belief that minute particles formed *corpuscles* of various weights and sizes which, in turn, imparted physical and chemical properties to all physical substances. Although he was unable to prove his theory, his ideas undermined contemporary theories of alchemy and prepared the way for further discoveries in chemistry and physics. Besides his own contributions to science, Boyle stimulated the practice of precise and logical scientific inquiry among his colleagues in the Royal Society.

HARVEY. William Harvey (1578–1657) received his education at Padua's renowned school of medicine. Returning to England, he devoted years of study to the mysterious operation of the heart. The results of his painstaking experimentation were published in a concise treatise entitled *On the Motion of the Heart and Blood* (1628). He demonstrated conclusively that the heart provided the impetus for the circulation of the blood in a closed system in which the arteries carried blood to the extremities and the veins returned it to the heart. A gap in this theory was closed with Marcello Malpighi's discovery in 1661 of the microscopic capillaries that connect the arteries and veins. Harvey's discovery opened the way for a more accurate explanation of human physiology, including digestion and respiration, although many decades passed before the implications of his work were fully understood.

Mathematics. The complex problems studied during the seventeenth century required precise new mathematical techniques. Developments in mathematics also provided the analytical tools necessary to deal with problems that could not readily be subjected to laboratory analysis. The most significant accomplishments in the development of arithmetic language include John Napier's discovery of logarithms, René Descartes's analytical geometry, and Pierre de Fermat's differential calculus. Blaise Pascal played a major role in developing probability theory and the properties of conic sections. Isaac Newton (1666) and Gottfried Leibniz (1676) arrived independently at the formulation of integral calculus.

The Newtonian Synthesis. The work of Isaac Newton (1642–1727) was a fitting crown to seventeenth-century science. It is certainly true that Newton drew upon the discoveries of Descartes, Kepler, and Galileo, but his concept of the universe surpassed their individual efforts. As a young Cambridge scholar, Newton formulated the binomial theorem and experimented with the nature of light. Although many of the conclusions contained in *Optics* (1704) proved erroneous, the work formed the basis of further investigation.

Newton's greatest achievements were presented in the *Mathematical Principles of Natural Philosophy* (1687). In the *Principia* he formulated his laws of motion and gravitation. His three laws of motion state that: (1) bodies maintain their velocity unless acted upon by a force, (2) acceleration (that is, a change in velocity) is directly proportional to the force applied, and (3) for every action there is an equal and opposite reaction. Newton's universal law of gravitation states that the mutual attraction of two bodies is directly proportional to their respective masses and inversely proportional to the distances between them. Newton's theorems demonstrated that Kepler's celestial mechanics and Galileo's terrestrial mechanics were part of the same universal set of laws and that all bodies, whether large or small, on earth or in the heavens, operated together in a gigantic world machine.

Study of Man and Society. A procession of great scientists created a vision of the universe controlled by natural law, whose secrets could be revealed by rational analysis. In the minds of the literate public, mankind and society came to be regarded as natural phenomena whose basic laws could also be discovered if they were subjected to the same probing analysis once reserved for the planets.

PASCAL. Blaise Pascal (1623–1662) was an eminent French mathematician and religious mystic who pondered the implications of the scientific discoveries. He was stunned by the contrast between the immense and complex universe on the one hand and man's insignificance on the other. Although he despaired of finding his way to God through reason, he saw man's intellect as an ennobling quality. In his *Thoughts*, published posthumously in 1670, he described man as a weak reed buffeted by the forces of nature and yet standing heroically alone in possession of consciousness, which could ponder the forces of nature.

SPINOZA. In a world where orthodoxy was crumbling, Baruch Spinoza (1632–1677) was expelled from the synagogue of Amsterdam for his unorthodox views. By carrying Descartes's natural philosophy to its logical conclusions, he arrived at the pantheistic view that the physical world was not a creation of God but rather a visible manifestation of his all-encompassing attributes. In *Ethics Demonstrated in a Geometrical Manner* (1677), he argued that mankind as part of the universal order should be studied in a scientific way: "I shall consider human actions and desires in exactly the same manner as though I were concerned with lines, planes, and solids."

BAYLE. Like Pascal and Spinoza, French philosopher Pierre Bayle (1647–1706) absorbed Cartesian skepticism. Both his intellect and his observations of the bloody consequences of religious intolerance led him to the conclusion that theological certainty was impossible and religious tolerance essential. In his *Historical and Critical Dictionary* (1697), he applied the tenets of logic to the study of history and in the process rejected the Bible as a sound guide to ethical conduct. Thus he opened the way for scientific study of history stripped of its theological underpinnings.

HOBBES. In England Thomas Hobbes (1588–1679) applied the scientific outlook to the study of politics in his monumental treatise *Leviathan* (1670). Behind his political theory lay a thoroughly mechanistic view of mankind. Hobbes began his study with an examination of man as a human animal in a hypothetical "state of nature," without either government or other cultural constraints. Hobbes believed that man had a limited capacity to reason but employed it only to satisfy basic appetites and to avoid pain. This individualistic search for pleasure and security led to a "war . . . of every man against every man," with the result that the "life of man [is] solitary, poor, nasty, brutish, and short." In order to end anarchy and secure tranquility, Hobbes held that men surrender their natural rights to a sovereign state, which he called the Leviathan. It maintained absolute control through the threat of force, and its only obligation to its subjects was to protect them from their fellowmen. Although Hobbes supported the concept of absolutism, monarchists did not like his ideas because they were based on secular utilitarianism rather than on the concept of divine right.

LOCKE. John Locke (1632–1704) shares with Hobbes the distinction of being one of the most influential political theorists of modern times. The ideas expressed in his *Second Treatise on Civil Government* (1690) had a significant impact on the development of English parliamentary democracy, French political theory, and the American Declaration of Independence.

Locke agreed with Hobbes that government is not divinely ordained but rather is the direct outgrowth of natural human activity. However, Locke's political theories differ sharply from those developed in *Leviathan* because he disagreed with Hobbes's view of human nature. Locke believed that men in a "state of nature" (that is, without government) were guided more by reason than passion and enjoyed the inalienable rights of life, liberty, and property. He argued that government arose primarily from a need to adjudicate property rights and that when forming governments, men gave up their unlimited freedom of action for a well-ordered society but did not surrender their inalienable rights. Thus, while Hobbes's contract theory lead to absolutism, Locke's postulated limited government.

At a time when religious and scientific dogmatism continued to wrack Europe, Locke pleaded for a more balanced outlook. In his *Essay concerning Human Understanding*, he denied the existence of innate ideas or truths in the mind of man. He argued that all knowledge comes from sense impressions and thus no one can hope to obtain absolute truth. His *Letter concerning Toleration* extended this reasoning to religion, arguing that each individual should be free to find his own way to God without persecution so long as he did not disturb the political order.

GROTIUS. Dutch scholar Hugo Grotius (1583–1645) attempted to apply the same cold logic to the examination of international affairs that Hobbes and Locke applied to the government of individual states. Amid the bloody anarchy that constituted the international relations of the age, he hoped to discover those natural laws that would promote harmony among states or, failing that, at least substitute controlled violence for indiscriminate slaughter. Although his treatise *On the Laws of War and Peace* (1625) had little immediate impact, Grotius may be credited with formulating the tenet that sovereign states must be restrained in their dealings with other states by the same natural laws that guide men in society.

Baroque Consciousness

The seventeenth century is often called the baroque age. The term *baroque* is difficult to define, but examples of this style are usually immediately recognizable. No longer satisfied with the orderly constraint of Renaissance classicism, artists, architects, and writers began to explore new avenues of expression. Their work is marked by a flamboyance and exuberance that many critics have condemned as extravagant. However, it is just those qualities that reflect the dynamism of the seventeenth century. This section will trace the main currents of baroque art as well as the work of those men whose mode of expression did not fit within that dominant movement.

Architecture. The baroque spirit found fulfillment in seventeenth-century architecture. The monumental palaces, public buildings, and churches, with their grandiose exteriors and brilliantly decorated interiors, reflect the sense of majesty and power of those who controlled society.

ITALY. Rome was the center of Italian baroque architecture, and its new buildings set the style for Europe. Giovanni Bernini (1598–1680) was the incomparable master of this style. He completed the exterior design of Saint Peter's Basilica with a piazza enclosed by the sweeping oval colonnade and with interior decorations whose focal point is the great canopy over the high altar.

As a sculptor Bernini ranks among the great masters. His *Ecstasy of Saint Teresa* decorates the Santa Maria della Vittoria in Rome, and his busts of Cardinal Borghese and Louis XIV demonstrate why his talent was in such great demand. Among the other renowned seventeenth-century Italian architects who are remembered for their part in the revival of church building were Carlo Maderna, Carlo Rainaldi, and Francesco Borromini.

FRANCE. French architecture in the seventeenth century reflected the triumph of absolute monarchy in the same way that Italian building reflected the resurgence of Roman Catholicism. François Mansart's work on the châteaux of Balleroy and Blois shows the strong influence of classicism, which resisted the influence of less restrained Italian baroque. The Versailles Palace is the greatest example of seventeenth-century monumental architecture and demonstrates the taste of Europe's most powerful monarch. It was constructed under the supervision of architect Louis Le Vau, interior designer Charles Le Brun, and gardener André Lenôtre and completed by Jules Hardouin-Mansart. Although its exterior design retains the classical style, its enormous size and the richness of its interior decoration place it within the context of the baroque age.

ENGLAND. English Gothic architecture adapted slowly to Continental modes, but by the beginning of the seventeenth century, its architects began to respond to Italian influence. This development is evident in the work of Inigo Jones, who studied in Italy and became court architect of James I and Charles I. Christopher Wren was

the most prominent English designer of the century. He is best remembered for his numerous parish churches, which he built after the
great fire in 1666 and for Saint Paul's Cathedral, the most magnificent example of baroque architecture in England. The adaptation
of Italian baroque techniques reached their peak in the work of John
Vanbrugh whose grandoise Blenheim Palace and Castle Howard
enjoyed only short popularity.

CENTRAL EUROPE. Architectural trends in the Germanies reflect the
continuing Hapsburg rivalry with France and the rejuvenation of
Catholicism as a result of the Catholic Reformation. The most renowned Austrian architect was Johann Fischer Von Erlach, who designed the Viennese Karlskirche and the Schönbrunn palace.

Painting. The self-assurance and optimism reflected in High
Renaissance classicism gave way to a sense of impending doom as
religious controversy and dynastic wars conspired to shred the fabric
of European culture at the beginning of the sixteenth century. The
attempt to draw meaning from the engulfing chaos, using techniques
inherited from the Renaissance, is known as *mannerism*. Bronzino
(d. 1572), Tintoretto (d. 1594), and El Greco (d. 1614) (see p.
58) were among the most brilliant practitioners of this style, which
relied on complexity and movement to generate a sense of suspense
and wonder.

The baroque style emerged at the beginning of the seventeenth
century, as the intellectual community began to regain its equilibrium.
The baroque mentality came to accept the operation of powerful and
complex natural forces that controlled the universe, while at the same
time it reaffirmed the unique power of human reason to understand
and manipulate those mute forces. The art arising from this outlook
stressed contrasts, dynamic tension, and movement.

ITALY. There were several major avenues of development in Italian
baroque painting. Michelangelo Caravaggio (ca. 1565–1609) produced powerful works by relying on visual realism and the sharp
juxtaposition of light and shadow. His down-to-earth treatment of
Christian subjects was often criticized as irreverent. Annibale Carracci
(1560–1609), best remembered for his frescoes in the Farnese gallery,
led a school that returned to the strict application of classical rules.
Decorative ceiling art, a hallmark of seventeenth-century church
decoration, found vivid expression in the work of Giovanni Gaulli and
Giovanni Tiepolo.

SPAIN. Diego Velásquez (1599–1660) was Spain's greatest seventeenth-century artist. His portraits, including those of the Spanish
royal family and Pope Innocent, project both a vivid visual reality
and strong psychological insight. Other Spanish artists of the period

include José Ribera, noted for realistic religious works, and Bartolomé Esteban Murillo, known for his sentimental genre paintings and religious works.

FRANCE. Among the most significant French artists of the period were Nicolas Poussin (1594–1665) and Claude Gellée (Lorrain) (1600–1682). Both lived in Rome, where they adopted a classical technique and outlook. Of the artists who worked in France, the most significant were Georges de la Tour (1593–1652) and Louis Le Nain (1593–1648).

LOW COUNTRIES. The seventeenth century witnessed a golden age of Dutch and Flemish art. The Fleming Peter Paul Rubens (1577–1640) was most representative of the baroque consciousness. He was a master in depicting human action, and his skill in producing vibrant flesh tones has rarely been equalled. Rembrandt van Rijn (1606–1669) raised Dutch art to the pinnacle of greatness. He played down movement while heightening emotional drama with lighting and shadow. Rembrandt's most familiar masterpieces include *The Night Watch* (1642), *Aristotle Contemplating a Bust of Homer* (1653), and *The Syndics of the Draper's Guild* (1661). Other Dutch masters that deserve mention include Frans Hals (1580?–1666), noted for his group portraits of bourgeois dignitaries, and a host of genre and landscape artists including Jan Steen (1626–1679), Jacob van Ruisdael (1628?–1682), Pieter de Hooch (1629–1683?), and Jan Vermeer (1632–1675).

ENGLAND. The most important names associated with English art in the seventeenth century were both Dutchmen. Anthony van Dyck (1599–1641) was court painter to Charles I, and Sir Peter Lely recorded for posterity the images of England's aristocracy, setting a style for portrait painting that lasted through the next century.

Literature. Seventeenth-century European literature met the same high standards set by the other arts. Dramatics dominated the French scene. Pierre Corneille (1600–1684) attempted to break away from classical rules in his idealist drama *Le Cid*. Molière (Jean Baptiste Poquelin, 1622–1673) was a realist whose comedies (for example, *Tartuffe*) could gently mock human foibles or scathingly denounce mankind's rapacity. Jean Racine (1639–1699) wrote tragedies whose themes, as in *Phèdre*, dealt with the destructive force of uncontrollable passion.

In England John Milton (1608–1674) wrote *Paradise Lost* (1667) and took his place as the greatest epic poet in the English language. The poem deals with issues at the heart of baroque intellectual ferment, including the relationship of man to God, the dynamic tension between reason and passion, and the delicate balance between universal order and chaos. John Dryden (1631–1700) achieved fame as a satiric poet and literary critic. John Bunyan (1628–1688), a poorly educated ex-soldier, wrote *Pilgrim's Progress,* a Christian allegory that spoke directly to England's common man with powerful images constructed in simple language.

Music. The innovation of musical expression was the most novel development in the seventeenth-century arts. The opera, combining elaborate staging, music, and librettos, came into its own. Among the greatest operatic composers of the period were Monteverdi, Lully, and Purcell. Instrumental music, relying on the variation inherent in the chromatic scale, was also developed by such composers as Alessandro Scarlatti, Antonio Vivaldi, and Girolamo Frescobaldi. They were aided by the improvement of musical instruments, including the violin and the piano, and refinements of the organ. Baroque composition reached its peak in the work of Johann Sebastian Bach and George Frederick Handel (see p. 172).

14

The Enlightenment

The scientific achievement of the seventeenth century, capped by the Newtonian synthesis, altered the presuppositions of the European intellectual community. The rationalist spirit broke the confines of science and expanded to encompass all areas of human interest. This eighteenth-century phenomenon by which every question was subjected to the test of reason created a cultural climate known as the Enlightenment.

The Philosophes

The leaders of the Enlightenment were know as *philosophes* (a term not synonymous with philosophers). Although as a group the philosophes included such great intellects as David Hume and Immanuel Kant, they were most influential as the popularizers of rationalist concepts. What they lacked in depth they made up for with clarity, wit, incisiveness, their ability to turn a phrase, and an amateur's enthusiasm for any activity that would put their credo of rationalism to the test. Although as the name implies, the philosophes predominated in France, their group contained brilliant representatives from every area of Europe and from America. They moved easily from one country to the other, even in wartime, for they considered themselves citizens of the "republic of letters." Physical absence of a philosophe from the social circle of salons and reading rooms stimulated voluminous correspondence that maintained intellectual contact and sustained the flow of ideas.

Beliefs of the Enlightenment

The character of the Enlightenment can best be understood by examining the presuppositions most widely held by those who fostered the movement.

Natural Law. Newton's greatest achievement had been to demonstrate that the physical world functioned through the universal operation of certain natural laws. The interaction of matter and force thus produced eternal and immutable patterns. The search for natural laws governing the operation of human activity soon permeated to the very core of the eighteenth-century intellect.

Rationalism. Reliance on reason was another hallmark of the age. Newton and his colleagues had reinforced the growing belief in man's capacity to find truth through the agency of human reason. At the same time, there was a tendency to abandon abstract metaphysical constructions and to concentrate on empirical knowledge within the finite realm of experience. It should be remembered, however, that despite their skepticism, the philosophes themselves were often guilty of jumping to erroneous conclusions based upon a priori beliefs.

Optimism. The possibility of virtually limitless human progress followed logically from the acceptance of natural laws and the rational capacity to discover them. Among some philosophes, this optimism became utopianism. However, optimism was tempered by men like Voltaire, who pointed out that the world was inhabited by people, not by disembodied reason, and that where there are people logic often fails.

Activism. Another characteristic that set the philosophes apart from the role of traditional philosophers was their activism. Seeing the possibility of making a better world, they set out to do it. The philosophes became propagandists against the obscurantism of established religion and the inefficiency of hidebound governments. They strove to strip away every impediment to the full development of human nature. The corrosive effects of these attacks on the institutions and values of European society no doubt played an important part in the ultimate collapse of the ancien régime.

The Philosophers

Voltaire once referred to himself as a sparkling stream that did not run deep. During the Enlightenment, however, there were philosophers of profound intellect who altered man's understanding of human consciousness and its relationship to the physical world.

Locke. John Locke (1632–1704) was the most influential philosopher of the Enlightenment. At every turn one discovers either acceptance and elaboration of his ideas or critical analysis of them. In any case it was impossible to ignore him. His political theories have already been discussed on page 158. Of more central concern for the Enlightenment was his *Essay on Human Understanding* (1690). The basic premise of this work is the repudiation of innate ideas. For Locke the mind at birth is a "blank page" (*tabula rasa*), which throughout life passively receives sense data from the outside world. Even the most complex ideas are simply elaborate constructions derived from a myriad of experiences. This empirical theory, coupled with Locke's belief that human nature was essentially good, being devoid of the Original Sin of traditional Christianity, had wide-ranging implications. If man were rational and receptive to all ideas, then environmental reform and universal education could lead to a perfect human society. This notion was elaborated in Étienne de Condillac's essay *Origins of Human Knowledge* (1754), and in Claude Adrien Helvetius's *On the Mind* (1758).

Berkeley. Despite the influence of Locke's psychology, certain logical inconsistencies in his empirical analysis soon came under scrutiny. While Locke argued that all knowledge of the real world was filtered through the senses, he nevertheless believed that the mind could formulate general laws with certainty. This was possible because primary qualities of objects (size, shape, number, and so on) were not distorted by the senses, while secondary qualities (taste, smell, color, and so on) could be. Anglican Bishop George Berkeley (1685–1753) denied Locke's distinction between qualities and argued in his *Dialogues* (1713) that physical reality exists only because it is perceived by the individual's mind—that is, only minds and ideas resulting from sense data exist in the physical world. However, Berkeley added that sense data recorded by the finite mind are emanations from the infinite mind of God.

Hume. The Scottish philosopher David Hume (1711–1776) carried Berkeley's criticism of Locke to its stark conclusion. In an *Enquiry Concerning Human Understanding* (1752), Hume denied the existence of the mind as a distinct entity capable of perceiving reality. He argued that sensations tell us nothing about the real world and that even the phenomenon of cause and effect, taken for granted by common sense, was at best a possibility and at worst an illusion. As for Berkeley's God, he might be fabricated to assuage fear but certainly could not be found among the random collection of distorted sensations with which the human brain operated. And without God, or support of reason or natural law, upon what did man base his moral decisions except upon the changing tides of his fellowman's approval or disapproval? Although Hume had followed Locke into a cul-de-sac of total skepticism, it was Locke's optimistic empiricism that inspired the eighteenth century. Hume won the plaudits of some of his contemporaries for his erudition, but the full import of his words were realized only in the more skeptical twentieth century.

Kant. Immanuel Kant (1724–1804) was a German professor of metaphysics and logic who ranks with Hume among the seminal thinkers of the eighteenth century. He attempted to rescue philosophy and moral order from the abject relativism into which Hume had plunged it. In his *Critique of Pure Reason* (1781), Kant dealt with the problem of mind and experience. Like the empiricists, he admitted that the senses are capable of reporting only appearances. Contrary to Locke, however, he argued that the mind is an active agent whose natural structure of categories and logical patterns exists prior to external stimulation. It is the active sifting and categorizing of the mind that creates order and understanding out of what would otherwise be random sensation. Since the physical world objectively exists and is always perceived in the same way because of the structure of the human mind, it followed for Kant that science is a useful technique to produce practical knowledge concerning the everyday world of appearance (the *phenomenal* world). However, knowledge of ultimate reality (the *noumenal* world) has to be derived from a totally different source. It is *practical reason* or intuition that provides knowledge of this reality, including the existence of God and ethical principles. Man is duty bound to make moral decisions based on his faith in free will, immortality, and the existence of God. The basis for moral judgments must not be whether they will benefit the individual but whether they would be reasonable if universally applied.

The Religious Debate

The critical analysis of traditional Christianity and the formulation of new religious concepts formed a significant part of Enlightenment thought. The philosophes condemned the corpus of Christian dogma as a collection of ancient folktales and obscurantist witchcraft, and they attacked the Catholic church as spiritually, intellectually, and socially oppressive. Voltaire condensed his feelings with the battle cry *"Écrasez l'infâme!"* ("Crush the infamous thing") and subjected Christian ritual, bigotry, and superstition to scathing ridicule.

Deism emerged as the most popular substitute for Christianity for many philosophes. The deist philosophy accepted God as a Creator who had set the world machine in motion in accordance with the natural laws elucidated by Isaac Newton. Alexander Pope put the deist view succinctly when he wrote, "Nature and nature's laws lay hid in night:/God said, let Newton be! and all was light." The Deity did not interfere in human affairs. He had endowed every human with a beneficent nature and the mental faculties to set his own life in harmony with all nature. Thus, while Locke and the rational Christians argued that nothing in their faith was contrary to nature, the deists argued that Christian faith was irrelevant and that morality could be discovered by reason. Deism was thus a highly intellectualized movement whose followers demonstrated little religious zeal. A few empiricists denied the possibility of knowing the existence of God, and Baron Holbach was the best known of a handful of outspoken atheists. Voltaire's epigram "philosophy for the classes, religion for the masses" shows that even he regarded organized religion as a necessity to control the unenlightened multitude.

While the intellectual elite accepted the deist position, the majority were moved by the need for a more personal God. The German Pietists drew large numbers of devout Christians to their ranks. The Pietists rejected both the theological authority of the Lutheran church and the cold detachment of rationalist deism. They turned instead to biblical study and quiet contemplation in an effort to foster personal contact with God and through it moral rejuvenation and a virtuous life. In England John Wesley (1703–1791), under the influence of Pietism, founded the Methodist movement. Methodism was based upon a belief in free will and a rigorous code of self-improvement through group activity, including public confession, prayer, and worship. As an Anglican priest, Wesley had no intention of establishing a separate sect, but growing disapproval of his movement, particularly its uninhibited emotionalism, led to a withdrawal of church support. Undaunted, Wesley continued to preach at thousands of open-air rallies, where his converts experienced a spiritual renewal that the staid established church could not provide. By 1784 the Methodist church had set off on its own course. Methodism must be regarded as one of the most significant social and religious phenomena of eighteenth-century England.

Social Criticism and Political Theory

The philosophes were almost consumed with a desire for order and efficiency. In their most optimistic moments, they often projected the possibility of a perfectly harmonious society of enlightened citizens. Among the most brilliant social critics and political theorists, however, there emerged the realization that reason is a limited force in the complex interaction of men in society.

Montesquieu. Charles de Secondat, baron de Montesquieu (1689–1755), was a member of the Gascon nobility, born to wealth, social position, and political office. Despite his vested interest in the regime, his lifelong inquiry into the nature and application of political power led him to conclusions that undermined its authority. Montesquieu's first great success was the *Persian Letters* (1721), a satire in which two Persian visitors reveal constant amazement at the incongruities of Western culture. Here at their best are the Enlightenment's witty attack on pompous authority and a cosmopolitan plea for toleration. In his greatest work, *The Spirit of the Laws* (1748), Montesquieu applied an empirical method to discover both the underlying principles of political organization and the factors that promoted diversity in political experience. He reserved his greatest admiration for the checks and balances of the English constitution, which, he concluded, protected aristocratic rights from a capricious monarch. Although his analysis may have produced erroneous judgments, the English constitutional system came to be praised as a model of enlightened government, and the French monarchy suffered by comparison. Because of his empirical approach, Montesquieu is often regarded as the founder of the social sciences.

Voltaire. François Marie Arouet (1694–1778), known as Voltaire, was the leading figure of the French Enlightenment. His intellectual productivity ranged across a spectrum that included philosophy, science, political theory, history, drama, and prose. His best-known works include *Letters on the English* (1733), which analyzes English institutions to the detriment of France; *Elements of Newtonian Philosophy* (1738), an explication for laymen; a biography of Charles XII; a multivolumed *Essay on General History* (1756); and *Candide* (1759), a satirical romance in which the misadventures of its hero demonstrate that this is hardly "the best of all possible worlds."

Voltaire, the archcritic of the age, has been criticized for his negativism. But his outlook was a combination of both hopes and doubts. Although he believed that reason was man's greatest asset and intellectual freedom its prerequisite, he regarded history as a chronicle of man's folly and vice. He was personally intolerant of ideas with which he disagreed and saw little possibility for general human enlightenment. At the same time, he attacked the arrogance of dogmatic intolerance, the Byzantine inefficiency of government, and the naive optimism of rationalist utopianism. Ultimately he staked his hopes for the improvement of the human condition on the slow spread of reason and the enlightened despotism of such philosopher kings as Frederick the Great of Prussia.

Rousseau. Jean Jacques Rousseau (1712–1778) is the most controversial figure in the Age of Enlightenment. Painfully shy and morose, he did not fit into the brilliant life of salon society. He scorned

Voltaire's flippant skepticism and maintained an abiding faith in man's essential goodness. While he honored the work of rational empiricists, he considered intuition and emotion to be better sources of truth.

Rousseau, as Locke and Hobbes before him, built his social and political theories upon hypotheses concerning man's nature. In his *Discourse on the Origin of Inequality* (1755), he wrote that in a state of nature (before political organization) man was essentially good and happy. Contrary to Locke and Hobbes, however, he rejected the view that men had ever left this condition by entering into a legitimate social contract. On the contrary, they had been forced into an illicit political and social organization by covetous oppressors who robbed them of their freedom and appropriated the commonwealth for personal gain. Constructed upon these evil grounds, society had become the source of man's corruption and debasement.

Rousseau developed his argument in *The Social Contract* (1762), his greatest work and one of the most influential books of modern times. In this treatise he reiterated the essential goodness of man in the state of nature but reasoned that mankind required social organization to achieve full potential. He therefore advocated a true social contract—a perpetual agreement that would form a tight community akin to a biological organism resulting in both individual fulfillment and the common good. The community was to be guided and regulated by a sovereign power, which was neither the limited government of Locke nor the Leviathan of Hobbes but the "general will." By this Rousseau meant not the rule of the majority but a mystical summation of the people's collective will voluntarily established by common consent. This nebulous concept has provided arguments for both democracy and totalitarian dictatorship, a paradox that arises from the ambiguities and contradictions of Rousseau's thought.

Economic Theory

The eighteenth-century presuppositions that natural law guides all activity and that men are capable of making rational decisions in their own best interest had a great impact on economic theory. During the seventeenth and early eighteenth century, mercantilism was the accepted view of political economy. Such proponents of this view as England's Oliver Cromwell and France's Colbert maintained that the government should regulate the economy for the best interest of the state.

Physiocrats. The traditional view was challenged by François Quesnay (1694–1774), around whom formed a group of economic thinkers known as the *physiocrats*. Quesnay held that only agriculture produces wealth and that individuals who attempt to gain the greatest possible profit make the most efficient use of their resources. He therefore called for an end to all economic regulation of agriculture and for the abolition of all taxes except those on agricultural production. This concept of government noninterference in the economy is summed up in the phrase *laissez faire, laissez passer* ("leave it alone, let it be"). The dogmatism of the physiocrats and the revolutionary implications of the single-tax system in a society dominated by aristocratic landowners undermined their position. In addition their agrarian outlook would soon be dated by industrialization. Nevertheless, "laissez faire!" became the economic battle cry of the future.

Adam Smith. Adam Smith (1723–1790) accepted the physiocrats' basic economic assumptions. He believed that the marketplace operated according to the law of supply and demand, that men were economically motivated, that they could make rational decisions in their own best interests, and finally that the sum total of individual well-being was the well-being of society. Government economic interference was therefore illogical and bound to be disruptive. He broke with the physiocrats, however, in concluding that commerce and industry can both be rightly considered as truly productive economic sectors. Smith's ideas are contained in *The Wealth of Nations* (1776), one of the most influential works of the nineteenth century.

Arts and Letters

The fine arts of the eighteenth century reflect the philosophy of the Enlightenment and the patronage of an aristocratic elite determined to stop time on a beautiful spring morning. Reason and nature were combined in an outlook that stressed the classical characteristics of order, form, and balance. At the same time, the aristocracy nurtured a life style of lightheartedness and graceful elegance. At its best eighteenth-century art expressed the human spirit in civilized equilibrium, and at its worst it reflected a heartless and shallow hedonism.

Literature. Alexander Pope (1688–1744) was the most highly acclaimed literary figure of the first half of the century. He won his reputation and fortune as a translator of the *Iliad* and the *Odyssey*. His *Essay on Man* (1744) not only reflects his optimistic philosophy but is a showpiece for the measured cadence of the couplets that were his trademark. Pope's friend Jonathan Swift (1667–1745) did not share his optimism; *Gulliver's Travels* (1726) is a political and social satire that places Swift more in the camp of Voltaire.

The eigtheenth century witnessed the emergence of the modern novel. Representative of English prose are Samuel Richardson's sentimental *Clarissa* (1747) and Henry Fielding's raucous *Tom Jones* (1749), while French contributions include Pierre de Marivaux's *La Vie de Marianne* (1741) and Jean Jacques Rousseau's *La Nouvelle Héloïse* (1761).

Painting. Eighteenth-century painting provides a clear reflection of aristocratic taste and life style. The French Rococo style at its best can be seen in the work of Antoine Watteau (1684–1721). In his *Embarkation for Cythera,* the wilderness becomes a garden where cupids flit among the trees and elegantly clothed lovers whisper. François Boucher (1703–1770) and Jean Honoré Fragonard (1732–1806) continued this motif through the century. Their paintings reflect a sense of the sweetness of life that, as in Boucher's work, often borders on the salacious. Jean Baptist Chardin (1699–1779) concentrated on solid middle-class subjects in whom he perceived the stability of French society. Across the English Channel, Thomas Gainsborough (1727–1788) and Sir Joshua Reynolds (1723–1792) portrayed the gentry as they saw themselves and hoped others saw them. William Hogarth (1697–1764), on the other hand, shared Fielding's view of life and the English aristocracy, which was more human and less respectful. His narrative sequences *Marriage à la Mode* and *The Rake's Progress* poke fun at aristocratic affectation and decadence.

Music. German composers challenged Italian musical dominance by the middle of the eighteenth century. Johann Sebastian Bach (1685–1750) is best known for his religious themes, which remain a high point of baroque music. His life and work greatly influenced the German composers who followed him. Joseph Haydn (1732–1809) created a prodigious body of instrumental music. Over one hundred symphonies reflect his lifelong effort to mold the symphony orchestra into a body of many tongues that spoke with one voice. Wolfgang Amadeus Mozart (1756–1791) followed Haydn's lead. The sheer brilliance of Mozart's gifts stunned the musical world. His symphonic masterpieces and string quartets built upon the work of Haydn; his operas, including *The Marriage of Figaro* (1786), *Don Giovanni* (1787), and *The Magic Flute* (1791), integrated voice and orchestra at a level never before attained. In England the German expatriate George Frederick Handel (1685–1759) failed in his efforts to popularize the Italian operatic style, but his oratorios, particularly *The Messiah* (1742), made him a national hero. In the effort to develop symphonic music, composers were limited particularly by the horn instruments, which were primitive by today's standard. On the other hand, the violins of Antonius Stradivarius (1644–1737) have never been surpassed, and many are still in use today.

Scientific Discoveries

The spectacular theoretical achievements capped by Newton in the seventeenth century were not repeated in the eighteenth. However, much of importance was done in the realm of theoretical refinement and in the laboratory.

Physics. In physics Pierre Laplace (1749–1827) refined the Newtonian mechanics to demonstrate that the solar system was a self-regulating mechanism. Joseph Lagrange (1736–1813) developed applications for differential calculus and was instrumental in the formulation and adoption of the metric system. Benjamin Franklin (1706–1790) advanced the study of electricity with his demonstration that lightning is an electrical discharge. In Italy Luigi Galvani (1737–1798) studied the effect of electrical shock on muscles and Alessandro Volta (1745–1827) developed the voltaic cell or battery.

Chemistry. Advances in chemistry were among the most notable of the eighteenth century. Laboratory experimentation brought a clearer understanding of the complex gaseous makeup of the air and of the phenomenon of combustion. Joseph Black (1728–1810) isolated carbon dioxide; Henry Cavendish (1731–1810) followed with the separation of hydrogen; and Joseph Priestly (1733–1804) shared with Carl Scheele (1742–1786) the discovery of oxygen. In France Antoine Lavoisier (1743–1794) gave theoretical structure to the experimental work already performed, which earned for him the title "Father of Chemistry."

Botany. Metaphysical assumptions concerning the creation of the universe blocked developments in the biological sciences, which thus lagged behind physics and chemistry. The debate over the proper technique of biological classification reflected a clear philosophic division. Carolus Linnaeus (1707–1778), a Swedish naturalist, used sexual characteristics to classify plants into distinct species and genera. However, Georges Buffon (1707–1788), a French botanist, argued that such a classification fostered artificiality and did not reflect the continuity of the *great chain of being*, in which all living things are linked. The issue was not resolved in the eighteenth century.

Technology. Two technical innovations of the era had a profound practical impact. In both cases the work was done primarily by skilled artisans rather than by theoretical scientists. Thomas Newcomen (1663–1729), a blacksmith, developed a practical steam engine that came into general use in the second decade of the century. Improved versions of the engine provided the motive force for the industrial revolution. John Harrison (1693–1776), a watchmaker, perfected the chronometer that enabled seamen to ascertain their longitude and thus their exact location. This single development had enormous ramifications for worldwide commerce.

Dissemination of Knowledge

The Enlightenment encompassed a small literate elite who lived in a select world, psychologically if not physically apart from the toiling masses. This world was one of leisure and physical comfort, and it allowed the time and resources for intellectual cultivation.

The Salon. The *salon* became a focus of intellectual life in France. Within the rococo setting, intellectually gifted hostesses would draw a group of sparkling intellects into brilliant conversation. The salon, though often catering to affectations, became an important arena for the cross-fertilization of ideas.

Journalism. In England the male-dominated coffeehouses and reading rooms provided sharper and coarser sounding boards, but the impact was the same. English society was remarkably liberal for its day, and journalists like Joseph Addison (1672–1719) and Richard Steele (1672–1729) were a constant marvel to the French if for no other reason than their ability to stay out of jail. Their *Spectator* was among the most popular of early English newspapers that provided a forum for the avalanche of ideas and opinions hawked by men of affairs. The same can be said for the *Gentlemen's Magazine* and the *Edinburgh Review;* they both set a very high standard for periodical literature.

The Encyclopedia. The greatest single accomplishment in the effort to disseminate the ideas of the Enlightenment came with the publication of the *Encyclopedia* edited in France by Denis Diderot (1713–1784). The mammoth work, produced in twenty-eight volumes between 1751 and 1772, was designed as a compendium of all useful knowledge. Contributions included so many leading intellectuals that the terms *encyclopedist* and *philosophe* became virtually synonymous. Though expensive, the *Encyclopedia* was widely disseminated, and it provided a self-contained library of fact and opinion for members of the "republic of letters" scattered across the Continent.

15

Enlightened Politics
in Europe

Enlightened despotism is the term used to describe a theory of monarchical government practiced generally in central and eastern Europe in the period from 1740 to 1800. The enlightened despot was expected to promote governmental efficiency and the well-being of his people through the autocratic application of rational policies—an outlook best summed up in the aphorism "Everything for the people, nothing by the people."

Rationalized governmental operations enhanced the power of the monarchy and its war-making potential, but the cultured court life was usually a luxury of the monarch and his small circle of favorites. It brought no political or intellectual liberalization and usually did little to benefit the social or economic standing of the great mass of people.

War of the Austrian Succession

The War of the Austrian Succession (1740–1748) was the first round in the long contest between Frederick II of Prussia and Maria Theresa of Austria for dominance in the Germanies. Prussia, France, and Bavaria all hoped to take advantage of the inexperienced archduchess Maria Theresa even though they had recognized her right to rule the Hapsburg domains when they accepted the Pragmatic Sanction (see p. 133).

Laying claims to Silesia, Frederick II invaded the province and defeated the Austrians at Mollwitz (April 1741). This victory led to an alliance of Prussia with France, who hoped to seize the Austrian Netherlands; with Elector Charles of Bavaria, who claimed the imperial throne; and with Spain, who sought Italian gains. England and Holland were determined to thwart French ambitions and allied themselves with Maria Theresa. (The North American phase of the conflict, known as King George's War, is discussed on p. 148.) Frederick sealed his conquest of Silesia with a victory at Chotusitz (May 1742). Maria Theresa, realizing that she could not cope with so many enemies at once, acknowledged the loss of Silesia and made peace with Frederick at Breslau (11 June 1742).

The French, deserted by their powerful ally, were forced to abandon Prague (December 1742). They withdrew from Germany entirely after being defeated by the English at Dittingen (June 1743). Marshal Saxe, Louis XV's greatest general, maintained himself in the Netherlands and defeated the English at Fontenoy, (May 1745).

Austria slowly regained its strength. The death of Emperor Charles VII removed the Bavarian threat and led to the election of Maria Theresa's husband as Emperor Francis I. Frederick, fearing the Austrian resurgence, reentered the conflict and maintained his hold on Silesia with a stunning victory at Hohenfriedberg (June 1745). A second defeat at Kesselsdorf (December 1745) convinced Maria Theresa that further hostilities were futile. In the subsequent Peace of Dresden (25 December 1745), Frederick retained Silesia while recognizing Francis I's imperial title. Bloody but indecisive fighting continued in Italy and the Netherlands until a general settlement reached at Aix-la-Chapelle (October 1748) restored the status quo ante bellum with the exception of Silesia and a few Italian territories.

The Seven Years' War

The years from 1748 to 1756 marked a period of "cold war" in central Europe. Maria Theresa worked to restore her state in the hope of regaining Silesia. Count Kaunitz, her able foreign minister, negotiated a new anti-Prussian alliance that included not only Russia but also France, the Hapsburg dynasty's hereditary enemy. Frederick II, realizing the danger of isolation, finally allied himself with England. This "diplomatic revolution" resulted in the realignment of the great powers shown below. Note that the imperial conflict of France and England and the rivalry of Prussia remained constant despite the reversal of allies.

War of the Austrian Succession (1740–1748): France, Prussia, and Russia vs. Austria and England
Seven Years' War (1756–1763): England and Prussia vs. Austria, France, and Russia

The war began in August 1756 when Frederick II, sensing imminent attack, seized the initiative by invading Saxony. This was the first campaign in a series that raged unabated until the fall of 1760. What Frederick lacked in numbers he made up for with his tactics. When he gave battle, his well-drilled Prussians usually inflicted more punishment than they received. Even when he was beaten, Frederick's enemies were often so badly mauled that pursuit was impossible. The Prussians won stunning tactical victories against the French at Rossbach (November 1757) and against the Austrians at Leuthen (December 1757), but Frederick was unable to convert them to his strategic advantage. The tide began to turn against him in 1758. The Russians fought him to a bloody standoff at Zorndorf, and the Austrians defeated him at Hochkirch. The year 1759 saw Frederick at the brink of disaster. The allies won their greatest victory of the war at Kunersdorf (August 1759), where the Prussians sustained 50 percent casualties. The last important pitched battle took place at Torgau (October 1760), where the Austrians, enjoying numerical advantage, gave ground only after inflicting severe punishment. The campaigns had drained Prussia of men, materiel, and money; and the allies seemed ready to deliver the coup de grace when Frederick was saved by what Germans would henceforth consider a miracle. The death of Empress Elizabeth (January 1762) brought Peter III to the Russian throne. He withdrew from the war, and Sweden followed suit. The Austrians, too weary to continue alone, agreed to a settlement. A peace of exhaustion was signed at Hubertusburg on 15 February 1763. After seven years of slaughter, the signers agreed to a return to the status quo ante bellum. The decisive phases of this war, fought between England and France in North America (the French and Indian War) and in India, are discussed on page 148.

Brandenburg-Prussia 1740–1786

Frederick II, "the Great," was the archetype of an enlightened despot. He totally dominated an efficient garrison state, and by drawing upon his military genius and statecraft, he raised Bradenburg-Prussia to the first rank among European states. However, the price he paid for these short-term gains was stagnation among the most innovative segments of the society.

Frederick the Great's Early Years. Frederick grew up under the tutelage of his father, Frederick William I, a severe taskmaster, but he rebelled against his father's crude barracks mentality. From a French tutor and his English mother he gained a knowledge and appreciation for arts and letters, became an accomplished flutist, and corresponded with Voltaire and other French intellectuals. At first his father regarded him as an effeminate dandy of whom little could be expected, but Frederick was slowly reconciled to his father's harsh treatment.

Frederick's Reign (1740–1786). It is impossible to separate Frederick's domestic and foreign policies. He was determined to enhance Brandenburg's status, and to do that he needed to expand the well-drilled army he had inherited from his father. The overriding consideration of Frederick's domestic policies, in turn, was to maintain the army at the peak of efficiency.

CLASS SYSTEM. Frederick promoted a rigid class system and assigned a definite role to each class. The Junkers (landed nobility) were the backbone of the garrison state. They were required to serve the state and supplied the overwhelming majority of its professional officers and civil servants. In return for this service, Frederick maintained their social status and guaranteed their economic well-being. The Junkers controlled the peasantry, whose function was to raise food, pay taxes, and supply recruits for the army. Frederick was contemptuous of the bourgeoisie, but he recognized that commerce and industry were indispensable. He excluded them from government posts and the officer caste but, in return, supported their commercial interests with tariff barriers and subsidies. The merchant class was also exempted from military service.

FOREIGN POLICY. This rigid social structure provided Frederick with the resources he needed to carry out an active foreign policy despite Prussia's relative poverty. He conquered Silesia and held it through the bitter campaigns of the War of the Austrian Succession and the Seven Years' War (see p. 175). Frederick II and his successor Frederick William II also participated in the partitions of Poland. As a result, their state was expanded to include West Prussia, with the seaport of Danzig, New East Prussia, and the province of Posen (see p. 187).

ENLIGHTENED DOMESTIC POLICY. Despite the territorial gains won by Frederick II, Prussia suffered from his wars. He earned his credentials as an enlightened despot during the decades of reconstruction that followed his last campaigns.

Even before the Seven Years' War, Frederick had directed reclamation of the Oder River swamps and colonized the area with fifty thousand immigrant peasants. He followed the same procedure after 1763 in the devastated areas of Prussia, where he supplied over three hundred thousand settlers with land and equipment. He supported the Junkers with subsidies and took an active interest in agronomy, particularly the introduction of such new crops as potatoes, sugar beets, and turnips. The acquisition of Silesia resulted in a significant increase in Prussia's natural resources and industrial base, which Frederick nurtured under a tightly controlled mercantilist policy.

CONCLUSION. Frederick II earned his title "the Great" as a result of his brilliant battlefield exploits and his skill as a diplomat. His reputation as an enlightened despot emerged from his single-minded devotion to duty in streamlining the Prussian state in pursuit of his interests. As a result, Prussia took its place among the great powers in the decades before the French Revolution. In the long run, however, his successes proved ephemeral. His reign may be criticized for having reinforced Prussia's backward social structure, for having maintained a political system that only an autocrat of his ability could operate, and for having sapped the vitality of the most creative segments of the society.

Austria 1740–1792

The Hapsburg state was Prussia's chief rival for dominance in central Europe. It contained approximately 25 million inhabitants, of whom the most significant groups were the Germans, Slavs, Magyars, and Belgians. They were held together not so much by common interest as by the age-old habit of obedience to the Hapsburg dynasty. These loyalties were put to the test in the last decade of the eighteenth century.

Maria Theresa (r. 1740–1780). Maria Theresa is not included in the list of enlightened despots. She rejected the enlightenment as foreign and atheistic and maintained the Catholicism of her forefathers. In addition, she recognized that the ideological commitment to rationalism on the part of the philosophes was often impractical when applied to the intricacies of a functioning political system.

From the invasion of Silesia that accompanied her accession until her death, Maria Theresa retained personal control of her government. However, she had the ability to choose competent advisers and the wisdom to rely on their advice. From her husband, Emperor Francis I, to whom she bore sixteen children, she obtained moral support and guidance until his death in 1765. He also provided military advice, but he did not play an important role in the government. She succeeded him as ruler of the Holy Roman Empire in 1765.

DOMESTIC AFFAIRS. Maria Theresa realized that the humiliation suffered at the hands of Frederick II in the War of the Austrian Succession was as much a result of Austrian weakness as of Prussian strength. Thus she strove to eliminate governmental deficiencies. Count von Haugwitz undertook the primary responsibility for executing these reforms and remained the queen's chief domestic adviser until his death in 1765.

Haugwitz created the Directory to supervise the joint administration and finances of Austria and Bohemia in 1749. In 1761 these functions were divided between the Court Chancellery for administrative affairs and the Court Chamber for fiscal affairs. Overall supervision of the Hapsburg domains was bestowed on the Council of State in 1760. The decisions of these policy-making bodies were enforced in the provinces by district prefects.

The primary purpose of these bureaucratic reforms was to ensure financial solvency. They were reinforced by the elimination of ecclesiastical and aristocratic tax exemptions and the creation of a universal income tax. The result was a vast increase in state revenue, which, in turn, ensured the maintenance of a strong standing army.

Despite the extensive remodeling of the administrative structure, Maria Theresa never ruled a centralized state. The Hungarian nobility retained their traditional liberties, including tax exemptions, and her Italian and Belgian territories successfully resisted innovations that would have ended their autonomy.

FOREIGN AFFAIRS. Maria Theresa's most trusted adviser was Wenzel, Prince von Kaunitz-Rietberg. During the reassessment of Austrian foreign policy following the defeat in the War of the Austrian Succession, Kaunitz argued that Prussia was Austria's greatest enemy, and that the task of recovering Silesia would be best served by an alliance with France. The alliance was consummated in 1756, and it placed Austria in a far stronger position in her struggle with Prussia (see p. 176). Austria failed to regain Silesia in the Seven Years' War, but Kaunitz effectively maintained Austria's international position. The foreign minister feared Russia's growing influence in Poland and, when he could not prevent its partition, took part in the agreements by which Austria annexed Galicia (see p. 189).

CONCLUSION. At midcentury Austria had been in danger of internal disintegration and international decline. Through the work of Maria Theresa and her two able ministers, Haugwitz and Kaunitz, these trends were reversed, and Austria reasserted itself as an important European power.

Joseph II (r. 1780–1790). Joseph II embodied all the strengths and weaknesses of enlightened despotism. He was both a tyrant and a reformer. Although he became coregent in 1765, he held a subordinate position until the death of his mother, Empress Maria Theresa, in 1780. His reign was marked by a consuming desire to create a rational and centralized state. To accomplish this he attempted to renovate the political, economic, and social structure of his diverse domains.

His autocratic programs were initiated against the advice of his ministers and in the face of adamant resistance by a cross section of his subjects. His attempts to carry out massive domestic changes, coupled with his aggressive foreign policy, resulted in ultimate failure.

DOMESTIC REFORMS. Joseph tried to destroy or regulate all those institutions that had traditionally maintained corporate autonomy at the expense of uniformity and state power.

The administrative reforms carried out by Maria Theresa in Austria were extended to the Italian provinces, Hungary, and Belgium. Royal officers were assigned to administer these areas, thus usurping power formerly exercised by provincial estates or local magnates. The Hungarian nobility sabotaged this effort by passive resistance, and the Belgians rose in open revolt (1789).

Though a Catholic, Joseph also attacked the secular power of the Church. He restricted papal control within his domains, expropriated monastic lands, eased censorship, and granted religious toleration to non-Catholics, thereby easing the plight of the Jews. These reforms alienated a large majority of Joseph's Catholic subjects.

The emperor's most revolutionary reforms centered on his attempt to end serfdom and bring the landed nobility to heel. He abolished the personal servitude of serfs in 1781 and followed this action by a series of decrees guaranteeing them land tenure and a greater share of their production. Had the program been successful, it would have increased state revenues, reduced the power of the nobility, and created a relatively prosperous, loyal landowning peasantry.

Despite his good intentions, Joseph's reform failed. His attempts to change everything at once without consultation or compromise embittered his most powerful subjects, leaving him without support and without the power to enforce his decrees. When he died in 1790, his realm was in disarray. His successor, Leopold II (r. 1790–1792), restored order only at the expense of Joseph's reforms. Hungary thus reverted to its former autonomy, the Church regained its power, and the serfs sank back to their former status.

FOREIGN POLICY. Despite his enlightenment at home, Joseph was an aggressive and inept power politician in foreign affairs. His effort to annex Bavaria in 1777 led to a showdown with Prussia, but before any actual combat, Joseph realized his folly and abandoned the scheme. In 1782 he undertook a second adventure. He hoped to reinvigorate the Belgian economy by opening the Scheldt River, which had been closed to seaborne traffic by the Treaty of Westphalia. France, England, and Holland would not tolerate a change in the international status quo, and again Joseph renounced his plans. His last failure came as an ally of Russia in war with Turkey (1787–

1790). Russia gained the Crimea, but Austrian mismanagement resulted only in heavy casualties and the devastation of southern Hungary.

Russia 1725–1796

A succession of weak monarchs occupied the Russian throne from the death of Peter the Great in 1725 until the accession of Catherine II in 1762. The period was marked by palace intrigue and and factionalism instigated by the imperial guards regiments and cliques of powerful noblemen. Catherine II reasserted the imperial authority, enhanced Russia's international position, and brought the Enlightenment to her brilliant court; but in the process she compromised the well-being of the Russian people.

Era of Palace Intrigue (1725–1762). The Romanov dynasty had no fixed rule of succession, and Peter the Great died without naming an heir. Intriguers within the court were determined to protect their own interests. The guards regiments played an important role in these events. Noblemen were willing to serve in the ranks of these units assigned to protect the monarch both from a sense of duty and in hopes of personal advancement. Thus the guards were the most prestigious and powerful military units stationed in the capital.

POLITICAL TRENDS. As the following genealogical table shows, Russia changed rulers seven times between 1725 and 1762. The three emperors were unable to solidify their positions and were overthrown by palace coups. The empresses, on the other hand, had relatively long reigns. They were usually uninterested in affairs of state and left control of the government to court favorites, often Germans. The guards remained a pervasive influence in the selection of rulers.

ECONOMIC AND SOCIAL TRENDS. The aggressive Westernization program initiated by Peter the Great atrophied after his death. Although many of the enterprises that he had founded continued to operate, industrial development practically ceased. Prices rose with the reinstitution of private commercial monopolies and restrictive tariffs. The government suffered constant fiscal embarrassment because of large military expenditures, corruption, and widespread tax exemptions among the privileged.

A clear indication of imperial weakness can be seen in the rising power of the nobility (*dvorianstvo*), which slowly broke away from the obligations of state service and at the same time extended its power over the peasantry. The following decrees increased the nobility's power: (1) an initial decrease in the term of state service to twenty-five years (1736) followed by the abolition of the require-

Succession to the Russian Throne

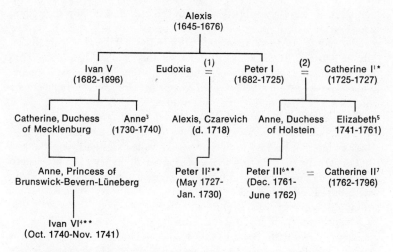

Superscripts indicate order of succession after Peter I.
**Czars overthrown in palace coups*

ment altogether (1762); (2) the exclusive right to own private serfs (by 1760); (3) the right to assess and collect the head tax (1731); (4) the right to try and punish serfs for all offenses except murder and robbery, including the right to use the knout, a whip that often caused death. Without their lord's consent, serfs could no longer enlist in the army, enter business, acquire land, or marry outside the estate. Thus, at a time when serfdom was disappearing in western Europe, it acquired its most onerous form in Russia.

FOREIGN AFFAIRS. Russia's attempts to increase her influence in southern and central Europe met the resistance of Poland, Sweden, and Turkey. In the conflicts that followed, Russia generally encountered French hostility and had Austrian support.

War of the Polish Succession (1733–1736). In the struggle for control of the elective crown of Poland following the death of King Augustus II (1733), Russia successfully supported the candidacy of Frederick Augustus, elector of Saxony, who became Augustus III (see p. 187).

Russo-Turkish War (1735–1739). The intermittent conflict between Russia and Turkey broke out again in 1735, primarily over territorial disputes along their common border. Russia gained control of Azov, at the mouth of the Don River, but in the Treaty of Belgrade (1739) agreed to dismantle all fortifications in the area and to ship its trading goods in Turkish ships.

War of the Austrian Succession (1740–1748). Though nominally an ally of Austria, Russia took little part in this conflict. The court contained Prussian sympathizers, and for a time Russia was preoccupied with Sweden. The war was virtually over when Russia intervened in 1748, and its troops saw no action.

Russo-Swedish War (1741–1743). Sweden still hoped to recoup the losses it had suffered under Peter the Great and took advantage of Russia's internal turmoil to declare war. Sweden was badly beaten and in the Treaty of Abo (1743) ceded a small piece of southeastern Finland to Russia. In addition it accepted the Russian candidate, Adolphus Frederick, duke of Holstein, to fill its vacant throne. Adolphus, however, was an unreliable Russian puppet.

Seven Years' War (1756–1762). Russia played an erratic role in the conflict. Allied with Austria and France against Prussia, its troops won a stunning victory at Kunersdorf (August 1759) and briefly occupied Berlin (1760); but it did not press the attack. The death of Empress Elizabeth in 1762 brought to the throne Peter III, an ardent admirer of Frederick the Great, who withdrew Russia from the war (see p. 177).

Catherine II, "the Great" (r. 1762–1796). Catherine II is usually included in a list of enlightened despots. She personally controlled the government throughout her long reign, conducted an aggressive foreign policy, and maintained a brilliant court graced by intellectuals and artists. But although Catherine was held in high esteem by the philosophes, her tentative steps to streamline Russian government proceeded on a veneer of platitudes covering a policy of personal gratification.

DOMESTIC DEVELOPMENTS. Catherine was a German princess whose husband ascended the throne in 1761 as Emperor Peter III. Her personal estrangement from Peter and her lust for power led Catherine to conspire with the guards to overthrow her husband. Peter was arrested and assassinated (June 1762), and Catherine was proclaimed empress by the guards. However, Catherine's foreign birth and tainted claim to the throne left her in a tenuous position that she could strengthen only by catering to the demands of the nobility.

A flurry of reform activity marked the first years of Catherine's reign. The empress convoked the Legislative Commission in 1767.

Its agenda was set by an *Instruction* that called for a vast governmental study and reforms along lines recommended by Western philosophes. But the excitement quickly subsided, and the Legislative Commission failed to produce even proposals for reform.

Catherine did carry out significant changes in provincial administration. The Petrine colleges (ministries) were slowly abolished and replaced by functional agencies, including those of justice, education, and finance. These agencies, dominated by the nobility, operated under the direct supervision of appointed provisional governors and under the overall control of the Senate, an administrative board in the capital. This elaborate new system looked efficient on paper, but Catherine was reluctant to be bound by bureaucratic constraints and continued to rule by caprice rather than by law.

The nobility benefited most from Catherine's programs because she bought their support by promoting their interests. This policy was capped in 1785 with the Charter of the Nobility, which confirmed and expanded its privileges. The charter guaranteed the nobility that their titles would not be revoked without due process, that they would suffer neither corporal punishment nor confiscation of estates if convicted of a crime, that they would henceforth be exempt from the poll tax, and that they were free to punish serfs with Siberian exile, which they could terminate at will.

Thus the peasantry sank even lower within the system. Even their legal rights, which were often vaguely defined, were unenforceable in the face of powerful local nobles. As a result of their degradation, Russian history is punctuated with recurrent peasant revolts. The most remarkable insurrection of this period was led by Emelyan Pugachev during 1773–1775. Leading a force of Cossacks, Old Believers (see p. 134), and peasants, Pugachev seized much of southern Russia. Within a year his revolt was liquidated in a sea of blood, and he was executed in 1775.

CATHERINE'S FOREIGN POLICY. The most obvious result of Catherine's long reign was the steady westward advance of Russian frontiers. To facilitate her expansionist policy, she negotiated and then sustained a close working relationship with Frederick II of Prussia. She met resistance from Turkey and Poland, her intended victims, and from Austria, France, and Sweden, who viewed her designs with alarm.

Catherine was determined to reduce Poland to the status of a docile Russian puppet. In 1764 she secured the election of Stanisław Poniatowski, a former lover, to the vacant Polish throne. Catherine's heavy-handed tactics, including the use of troops, incited a faction of Polish noblemen to revolt; they were soon supported by France. The Turks also feared Russia's growing strength and declared war on Russia in 1768. Russia quickly conquered the Turkish provinces of Moldavia and Wallachia (1770). The growing apprehension that Russia would soon control not only Poland but the littoral of the Black Sea led Austria into alliance with Turkey. Frederick II of Prussia, fearing the outbreak of a general war in eastern Europe for which he was not prepared, suggested a negotiated settlement.

The result was the first Partition of Poland (1772). Russia relinquished Moldavia and Wallachia and was compensated with Polish territory lying east of the Dvina and Dnieper rivers. The Treaty of Küchück Kainarja (1774) ended the Russo-Turkish War. Under its terms Russia obtained possession of the Black Sea coast from the straits of Kerch westward to the mouth of the Bug River. In addition Russian ships gained the right of passage through the Bosporus and Dardanelles. Catherine subsequently annexed the Crimea (1784), thus ending its short-lived status as an independent Tartar state. Turkey renewed hostilities in 1784 but against the combined forces of Russia and Austria was forced to accept the Treaty of Jassy (1792), in which it recognized the Russian annexation of the Crimea and ceded the province of Ochakov lying between the Bug and the Dniester rivers.

While Russia had been preoccupied with Turkey, Poland attempted to reassert her independence. Catherine moved to end Polish resistance, and in league with Prussia carried out the second and third partitions of Poland (see p. 187). Poland ceased to exist, and Catherine rounded out her westward expansion by the addition of one hundred and eighty thousand square miles of territory and six million new subjects.

Dismemberment of Poland

Poland failed to keep pace with the autocratic centralization carried out in the surrounding states of Prussia, Austria, and Russia. It had declined as a great power following the demise of the Jagellonian dynasty in 1572. As its strength dissipated, Poland became a pawn in eastern European power politics. Its leaders were unable to reinvigorate the kingdom or to withstand the pressure from its aggressive neighbors. As a result Poland disappeared from the map of Europe.

Roots of Polish Weakness. The reasons for Poland's demise are complex. Though indefensible borders are often given as a major cause of its difficulties, the same could be said of Prussia, which did not suffer a similar fate. Poland's elective monarch is also cited as a grave defect, but the practice of election by a diet of nobility was not necessarily incompatible with a strong executive and centralized administration. It is certainly true, however, that the elective throne presented a tempting prize for foreign intriguers.

The Polish nobility contributed to Poland's destruction. A handful of powerful families, including the Czartoryskis and the Potockis, dominated the aristocracy, which numbered nearly a million people. Although a large part of this caste was impoverished, it monopolized the land and ruthlessly controlled the servile population.

Two institutions reinforced aristocratic dominance. The *pacta conventa*, which prescribed limitations on the royal power of each newly elected monarch, was used by the nobility to strip the king of power. This negative influence was carried to absurd, and ultimately tragic, lengths in the seventeenth century through the use of the *liberum veto*, which permitted any nobleman to veto a legislative bill and dissolve the Diet in a single stroke. To this political disarray must be added an inefficient administrative structure, a weak army, and a backward economy. Finally, Poland found itself surrounded by states that were both able and eager to take advantage of its weakness.

First Partition (1772). The Czartoryski clan hoped to obtain the throne following the death of their ailing Saxon king, Augustus III. Their candidate was Stanistaw Poniatowski, who was well known in the Russian court as a former envoy and lover of Catherine II. Catherine believed Stanistaw would support Russian policies and promoted his candidacy. When Augustus died in 1763, Stanistaw was elected by the Diet, which was impressed both by well-placed bribes and the ominous presence of Russian troops. The election of a Russian puppet worried both France and Austria and led to a Turkish declaration of war on Russia.

When the Russo-Turkish war threatened to engulf all of eastern Europe, Frederick II, the unprepared ally of Russia, suggested that Prussia, Austria, and Russia avoid war by a multilateral annexation of Polish territory. Russia seized the area of Poland lying north of the Dvina River and east of the Dnieper River. Austria annexed Galicia; Prussia annexed West Prussia. As a result of the first partition, Poland lost over a quarter of its 283,000 square miles of territory and 20 percent of its 8.75 million inhabitants.

Second Partition (1793). Stanistaw II made a determined effort to save his kingdom from destruction. Most of the nobility realized that their constant intrigues threatened Poland's existence and submitted to reforms. The king instituted administrative reforms, and the economy experienced healthy growth. In 1791 Stanistaw promulgated a new constitution. Its most significant articles abolished the *liberum veto*, made the succession to the crown hereditary in the house of the

THE PARTITIONS *of* POLAND
1772 ~ 1793 ~ 1795

Saxon electors after the death of the childless Stanistaw, and permitted townsmen to take part in the administrative and political life of the state. Prussia and Austria both accepted these constitutional changes, but Catherine foresaw the loss of Russian influence in the revitalized kingdom. At the prompting of a few Polish malcontents, she invaded the country, and in alliance with Frederick William II, successor to Frederick the Great, she agreed to a second partition of Poland. Russia obtained the Ukraine and the remainder of White Russia, while Prussia seized the western province of Great Poland and the cities of Danzig and Torun. Austria did not participate in the second partition. Poland retained approxiamtely 3.5 million inhabitants and one third of its original territory.

Third Partition (1795). Immediately following the second partition, a group of Polish patriots, led by Tadeusz Kosciuszko, began organizing to reassert Poland's sovereignty. Kosciuszko, who had been General Washington's adjutant during the American War of Independence, raised the standards of revolt at Cracow in March 1794. Though without the support of France or Prussia, the rebels inflicted several severe defeats on the Russian army before being overpowered. The third partition followed quickly after the Russian victory. Russia annexed Kurland and the remainder of Lithuania and Black Russia. Prussia seized Podlachia, adjoining East Prussia, and the city of Warsaw. Austria obtained the area of western Galicia. The third partition eradicated Poland from the map of Europe. It did not reappear until the World War I settlement in 1919.

The Iberian Peninsula

Enlightened despotism was not confined to the powerful states of eastern Europe. The rulers of the Iberian Peninsula were also influenced by the rationalist spirit and attempted to put enlightenment theories to practical use.

Spain. Carlos III (r. 1759–1788) served his apprenticeship as an enlightened ruler in the duchy of Naples and Sicily, beginning in 1738. There he abolished serfdom, reformed the legal code, initiated a more equitable tax structure, and limited aristocratic power. He carried this reforming spirit with him when he ascended the Spanish throne. He reduced clerical dominance in Spain by expelling the Jesuits and by limiting the authority of the Inquisition. He took a personal interest in the advancement of commerce and industry, which he stimulated through a reduction of internal tariffs, regulation of the guilds, and subsidies to textile manufacturers. Carlos III demonstrated the influence an energetic ruler can have upon a state. Unfortunately for Spain, he was not succeeded by men of his caliber.

Portugal. The brief regeneration of Portugal was carried out not by Joseph I (r. 1750–1777) but by his chief minister Sebastian José de Carvalho e Mello, marquis of Pombal. Pombal earned his monarch's favor by directing relief operations in Lisbon after the catastrophic earthquake of 1755. Thereafter he virtually ruled the country. Working against the opposition of both Church and nobility, he raised educational standards, promoted industry and trade, and reformed the state administration. Pombal's programs relied upon the king's support, and when Joseph died the marquis fell from power, and Portugal settled once more into quiet stagnation.

16

The Ancien Régime in France and England

The French expression *ancien régime* ("old order") is used to denote the prerevolutionary societies of eighteenth-century England and France. This chapter will discuss the political developments within these countries and the American Revolution, which, seen from a European perspective, is the last colonial war fought between England and France. Politically and socially, the period is marked by the revival of aristocratic power in both countries. It was the last flowering of a privileged class of landed nobility whose dominance would soon be ended by revolution and industrialization.

France 1715–1788

The history of eighteenth-century France reveals a series of paradoxes. Although Louis XIV had created a pervasive absolutism, his successors were burdened with a government so corrupt, inefficient, and constrained by traditional practices that they could not carry out a coherent program or institute meaningful reforms. Although the French economy prospered and expanded, the government constantly hovered on the brink of financial disaster. Although the privileged classes maintained a virtual monopoly of wealth and social position, they undermined the authority of the monarchy that guaranteed their status. The greatest paradox, common to many other societies, was the conservatism that gripped the overwhelming majority of Frenchmen. They remained loyal to traditional institutions despite the blatant corruption and inefficiency of government, the rigid caste system that ensured the dominance of a small elite, and the growing disparity between rich and poor.

Social Structure. Frenchmen were divided into three legal categories called *estates*. Membership within an estate defined a man's civil rights and obligations, and it tended to divide the nation into three broad social categories. However, within each category there existed a wide diversity of wealth and social status.

FIRST ESTATE. The clergy, which because of its exalted function was designated the first estate, included approximately one hundred and thirty thousand members in 1750. In preceding centuries the hierarchy had provided an avenue of upward social mobility for the devout and intelligent sons of the lower classes, but by the mid-eighteenth century, social stratification within the Church was clearly evident. The nobility controlled all the bishoprics; the bourgeoisie provided the lower-ranking administrators; and the parish priests were drawn from the lower middle classes and sometimes the peasantry. As a result, there was a great disparity of wealth and interest among the clergy. The churchmen paid no taxes on income or church property but through a periodic convocation made a monetary gift to the crown.

SECOND ESTATE. The second estate consisted of approximately four hundred thousand aristocrats who controlled approximately 25 percent of the land. They can be placed in two broad categories.

The nobility of the sword were the descendants of the feudal warrior caste, which during the Middle Ages had exercised virtual sovereignty in the provinces. They had been deprived of their military power and political functions by Louis XIV. Those with the most exalted titles lived at court, where they basked in the reflected glory of the crown and received the king's monetary favors. The majority of the group, however, lived on their provincial estates in dignity though without great wealth.

The nobility of the robe were administrative officers originally drawn from commoners, whose bureaucratic skills and loyalty to the crown had been rewarded with noble titles and estates. Louis XIV had employed this group in his struggle to overpower the old nobility. They served as provincial intendants and controlled the parlements. Despite their humble origins, several generations of power had raised them to the status of the old nobility. Although they were royal officers, they came to be the most outspoken supporters of the nobility's status and privileges.

Although the nobility had not always formed a closed caste, by the middle of the century, it had become extremely difficult for a commoner to join the privileged group.

THIRD ESTATE. The third estate contained the remaining 24 million Frenchmen and encompassed the greatest social and economic diversity. At the top of this unprivileged category stood the *bourgeoisie*, who controlled 20 percent of the land and who also controlled the country's commerce and industry. They resented their exclusion from political power and felt stifled by the archaic economic structure, particularly during the economic stagnation that set in during the 1780s. Below the bourgeoisie was a middle class of small merchants, artisans, and the semiskilled and unskilled urban workers. The economic status of the working class generally declined throughout the period.

At the bottom of the social structure were the peasant masses. Compared with their counterparts throughout Europe, they were relatively well-off. Only a small minority was still bound by obligations of serfdom. As a group they may have owned as much as 40 percent of the land (although, of course, they comprised over 90 percent of the population). For centuries the peasants had stolidly produced the nation's wealth and borne its financial burdens. During the eighteenth century, they became increasingly restive as the nobility attempted to reimpose outdated manorial obligations.

Economic Trends. The economy of eighteenth-century France was primarily agricultural. During the century the population increased by an estimated 6 million persons to approximately 24 million. As a result, French agricultural production remained the highest in Europe, although productivity was low by modern standards. Foreign trade also showed gains that compared favorably with England despite the loss of French Canada and India in 1763, and merchant capitalists emerged as an important economic group. France began to fall behind England in the production of coal and iron at the end of the century. Despite Colbert's subsidization of textiles during the reign of Louis XIV, the industry did not keep pace with England's.

Several factors retarded French growth. Land remained the symbol of genteel wealth, and a social stigma attached to commercial and industrial activity. The guild system, though moribund, restricted manufacture, while the heavy fiscal burdens borne by the peasantry precluded capital accumulation necessary for agricultural improvements. The development of credit facilities also lagged behind the Low Countries and England. The attempt of John Law to combine a national bank with his Company of the West (an American trading company) resulted in frenzied speculation during 1719 until the Mississippi Bubble burst. The crash led to a lingering distrust by French investors in banks, stock companies, and paper notes and securities, all of which are essential for the growth of a commercial, industrial society.

Political and Administrative Structure. The French monarchy reached the peak of its power and prestige during the reign of Louis XIV (1643–1715). The Sun King's absolutism was derived primarily from the strength of his personality and the seventy-two-year duration of his reign. The failure to institutionalize royal absolutism by a thorough reform of the state bureaucracy became painfully obvious to the crown during the eighteenth century when the first and second estates attempted to maintain their privileges and reassert their lost authority. Louis XV and Louis XVI found themselves saddled with an archaic, disorganized, and overlapping administrative system manned by royal officials and members of the aristocracy who could neither be removed from office nor coerced into obedience.

GÉNÉRALITÉS. Administratively, France was divided into thirty-four districts (*généralités*), each controlled by a royal intendant. Originally intendants had been commoners raised to high office to guarantee their loyalty to the crown. Their chief functions had been to control the local nobility and carry out the king's orders. With the passage of time, they became hereditary nobles who identified with local interests. In addition their offices came to be regarded as personal property, which they bequeathed to their sons. Although from their provincial strongholds, they could not openly defy the king, they could covertly obstruct and sabotage his programs.

PARLEMENTS. France had no unified legal code; common law prevailed in the north, and Roman law was applied in the south. There was a *parlement* (high court) for each of thirteen distinctive regions, with the most powerful being the Paris Parlement. The *parlementaires,* or judges, were members of the nobility of the robe and had a hereditary right to their offices. Besides their legal functions, the parlements had the right to question royal decrees (*droit de remonstrance*), which could not become law until registered by the court. The parlements became the most powerful obstruction to royal absolutism.

PROVINCIAL ESTATES. The Estates General, a convocation of representatives from the three legal orders, formed the national legislature. But between 1614 and 1789, the Estates General never convened. Several provincial estates did, however, continue to function during the eighteenth century; the most powerful of these were in Brittany and Languedoc. These assemblies were dominated by upper-class representatives who gained important privileges for their areas, particularly in the form of tax relief. These institutions greatly diminished the king's prerogatives, but in place of absolutism, they simply imposed oligarchy.

Reign of Louis XV (1715–1774). Louis XV, who was only five years old when he succeeded his great-grandfather Louis XIV, demonstrated neither interest nor talent in affairs of state. Throughout his long reign, he centered his attentions on hunting and womanizing. As a result his reign was marked by a resurgence of aristocratic influence among both his courtiers and his royal administrators. Attempts were made to strengthen the administration and fiscal structure, but they ultimately failed. The reign can be divided into three distinct phases.

REGENCY (1715–1723). During the king's minority, France was controlled by Philippe, duc d'Orléans. Orléans's effort to reinstate the nobility of the sword to a position of political prominence failed due to the general incompetence of these nobles. Noblemen of the robe thus retained their prerogatives as ministers of state. As parlementaires, they demanded that the crown submit its actions to greater scrutiny. Royal decrees were often delayed by parliamentary remonstrances. The regent could enforce his will by convening a special session (*lit de justice*) of the parlement, at which it was required to register royal edicts. Government by coercion could not succeed in the long run, however, and the parlements grew more recalcitrant with each passing year. The financial ministry of John Law momentarily eased the treasury's plight, but the collapse of the Mississippi Bubble opened a new financial crisis. The most successful undertaking of the regency was the alliance with Britain that for a generation halted the long struggle for imperial hegemony.

FLEURY ADMINISTRATION (1726–1743). André Hercule de Fleury had been Louis's tutor and in 1726 became his chief minister. As the virtual ruler of France for seventeen years, Cardinal Fleury provided the country with honest and intelligent leadership. The maintenance of peace, which alone could insure prosperity, and fiscal equilibrium became the keys to his policy. He avoided religious controversy and confrontations with the parlements and made no attempts to alter drastically the status quo. As a result of his policies, France experienced general prosperity and slowly recovered from the effects of Louis XIV's continual wars.

THE KING'S PERSONAL RULE (1743–1774). Louis took the reins of government into his own hands after the death of Fleury in 1743. Despite his good intentions, supervision of the complex machinery of state was beyond his capabilities. His inept handling of foreign affairs triggered a fiscal crisis, which, in turn, brought him into direct confrontation with the Church, the parlements, and private interests at court.

Louis's direction of foreign policy can only be described as inept. He abandoned Fleury's peace policy and plunged France into two disastrous wars. The War of the Austrian Succession (1743–1748) was fought at great cost for no gain. The Seven Years' War resulted in humiliating defeats and the cession of Canada and India. In addition it precipitated a financial crisis.

The financial demands of Louis's wars demonstrated the inadequacy of the fiscal system. At the root of the problem was the tax exemption enjoyed by the privileged estates. In 1749 Jean Baptiste Machault d'Arnouville, the comptroller general, instituted the *vingtième*, an income tax on all property. Opposition from the nobility and the clergy supported by the parlements was so strong that Louis allowed the issue to go unresolved. The Seven Years' War reopened the controversy. The parlements presented a united front in their adamant refusal to accept equal taxation, but the king's new advisers convinced him that a firm stand must be taken if the crown wished to maintain its authority. In 1771 the Paris Parlement was abolished and its members sent into provincial exile. The *vingtième* was collected, and the rates of the *capitation*, another income tax, were increased. However, the king's sudden death in 1774 ended this vigorous program and gave the privileged orders a chance to counterattack.

Reign of Louis XVI to 1787. Louis XVI, the grandson of Louis XV, reigned from 1774 until his execution in 1793. He was morally upright but lacked the intelligence and strength of will to provide the imaginative and forceful leadership France needed. Queen Marie Antoinette discredited herself, the king, and the monarchy by her scandalous behavior and frivolous disregard of popular opinion. The privileged orders, abetted by the queen, successfully challenged the king's authority and undermined his prestige but avoided taking any responsibility. The philosophes, though not opposed to monarchy, became increasingly critical of the poorly managed regime. The bourgeoisie chafed under their legal disabilities and their diminishing status. The unprivileged and dispossessed, who bore the greatest burdens, approached the limit of their endurance.

Although Louis XVI reinstated the parlements, his appointment of the physiocrat Turgot as comptroller general indicated his desire to continue reforms. Turgot hoped to carry out a complete renovation of the economic and fiscal structure, but his programs evoked such an outcry that he was dismissed in 1776. His successors, Necker, Calonne, and Loménie de Brienne, all realized the necessity of fiscal reform, but they could make no headway. Despite the financial crisis resulting from French intervention in the American Revolution (see p. 206), the aristocracy adamantly refused to accept any reforms that would undermine their privileged status. By the mid-1780s the nobility held a virtual monopoly not only as parlementaires but as ministers, bishops, and army officers. The king lost control of events at a time when only decisive action could have saved his regime from disaster.

England in the Eighteenth Century

England emerged from the ferment of the sixteen hundreds into a period of relative political tranquility and economic growth. The island kingdom consolidated its hold on Scotland and Ireland. Its unrivaled commercial activity was the envy of Europe. Innovations in agriculture and industrial technology buttressed a growing economy. The eighteenth century was a golden age for aristocrats, who exercised power from the Parliament, the royal administration, and their country estates. At the other end of the scale, life became increasingly difficult for the great mass of unprivileged and unpropertied lower classes.

Social Structure. At the beginning of the eighteenth century, England had a population of approximately 5.5 million. The census of 1801 indicates that the number had risen to 9 million and that an internal migration had shifted the center of population northward into the Midlands. By 1801 London had nearly nine hundred thousand inhabitants, making it the largest city of Europe; Liverpool thrived on the slave trade; and Manchester and Leeds, though only towns by modern standards, were burgeoning industrial centers. Despite urban growth 75 percent of the population still lived in rural hamlets, and 50 percent earned their living directly from agriculture.

NOBILITY. A small nobility formed the dominant class, whose nucleus contained approximately seventy powerful Whig peers. The dukes of Devonshire, Bedford, Newcastle, Northumberland, and Rutland exemplified men whose estates covered whole counties and whose rank and wealth brought them social status and political power. The English nobility hardly resembled the irresponsible caste prevalent in France. They played a dominant role in national politics and local administration and supported the government with their taxes. The gap between lords and commons was bridged by commoners whose wealth bought them titles and position and by the inclusion of all but a peer's eldest son in the ranks of commons.

GENTRY. The gentry formed the backbone of rural society. Though lacking titles and great wealth, the squires lived comfortably on their estates, where they set the tone for polite society and served as local administrators. The House of Commons drew its membership from this group, and as their economic position declined, many joined the Tories to challenge the power of the Whig oligarchy.

YEOMEN, TENANTS, AND RURAL LABORERS. Land consolidation, discussed on p. 199, disrupted the traditional life style of the mass of country dwellers. The yeomen, or small landowners, could not compete with more efficient large farmers and gradually disappeared. They were slowly replaced by tenant farmers, who might be moderately prosperous but had neither the security, social standing, nor political rights that accompanied land ownership. The increasingly numerous but the least fortunate class included men who eked out a living from day labor, sought refuge and jobs in the cities, or joined the growing number of vagabonds.

URBAN ELITE. England was a world power by virtue of her trade and industry. As a result, her merchant capitalists took their place beside the landed nobility as men of substance and influence. The economic significance of commerce relieved it of the social opprobrium attached to business in France. The English nobility could thus engage in business partnerships without fear of derogation, while the merchants gained entrance into polite society through partnership, marriage, or purchase of position. This alliance of land and commerce strengthened the ruling class and broadened its outlook.

URBAN WORKING CLASSES. A wide disparity existed among the urban working classes. Skilled artisans could maintain their families in moderate comfort during normal times. The growing number of semi-skilled industrial workers and unskilled day laborers, on the other hand, lived amid poverty, squalor, and crime even in the best of times. Crop failure, war, or depression could rob them of even bare subsistence. The urban disorders that often resulted were suppressed with severity.

Economic Trends. The phrases *agricultural revolution* and *industrial revolution* are used to describe the accelerating economic growth experienced in England during the second half of the eighteenth century. The term *revolution* is warranted because a profound transformation of English society took place in a relatively short time. These changes resulted from the application of science and technology to production and required a reordering of basic social and political relationships. The agricultural transformation, which began first in England, is discussed on p. 199, while an examination of the overall process of industrialization and its impact upon Europe is reserved for chapter 19.

At the beginning of the eighteenth century, English agriculture employed the traditional open-field system and followed the time-honored practice of crop and field rotation as a means of maintaining fertility. Productivity was very low by modern standards. The transformation of this system began with the uncoordinated experimentation of gentlemen farmers and amateur scientists in an effort to increase yields. Viscount Charles Townshend (1674–1738), experimented with root crops and demonstrated that the turnip could be sown in fields previously left fallow, thus returning nitrogen to the soil while also producing fodder for cattle that had previously been slaughtered for want of winter feed. Jethro Tull (1674–1741) published his theories on new cultivation techniques in *Horse-hoeing Husbandry* (1731) and developed the seed drill and the horse hoe, which increased productivity over the old broadcast methods. Robert Bakewell (1725–1795) was the most prominent figure in the scientific study of animal husbandry. His experiments in selective breeding led to the development of heavier and more compact sheep and cattle. Although widespread changes in agricultural methods did not take place overnight, the idea that scientific management and the application of technology could increase production and profits was not lost on the relatively small landowning class. However, such reforms were expensive and profitable only when applied to large blocks of lands. This knowledge increased the process of enclosure. Landowners could petition Parliament to allow enclosure, or fencing, of their share of community wasteland and common fields and the consolidation of their separate strips into large blocks. By this process 6 million acres were enclosed between 1700 and 1844. In the long run, the English economy certainly benefited from enclosure, which increased both production and productivity, and in the process freed rural labor for industry. But the short-term results were tragic for the small farmer, who could not survive without the benefit of the common lands and who could not compete against the more efficient large landowners. Thousands of families were driven from their homes and deprived of their livelihood in a society that provided no system of social security, save the infamous workhouse.

Political Trends. The Whigs had been the primary beneficiaries of the constitutional struggle during the seventeenth century (see chapter 9). Once in power they wanted to avoid controversial issues and devote their full attention to the enjoyment of their wealth and status. Despite the venality and personal indulgence that resulted, important constitutional changes continued. The most significant was the unique development of ministerial responsibility, which became the hallmark of the British parliamentary system. Scotland was finally subdued and integrated, but Ireland remained a bloody battleground.

HANOVERIAN DYNASTY. According to the Act of Settlement (1701), Queen Anne was to be succeeded by her nearest Protestant kin. When she died in 1714, the crown thus passed to the elector of Hanover, a descendant of James I, who ascended the throne as George I (r. 1714–1727). George I and his son George II (r. 1727–1760) took a greater interest in Hanover than in England. Both generally left English affairs in the hands of English ministers. George III (r. 1760–

1820) was proud to be an English king and attempted to reassert royal authority, but parliamentary power and his recurrent insanity limited his role.

Although the king's powers had been severely curtailed in the seventeenth century, the monarch still held significant prerogatives. He appointed ministers, controlled membership in the House of Lords through his right to reward supporters with peerage, and wielded considerable influence in the House of Commons through control of patronage.

SCOTLAND. Scotland was a bleak and impoverished country at the beginning of the century. In the Lowlands the Presbyterian kirk and the great lairds maintained control over a peasant people who scratched a bare living from the spare soil. In the Highlands the clan system maintained a warrior society in which impoverished cotters and herdsmen often supplemented their meager incomes with foraging raids into the Lowlands. Against this background the long struggle with England was finally resolved.

Act of Union. The crowns of Scotland and England had been united in 1603 when James VI of Scotland succeeded Elizabeth as James I of England. This personal union was confirmed in 1707 when negotiations were sealed with the Act of Union that created Great Britain. Under its terms the Scots retained their own legal system and the independence of the kirk. Most significantly they were admitted into England's lucrative mercantile system. Although they ceded their independence and lost their parliament, they obtained forty-five seats in the British House of Commons and sixteen seats in the House of Lords.

The Fifteen. The Act of Settlement (1701) had prescribed the Protestant succession to the English throne, thus denying the claim of James, "the Old Pretender," son of the deposed Stuart ruler James II. Upon the death of Queen Anne, James attempted to regain his throne in a rebellion known as the Fifteen. Promises of French aid were not forthcoming after the death of Louis XIV, and few Jacobites rallied to James in England and the Lowlands. On 13 November 1715, one of the Pretender's armies surrendered at Preston, while the other fought to a draw at Sheriffmuir. As a result the adventure collapsed, James fled to the Continent, and George I settled more securely upon the British throne.

The Forty-five. The Stuarts made a second armed attempt to regain the throne during the Forty-five. Taking advantage of England's involvement in the War of the Austrian Succession, Prince Charles Edward Stuart, the Old Pretender's son, landed in western Scotland in July 1745 and "called out" his Highland supporters. Bonnie Prince

Charlie, as he was known, captured Edinburgh and then led his army deep into England, where to his surprise the people failed to rally to his cause. He fell back and was pursued into Scotland by the duke of Cumberland, who commanded the forces of his father, George II. Charles finally stood his ground at Culloden (16 April 1746), where his army was destroyed. Charles became a hunted man, while his supporters paid the price of traitors. The clan system was abolished, and after centuries of warfare, the Highlands were finally subdued.

IRELAND. Even by eighteenth-century standards, the Irish lived in incredible poverty. The country had been controlled and exploited by England for time out of memory. English landlords owned 75 percent of the land and lived comfortably in London or within the *pale* surrounding Dublin. Beyond the pale the peasants, enchained by law and their own customs, lived in abject poverty on farms often no bigger than gardens. Only the introduction of the potato saved the country from more frequent famines than it endured. After the insurrection of 1689, promises of equitable treatment were repudiated, and Poynings's Law divested the Irish of civil rights. The economy was milked by English interests. Government and ecclesiastical posts became sinecures for England's idle rich. Although England's harsh treatment of Ireland stemmed in large measure from English contempt for Catholicism, solidarity developed in Ireland between the predominantly Catholic masses and the Anglo-Irish Protestant landowners, who identified with their Irish interests rather than with England.

Beginning in the 1770s, demands for reform began to grow. During the American War of Independence, Britain withdrew her troops to the colonies. Henry Grattan organized the United Volunteers, ostensibly to protect the country from French invasion, but he used this armed force to blackmail Britain for reforms. Poynings's Laws were repealed (1783), and an Irish Parliament (Grattan's Parliament) was created. However, the British Parliament refused to grant Ireland any significant relief from the Navigation Laws, which kept Ireland at the mercy of English commercial interests, while the land reform and Catholic disabilities were not even considered.

England's failure to respond to the overtures of moderates like Grattan and the outbreak of the French Revolution raised Irish demands to a fever pitch. The republican Society of United Irishmen, led by Wolfe Tone, attempted to free Ireland with French aid, but his movement was betrayed. Tone committed suicide before execution, and his followers were subdued in a bloodbath (1798).

The Act of Union (1801) brought Ireland into the United Kingdom of Great Britain and gave her one hundred seats in the House of

Commons and thirty-two seats in the House of Lords; but to the impoverished, disfranchised Catholic masses, this provided no relief. Britain's refusal to deal with Irish grievances prevented reconciliation and led to increased Anglo-Irish hatred, punctuated by periodic outbursts of violence, throughout the nineteenth and twentieth centuries.

ROBERT WALPOLE AND MINISTERIAL RESPONSIBILITY. Throughout his reign George I remained preoccupied with the interests of Hanover. Since he could not speak English, he avoided cabinet meetings and delegated authority for the government of Britain to the cabinet of his chief minister, Robert Walpole. Although it was not obvious at the time, Walpole's tenure from 1721 to 1742 marks an important stage in the development of the British political system.

Walpole did not hold the title Prime Minister, but during his long administration, he developed the prerogatives of the office. Although he held his post by virtue of royal appointment, he could not hope to carry out his executive duties without maintaining a parliamentary majority. His dual function as executive officer and majority leader became a unique feature of Britain's parliamentary system. Although the system remained in the embryonic stage during Walpole's administration, the following features of parliamentary government slowly developed: (1) the prime minister and members of his cabinet are collectively responsible for their actions to a majority in the House of Commons; (2) the cabinet usually contains only members of the majority party, and the prime minister is the parliamentary leader of that party; (3) should the cabinet lose the confidence of the parliamentary majority on an important issue, it must resign as a group and either give way to a new ministry or call for a national election to resolve the issue.

Unlike his modern counterpart, an eighteenth-century prime minister had no tightly knit party to supply a parliamentary majority and thus had to rely on a variety of expedients to maintain his position. Walpole kept the king's favor through the constant intercession of his close friend Queen Caroline. His control of royal patronage enabled him to dispense government posts and sinecures to his supporters. The duke of Newcastle, Walpole's secretary of state, became the greatest boroughmonger in the realm. Because a relative handful of men controlled elections in the many rotten (unrepresentative) boroughs, Newcastle's influence, favors, threats, and bribes ensured the government's parliamentary majority.

There are several outstanding characteristics of Walpole's administration. At the outset, he was concerned with completing the destruction of the Tories and thereafter with promoting the personal fortunes of his supporters within the Whig faction. Secondly, he took an active interest in financial and economic affairs. A speculative boom promoted by the South Sea Company, hence known as the South Sea Bubble, collapsed in 1720 amidst mismanagement and fraud. Walpole played a decisive role in restoring confidence during the financial panic that followed. In addition, he overhauled the tariff system to promote manufacturing and commerce while lowering land taxes. Finally, he was determined to keep England from expensive foreign adventures, which he believed would bring no benefit and whose cost would be borne by the merchant class and the landed aristocracy. He succeeded in maintaining peace for twenty-five years, but popular opinion drove the government to war in 1739, and Walpole retired from office in 1742.

WILLIAM PITT AND THE QUEST FOR EMPIRE. William Pitt (often referred to as the earl of Chatham to distinguish him from his son and namesake) was the dominant spokesman for the expansionist attitude Britain adopted during the middle of the century. He was one of the most influential politicians of the day, although he served as prime minister for only a few months in 1766. He sat for Old Sarum, the rottenest of the rotten boroughs, yet won the nickname "the Great Commoner" for his support of honest government and constitutional reform. In foreign affairs he viewed France as the greatest threat to England's imperial greatness and joined the "patriot" faction that belittled Walpole's weak foreign policy. Pitt reached the peak of his influence from 1757 to 1761 when, as secretary of state and majority leader in the Commons, he successfully directed England's efforts in the Seven Years' War (see page 176). By his constant attacks on the ministry during his long periods of opposition and by his appeals to public opinion to support his positions, Pitt undermined the attitude that the Parliament was an aristocratic preserve and helped foster the respectability of parliamentary opposition.

The American Revolution

Britain's victory in the Seven Years' War (1756–1763) seemed to confirm its position as the dominant imperial power. The Union Jack flew from Lake Superior to Calcutta, and English merchantmen and men-of-war ruled the waves. However, in just over a decade, the thirteen American colonies were in revolt, and Britain found itself confronting the rebels and a hostile Europe in the North Atlantic's last great colonial war.

The Thirteen Colonies in 1763. The colonists were not primed for revolt in 1763. They had long enjoyed the relative autonomy of a benevolent government. Restrictive trade legislation was laxly enforced, and British merchants had been left to handle their own affairs with colonial customers. Each colony had its own assembly whose self-regulatory legislation was usually sanctioned by the Privy Council. The defeat of France and its Indian allies opened the prospect of cheap, bountiful lands to the west.

In 1763 the colonies contained approximately 1.5 million inhabi- tants. Aided by a high birth rate and immigration, by 1775 the population had risen to 2.5 million, approximately one third the population of Britain. The colonies, however, remained almost en- tirely rural with only Boston, Philadelphia, New York, and Charles- ton having more than ten thousand inhabitants. Although the colonies shared a primarily British stock and a culture that included Protestant- ism and the common law, to which was added the leaven of the frontier experience, each formed a fairly compact community that cooperated with its neighbors only in times of greatest danger.

Roots of Conflict. Britain's victory in the French and Indian War failed to consolidate its imperial position. Discord soon racked North America. Sources of conflict arose directly from Britain's recent victory. After concentrating for decades on imperial defense, George III's government was determined to organize an effective mercantile system that would ensure a colonial contribution to imperial defense and administration. The decision was made at the very time when the colonies, no longer facing the threat of French attack, were unlikely to accept increased taxation or interference from Britain. The diver- gence of British and colonial interests after 1763 generated antagon- ism and then open conflict.

PROCLAMATION OF 1763. The defeat of France did not bring imme- diate peace to the western wilderness. Pontiac, the Ottawa chief, angered by British neglect and the westward movement of settlers, formed a great alliance of the western tribes. They launched a co- ordinated attack on Britain's outposts beyond the Alleghenies and overwhelmed all but forts Detroit, Niagara, and Pitt (1763). But they were unable to capitalize on their victories, and their alliance disin- tegrated in 1765. At the outbreak of hostilities, the English govern- ment issued a proclamation (1763) prohibiting the movement of colonists beyond the Allegheny divide, an action intended to ease tensions, prevent costly hostilities, and protect the settlers. But Eng- land could not prevent westward expansion, and its attempts caused resentment among colonists who wanted to develop the territory.

THE SEARCH FOR REVENUE. George Grenville became prime min- ister and chancellor of the exchequer in 1764. He and his successors were determined that the colonies would begin to pay for their up- keep and form an integral part of a mercantile empire designed to promote England's well-being. Their attempts served only to raise the political temperature in the colonies.

Sugar Act (1764). The Sugar Act revised the Molasses Act (1733). While lowering the tariff on molasses (the raw material of rum), the government was determined to eliminate smuggling and collect the duties, thus curbing the colonial traffic with the French West Indies.

Stamp Act (1765). This act required placement of revenue stamps on all legal documents and many luxury items. The tax was low, easy to collect, and expected to provide substantial revenue. There was an immediate outcry from the colonies, who had not been consulted. The Virginia House of Burgesses condemned the act as illegal taxation. The Stamp Act Congress, an ad hoc convocation with delegates from nine colonies, condemned the tax and denied Parliament's right to tax the colonies. The colonists harassed tax-stamp agents and refused to buy English goods. The British government gave way, and the act was repealed in March 1766. While repealing the Stamp Act, the Parliament did not concede in principle. The Declaratory Act reaffirmed the Parliament's right to tax the colonies.

Townshend Duties (1767). The colonists had denied Parliament's right to levy internal taxes in the colonies. Chancellor of the exchequer Charles Townshend thus sought a remedy in the imposition of new customs duties and tighter monitoring of trade. The new duties were imposed on tea, lead, paper, paint, and glass. Although American propagandists had drawn a fine distinction between internal and external taxation in their attacks on the Stamp Act, their denunciation of the Townshend duties made it obvious that they were adverse to paying taxes of any kind levied at Westminster. Again a public outcry and a boycott of English imports led the government to repeal the duties in 1770.

COERCION AND RESISTANCE. The question of revenue was soon overshadowed by the more fundamental issue of who controlled colonial affairs. The British pressed the issue, and the colonists dug in their heels.

Boston Massacre (1770). Friction between Bostonians and Redcoats turned to hatred in 1770 when British sentries were provoked by snowballs and hecklers to fire into a crowd, killing five.

Boston Tea Party (1773). Under the terms of the Tea Act, the East India Company was permitted to sell its tea in America, directly to retailers. The inexpensive tea carried a tax and hurt American wholesalers. On the night of 16 December 1773, the "Sons of Liberty," costumed as Indians, boarded ships in Boston Harbor and destroyed their cargoes of tea. The "Tea Party" resulted in severe reprisals.

Intolerable Acts (1774). In response to Bostonian vandalism, Parliament was determined to bring the colonials to heel. The Intolerable, or Coercive, Acts closed the Boston port, placed Massachusetts permanently under martial law, permitted the quartering of troops in homes, and suspended the jurisdiction of colonial courts over royal officers. The Quebec Act, which placed the territory west of the Alleghenies under Canadian jurisdiction, is often included in this list. These acts galvanized opinion against British rule.

The War of Independence (1775–1783). At the outbreak of hostilities, Britain had economic and military superiority; but British opinion was divided, and the rebels, though lacking in training and discipline, ranged easily over a large, familiar, and generally hospitable country. The British army performed well, as expected, but it is difficult to imagine how it could have converted battlefield success into lasting political control of the colonies after the shooting began in 1775. American victories, though scattered, came at crucial moments. The opening rounds at Concord (April 1775) and Bunker Hill (June 1775) gave the colonists' cause a psychological boost. The Declaration of Independence by Congress in Philadelphia (4 July 1776) brought no insurance of military success, and the British occupied New York City (September 1776) and Philadelphia (September 1777). But American morale rebounded with the capture of General Burgoyne's army at Saratoga (October 1777). This victory ensured open French support, which was formalized by a treaty of alliance (February 1778). Britain soon found herself at war not only with France but also with Holland and Spain. In addition Russia made it clear that it would protect its neutral status against Britain's blockade with force if necessary. In 1779 the war shifted to the Carolinas, where after initial successes the British army of George Cornwallis retreated to Yorktown, Virginia, to await support from the fleet. The British fleet was defeated, and Cornwallis surrendered after being encircled by an Anglo-French army commanded by George Washington (19 October 1781). This campaign ended the fighting, but the peace terms were not agreed on until 1783. Under the terms of the Peace of Paris (20 January 1783), the former colonies were recognized as the sovereign United States. The United States became a testing ground for republicanism in a world of monarchies, and the experiment was followed closely by European men of affairs. Although Britain lost this phase of its colonial wars, it was not seriously weakened. The French, on the other hand, had won the war, but soon reaped a financial crisis as the result of its cost.

17

The French Revolution

Although historians divide their work into chapters, epochs, and ages, the story of man is a continuum that stretches unbroken into the past. There are, nevertheless, some periods whose drama and impact seem to set them apart; the French Revolution is such a time. The drama began in France in 1789 but soon overflowed its boundaries and engulfed Europe. When the revolutionary flood subsided, it revealed not only the debris of broken institutions and values but also the foundation of a new Europe whose ideas and institutions still buttress Western civilization.

Collapse of the Old Regime

The French Revolution took both its participants and foreign observers by surprise. On the surface France seemed to be the most stable and powerful state in Europe. Her economy was strong and her intellectual life vibrant. But hidden fissures weakened the edifice, and only a sudden shock was needed to bring it down. The class structure had become increasingly rigid; the aristocracy and bourgeoisie, who despised one another, grew increasingly frustrated in their attempts to enhance their position. The standard of living among the urban workers and peasantry deteriorated even as the economy flourished. During times of crisis, the latest of which occurred in the winter of 1788–1789, they were pushed to the brink of starvation and despair. The intellectuals gave voice to the general malaise, attacking the archaic institutions and calling for sweeping reforms. The king and his ministers, along with his detractors within the privileged estates, failed to perceive the danger and the potential for revolt. Louis XVI hoped that mere tinkering with the financial system would resolve his difficulties. In the process he triggered a revolution that swept away his regime.

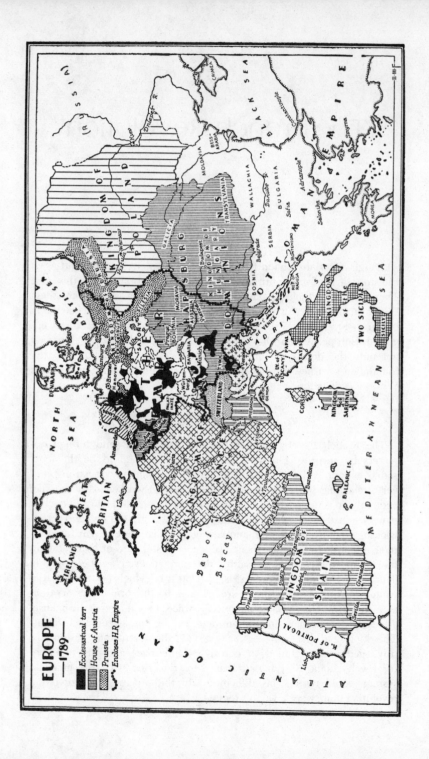

Assembly of Notables. Louis XVI hoped to negotiate fiscal reforms without a renewed confrontation with the parlements. He convened the ad hoc Assembly of Notables in February 1787, before which Comptroller general Calonne laid out the crown's program. Its most significant features were (1) a universal land tax to be assessed by elected provincial assemblies; (2) abolition of internal tariffs; (3) redemption of the Church debt in return for forfeiture of its manorial rights; and (4) a reduction and reorganization of the *taille* (direct tax), *gabelle* (salt tax), and the *corvée* (labor duty). The assembly, made up of peers, municipal officers, and bishops, demanded a full accounting of the government's finances in the hope of increasing their powers, and they rejected as illegal the king's attempt to levy new taxes without the consent of the Estates General. Thwarted in his attempted reform, Louis XVI dismissed Calonne and dissolved the Assembly of Notables in May 1787.

Confrontation with the Parlements. Louis XVI, determined to enforce his will, demanded the registration of his decrees by the Paris Parlement in a *lit de justice* (July 1787). This act began a confrontation with the parlements that continued until August 1788. The Paris Parlement denounced as unconstitutional the enactment of new taxes without the consent of the Estates General. Although they were in fact simply trying to preserve their privileged status, the parlementaires won wide popular support for their defense of traditional liberties against the usurpation of the king. Louis responded first by exiling the justices (August 1787) and then by stripping the parlements of their political and judicial authority (May 1788). The crown could not maintain its position against the resistance of the aristocracy, the clergy, the parlements, and public opinion. In August 1788 Louis agreed to summon the Estates General.

The Calling of the Estates General. The estates of the realm had not been convoked since 1614, and the king's summons was an admission of the gravity of the crisis. The first and second estates had demanded this extreme measure. They were certain that with the enforcement of traditional procedures, which required the estates to meet in three separate assemblies each casting one vote, they could increase their own authority while maintaining their privileged position above the third estate. But the commoners refused to accept this inferior status, and a ground swell of popular sentiment demanded a doubling of the representation for the third estate and the convocation of the Estates General in a single body. When the Paris Parlement officially condemned this proposal, thereby revealing its members' desire to maintain their privileges rather than to protect liberty, public opinion turned against it. Popular sentiment was probably best expressed by Abbé Sieyès in his pamphlet "What Is the Third Estate?" in which he demanded that the third estate, which included 98 percent of the people, stand on an equal footing with the other two estates. The king's council acquiesced. The nobility elected approximately three hundred members primarily from the provinces; the clergy elected the same number, drawing heavily upon parish priests; and the commoners elected six hundred representatives, drawn primarily from the upper-middle classes through a process of indirect election. During the campaign the electoral assemblies produced lists of grievances (*cahiers de doléances*) for consideration. The wide range of these demands, covering basic constitutional issues, made it clear that the estates would not simply deal with the financial crisis but would direct itself toward reforming the government.

The Revolution of Lawyers. The Estates General convened on 5 May 1789. The king missed a unique opportunity to present a comprehensive reform program and to make a personal appeal for national support. Instead he limited himself to a welcoming address and left to Necker, his newly reappointed director general of finances, the task of presenting a long and detailed financial statement. The three estates were then directed to adjourn to separate meeting halls to prepare for working sessions. At this juncture the expectations of the privileged were challenged by the third estate, which refused to meet in a separate session where their six hundred delegates would still cast only a single collective vote.

CREATION OF THE NATIONAL ASSEMBLY. For five weeks the third estate refused to verify the credentials of its members while calling upon the delegates of the other estates to unite with them in a single assembly. Although only a few members of the lower clergy accepted the invitation, the commons finally resolved to act. On 17 June 1789 the third estate declared itself to be the National Assembly and, as such, the only true representatives of the nation.

TENNIS COURT OATH. In his attempt to regain control of the situation, Louis ordered the temporary closing of the assembly's meeting hall. The commoners took this as a threat. On June 20 they met in an indoor tennis court, where they vowed to continue to meet until they had given France a constitution. The Tennis Court Oath enunciated the idea that the representatives of the people in national assembly had a right to determine the constitution of the state. On July 9 the National Assembly confirmed this belief by declaring itself to be the Constituent Assembly (that is, the constitution-making body). Louis XVI's inept handling of the affair had allowed the opportunity for controlled reform to slip through his grasp. He now faced a determined delegation of the people resolved to enforce its will.

The Popular Revolt. The confrontation between the third estate and the crown at Versailles was reflected in the growing unrest that soon gripped Paris and swept across rural France.

STORMING OF THE BASTILLE. Apprehension gripped Paris with the arrival of news that Necker had been dismissed from the king's service and that Louis was gathering troops around the city. Despite reassurances from the king that these steps had been taken for their own protection, the Parisians feared counterrevolution and responded by forming a municipal guard. On July 14 a crowd searching for arms confronted a small garrison of royal troops manning the Bastille. When parley failed they stormed the fortress. The taking of the Bastille had far-reaching implications; it demonstrated, first, the willingness and the ability of the Parisians to attack the king's troops and, second, his inability to make reprisals. A revolutionary city government, the *Commune*, with an elected mayor was formed and adopted as its standard the new tricolor flag. The events in Paris also lent support to the Constituent Assembly at Versailles, which could continue its work without fear of dissolution.

THE GREAT FEAR. The lean harvest of 1788 and the harsh winter that followed had cast the specter of famine across France. Apprehension turned to mass hysteria as desperate men fell prey to rumors that counterrevolutionary brigands stalked the land. Throughout July and August, mobs put the torch to the châteaus of the hated aristocrats, refused to pay taxes, and looted grain convoys. In the provincial towns, the bourgeoisie followed the lead of the Paris Commune, reorganizing their own municipalities and forming militia to protect themselves both from royal authorities and the rabble.

Fall of the Ancien Régime. After Bastille Day many aristocrats, including the king's brother, emigrated to the safety of neighboring states. Those who remained realized that for the time being at least they must reconcile themselves to the new circumstances if they hoped to save anything.

THE NIGHT OF AUGUST 4. The feudal regime was struck down by the National Assembly on the night of August 4. The move was led by the liberal vicomte de Noailles, who renounced his right to feudal dues and many of his seigneurial rights. He was imitated both by fellow liberals and by conservatives who feared that rural anarchy would sweep away their property rights. This wholesale abnegation of privilege that arose both from altruism and fear marked the first step in acceptance of the concept of equality before the law.

DECLARATION OF THE RIGHTS OF MAN AND CITIZEN. Having dissolved the theoretical basis for the old regime, the assembly formulated a new credo. The Declaration of the Rights of Man and Citizen, adopted on August 27, proclaimed liberty, property, security, and resistance to oppression as inalienable natural rights and endorsed the concept of popular sovereignty. Although the declaration confirmed a belief in monarchy and the inviolability of private property, taken in the context of the eighteenth century, it is a truly revolutionary document.

THE OCTOBER DAYS. The first phase of the revolution was climaxed on October 5, when a mob of Parisian women marched on Versailles demanding bread and regular provisioning for their city. The following day they forced the king to return with them to Paris, and on October 17 the assembly followed. As a result emigration of conservatives accelerated, and henceforth both king and assembly were under the scrutiny and influence of Paris.

The Constitutional Monarchy

The first phase of the revolution had destroyed royal absolutism and class privilege and had substituted the concept of popular sovereignty and equality before the law. The second phase, which lasted from October 1789 to September 1792 was an attempt to formalize these new ideas within the framework of a constitutional monarchy. Such a regime might have permanently bridged the gap between revolutionaries and the adherents of the old order, but Louis XVI was unable to adjust to his new role or to provide positive leadership. His intrigues destroyed all hopes for a balanced monarchical system and ultimately led him to the scaffold.

The Constituent Assembly. The October Days had removed the threat of dissolution that had hung over the assembly, a bountiful harvest removed the threat of famine, and civil disorder subsided. In relative calm the Constituent Assembly set to work to formalize the revolutionary gains by providing France with a new set of institutions.

POLITICAL REFORM. The immediate political issue facing the Constituent Assembly was the king's role in the new political system. Although all the representatives were professed monarchists, the majority were determined to destroy absolutism by bringing the monarchy under the constraints of law and by emphasizing the concept of popular sovereignty. The crown remained hereditary in the royal family, but amendment of the sovereign's title from King of France and Navarre to King of the French indicated that his right to rule was derived from the nation. The king was granted a four-year suspensive veto but denied the right to introduce legislation. He retained his control of the armed forces and foreign affairs. The delegates were also careful to protect themselves from radicalism. All men were given the rights of citizenship, but a distinction was drawn between "active" and "passive" citizens. Active citizens were accorded the franchise and the right to hold public office on the basis of the direct taxes they paid, while passive citizens were accorded only civil rights.

ADMINISTRATIVE REFORM. The patchwork of administrative, political, judicial, and fiscal jurisdictions was swept away. France was divided into eighty-three *départements*, which were subdivided into *districts*, *cantons*, and *communes* (municipalities). These subdivisions were to be governed by elected officials who were responsible for the local affairs. Jurisdiction of the new courts corresponded to the new administrative boundaries. Civil cases were to be tried by elected justices of the peace and appellate judges, while jury trials were retained for criminal cases. The system was capped by a high appellate court.

FISCAL REFORM. The fiscal crisis had worsened during the revolution. Although tax equalization insured long-range solvency, immediate steps were needed to meet current expenses and avoid bankruptcy. This was accomplished through confiscation of all ecclesiastical property, which was then used as backing for *assignats* (bonds). The idea of retiring the debt through projected exchange of assignats for land was theoretically sound, but it broke down as more and more assignats were issued to cover mounting expenses. They soon were accepted as legal tender and depreciated rapidly after 1793.

CIVIL CONSTITUTION OF THE CLERGY. By early 1790 the assembly had already taken steps to end what it considered Church abuses. It had instituted toleration of Protestantism, abolished monasticism, confiscated all ecclesiastical property, and ended the Church's financial autonomy. The decrees promulgated in July 1790 to reform the structure of the Church were known collectively as the Civil Constitution of the Clergy. Among its most important provisions were: (1) redistricting of dioceses to coincide with the new départements, (2) election of all clerics and payment of their salaries by the state, (3) abolition of the papacy's administrative and judicial jurisdiction within France. In November 1790 all priests were required to take an oath to support the Constitution of France. Those who refused to take the oath, including most of the bishops, became known as *nonjurors* and as such were required to give up their posts and public functions. Although the assembly had no desire to tamper with theology, its heavy-handed approach to Church affairs turned a large portion of the peasantry against the revolution. Henceforth the nonjuring clergy became an important force in counterrevolutionary activity.

FLIGHT TO VARENNES. Distressed by the Church reforms, which he considered sacrilegious, and by the deterioration of his authority, the king decided to flee to Luxembourg. There he hoped to rally the émigrés, win the support of other monarchs (including Emperor Leopold II, brother of Queen Marie Antoinette) and then march back to France and reclaim his throne. The elaborately laid plan miscarried the day after the royal party left Paris on 20 June 1791. The king was recognized in the border town of Varennes, placed under arrest, and returned to Paris.

CONSTITUTION OF 1791. Despite the king's attempt to abandon the revolution, the assembly completed work on the new constitution incorporating the principles of constitutional monarchy. This document, which received the king's signature on 14 September 1791, was the first written constitution adopted by a major European state. It confirmed the concept of popular sovereignty and affirmed that the King of the French should rule with the constraints of the law. Legislative power was vested in a unicameral legislature with the power to override the king's suspensive veto. At the same time the constitution reflected fear among the moderate Feuillant faction of growing republican and democratizing sentiments. The franchise was restricted to property-owning active (taxpaying) citizens. Constitutional amendment was made extremely difficult.

The Legislative Assembly. The Legislative Assembly stipulated by the Constitution convened on 1 October 1791. Under the terms of a "self-denying" decree adopted in May, members of the preceding assembly were excluded. The new assembly sat until the collapse of the monarchy in August 1792.

POLITICAL FACTIONS. Although there were no political parties in the modern sense, factions began to coalesce both inside and outside the legislature. The Feuillants, originally the strongest group in the assembly and the mainstay of the ministry, hoped to maintain constitutional monarchy favorable to bourgeois interests. More radical was the Jacobin Club, whose powerful right-wing members were first known as Brissotins and later as Girondins. The Jacobins contained the nucleus of later republican leadership. However, it is impossible clearly to differentiate political attitudes between the groups at this time. Their single common goal was the conquest of power.

OUTBREAK OF WAR. No clear-cut cause can be cited for the outbreak of war that was to ravage Europe for twenty-five years. Relations between the king and the legislature deteriorated throughout the winter of 1791–1792. In the legislature there was growing hostility to obstructionism and suspicion of the king's complicity with émigré plans to mount a counterrevolutionary invasion of France. The Girondins supported war to expose the royal treason and in the hopes of carrying the revolution into the Germanies and Austria. Louis also hoped for war because he felt that the French army, deprived of its aristocratic officers, would fall easy prey to the Austrians. Outside of France there was a growing belief that Louis's authority had to be restored before France set all of Europe aflame.

The outbreak of hostilities in April soon confirmed Louis's hopes. All along the frontier, French armies fled before numerically inferior Austrian and Prussian forces. The panic quickly spread to Paris, where massive demonstrations erupted for the first time since the summer of 1789. The king expended the residue of his prestige by use of his suspensive veto. Suspicions of the royal conspiracy with the enemy seemed to be confirmed when the duke of Brunswick, commander of the invading armies, issued a manifesto on 25 July 1792 threatening to destroy Paris if the royal family were harmed.

OVERTHROW OF THE MONARCHY. Military defeat and fear of counterrevolution were the primary causes of the Parisian insurrection that began in the predawn of August 10. Jacobin-led *sans-culottes* seized the city hall and installed a revolutionary commune in the place of the defunct municipal government. Next they stormed the Tuileries, where they massacred the king's Swiss bodyguard. Meanwhile, the royal family had escaped and thrown itself on the mercy of the Legislative Assembly. The assembly, however, had lost control of events. Acceding to the Commune's demands, it placed the king under arrest and called for a National Convention elected by universal manhood suffrage to determine the fate of the monarchy.

SEPTEMBER MASSACRES. Fear of counterrevolutionary sentiment and the panic generated by the fall of Verdun to the Prussians led to five days of uncontrollable rioting, beginning on September 2. The rioters threw themselves upon the suspected counterrevolutionaries packing the city's prisons. Before the frenzy subsided, over twelve hundred inmates had been slaughtered.

BATTLE OF VALMY. A string of domestic and foreign disasters had sapped revolutionary morale, but good news arrived from Valmy in the Argonne, where on September 20 French artillery, firing through an obscuring fog, had forced the Prussians to withdraw. Though of slight military significance, the battle gave an important psychological boost to the beleaguered French.

The Revolutionary Republic

The experiment in constitutional monarchy had failed. The National Convention ruled France from September 1792 until August 1795. It was a revolutionary regime, devoid of a constitution, that attempted to found a republic, fend off invaders, and defeat the real and imagined "enemies of the people" at home and abroad. In the process the revolution went through its most violent stage and, like Saturn, devoured its own children.

The Convention Takes Power. The National Convention convened on 21 September 1792. Many of its 749 representatives, elected by a small fraction of the eligible voters, were republicans. They can be divided into three broad categories. On the left were the Jacobins, who controlled the Paris commune and had swept the Parisian elections. They were led by Maximilien Robespierre, Jean Marie Collot d'Herbois, Georges Danton, and Jean Paul Marat. On the right were the more numerous Girondins, whose strength was drawn primarily from the provinces. Their most important spokesmen were Pierre Vergniaud, Jacques Pierre Brissot, François Buzot, Jérôme Petion de Villeneuve, and in the ministry Jean Marie Roland de la Platière. These factions were divided more by personalities and their aspirations for power than by ideology, although the Girondins tended to be drawn from a slightly higher social class, whose interests they reflected. These two factions vied for the support of the majority, known as the Plain or, more derisively, as the Belly. This majority drifted without leadership, its individual members attempting to maintain their safety and end up on the winning side.

BIRTH OF THE REPUBLIC. The convention's first order of business on September 21 was the dissolution of the monarchy and the declaration of the republic. September 22 was declared the first day of the year One of the republican epoch. In November 1793 the convention adopted a revolutionary calendar of twelve thirty-day months named for the seasons. Although France later reverted to the Gregorian calendar, many events of this period are still referred to by their revolutionary dates (for instance, 9 Thermidor year 2 and 18 Brumaire year 8).

TRIAL AND EXECUTION OF LOUIS XVI. Louis Capet, as the dethroned king was known, was brought to trial for treason before the convention in December 1792. After his conviction in January 1793, the Jacobins demanded and obtained the death penalty, while the badly divided Girondins feared the consequences of capital punishment. The king's execution on January 21 had far-reaching political implications. It ended all hope of reconciliation between republican France and the monarchies of Europe. It permanently alienated a large part of the still monarchist French peasantry, who, under the leadership of refractory priests and nobles, rebelled against the Parisian government. Finally it undermined the position in the convention of the Girondins, who were now attacked as counterrevolutionaries and federalists. Marie Antoinette's execution followed on 16 October 1793, and in 1795 the dauphin (who would have been Louis XVII), while in custody, disappeared without a trace. Louis's two brothers, the counts of Provence and Artois, continued the fight from exile and survived to rule after the revolution (see p. 253).

War of the First Coalition. Even before Louis's execution, the convention took several actions that made general war virtually inevitable. Dumouriez's victory at Jemappes on 6 November 1792 exposed the Austrian Netherlands to French conquest. France then opened the Scheldt River in violation of the Peace of Westphalia (1648), thus antagonizing both Britain and Holland. Of more ominous significance was the convention's proclamation offering the oppressed peoples of Europe aid in overthrowing their tyrannical masters, thereby throwing a gauntlet at the feet of Europe's monarchs.

On 11 February 1793 France declared war on Britain, Holland, and Spain, adding them to a list of enemies that already included Prussia and Austria. Her enemies formed the first of five coalitions that would be ranged against France for the next twenty-two years. Though at first poorly organized, the French armies were whipped into shape by Lazare Carnot. They fought desperately to hold their enemies at bay until 1795 when the coalition, war-weary and riven by separate interests, dissolved. Although the war continued, France was able to cope with her enemies piecemeal, and the time of greatest danger passed.

Jacobin Dictatorship. In the spring of 1793, the French Revolution entered a new phase. Having jettisoned the monarchy and their traditional economic and social institutions, the revolutionaries faced domestic turmoil and a growing foreign threat. At this juncture the Jacobins emerged as the dominant political force. They eliminated their domestic foes, restored order, and carried the war to the enemy. However, to achieve these results, they instituted a reign of terror that undermined the dream of a free society.

DEFEAT OF THE GIRONDINS. After the execution of Louis XVI, the Girondins controlled both the ministry and the convention. With this control came the responsibility for overwhelming problems. The Girondins could not bring themselves to take extreme measures to alleviate their problems, and they gained a reputation for hostility toward Paris.

The war generated not only fear and administrative problems but also a recurrence of food shortages. The *enragés* in the Parisian *sections* led the working class in their demands for immediate and drastic action, including economic controls. The Jacobins in the convention joined the chorus condemning the government. In March 1793 the peasants of the Vendée, led by royalists and nonjuring priests, refused to submit to the draft and rose in revolt. Almost simultaneously, General Dumouriez, the French commander in the Netherlands (who had close Girondin connections), defected to the Austrians.

As their opponents closed in, the Girondins lashed back. They tried unsuccessfully to condemn the popular Jacobin journalist Jean Paul Marat on charges of treason. During May they further infuriated the sans-culottes by attempting to abolish the Parisian municipal government and by actively supporting the federalist revolt against Parisian dominance. On 2 June 1793 the National Guard surrounded the convention and demanded the expulsion of the Girondin leaders, twenty-nine of whom were placed under house arrest. With this coup Girondin control ended, and the Jacobins emerged as the dominant political force.

JACOBINS. The Jacobins were the most radical group that was able to hold power during the Revolution. Their name was derived from a Jacobin convent where they met nightly under the leadership of Marat, Maximilien Robespierre, and Louis Antoine de Saint-Just, among others, to plan policy and strategy. Though initially a minority in the convention, they held sway in the sections and steadily organized a vast complex of clubs in every département. Despite the Jacobins' radicalism, their leadership was drawn from moderately successful middle-aged professional men, and their rank and file contained hardworking merchants and craftsmen.

Jacobin political beliefs included democratic republicanism that stressed nationalism and a strong centralized government. Many Jacobins were violently anticlerical and rejected Christianity for deism. Although they later instituted economic controls as emergency measures, they were committed to private property and laissez-faire. The keystone of their ideology was the conviction that a well-ordered, humane, and just society would emerge through the judicious application of human reason.

REVOLUTIONARY GOVERNMENT. The convention completed the draft constitution on 24 June 1793. However, the democratic Constitution of the Year 1 (1793) was never promulgated, and in October it was officially suspended for the duration of the war. In its place the convention sanctioned revolutionary government to deal with the national emergency. The convention remained in session as the repository of the general will but delegated its authority to its committees and representatives. The Jacobins controlled this ad hoc administration at all levels. This revolutionary government became a frightening prototype for the ideologically committed totalitarian regimes that emerged in the twentieth century.

Committee of Public Safety. The Committee of Public Safety was constituted on 6 April 1793. After September it contained twelve Jacobins who exercised a virtual dictatorship until July 1794.

Committee of General Security. Originally created in October 1792, the Committee of General Security was strengthened in September 1793. Its nine members, who were nominated by the Committee of Public Safety, controlled the police apparatus and were concerned primarily with eliminating counterrevolutionaries.

Revolutionary Tribunal. The regular legal system, which was not structured to deal with antirevolutionary crimes, was augmented in August 1792 by the Revolutionary Tribunal. Amid the general hysteria in the summer of 1793, when almost any crime could be viewed as detrimental to the state and thus treasonous, the tribunal became a summary court before which were paraded all manner of suspects. Only a perfunctory defense was allowed, and there was no appeal. After September the only sentence was death by guillotine, which was carried out within hours.

Representatives on Mission and National Agents. To enforce its authority and maintain order in the provinces and the army, the convention dispatched representatives on mission. The representatives, often members of the Committee of Public Safety, had unlimited authority and carried out their missions with ruthless dispatch. Permanent local administrators, known as national agents, were responsible to the convention and carried out its routine orders.

Surveillance Committees. The surveillance committees were originally established to monitor the activities of foreigners. Later known as revolutionary committees, they expanded their role and reported all suspected activities to local authorities and the Committee of General Security.

Jacobin Clubs. Finally a word must be said about the thousands of Jacobin clubs that formed a vast network throughout France. They served to spread republican ideology and reported to the Paris club to protect Jacobin control of the entire revolutionary apparatus.

REIGN OF VIRTUE AND TERROR. The Jacobins directed their energies toward four major tasks: (1) the prosecution of the war, (2) the reordering of the economy, (3) the elimination of counterrevolutionaries and spies, (4) the creation of a constitutional republic. The means they employed was terror, encompassing not only the cold-blooded elimination of all opposition but also the physical and psychological mobilization of the entire society. For Robespierre, whose presence dominated the government, the ultimate goal was the Republic of Virtue, a utopian existence of liberty, equality, and fraternity built upon the rational cooperation of all men. Those who stood in the way of this dream he denounced as enemies of mankind and condemned to the guillotine.

Levée en Masse. By the end of July 1793, the military situation was grim. Austrians advanced from the north; Prussians attacked from the east; the Spaniards approached from the south. The convention met this threat by the adoption of the extraordinary decree of 23 August 1793, which called the entire nation to arms. The *levée en masse* went far beyond universal military service. For the first time in European history, it called forth a citizen army and mobilized an entire nation for war. Not only were all able-bodied men called to the colors, but women were ordered to make supplies, old men were admonished to rally the youth, and private property was requisitioned for the defense of the *patrie*. At first the citizen army had to pit spirit and sheer numbers against Europe's well-drilled professionals, but under the guiding hand of Lazare Carnot, the "Organizer of Victory," they became a juggernaut that by December had turned the tide.

Economic Terror. By 1793 the economy was in chaos: Short supplies had driven up prices; speculators attempted to make a profit on the distress; and ordinary citizens, hedging against the future, hoarded goods. The convention adopted many measures to control speculation and inflation. The most important was the Law of the Maximum, adopted on 29 September 1793, which fixed prices on essential items and salaries. Prices nevertheless continued to rise, a black market flourished, and Parisian workers became increasingly hostile to limitations on their income.

One permanent benefit that came from this attempt to rationalize commerce was the adoption in August of a new system of weights and measures. The metric system, which employs decimal increments and relates linear to volume measurements, is now in worldwide use.

Political Terror. To enforce their policies and eliminate the opposition, the Jacobins imposed a political terror. The Law of Suspects (17 September 1793) permitted the jailing of "suspected persons," a category so broad that it gave the authorities a free hand.

In the provinces the representatives on mission subdued the disorganized federalists one city at a time. Some capitulations resulted in reconciliation, while in Lyons, Bordeaux, and Toulon, surrender precipitated a bloodbath in which innocent bystanders suffered the same fate as rebels. By December the insurrection in the Vendée was subdued in the same manner. At Nantes thousands were executed by drowning without a trial.

Marie Antoinette died under the guillotine in October and was followed by a growing procession of unfortunates, including not only antirevolutionaries, but Girondins, thieves, hoarders, speculators, and hapless "suspects." The Jacobins, fearful of their position, also turned against their erstwhile allies. On the left the Hébertists, who maintained the loyalty of the Parisian sans-culottes, wanted an accelerated terror directed against speculators and hoarders, the remaining nobility, and Christianity. The Jacobins isolated Jacques Hébert and his supporters and sent them to the scaffold on 24 March 1794. On their right the Jacobins faced a growing faction, led by Georges Danton and known as Indulgents, who felt that the greatest danger had passed and that the time had come for a diminution of the terror and a national reconciliation. They in turn were executed on 5 April 1794.

Thermidorian Reaction. Robespierre and his more extreme colleagues in the Committee of Public Safety grew increasingly isolated from the sources of their support. The Parisian sans-culottes, deprived of their leaders and trapped between fixed wages and rising prices, grew sullen. In the countryside the majority remained Christian and probably monarchist. Even the Jacobin convention began to crack under the relentless psychological pressures. The Law of 22 Prairial (10 June 1794) accelerated the procession to the guillotine, which now cast its long shadow over the convention itself. On 9 Thermidor (July 27) the convention rose against the dictatorship of its own committee, and the following morning Robespierre, Saint-Just, and Couthon met their fate in the *Place de Revolution*. As a result of this coup, the term *thermidor* now refers to any similar series of events that signals the end of the most violent stage of any revolution and the return to a more moderate course.

Although a Jacobin majority still controlled the convention, the survivors of successive purges returned and asserted their influence. The machinery of the terror was slowly dismantled. Paris, released from the constraints of patriotic puritanism, returned to its old pleasures. Although the republican regicides did not want to go back to 1789, the experience of the terror tempered their outlook. The convention used force to suppress Jacobin-inspired mobs in April and May of 1795 and ordered General Bonaparte to turn his guns on royalist insurgents at the head of hungry sans-culottes. The "whiff of grapeshot" saved the government, enhanced the reputation of Bonaparte, and permitted the implementation of a moderately conservative constitution.

The Constitutional Republic

Having destroyed the Jacobin dictatorship, the convention installed a constitutional regime, termed the *Directory*, which ruled France from October 1795 to October 1799. Although the frenzy of the terror subsided, France did not return to normalcy. The moderate republicans who controlled the regime were threatened on the left by radicals who wished to continued the Revolution and on the right by reactionaries who conspired to restore the monarchy. Thus preoccupied with its own survival, the Directory failed to solve the economic, religious, and social problems that still plagued the country. In addition France's increasingly aggressive foreign policy prevented a reconciliation with her foreign enemies. A military coup ended this first constitutional republic.

CONSTITUTION OF THE YEAR 3 (1795). The Thermidorians, having survived the terror, were determined to prevent a recurrence of Jacobin democracy and mob rule. On the other hand, as republicans and regicides, they could not permit the restoration of the monarchy. The new constitution, which took effect in September 1795, clearly reflected both their conservative republicanism and their instinct for survival.

The legislative function was vested in the *Corps législatif*, containing the Council of Five Hundred and the Council of Elders, which took office on 27 October 1795. The *five hundred*, all at least thirty years old, introduced and debated all bills. The *elders*, married men or widowers, at least forty years old, approved or rejected all legislation. To ensure stability the legislature was selected by electoral assemblies of property owners or tenants of substance, who in turn were elected by the citizenry.

Five directors elected by the elders had the power to make war and peace, controlled the armed forces, and were responsible for internal security. To prevent a new dictatorship, severe limitations were placed on their tenure and actions.

The constitution included not only a declaration of rights but a statement of duties, which emphasized obedience to the law and the inviolability of private property. In a final effort to protect their position, the Thermidorians also stipulated that two-thirds of the convention must sit in the new assembly. They were thus dubbed the Perpetuals.

THE DIRECTORY AND DOMESTIC AFFAIRS. The new government faced staggering difficulties. To end the financial chaos, the Directory repudiated the worthless assignats in favor of metallic money and through a forced conversion of government bonds, repudiated a large part of the national debt. The action, although necessary, benefited land speculators at the expense of honest investors and undermined public confidence.

The regime also tried to restore morality by stressing civic responsibility while attempting to prevent the revival of Catholicism. Little was accomplished, however, given the psychological release from the terror and the dissolute lives of several of the directors.

The greatest difficulties were posed by political opposition. On the left Gracchus Babeuf, a romantic communist, formed the Society of Equals, which conspired to replace the regime with the democratic constitution of 1793. Babeuf was arrested in May 1796 and executed in April 1797. Having disposed of this threat, the government faced a resurgence of royalism, whose adherents won a stunning victory in the legislative elections in April 1797. Fearing a royalist coup, the government struck first. In the coup of 18 Fructidor (4 September 1797), loyal troops supported the government, while royalist deputies were expelled from the legislature and their leaders arrested. Although dictatorship had been reinstated, for the moment the regime was safe.

Foreign Policy. France had made peace with Spain, Prussia, and Holland in 1795. Russia was preoccupied with Poland. However, England and Austria were still in the field. To secure peace, the Directory was willing to abandon France's republican crusade but was determined to maintain its "natural frontier," the west bank of the Rhine. England, though under a strain from the long conflict, was unwilling to allow France to retain Antwerp and reopen the Scheldt River, and Austria was not ready to cede the Netherlands (Belgium). The Directory launched a campaign in 1796, hoping to end the conflict, but it succeeded only in widening the war.

ITALIAN CAMPAIGN. The primary mission in the spring campaign was given to the armies of the Rhine, but it was the Army of Italy, commanded by Napoleon Bonaparte, that scored spectacular successes. In a lightning campaign launched in April, it defeated both Sardinia and Austria. The lesser powers, including Sardinia, Lombardy, Naples, and the papacy, scrambled to make peace, and after long negotiations, during which Bonaparte excluded the Directory, the Austrians signed the Treaty of Campoformio (17 October 1797). Under its terms Austria ceded Belgium and Lombardy in return for Venetia and the Dalmatian coast. Bonaparte formed the Cisalpine republic with Lombard territory and the Ligurian republic from the defunct republic of Genoa. He thus violated the Directory's policy by reopening the revolutionary attack upon the principle of monarchy, but the Directory could not repudiate a general who had filled French coffers with war indemnities and booty and who had gained such popularity with the public.

EGYPTIAN CAMPAIGN. Throughout his brilliant career, Napoleon Bonaparte's policies were marred by a flaw that ultimately destroyed him. He was unwilling to place limits on his power, and his dreams of glory were not balanced by a rational appraisal of his limited resources. Unable to cross the channel to attack England, France's only remaining enemy, Bonaparte embarked on an Egyptian campaign in May 1798. His aims were to control the eastern Mediterranean, conquer Egypt and the Levant, and drive the English from India. Despite his brilliant victories, his logistical support was inadequate for the vast undertaking. Admiral Nelson ended the dream in a stroke when he destroyed the French fleet at Aboukir Bay (1 August 1798), thus leaving the conqueror of the Turks stranded two thousand miles from home.

SECOND COALITION. Bonaparte's victory in Italy, his Egyptian adventure, and French reconquest of the Netherlands eroded chances for peace. Buoyed by success, the French sanctioned the creation of republican puppet states: the Batavian (Holland), Cisalpine (Lombardy), Helvetic (Swiss cantons), Ligurian (Genoa), Parthenopean (Naples), and the Roman (Rome) republics. Faced with the resurgence of the republican crusade against monarchism, England, Austria, Russia, Turkey, Sardinia, Portugal, and Naples formed the Second Coalition (September 1798). Russia withdrew in October 1799, while Prussia and Spain remained neutral. The spring of 1799 witnessed nothing but French defeats. Its conquests were lost and its frontiers threatened.

The Brumaire Coup d'Etat. Factionalism posed an increasing danger to the regime after 1798. The Jacobins' resurgence at the polls in 1798 and 1799 strengthened their position in Paris and the councils. The royalists were reinvigorated by French defeats in 1799 that seemed to forecast a Bourbon restoration. The conservative republicans, primarily among the Council of Elders and led by the directors Sieyès and Ducos, defended themselves against right and left. In these circumstances Sieyès, with the help of loyal troops, organized a conspiracy to destroy both royalism and Jacobinism in order to create a new and more stable republic. Bonaparte made himself available for this task when he abandoned his ill-fated army in August 1799 and made a triumphal return through France, where only news of his victories had preceeded him. The conspirators seized the government on 18 Brumaire year 8 (10 November 1799). The term *brumaire* is now used by historians to refer to any right-wing militarist coup. Although Sieyès had hoped to maintain the republic, he misjudged both the character and talent of Bonaparte. Within a few months, the ten-year search for liberty, equality, and fraternity ended in military dictatorship.

18

The Napoleonic Regime

The role of the great man in history has always fascinated historians. Is the great man a combination of such wisdom, charisma, fortitude, and willpower that he can shape events and change the course of history, or is he simply the symbol for an age—a figurehead borne on the crest of an irresistible wave of social forces that he is powerless to control? If neither of these, then what? Nowhere has the question been more intriguing than around the person of Napoleon Bonaparte, who from 1799 to 1815 held center stage of Europe's international affairs.

The Consulate

The first phase of Bonaparte's rule, from 1799 to 1804, is known as the *Consulate*. For a brief period, he shared power in a triumvirate, but after ratification of the Constitution of the Year 8, he exercised the executive authority alone. In 1802 Bonaparte became consul for life. During the Consulate, he restored law and order, made peace with Europe, and instituted domestic reforms that have survived to the present.

Napoleon Bonaparte's Youth and Early Career. Napoleon Bonaparte was born the son of a poor Corsican nobleman in 1769. Although his family had no influence in France, which had acquired Corsica in 1768, he was able to attend French military schools, from which he was commissioned a second lieutenant of artillery in 1785. But he did not consider himself a Frenchman, and even after the outbreak of the Revolution, he devoted himself to Corsican politics. Nevertheless, it was the Revolution that removed the barriers to advancement that had blocked talented but unprivileged men under the ancien régime. Bonaparte first came to national attention in 1793 when, by chance, he was given command of artillery at Toulon and played a decisive role in driving off the British attackers. He was briefly imprisoned after Thermidor because of his Jacobin connections but later cultivated friendships within the Directory. On 13 Vendémiaire (5 October 1795) he saved the Directory and the convention from a Paris mob, and was rewarded with command of the Army of Italy. The victories that followed further enhanced his reputation and set the stage for his participation in the coup d'etat of 18 Brumaire (9 November 1799), discussed on page 224.

Constitution of the Year 8 (1799). The constitution drafted by the conspirators of 18 Brumaire closed the revolutionary era. For the most part, its clauses served as window dressing for what became a Napoleonic dictatorship. Executive authority was vested in three consuls, but First Consul Napoleon Bonaparte was given ultimate authority. The legislative functions were divided among the Senate, the Legislative Body, the Tribunate, and the First Consul, who initiated all legislation. Although originally the tricameral legislature was not a rubber stamp, the arrangement was so cumbersome that it provided no real check on executive power. The dictatorship implicit in this document was consummated in the Constitution of the Year 10, adopted by plebiscite on 2 August 1802. Under its terms Napoleon became consul for life and dictator of France.

Domestic Reform. The inability of the prerevolutionary government to rationalize the malfunctioning bureaucracy and reform the archaic system of class privilege had led to the overthrow of the monarchy. Although many of the reforms instituted between 1789 and 1799 had miscarried, the revolutionary decade had cleared away obsolete practices and prepared the ground for new construction. The Napoleonic regime surpassed the ancien régime in dictatorial power, but at the same time, Napoleon Bonaparte presided over the establishment of those institutions that form the basis of modern French life.

NAPOLEONIC CODE. Prior to 1789 France had not possessed a unified legal system. Napoleon considered his greatest accomplishment the creation of a comprehensive and uniform set of laws and procedures. Although the restructuring of the legal system had been under consideration for years and the primary work was performed by legal scholars, Napoleon took an active part in the deliberations and brought the work to completion. The Civil Code was completed in 1804, followed by the Code of Civil Procedure (1806), the Commercial Code (1807), the Code of Criminal Procedure (1808), and the Penal Code (1810). In some respects the codes reflected the practices of prerevolutionary France. For example, the legal dominance of the father and husband was maintained within the family and the legal subservience of women confirmed. (Frenchwomen obtained suffrage only in 1946 and legal equality not until 1965.) On the other hand, the codes accepted the revolutionary credo of equal justice and careers open to talent, thus confirming the destruction of caste privilege.

ADMINISTRATIVE REFORM. The centralization of authority that became a cornerstone of French government was embodied in the law of 29 Pluviose (17 February 1800). The elective principal adopted by the Revolution was abandoned, and the First Counsul was empowered to appoint a prefect to administer each département, a subprefect for each *arrondissement*, and a mayor for each commune. Thus the political subdivisions became mere administrative areas whose officials were linked in a chain of command to Paris rather than being responsible to the local inhabitants.

FISCAL REFORM AND ECONOMIC POLICY. Poor fiscal management had ruined the Bourbon regime and undermined the revolutionary governments that followed it. Bonaparte undertook a sweeping program to create a stable financial structure. Through a new fiscal bureaucracy that paralleled the administration down to the local level, he was able to levy and collect direct personal and property taxes equitably. Indirect taxation was increased on alcoholic beverages, tobacco, and salt. To end monetary chaos, he established a fixed bimetallic currency and in January 1800 chartered the Bank of France. The bank was controlled by private shareholders, but its governors were appointed by the government. It issued the nation's currency, floated government bonds, set the discount rate, and in times of crisis advanced funds to the government.

EDUCATIONAL REFORM. The dream of universal enlightenment through education was a basic goal of eighteenth-century rationalists. By 1795 the National Convention had taken preliminary steps toward this goal. However, the centralized system that still exists in France was created under the direction of Napoleon. His primary concerns were to promote devotion to the regime, to provide basic vocational training, and to foster higher education for civil servants and army officers. Napoleon was not interested in mass education, and the elementary schools financed by the communes served primarily the middle class. Secondary education was provided by the popular communal *collèges* and the regional state *lycées*. Successful completion of this *baccalauréate* course opened the door to higher education in the humanities, law, medicine, science, and theology. Napoleon took a special interest in the *École Polytechnique,* which educated engineers, and Saint-Cyr, the military academy. The entire structure of French education was under the administrative control of the Imperial University created in 1808. Although tightly controlled secular education replaced the educational near monopoly exercised by the Church before 1789, Catholic educators continued to play a significant, though closely supervised, role.

THE CONCORDAT. Religious controversy had been one of the most divisive aspects of the Revolution. Bonaparte ended the insurrection in the Vendée and Brittany through a combination of military forces and conciliation. He then negotiated a settlement with the Vatican to heal the break with Rome. The Concordat, ratified in April 1802, established a church-state partnership until 1905. Under its terms France recognized Catholicism as the religion of the majority of Frenchmen and assumed financial obligation for the payment of clerical salaries and the maintenance of Church property. The clergy, who had been divided into warring factions by the Revolution, were drawn together. Henceforth, they were appointed by bishops who, in turn, were to be nominated by the government and confirmed by the pope. The Concordat gave the French government wide latitude in its control of public worship and religious education, while the Church regained its status at the arbiter of faith and morals.

International Affairs. Bonaparte took power when France was still at war with the Second Coalition (see page 224). Although he negotiated very favorable settlements with Austria and Britain, he undermined hopes for lasting peace and stability by his clearly aggressive designs in central Europe.

PEACE OF LUNÉVILLE. Finding Austria reluctant to negotiate, Bonaparte struck into Italy. He captured Milan, but at Marengo (June 1800) it was brilliant subordinate, General Desaix de Veygoux, who turned imminent defeat into a stunning victory. Caught in a pincers formed by the French armies of Germany and Italy, the Austrians sued for peace. Under the terms of the Peace of Lunéville (February 1801), Austria reconfirmed the Treaty of Campoformio (page 223), surrendered all her Italian possessions save Venetia, and recognized the French puppet republics in Italy and the Netherlands.

PEACE OF AMIENS. Britain was the last power to come to terms with France. Both nations wanted peace. Britain, despite its strong naval posture, was feeling the financial and commercial effects of the protracted conflict. Bonaparte desired peace in order to consolidate his position in central Europe. The Peace of Amiens (March 1802) ended the War of the Second Coalition. Britain returned all the conquered colonies of France and its allies except Ceylon and Trinidad. France, in turn, restored the independence of Naples and agreed to evacuate the naval station of Malta. Thus, after the end of hostilities, France controlled the west bank of the Rhine and dominated its client republics in the Netherlands, Switzerland, and northern Italy.

FRENCH REORGANIZATION OF GERMANY. Under terms of the peace

settlement, those German princes who had lost territory to France were entitled to indemnification in the other areas. Bonaparte used his prerogatives and power to redraw the map of Germany. With the exception of the archbishopric of Mainz, the ecclesiastical states disappeared. The same fate befell most of the imperial cities. Prussia and Bavaria were given much more than they had lost elsewhere so that they might form a counterweight to Austria. These transfers were confirmed in the Imperial Recess of 1803.

The Empire

As the Consulate is often characterized as a period of domestic reform, the imperial era (1804–1815) reflects Bonaparte's attempt to legitimatize his rule and his efforts to reorder the state system in such a way as to make France the unchallenged arbiter of European affairs. Although he was a diplomatic tactician of high caliber, Bonaparte failed as a statesman. Because he did not subject his grandiose schemes to rational analysis, his goals far surpassed his resources. By attempting to make France master of Europe, he challenged the balance-of-power system and thus ultimately placed France at war with all the rest of Europe.

Creation of the Empire. From the beginning of his rule, Bonaparte had hoped to become a hereditary ruler. He took the decisive step in 1804. In May he was proclaimed Emperor of the French Republic and in December, as Pope Pius VII presided, he crowned himself emperor in Notre Dame Cathedral.

War of the Third Coalition. The great powers had acquiesced in French expansion to its "natural frontiers" but refused to accept Napoleon's attempts to gain hegemony in western Europe and the Mediterranean. Britain was the first to perceive the danger to its strategic position in the Mediterranean and resumed hostilities in May 1803. Austria was also alarmed not only by French expansion in Italy (including the annexation of Piedmont, Elba, and Genoa, as well as Napoleon's assumption of the presidency of the Cisalpine republic [1802] and the title King of Italy [1805]) but also by the reorganization of Germany (1804). In response to this threat, Britain, Austria, Russia, and Sweden formed the Third Coalition.

The campaign of 1806 is the finest example of Napoleon's military genius. Relying on organization, speed of maneuver, economy of force, and his ability to mass his forces at the critical point, Napoleon fell upon his enemies. He surprised and captured thirty thousand Austrians at Ulm (October 1805) and then continued into Austria, where he met an Austro-Russian army and on 2 December 1805 won his greatest victory at Austerlitz. Austria capitulated under the terms of the Treaty of Pressburg (December 1805). It recognized French dominance in Italy and ceded territory in Germany to Bavaria, Württemberg, and Baden, which were now French puppets. Napoleon's triumph was tarnished only by the decisive naval battle of Trafalgar (31 October 1805); Lord Nelson's victory ended French hopes of defeating England by destroying its naval supremacy.

War of the Fourth Coalition. Napoleon's lack of statesmanship was evident in the wake of his military triumph. Displaying a total disregard for the traditional state system, he bestowed upon his brother Joseph the kingdom of Naples and upon his brother Louis the kingdom of Holland. He dissolved the Holy Roman Empire (August 1806) and in its place set up the Confederation of the Rhine, a loose assemblage of weak German states under French tutelage.

Prussia, which had held aloof from the previous conflict, now perceived its danger and joined with Russia in the Fourth Coalition. The Prussians offered battle without waiting for Russian support and were routed in simultaneous defeats at Jena and Auerstedt (14 October 1806), after which Napoleon occupied Berlin. Russia continued the war and fought the French to a bloody standoff at Eylau (February 1807) but requested a truce following its defeat at Friedland (June 1807).

The Treaty of Tilsit (July 1807) raised France to a position of unprecedented power. The Russians and Prussians recognized Napoleon's previous gains and acquiesced in the creation of the puppet kingdom of Westphalia ruled by Jérôme, Napoleon's youngest brother. Czar Alexander I agreed to cooperate with Napoleon's plans for economic and political reorganization. Now only Britain, protected by its fleet, continued the struggle.

Apogee and Decline of the French Empire. From 1807 through 1810, Napoleon was in an unassailable position. The Austrians tried once again to bring him to heel, but after victory at Aspern (May 1809), they were defeated at Wagram (July 1809) and once more capitulated. The emperor again divested Austria of large pieces of territory. He sealed his triumph by divorcing the empress Josephine in 1809 and marrying Marie Louise, archduchess of Austria, in 1810. At this time France exercised virtual hegemony in western and central Europe (see map on page 232). The grand empire stretched from the North Sea to the Adriatic. Napoleon controlled central Europe from Norway to Naples and was allied to Prussia and Austria. The emperor saw himself as a benefactor of European civilization who would inaugurate a golden age unparalleled since the time of Augustus Caesar.

The peoples under French control soon became disenchanted with their status. Despite the benefits to them of French administration, it became obvious that their countries were being manipulated purely for French interests.

THE CONTINENTAL SYSTEM. In an effort to destroy English commerce, Napoleon initiated his Continental System in 1806. Lacking the navy to blockade English ports, he attempted to enforce an embargo of English trade in Continental ports. The system worked a severe economic hardship throughout Europe and caused bitter resentment. Napoleon dethroned his brother Louis and annexed Holland for refusal to enforce the regulations (1810). Czar Alexander I declined to ruin his economy to benefit Napoleon, and the understanding reached at Tilsit dissolved. The annoyance felt by Europeans was accentuated by the fact that Napoleon himself violated the system when it was in France's interest to trade with Britain.

NATIONALIST UPRISINGS. The French Revolution had generated a strong sense of nationalism that was carried throughout Europe. In the wake of French aggression and domination, the subject nationalities began to stir. In Germany Johann Fichte's *Addresses to the German Nation* (1807–1808) called for German rejuvenation and liberation after the humiliation of Jena. In Italy nationalists formed secret societies to oppose French dominance. The greatest threat to French control came in Spain. Beginning in 1808 Napoleon tried to subjugate Portugal, Britain's last Continental ally. This required the replacement of Spain's Bourbon dynasty with his brother Joseph, the king of Naples. The result was a nationalist insurrection. The conflict, known as the Peninsular War, pitted the French against Spanish guerrillas and an army of British regulars commanded by Sir Arthur Wellesley (who as the duke of Wellington later faced Napoleon at Waterloo). Although the French controlled the cities, they could never corner and defeat their enemies who ranged the countryside. The French were driven out of Spain in 1813 after expending resources and lives to no avail for five years.

RUSSIAN CAMPAIGN. Determined to enforce his Continental System, Napoleon invaded Russia on 24 June 1812. The *Grand Armée* was a heterogeneous force of six hundred thousand men, of whom two hundred thousand were Frenchmen and four hundred thousand allied conscripts. The Russians were able to muster only two hundred thousand men and fell back before the French host. They finally stood their ground at Borodino on September 7, but they suffered fifty thousand casualties and were forced to abandon Moscow, which the French occupied on September 12. For the first time, however, the expected triumph eluded Napoleon. The Czar refused to capitulate,

Moscow was burned by either accident or arson, desertions and casualties had seriously reduced the French force, and winter approached. On October 19 the French began their retreat. Lacking munitions and forage, they fought desperate rearguard actions against the encircling Russians and after the beginning of November struggled simply to survive the freezing temperatures. Barely one hundred thousand survived to recross the Niemen River in December. The emperor, in the meantime, had returned to Paris to shore up his crumbling regime.

War of the Fifth Coalition. The fifth and last allied coalition against France took form during the spring and summer of 1813. The crowned heads of Europe finally realized that French revolutionary ideas and Napoleon's grandiose schemes for the reorganization of Europe posed a greater threat to their security than the threat from their potential allies.

METTERNICH'S DIPLOMACY. The prime architect of the coalition was Prince Klemens von Metternich, who since 1809 had been the foreign minister of Austria. Metternich's diplomacy encompassed two primary goals. First, he aimed to place Austria at the fulcrum of a reconstituted balance-of-power system. For this purpose he sought a negotiated settlement with Napoleon rather than his total defeat so that France would continue to serve as a counterweight to Russia and Prussia in central Europe. Second, he worked to maintain the ancien régime in central and eastern Europe. The Hapsburg domains were still ruled by a feudal system and contained many nationalities. Thus Metternich could not allow the appeal of liberalism or nationalism to be used against Napoleon. The coalition he created was an alliance of dynastic states rather than a crusade of peoples. During the spring of 1813, Metternich withdrew Austria from the alliance with France, negotiated the new coalition, prepared for war, and adroitly maneuvered to avoid a unilateral confrontation with Napoleon.

BATTLE OF LEIPZIG AND NAPOLEON'S ABDICATION. Napoleon believed that to make concessions would simply confirm his weakness. He rushed to rebuild his shattered army and in the spring of 1813 attempted to recoup his standing on the battlefield. But for the first time in the revolutionary epoch, he faced a coalition that included every major power in Europe. His military brilliance could not overcome the logic of numbers, and he was decisively defeated at the battle of Leipzig, a three-day struggle that ended on 19 October 1813. He fell back into France and fought on, winning tactical victories, but his enemies converged from all sides. Even then Napoleon refused to accept a settlement that would have left France with its frontiers at the Alps, the Pyrenees, and the Rhine. His marshals finally convinced him of the futility of further resistance. He abdicated in March 1814 and accepted exile as ruler of the island of Elba. The Bourbon dynasty, in the person of Louis XVIII, was restored in France, and representatives of the great powers met in Vienna to negotiate a peace settlement.

THE ONE HUNDRED DAYS. Napoleon brooded on Elba for ten months and then made a desperate effort to return to power. He slipped away from Elba in February 1815 and landed in southern France. Troops sent to arrest him rallied to his standard, Louis XVIII fled the country, and Napoleon reentered Paris in triumph. Despite assurances of his desire for peace, the allies immediately declared him an outlaw and moved against him. The climactic confrontation came at the battle of Waterloo, fought just south of Brussels, on 18 June 1815. In order to succeed, Napoleon would have had to destroy the coalition, and it is doubtful that even a stunning victory would have accomplished that. In any case, caught between the duke of Wellington's Redcoats and Blücher's Prussians, the French were first checked and then routed. Control of events slipped from Napoleon's hands, and he surrendered to the English on July 15. He was exiled to the forlorn island of Saint Helena in the South Atlantic, where he died in 1821.

The Napoleonic Legacy

Napoleon Bonaparte's meteoric career left Europe an ambiguous legacy. No one disputes his military genius, and it was with the sword that he carried the message of the French Revolution to the corners of Europe. No area that witnessed the passage of the Grand Armée was ever the same again. At the same time, his victories clearly demonstrate the hollowness of military power when it is detached from rationally conceived political goals. Napoleon's inability to place limits on his power resulted in the formation of a coalition that he could not defeat. Of all his battles, he lost the only three that really mattered—at Trafalgar, Leipzig, and Waterloo.

Within France he left a memory of national grandeur and institutions that still guide the nation; at the same time, he put the last nails in the coffin of revolutionary political liberty. *Bonapartism*, a form of dictatorship based on the myth of popular sovereignty, has maintained a powerful appeal in the twentieth century to those disenchanted with both republican liberalism and divine-right monarchy.

19

The Industrial Revolution

The Industrial Revolution was one aspect of a profound economic, social, political, and intellectual transformation that is often referred to as modernization. Beginning in Europe over two centuries ago, the movement gained momentum and has now touched all but the most remote regions of the world. This transformation has involved nothing less than the obliteration of the traditionally oriented, agricultural society that had served as the basic social organization throughout human history. In its place have evolved scientifically based, urban-industrial societies typical of twentieth-century Europe.

This chapter will deal primarily with England, where industrialization began and first reached maturity. It will examine the preconditions of industrialization, technological and organizational innovations, and the economic and social impact of these changes. The political ramifications of the Industrial Revolution will be discussed in chapters 20 and 21.

Many scholars object to the use of the term *Industrial Revolution* on the ground that it implies a sharp break with the past and a rapidity of change that are unwarranted by the facts. But there are several justifications for adopting the term besides the sanction of traditional usage. Economic and social change certainly do not occur with the speed of a political revolution. In fact, changes that involve the very fabric of society usually take place imperceptibly over long periods. Using the yardstick of historical time, however, the industrialization of western Europe proceeded with incredible speed, and the change was obvious even to the people caught up in it. In addition, the significance of the change must be considered. The impact of industrialization has rarely been equaled in the whole chronicle of human experience. For this reason alone, the word *revolution* seems appropriate.

Preconditions of Industrialization

A foundation of certain economic, social, political, and intellectual preconditions is necessary before any society can successfully begin to industrialize. The factors listed below are not comprehensive but serve to indicate why England's economic transformation preceded other European states.

Political Base. By the beginning of the eighteenth century, parliament had destroyed the absolutist pretensions of the Stuart dynasty and had emerged as the dominant political institution. Its victory ensured the operation of a rule of law essential to a well-ordered economic life. Parliament was controlled by a competent and self-assured oligarchy drawn from what America's John Adams would call the "rich, well-born, and the able." Although a majority of the aristocracy still represented landed interests, the sharp social separation and antagonism between land and commerce that typified the Continent did not exist in England. The oligarchy was acutely aware of the increasing importance of commerce as a factor in the nation's well-being. Members of the aristocracy thus protected England's business interests, and many took part in commercial ventures.

Economic Base. Until the 1780s England's economy grew at a rate no faster than that of its major Continental competitors. Nevertheless, certain factors ensured that England would have a distinct advantage in the early stages of industrialization. England had emerged from the long colonial struggle with Spain, Holland, and France as the dominant commercial power. Its large merchant fleet was protected by the world's strongest navy, and London was Europe's commercial and financial nerve center. Custom and progressive land law made English farmers among the most productive of Europe. In the towns the guild system had never been so pervasive in England as in Europe, and during the eighteenth century, it was a declining hindrance to manufacturing. The woolen-textile industry, though decentralized, provided a solid base for industrial growth in other sectors.

Social Base. England lacked the rigid class structure typical of Europe. Although the landed aristocracy dominated both the economy and the political structure, it did not form a closed caste. Younger sons of the nobility were commoners and had to find their own way in the world of law, banking, commerce, and politics. At the same time, rising merchant families married or bought their way into the ranks of the nobility. Thus, close family connections were forged between the old elite and the emergent classes. This less rigid structure provided for careers open to talent and for a flexible and mobile work force that later supplied the sinews for industrialization.

Intellectual Base. Perhaps the most significant precondition for industrialization is a favorable intellectual climate. The achievements of sixteenth- and seventeenth-century science had begun to unravel the mysteries of the universe, and with each new discovery had come a growing confidence in the power of human reason. The great minds of the eighteenth century began to apply the analytical techniques of science to the study of politics, economics, and social organization in the belief that change was possible and desirable and that with change would come a rational and well-ordered society.

Effect of the French Revolution. Although it was not a general precondition of industrialization, the French Revolution provided England with special advantages. Throughout the eighteenth century, the French economy had progressed at a rate comparable to England's. However, England was spared the disruption of the French Revolution and the dislocations that subsequently engulfed the Continent for twenty years. Thus, although England suffered commercial losses and bore a large part of the expense to subdue France, its economy prospered while those of both its enemies and allies stagnated. It was in these decades of revolution and war that England outstripped its rivals and moved to the threshold of industrialization.

Technological Innovation

The spectacular breakthrough in technological development was a primary factor in the first stage of development. The new inventions provided the capacity for mass production and distribution that formed the nucleus of an industrialized state.

Textiles. The manufacture of woolen cloth was the most highly developed industry in early eighteenth-century England. A cloth merchant, or draper, purchased the raw wool and had it carded, spun, woven, fulled, dyed, and finished by artisans who worked in their own homes or small shops. They were paid piece rates, and the draper kept ownership throughout the process. This method was known as the *domestic* or *putting-out* system. Cotton fabrics, produced primarily in India, came into vogue in the middle of the century but could not be produced profitably within the domestic system.

The technological developments that made the cotton-textile industry England's most valuable manufacturing sector resulted from the collective work of many inventors of whom only the most prominent can be mentioned. In 1733 John Kay developed the flying shuttle, which mechanically threw the thread of the woof across the warp, thus weaving wider cloth and greatly speeding the process. The rate of spinning was also increased by James Hargreaves's invention of the spinning jenny (1764), which allowed one operator to spin many spindles of thread simultaneously. In America Eli Whitney developed the cotton gin (1793), which mechanically separated the fibers from the seed and thus speeded the production of raw cotton needed to keep pace with the growing demands of English textile production. The flying shuttle and the spinning jenny were readily adapted to the domestic process, but Richard Arkwright's water frame (1769) and Samuel Crompton's improved *mule*, a waterpowered multiple spinner (1779), required waterpower to produce tough fine thread. The same was true of Edmund Cartwright's power loom, developed in 1785 and adapted to steam power after 1803. The result of these innovations was to draw the manufacturing process together into large mills where power was available and where the large, expensive machinery could be most effectively utilized. Lancashire and Derbyshire became the centers of this new industry. The woolens industry, located just to the east in Yorkshire, adapted more slowly to the new processes and was not mechanized until midcentury.

Although Britain maintained a large advantage in textiles during the nineteenth century, some Continental states also had healthy industries. The most developed sectors in Germany were Saxony and Rhenish Prussia, while the French centers were across the Rhine in Alsace and Lille. Belgium was also known for its textiles. Lyons, France, was the center of the silk industry, which thrived in southern France and northern Italy before the development of synthetic fibers. The woolens industry remained under the domestic system throughout most of the Continent until late in the century.

The Steam Engine. The most significant single development of the Industrial Revolution was the replacement of wind, water, and muscles, which had been the only sources of energy throughout history, with a new source of power. After a period of trial and error, the steam engine became a dependable source of efficient and extraordinary power that could be adapted to almost any piece of machinery. The most important figure in this development was James Watt, a Scottish instrument maker who improved the Newcomen engine that since 1706 had been used primarily as a water pump. Beginning in 1765, Watt transformed the primitive pump into an efficient engine by adding a steam condenser, a governor, and a sun-and-planet drive system that converted reciprocal motion to rotary motion. His experiments were financed by Matthew Boulton, a wealthy Birmingham hardware manufacturer. The partnership of Boulton and Watt produced thousands of engines that were adapted to the needs of every major industry.

Coal. Charcoal had provided the primary fuel for preindustrial

Europe, but as the hardwood forests were depleted, coal became the fuel for the Industrial Revolution. Vast deposits were first developed in England's Midlands, South Wales, and Northumberland, while on the Continent the Belgian deposits around Mons provided the greatest supplies. As the ninteenth century progressed, fields around Anzin, France, and the German deposits in the Roer and Ruhr valleys and in Upper Silesia were extensively exploited. The chief disadvantage of coal as a fuel in metallurgical industries was that its impurities combined wth the metal during the smelting process. By the 1730s the Darbys of Coalbrookdale had developed a coking process that drove the impurities out of bituminous coal by distillation. The remaining coke became the fuel for the manufacture of high-quality iron. Coal was also used to fuel steam engines, which were used extensively in mining operations to pump out ground water and to operate hoists and ventilating equipment.

Iron and Steel. The development of coke greatly increased the production of pig iron, but it was brittle and therefore in many respects less useful than malleable wrought iron. Henry Cort's rolling mill constructed in 1783 helped remove the impurities and also produced sheet iron. In 1784 Cort and Peter Onions simultaneously invented the *puddling* process by which impurities were burned out by stirring the molten iron in a reverberatory furnace.

Steel, harder but less brittle than iron, is made by adding controlled amounts of carbon and other metals to pure iron. Because of the expense of this process, it was produced in limited quantities until the late 1850s, when Henry Bessemer invented a converter to burn off the impurities in molten iron.

The greatest ironmaster in England was John Wilkinson of Straffordshire. His cannon-boring machine was used by Boulton and Watt to bore accurate steam-engine cylinders, and he, in turn, adopted the steam engine to drive the bellows, drop hammers, and rolling mills. Wilkinson manufactured weapons, pipe, and structural iron. His firm also fabricated the first iron bridge and one of the first iron boats, a barge to transport his products.

As in other industrial sectors, the British held a wide lead in iron and steel production during the first half of the nineteenth century. Continental entrepreneurs developed the necessary techniques by employing English inventors and mechanics. William Cockerill founded the Seraing Works in Belgium in 1837. In 1836 the Schneiders in France took over the faltering Le Creusot foundry and transformed it into an industrial giant. Iron-making establishments in Germany, including the Krupp Works in Essen, generally remained small during the first half of the century.

Iron was employed wherever hard, durable construction material was required. In heavy industry it replaced wood for machinery and was used for building construction. It was essential for the manufacture of railroad rolling stock and rails and, after 1860, in the construction of ships.

Transportation and Communication. One of the greatest constraints to commerce and industry in early modern Europe was the lack of adequate roads. Those that existed often became impassable during periods of bad weather and heavy traffic. This deficiency began to be remedied after 1750.

ROADS. New construction methods developed by the Scottish engineers Telford and McAdam gave impetus to a boom in road construction, and by 1850 England had an interlocking network of highways. While the English left the task to commercial turnpike companies or local governments, the Continental states controlled the financing and construction of their roads. The roads of Belgium and France were generally superior to those of England, while those of Germany, Austria, and eastern Europe were appreciably worse.

CANALS. After high initial cost, canals provided an inexpensive means of transporting freight. Between 1790 and 1840, two thousand miles of canals were constructed in England, primarily by private companies. As with road construction, the Belgian and French governments took an active part in financing canals. By 1850 the French had twenty-five hundred miles of canals linking their river system in a great transportation network.

RAILROADS. The railroad was the most significant transportation innovation of the nineteenth century. Eighteenth-century inventors had experimented with horse-drawn rail carts and steam tractors for road use. It was the Englishman George Stephenson who developed the first successful steam locomotive in 1825. With its smokestack glowing red-hot, it ran from Darlington to Stockton at eight miles an hour. In 1830 Stephenson produced the *Rocket*, which attained speeds of thirty miles an hour between Manchester and Liverpool and clearly demonstrated the practicality of steam transportation. It took nearly twenty years to develop efficient engines, rolling stock, and rails, but by the late 1840s, Europe was experiencing a railroad building boom. Britain's network was the most extensive, but sixty-five hundred miles of track (1850) came at a high cost because of haphazard private construction during the 1830s. By 1846, however, a standard gauge had been adopted, and working agreements arranged to provide through service among the many lines. Belgium employed state financing and a master plan to construct an efficient system, while France produced a unified system using planning and private financing. Germany probably benefited most from the railroad because its roads and canals were generally inadequate, but political disunity hampered its efforts.

TRADE AND SHIPPING. Britain had won a place as a maritime power during the colonial wars of the seventeenth and eighteenth centuries. It obtained a position of preeminence during the Napoleonic conflict and thus reaped commercial benefits from the boom in international trade during the first half of the nineteenth century. Of particular importance was the importation of raw cotton from the United States and Egypt and the export of cotton textiles to the Orient, particularly India. In addition, England imported other major commodities, including sugar, tea, and wool for home consumption or reexport. This trade stimulated banks, insurance companies, brokerage houses, and shipbuilding and thus brought enormous revenue to Britain.

The impact of industrialization was clearly evident in ship construction. The age of sail went out in a blaze of glory. American and British shipbuilders competing to capture passenger trade, mail routes, and the lucrative Far Eastern markets developed long, sleek clippers that could carry large cargoes and outrace anything afloat.

Ships like the *Lightning* and the *Cutty Sark* ruled the sea-lanes during the 1850s and 1860s, but they were gradually displaced by iron-hulled steamers. Robert Fulton successfully tested the steam-driven *Clermont* in 1807, and the first steam-assisted trans-Atlantic crossing was completed by the American ship *Savannah* in June 1819. The fuel consumption of the first steamers limited their cruising range and carrying capacity, but technological innovations slowly overcame these difficulties. The screw propeller was successfully used in 1839, and the compound-expansion engine, with greater power and efficiency than previous types, was introduced in the mid-1850s. All-iron construction supplanted iron-and-wood composite ships and provided strength coupled with increased usable space. Regular steam passenger service across the Atlantic began in the 1830s, and long freight haulers were developed by the early 1850s. It was not until the 1870s, however, that steamship tonnage surpassed that of sailing ships.

COMMUNICATIONS. Advances in communication kept pace with improvements in transportation. The most spectacular discovery was the invention of the telegraph. Attempts to perfect electronic communication were carried on simultaneously in many countries. Important improvements and discoveries were made by André Ampère, Wilhelm Weber, and Charles Wheatstone, among others. However, most of the popular acclaim went to the American artist Samuel F. B. Morse, who improved upon existing electric keys, developed a code, and transmitted the first telegraphic message from Washington, D.C., to Baltimore in 1844. Thousands of miles of telegraph lines were soon in use dispatching trains, carrying diplomatic messages, and transmitting business information. A telegraphic cable was laid between England and France in 1851, and a successful trans-Atlantic link was laid in 1866.

More mundane but of equal importance was the development of an efficient inexpensive postal system. Standard rates were adopted for letters by weight, and most countries established regular service by contracting with private rail and steamship carriers. England led in this field with the penny post, and continental countries quickly followed suit with their own national variations.

Industrial Capitalism

The technological innovations of the eighteenth century were not in themselves the reason for economic acceleration. More significant was the developing form of economic organization known as industrial capitalism that evolved to meet the increased needs of expanding markets.

The Captains of Industry. During the seventeenth and eighteenth centuries, English merchants and bankers had accumulated the financial reserves needed for industrialization. But although they invested in new ventures, the industrialists were not often drawn from their rather conservative ranks. The "captains of industry" were more often men who combined driving ambition, a willingness to take risks, administrative skill, and engineering ability in their struggle to rise above their humble origins. Once established, they often reinvested their earnings in business expansion, thus creating new capital and freeing them from outside control.

Industrial Production. At the heart of the new system was the industrial plant, where the workers were organized to supervise and supplement power-driven machinery. The machinery was expensive, but once installed it repaid its cost by mass-producing uniform, high-quality goods at high speed.

Mass production, requiring a disciplined semiskilled work force harnessed to the rhythm of machines, thus called into existence the industrial proletariat. Automation also dramatically altered the operations of the marketplace. The preindustrial economy produced a relatively small quantity of handcrafted goods for a small market. The industrial economy produced a large volume of machine-made goods for a very broad market. Industrial products were less expensive and, despite a popular myth to the contrary, of high quality. On the other hand, the new system was difficult to regulate. Wild fluctuations in market conditions occurred periodically. Unbridled expansive booms often triggered cyclic depressions resulting in bankruptcy, idle machinery, and mass unemployment.

Formulation of Capitalist Theory. The development of new economic theories accompanied the transition from a commercial to an industrial economy. The mercantilist belief in stringent regulation gave way to laissez-faire (literally, "let alone"), a conception that prosperity resulted from the unrestrained interplay of self-regulating natural economic forces. The most influential proponent of the new economics was Adam Smith, who presented his view in *An Inquiry into the Nature and Causes of the Wealth of Nations* (1776). Smith believed that each individual knew best how to regulate his own affairs and that the cumulative result of individual striving for personal gain was general prosperity. Government attempts to regulate the economy were condemned as futile obstructionism. Although Smith wrote during the heyday of English commercialism, his theories were tailor-made for the industrial age. Industrialists, needing elbowroom for expansion and experimentation, took up the theory of laissez-faire but ignored Smith's admonition that public welfare could not be totally abandoned to private profit. Laissez-faire thus became the battle cry of the propertied industrial classes while offering no solace to the proletariat.

In fact, Smith's successors seemed to marshal the laws of nature against an improved standard of living for the working masses. Thomas Malthus argued in his *Essay on the Principle of Population* (1798) that population growth would always outstrip increases in food production and thus reduce the vast majority to subsistence. David Ricardo seconded this opinion in his *Principles of Political Economy and Taxation* (1817). Ricardo's "iron law of wages" stated that wages would inexorably find their natural level at subsistence. It is not surprising that economics came to be known as "the dismal science."

The Social Impact of Industrialization

Industrialization was accompanied by profound changes in the social structure. The process is so complex and the statistical data from the eighteenth and nineteenth centuries so scanty that it is impossible to differentiate among causes, effects, and parallel developments. As a result there has been wide disagreement among historians regarding the impact of these changes on the people who lived through them.

Population Growth. Although figures are imprecise, it is clear that sometime after 1750 the population of Europe began to increase sharply. The consensus places the population of Europe at roughly 188 million in 1800 and at near 275 million by midcentury. A decreasing death rate and longer life expectancy rather than an increase in the already high birthrate were the primary ingredients of this growth. They in turn were influenced by a greater attention to personal hygiene, increased interest of the authorities in public health, and agricultural improvements that increased the quantity and quality of food. The population increase had an impact on industrialization by increasing the demand for goods. Industrialization spurred on population growth through the mechanization of agriculture.

Urbanization. Preindustrial societies do not generally produce a surplus large enough to maintain more than 15 percent of their population in cities. It was only after industrialization that a majority of western Europeans became city dwellers. As in other aspects of this transformation, England led the way. Agricultural changes, including eighteenth-century enclosures, and increased industrial activity brought workers to the factory towns in droves. Although less than one Englishman in four lived in towns of more than two thousand persons in 1750, by 1850 the urban population had reached 50 percent. Built upon coal, iron, textiles, and commerce, great cities arose at Newcastle, Liverpool, Manchester, Leeds, Sheffield, and Birmingham. They marked the spots where hamlets had stood barely a century before. Although every major power had an urban center, the process of urbanization was less pronounced the farther one traveled into southern and eastern Europe. Nevertheless, the urban population reached 30 percent in Germany and 25 percent in France by midcentury, and the increase was rapid enough to cause severe social stress.

Social Tension. The transformation of the European economy from an agrarian and handicraft base to an industrial base was naturally accompanied by a reordering of the social structure. Personal distress, bitterness, and disorientation are common features in such a transition and were clearly evident in nineteenth-century Europe.

The landed aristocracy and the gentry had formed the backbone of agrarian economies. Although commercial interests had begun to challenge their authority in the seventeenth century, it was not until the nineteenth century that they began to slip from their dominant position. They were slowly replaced by the industrialists and the burgeoning middle class, which arose to manage the industrial economy. Depite the economic decline of the aristocracy, the speed of their displacement should not be exaggerated, for this old elite maintained its social prestige and political power until the twentieth century in practically every European state.

It was the working classes, with few psychological or monetary reserves and no political power, that bore the brunt of industrialization. Driven from their land by enclosure or competition with large landholders or deprived of their livelihood by mechanization, these men could respond only with sporadic and ineffective violence. The Luddite riots, instigated by hard-pressed knitters and handloom weavers in the English Midlands between 1812 and 1816, were only the most spectacular instances of machine wrecking by men driven to desperation by the transition to automation. Ultimately the displaced farmer and the obsolescent artisan joined the throng that trudged to the mines or mills and became part of the industrial proletariat.

The price paid for industrialization by those who built the new society with their labor is well documented. Human life was used up as a commodity with no allowance made for sex or age except that the weak were exploited more often than the strong. A sixteen-hour day and a six-day week in the mills were not uncommon. The end of work meant only the right to return to the festering slums that mushroomed in the industrial towns.

Without discounting the wretched condition of the working classes in the first decades of industrialization and putting aside the question of whether actions could have been taken to mitigate the misery, other factors must be kept in mind. The ninety-six-hour workweek, child labor, grinding poverty, and early death were not inventions of the industrial world. They were the reality of life in every agrarian society. What was hard to bear for the new urban dwellers were the unfamiliar surroundings, the loss of psychological support provided by traditional ways, and the tyranny of the never-tiring machinery. It was, however, only through industrialization that the high standard of living enjoyed by the majority in twentieth-century Europe could ever have been obtained.

Political Effects. The alteration of political attitudes and activity during the first half of the nineteenth century will be discussed in the following chapters. It should be noted here, however, that this political activity did not take place in a vacuum. The movement of politics reflects a society's economic and social pressures as it swings across a wide spectrum from orderly evolution to violent revolution. It was in such a setting that the societies of Europe struggled to bring order to a world that was undergoing changes unprecedented in the memory of man.

20

Restoration and Reaction

As the allied armies closed in on Napoleon's beleaguered troops in the spring of 1814, the statesmen of Europe faced a dual task. They had to reconstruct the state system in such a manner as to restore the balance of power. They achieved this goal in a remarkably short time; the peace settlement reflected an unusual moderation and realism. The second task was to restore the social and intellectual equilibrium of Europe. This task was as important as the first, since the wars against France had been fought by the powers of central and eastern Europe to defend the ancien régime against the infectious ideas of liberty, equality, and fraternity loosed upon Europe by the French revolutionaries. However, it is much easier to defeat armies than to destroy dreams, and the statesmen of Europe showed a lack of imagination in trying to cope with the aspirations of the revolutionary generation. Censorship, prison, and bayonets only served as a stimulus to the idealists who still hoped to remake the world. As a result, successive waves of revolution buffeted Europe in 1820, 1830, and 1848.

The Peace Settlement

The peace settlement rested on three working principles: legitimacy, stability, and compensation. The concept of legitimacy was paramount. The victorious allies desired to restore the prerevolutionary regimes to their historical roles as far as possible. This principle permitted France to retain its prerevolutionary territory and regain its position in the councils of Europe more quickly than might have been expected. At the same time, it was recognized that twenty-five years of warfare had resulted in some irreversible changes and that attempts to alter the new status quo would in themselves be revolutionary acts liable to result in a renewal of hostilities. Thus, the principle of stability

PRINCIPAL EUROPEAN TERRITORIAL CHANGES IN 1815

0 100 200 300 400 500 MILES

- ▨ TO RUSSIA
- ▨ TO PRUSSIA
- ▨ TO AUSTRIA
- ▨ TO PIEDMONT
- ▨ TO NETHERLANDS
- ▪▪▪ GERMAN CONFEDERATION

FINLAND

RUSSIAN EMPIRE

WON IN 1793 AND 1795

NORWAY from DENMARK to SWEDEN

SWEDEN

DENMARK

SWEDISH POMERANIA

PRUSSIA

POSEN

KINGDOM OF POLAND

SAXONY

GALICIA

BESSARABIA

LUXEMBURG
SAAR

FRANCE

SALZBURG

SWITZ.

TYROL

AUSTRIAN EMPIRE

LOMBARDY

VENETIA

PIEDMONT

ISTRIA

DALMATIA

OTTOMAN EMPIRE

TUSCANY
ELBA

PAPAL STATES

CORSICA

NAPLES

SARDINIA

SICILY

IONIAN ISLANDS

MALTA (TO BRITAIN)

was invoked to preclude the revival of the Holy Roman Empire or the restoration of prepartition Poland. Even Joachim Murat, Napoleon's dashing cavalry commander and brother-in-law, retained the throne of Naples until his commitment to Napoleon during the One Hundred Days exhausted Europe's patience. Where the demand of stability precluded the claims of legitimacy, the diplomats provided territorial compensation in other areas to maintain the traditional balance among the states.

First Treaty of Paris. The peace settlement was drafted in Paris and signed on 30 May 1814. Agreement was facilitated by Napoleon's abdication in April and his withdrawal to the island of Elba. The Bourbon dynasty was restored in the person of Louis XVIII. In keeping with the principles of legitimacy and stability, the terms were moderate. France retained its 1792 boundaries, which included Belgium, part of the Rhineland, western Savoy, and the former papal territory of Avignon. It also regained all its colonies except Tobago, Mauritius, and Saint Lucia, which were ceded to Great Britain. France in turn recognized the independence of its conquered territories, including the Netherlands, the German and Italian states, and Switzerland. The allies waived any right to a war indemnity. Finally, they planned to settle central European issues at an international congress in Vienna.

Congress of Vienna. The brilliant assemblage in Vienna (September 1814–June 1815) heralded the victory of the monarchical principle. Czar Alexander I personally led the Russian delegation. Prussia was represented by Prince Karl von Hardenburg and Baron Alexander von Humboldt. The British ministers were Viscount Castlereagh and the duke of Wellington, who in the midst of the proceedings again had to take the field against Napoleon. France was ably represented by Charles Maurice de Talleyrand-Périgord. The host of the conference was Prince Klemens von Metternich, who had become the chief minister of Austrian emperor Francis I in 1809 and had subsequently forged the alliance against Napoleon. Metternich directed the proceedings and played such a dominant role in international affairs for three decades that the period from 1815 to 1848 is often referred to as the Age of Metternich.

While the lesser princelings and representatives of secondary states indulged in an exhausting round of entertainment, the ministers of Austria, Russia, England, and Prussia deliberated over the fate of Europe. The most significant territorial provisions were as follows: (1) Austria ceded the Austrian Netherlands and was compensated with Lombardy and Venetia, the Dalmatian coast, Polish Galicia, and the territory surrounding Salzburg; (2) Prussia retained Polish Posen, the northern two-fifths of Saxony and a large portion of the Rhineland bordering France; (3) Russia retained Finland and gained the Black Sea province of Bessarabia; in addition, the restored Polish kingdom passed to the Romanov dynasty; (4) Great Britain retained the French colonies of Tobago, Saint Lucia, and Mauritius, the Dutch outposts of Cape Colony, South Africa, and Ceylon, and the Mediterranean stronghold of Malta; (5) Holland was compensated for its colonial loss with the acquisition of Belgium, after the One Hundred Days; (6) Sweden was rewarded for its loyalty to the allied cause and was compensated for its loss of Finland with the acquisition of Norway, which was taken from Denmark in retribution for its constancy to Napoleon. The map on page 248 illustrates another important aspect of the settlement. Care had been taken to form a buffer around France with the additions to the Netherlands, Prussia, and Savoy.

In addition to the territorial settlement, several other significant decisions were reached. The Bourbons were restored in Spain and, after the One Hundred Days, to the kingdom of Naples. The loosely knit Confederation of Germany consisting of the remaining thirty-nine sovereign states replaced the Holy Roman Empire.

As a result of the settlement, Austria emerged as the fulcrum of the balance-of-power system. Its dominance reached from the Baltic through the German confederation to the weak states of Italy. France fared better than expected under the circumstances. Talleyrand took advantage of the bitter debate over the disposition of Saxony and Poland by taking Austria's side against the sweeping demands of Prussia and Russia. Thus, despite the existence of the Quadruple Alliance, France quickly regained its standing as a great power.

Finally, the great powers agreed to protect Europe from further French aggression through the implementation of the Quadruple Alliance and to resolve future problems by multilateral summit conferences. These agreements mark the formation of the Concert of Europe, an important step in the development of an international mechanism to resolve problems short of war.

Second Treaty of Paris. Napoleon's final attempt to regain his power ended disastrously at Waterloo. As a result a second less lenient peace settlement was imposed on France (November 1815). The Bourbons were once more restored to the throne but on this occasion were required to pay an indemnity of 750 million francs. An allied army occupied France until the debt was paid. France's boundaries were reduced from those of 1792 to those of 1790, thus excluding Belgium and part of Savoy.

The National Restorations

The international peace settlement was only the first phase in the reordering of post-Napoleonic Europe. The revolutionary events of the preceding quarter century had left a lasting imprint on Europe. Each country had to adjust its policies and attitudes to new realities. In some areas this was accomplished with ease, while in others the restoration era was marked by decades of bitter strife.

Victorious England. Restoration would be a misnomer if applied to England because the island nation had been an implacable foe of the French Revolution since 1793, and it had emerged from the wars with its political institutions, class structure, and values intact.

THE ENGLISH OLIGARCHY. The eighteenth century was the golden age of the English aristocracy. At the apex of the social pyramid were between one hundred and fifty and two hundred noble families who lived in splendor on estates that in some instances comprised whole counties. Below them stood the gentry, a wellborn untitled class whose affluence did not match the lords but who shared with the aristocracy a life of ease, influence, and culture restricted to the privileged few. Together these classes formed an oligarchy that controlled the political life of England.

For political purposes a distinction is usually made between Whigs and Tories. These groups did not form political parties but rather factions and cliques. By the middle of the century, these labels reflected family history, religious affiliation, or personal preference rather than political platforms. The one issue that divided them was the struggle for political power.

The foundation of the aristocratic dominance had been laid during the Whig ascendancy in the reigns of the first two Hanoverian kings, George I (1714–1727) and George II (1727–1760) because these monarchs were Germans who had little understanding of or interest in English affairs. Thus, political power and the spoils that flowed naturally from it fell to the Whigs, who controlled the ministry and the Parliament. The diehard Tories (Jacobites) made two vain attempts to restore the Stuarts through armed insurrection in 1715 and 1745, but when these failed they made their peace with the new dynasty.

The accession of George III (r. 1760–1820) marked a political turning point. The new king took an active interest in politics and supported the Tories in the 1760s when the Whig coalition was disintegrating. Lord North became prime minister in 1770, and except for a Whig interlude following the American Revolution, the Tories controlled the government until 1830. Many believed that the loss of the American colonies had stemmed in large measure from governmental inefficiency and widespread corruption. In response to demands for reform, many sinecures (positions carrying high pay for little or no work) were eliminated, the government revenue officers were disfranchised to prevent electoral corruption, and public contractors were barred from sitting in the Commons.

The greatest statesman of the age was William Pitt the Younger, who became prime minister at the age of twenty-four in 1783 and except for a brief retirement from 1801 until 1804 retained the post until he died in 1806. At the beginning of his administration, Pitt continued the reforms. He attempted with some success to put the government on a sound fiscal footing and tried unsuccessfully to remove the legal disabilities of Dissenters and Roman Catholics. The most significant constitutional change of his administration took place in 1801 when Ireland was incorporated into the United Kingdom.

ENGLISH REACTION TO THE FRENCH REVOLUTION. Many Englishmen supported the French Revolution when it began in 1789. They were flattered by what they perceived as a French attempt to destroy despotism and create a constitutional monarchy on the English model. However, this support soon vanished as the English ruling class witnessed the destruction of the French nobility, attacks on Christianity, and, finally, the abolition of the monarchy. The most famous denunciation of the Revolution was Edmund Burke's *Reflections on the French Revolution* (1790), which condemned the wholesale destruction of time-honored institutions as a misguided attempt to remake the world along "rational" lines.

The extremism of the French Revolution led to a backlash against the reformist tendencies in England. Parliament quickly enacted legislation that severely limited freedom of assembly, the press, and speech. Trade unions were outlawed. The Habeas Corpus Act was suspended in 1794, thus enabling the government to jail suspects without due process. Having effectively muzzled all but such prominent dissenters as Charles James Fox, the government turned its attention to the prosecution of the war with France.

POSTWAR REPRESSION. The victory in Europe did not bring Englishmen the stability and prosperity they had expected. Returning veterans could not find jobs in an economy disrupted by the long war. Landowners tried to protect their interests through parliamentary enactment of the Corn Laws (1815), designed to keep wheat prices high through an embargo of foreign grain. The act was ineffective but embittered the working classes.

As unemployment, rising bread prices, and the dislocation caused by industrialization brought England to the brink of class war, popular leaders, including Jeremy Bentham, William Cobbett, Francis Place, and Henry ("Orator") Hunt, emerged to demand political reforms. Their words were backed by popular agitation. The Luddite riots (see p. 246) continued into 1816, and mass meetings were organized. A rally held in the London precinct of Spa Fields in December 1816 degenerated into a riot. The Parliament responded to this lawlessness with the so-called Coercion Acts (1817), which among other things suspended habeas corpus and prohibited "seditious" meetings.

The confrontation reached a climax in August 1819 when cavalry were used to disperse a crowd of fifty thousand, which had gathered in Saint Peter's Fields, Manchester, to hear "Orator" Hunt demand parliamentary reform. Hundreds were wounded and eleven killed in the melee that came to be known as the Peterloo Massacre, a bitter pun on Wellington's great victory over Napoleon. Parliament again quickly responded by passing the Six Acts (December 1819), which banned unauthorized public meetings, placed a heavy tax on newspapers and journals, and threatened seditious writers with exile. Those who despaired of reform placed their hope in more desperate ventures. In 1820 the government uncovered the Cato Street Conspiracy, a plot to assassinate the entire Tory cabinet.

Although England seemed on the brink of revolution in 1820, the danger passed for a number of reasons. The government had demonstrated willingness to use force to protect itself against the unarmed populace. Returning prosperity eased unemployment and raised wages. The memory of the Jacobin terror began to recede in the public consciousness. Finally, a new generation of Tory leaders emerged, including George Canning and Robert Peel, who were better able to deal with the pressures of the postwar world.

The French Restoration. Restorations lack the drama of the revolutionary events that precede them. However, it would be a mistake to conclude that successful restorations are barren of significant achievement. It is the function of a restoration regime to reweave the intellectual, social, political, and economic fabric of a society and to replace those institutions and values that had failed to meet society's needs. The most difficult task of remolding a popular consensus in France was hampered by the long-standing animosity built by decades of revolution. The task of national reconciliation fell to the Bourbon dynasty.

REIGN OF LOUIS XVIII (1814–1824). Louis XVIII, the brother of the executed Louis XVI, had fled from France in 1791 and returned in 1814, a weary but wiser man. It has been said of the Bourbons that they "learned nothing and forgot nothing," but this aphorism does not apply to Louis XVIII. He was determined to restore the dynasty but recognized that he would have to come to terms with the revolutionary past.

Charter of 1814. The constitutional charter promulgated in June attempted to foster reconciliation. It proclaimed the dynasty's divine right to rule but guaranteed constitutional government in perpetuity. The new constitution retained the Napoleonic Code and the administrative apparatus created to enforce it. In addition, it granted religious freedom and accepted the revolutionary land settlement. The king also recognized the revolutionary heritage of popular representation by the creation of a bicameral legislature. The House of Peers included the Napoleonic nobility as well as the old Bourbon aristocracy, while the Chamber of Deputies, elected by limited suffrage, represented the propertied classes. The king had the exclusive right to introduce and veto legislation. The executive functions were placed in the hands of a ministry responsible to the king though not immune from parliamentary pressures, including the threat of impeachment. Designed as a compromise, the charter was attacked by the still unreconciled factions. The king was supported by moderate royalists, but to his right were Ultraroyalists, led by his brother the comte d'Artois, who demanded a complete repudiation of the revolutionary heritage. Also on the right were disgruntled Bonapartists, including thousands of army officers who had been retired on half pay. The left included the liberals in the business community who were appalled by the heavy taxes that soon appeared and diehard democrats who viewed the restoration as a rejection of all they had labored for from 1789 to 1799.

Second Restoration and the White Terror. When Napoleon returned to France in May 1815, no one rallied to the Bourbons, and Louis fled the country. Returning "in the baggage of the allied army" after the battle of Waterloo, the king briefly lost control of events to the Ultraroyalists. A "white terror" reigned in western and southern France, where royalist gangs hunted down and lynched republicans and Bonapartist sympathizers. The legislative elections in August 1815 produced an extremely reactionary majority. This *chambre introuvable* threatened to alienate large sections of the populace with its extreme policies. Louis XVIII soon dissolved it and won a more moderate majority in the subsequent election. Louis appointed the duc de Richelieu and Élie Decazes as his chief ministers, and under their direction the government steered a moderate course from 1816 to 1820. In 1818 the war indemnity was paid, the armies of occupation withdrew, and France rejoined the Concert of Europe. The parliamentary machinery worked reasonably well, and France seemed on the way toward a new political consensus based upon constitutional monarchy despite continued harassment by both radicals and Ultras.

Assassination of the Duc de Berry. Hopes of reconciliation were shattered in 1820 when a lone assassin killed the duc de Berry, the king's nephew, in a vain attempt to sever the royal lien of succession. The comte d'Artois laid the blame for his son's death squarely on Decazes's lenient policy. Louis could no longer resist Ultra pressure, and the government soon passed to the reactionary duc de Villèlé, who took his orders from the comte d'Artois. A severely restrictive electoral law guaranteed the election of a reactionary majority in the Chamber, who quickly passed legislation limiting freedom of speech and academic freedom. The ineptitude of such radical conspirators as the Carbonari only served to justify the repression. The government felt confident enough by 1823 to intervene in Spain to restore its tottering Bourbon regime. To the chagrin of liberals who remembered Napoleon's agony in Iberia, the French army scored a brilliant success, thus bolstering the Ultra government.

REIGN OF CHARLES X (1824–1830). Upon the death of his brother Louis, the comte d'Artois acceded to the throne as Charles X. The medieval splendor of his coronation at Rheims demonstrated his determination to restore the crown's prerevolutionary prerogatives. This policy soon dissipated the monarch's popularity.

The government indemnified the aristocracy for property confiscated during the Revolution with funds obtained by lowering the interest on government bonds. This indemnity law (1825) struck hardest at upper-class investors and cost the regime their influential support. Despite complaints, the act definitively resolved a nagging issue, for once the nobility accepted the indemnity, they forfeited any further claim on their old estates. Government support of the Church also antagonized a significant segment of the middle class, whose anticlerical attitudes had roots in the Enlightenment. The Law of Sacrilege (1826), which decreed the death penalty for certain sacrilegious acts, antagonized these anticlericals and freethinkers while doing nothing to strengthen the regime. Finally, the government antagonized the middle class by dissolving the national guard (1827), while failing to take the rudimentary precaution of disarming its bourgeois members.

Driven underground, the Liberals organized secret societies and were able to win a parliamentary majority. Charles refused to abide by this electoral mandate. The appointment of the reactionary prince of Polignac as prime minister in August 1829 and his obvious intention to rule without parliamentary support brought France to the brink of revolution. In four short years, Charles and his Ultras destroyed any hope that Frenchmen could be reconciled under the Bourbon banner.

The Spanish Restoration. Nowhere was the dichotomy between the ancien régime and the forces of liberalism more clearly evident than in postwar Spain. Between 1808 and 1814, the Iberian peninsula was the scene of a brutal conflict between the French troops, who maintained Joseph Bonaparte on the Spanish throne, and an English army supported by a nationalist guerrilla movement fighting in the name of the exiled Ferdinand VII. In May 1812 the Cortes (national assembly) that had been elected in the liberated zone adopted a constitution. While maintaining the monarchy, the charter stressed the concept of popular sovereignty. The popular will was to be expressed through a unicameral legislature elected by universal manhood suffrage. Ferdinand accepted the constitution to strengthen his support in the struggle against France, but events indicated that he had no intention of honoring his word.

The Bourbon dynasty was restored in Spain in March 1814, and Ferdinand immediately laid plans for an uncompromising restoration of the ancien régime. In May the king carried out a coup in which he simultaneously repudiated the constitution and ordered the arrest of all liberal leaders. He subsequently restored the aristocracy and the Church to all its prerevolutionary property and privileges. Orthodox was enforced by the reestablished Inquisition, and seditious ideas were controlled through total press censorship. Despite this reinstitution of monarchical absolutism and caste privilege, the country sank into chaos and depression.

Among the crown's greatest problems was the loss of revenue resulting from the revolt of Spain's South American colonies, which had begun during the reign of Joseph Bonaparte. Ferdinand was determined to restore his authority in South America, but in January 1820 the expeditionary force mobilized for the purpose at Cadiz, rose in revolt against his domestic policies and maladministration of the army.

A junta of liberal army officers forced the king to reinstate the Constitution of 1812, but their position deteriorated amidst bickering and managerial ineptitude. The revolution was suppressed in 1823 by a French army acting as a police force for the Continental powers (see p. 261). The reinstatement of Ferdinand aggravated relations between the old ruling class and the emergent liberals. Neither side was willing to compromise its principles, and nineteenth-century Spanish history is a dreary chronicle of coup and countercoup, while the people were left to fend for themselves.

The Hapsburg Domains and the Restoration in the Germanies. In 1815 the Austrian Empire reemerged as the dominant power of central Europe. It had not only survived a generation of diplomatic humiliation and military defeat but in the process had averted the contagion of rationalism, liberalism, and nationalism that could have destroyed the polygot empire from within. It was the task of Metternich from 1815 to 1848 to maintain the empire from physical and ideological danger, a task that he accomplished as much through diplomacy as through domestic regulation.

The political and territorial changes resulting from the Napoleonic wars were greatest among the German states. The Holy Roman Empire had been destroyed and replaced under terms of the Vienna Settlement by the Confederation of Germany, a loose union of the thirty-nine German states, whose primary connection was the weak Diet presided over by Austria. The states varied widely in terms of influence, culture, and outlook. Austria and Prussia were not only the most powerful but also among the most conservative. Liberal regimes existed in Baden, Nassau, Saxe-Weimar, and Württemberg. The rulers of these small states issued constitutions similar to the French Charter of 1814.

Despite the political and economic divisions, a sense of German unity was maintained by the intellectual community. Their liberalism and nationalism were to a great extent outgrowths of the Napoleonic era, and they were torn between a desire to rationalize their society and a nationalist fervor to protect Germany physically and culturally from French encroachments. The university student organizations (*Burschenschaften*) that originated at Jena in 1815 and spread to other universities were the most visible and vocal manifestations of these sentiments. The Wartburg Festival, held on 17 October 1817 to commemorate the three-hundredth anniversary of the Lutheran revolt and the fourth anniversary of the victory at Leipzig, demonstrated the widespread appeal of the movement for young intellectuals and alarmed the conservative and antinationalist rulers of Germany. More ominous was the assassination by a radical fanatic of August von Kotzebue, a dramatist and part-time intelligence agent in the pay of Czar Alexander I. His death provided Metternich with the opportunity he needed to move against the liberals. The Diet convened at Carlsbad in September 1819 and promulgated the Carlsbad Decrees, which ordered the dissolution of the Burschenschaften, imposed rigid press censorship, and created a system of monitors whose task was to eliminate subversive elements from Germany universities. The Diet also created the Mainz Commission, which throughout the 1820s investigated subversives and which at Metternich's insistence searched in vain to locate the nonexistent international revolutionary headquarters.

Restoration Italy. Postwar Italy, despite its sharply delineated natural frontiers, remained, as Metternich aptly remarked, a "geographical expression." The peninsula had probably gained more from the Napoleonic occupation than any other area and as a consequence suffered from the restoration.

The nine states of Italy shared several characteristics. Collectively, their governments were among the most reactionary in Europe. Order was maintained through the enforcement of Catholic orthodoxy, censorship, the presence of armed forces, and the operation of hordes of secret-police agents. The influence of the Hapsburg dynasty was pervasive. Lombardy and Venetia were integrated into the Austrian Empire, and the duchies of Parma, Modena, Lucca, and Tuscany were ruled by the emperor's kin. Thus, in northern Italy only the kingdom of Piedmont-Sardinia was ruled by an Italian dynasty, the house of Savoy. The Papal States sympathized with the Hapsburg outlook, and the kingdom of the Two Sicilies was bound to the Austrians by treaty. The pope reigned as both head of Roman Catholicism and temporal ruler of the Papal States. Ferdinand I, an older version of his inept nephew king Ferdinand VII of Spain, ruled the kingdom of the Two Sicilies. These rulers held sway over lands so impoverished, crime ridden, ill administered, and repressive that they were a scandal even to their reactionary friends.

As in Germany, the liberal elements among the professional and commercial classes were a small minority in a population of generally illiterate peasants still wedded to the conservative values that had bound them to their rulers for centuries. Unable to express their nationalist and liberal attitudes openly, the intelligentsia, including a large number of young army officers, formed secret societies. The most influential of these were the Carbonari in Naples and the Federati in Piedmont. Their primary goals were rationalized constitutional monarchy and national unification.

It took only the news of the outbreak of the Spanish insurrection to trigger a revolt among these dissident elements in Naples (July 1820) and Piedmont (March 1821). Ferdinand bought time by accepting demands for the promulgation of the Spanish Constitution of 1812. Regent Charles Albert of Piedmont followed suit. The revolutionaries failed to consolidate their position. They were poorly organized, untrained in public adminstration, politically naive, and most significant, they failed to appeal to the oppressed masses. As in Spain, Ferdinand and Charles Albert soon repudiated their concessions and relied on the Austrian army to put down the revolts. Italy once more sank into its decadent slumber.

Russia from Alexander I to Nicholas I. Czar Alexander I (r. 1801–1825) is one of the most intriguing and complex personalities of the restoration era. The early years of his reign are marked by a vague paternalistic liberalism that found little clear expression except in the abortive constitutionalism attempted in the kingdom of Poland. After 1810 he tended progressively to religious mysticism, coming to perceive himself as a divinely ordained emissary whose destiny was to deliver European civilization from the anti-Christ in the form of Emperor Napoleon and then to restore the unity and vigor of Christendom. He regarded the burning of Moscow and the subsequent deliverance of Russia in 1812 as a miracle. After Napoleon's defeat he fostered the Holy Alliance in an attempt to achieve his second goal.

Reaction set in after 1815. Alexander brushed aside the reform proposals of minister Mikhail Speranski and came to rely heavily on the advice of Aleksei Arakcheev, a ruthless but efficient reactionary devoted to autocracy. Alexander's desire to crush all trace of liberalism became so strong that Metternich regarded him as a threat to European stability.

The greatest threat to autocracy came from a small group of liberal aristocrats and army officers whose wartime experiences in western Europe had fostered hopes for a more open society. They formed the Union of Public Good (1818), which was soon driven underground and split into two factions. Although both factions agreed on the need to end autocracy and emancipate the serfs, the more conservative Northern Society, led by Nikita Muraviëv, sought to create a constitutional monarch, while Pavel Pestel's Southern Society demanded a republic.

The opportunity for action came in December 1825 with the death of Alexander I. Under terms of a secret family agreement, the heir apparent, Grand Duke Constantine, had waived his rights to the throne in favor of his brother Nicholas. The Decembrists, who took their name from the month of the revolt, capitalized on the public confusion, denouncing Nicholas as a usurper and demanding "Constantine and Constitution." The secrecy of the conspiracy precluded the marshaling of public support, and the lack of communication between the Northern and Southern societies prevented concerted action. The rebel leaders were disorganized, and the rank-and-file mutineers in the Saint Petersburg garrison sacrificed their lives in the mistaken belief that they were supporting the rightful heir. The Decembrist revolt collapsed within hours, and Nicholas I acceded to the throne.

The reign of Nicholas I (1825–1855) was a continuation of thoroughgoing repression. Nicholas distrusted even his own bureaucrats, and the government passed into the hands of his personal chancery. His direct supervision of its third section (secret police) was a hallmark of his regime. The most positive aspect of his domestic policy was the codification of the laws (1833), which provided the first coherent compilation of Russian statutes. Nicholas took a more independent position in foreign policy than Alexander. His support of the Greek insurrection in hopes of weakening the Turkish Empire placed him in opposition to Metternich. He successfully defeated the Polish insurrection of 1830 and for the rest of his reign carried out a policy designed to destroy Polish culture and to integrate Poland within the Russian Empire.

The Concert of Europe

The Quadruple Alliance had been forged to defeat Napoleon and restore the balance of power. Under the terms of the Second Treaty of Paris (1815), Austria, Prussia, Russia, and Britain agreed to extend the alliance for twenty years and to hold periodic conferences to formulate common policy for the maintenance of peace. However, it was soon evident that a significant difference of opinion existed between Britain and her Continental allies. Castlereagh and his successor George Canning were prepared to intervene in Europe to prevent any state from upsetting the balance of power by overt acts of military aggression. Metternich believed that revolutions were inherently aggressive since they challenged divinely instituted authority and that they could infect the entire continent without a single battalion crossing a frontier. He wanted to use the alliance to maintain the status quo even if it meant intervention in the domestic affairs of states, a step that even a Tory government in England was unwilling to take. This basic difference of opinion undermined the Concert of Europe, and within a few years, the great powers had returned to the traditional diplomacy in pursuit of national and dynastic interests.

The Congress System. Ambassadors participated in the first conference held after the war, but the four international congresses held between 1818 and 1823 involved the chief ministers of the great powers. Metternich dominated these proceedings and was able to overpower the revolutionary movements of 1820 despite the non-cooperation of Britain and the declining support of Russia.

CONGRESS OF AIX-LA-CHAPELLE. The first congress met at Aix-la-Chapelle in September 1818 to arrange for the readmission of France into the community of nations. In return for settlement of the war indemnity, the allies agreed to withdraw their army of occupation. France also became a partner in the new Quintuple Alliance, although the Quadruple Alliance remained in force.

CONGRESS OF TROPPAU. A second congress gathered at Troppau, Silesia, in October 1820 to deal with the revolution in Naples. The congress adopted a protocol clearly enunciating Metternich's position that revolution was an inherently aggressive act and that the legitimate regimes had a right to take any steps necessary to bring the guilty state back into the fold. The congress invited Ferdinand I to a subsequent meeting where he would act as a mediator between Europe and his rebellious subjects. While England recognized Austria's rights to protect its vital interests in Italy, it rejected the Troppau Protocol.

CONGRESS OF LAIBACH. Representatives of Austria, Prussia, Russia, and the Italian states met at Laibach, Austria, in January 1821 to receive Ferdinand I. Although he had promised before he left Naples to support the new constitution, at Laibach he repudiated the revolution and called on the powers to restore his authority. The Austrian army served as the expeditionary force that defeated the Neapolitan and Piedmontese revolutionaries (March–April 1821) and restored the old regime in Italy.

CONGRESS OF VERONA. The last congress of this kind met in Verona, Italy, in October 1822 to deal with the Spanish revolution. Metternich found it difficult to maintain his position. He had to control the erratic Czar Alexander, who wanted to send one army to Spain to suppress a revolution and one to Greece to support a revolt against the Turks. England, on the other hand, already opposed intervention in principle and was particularly opposed to aiding the Spanish Bourbons. Canning feared that a revived Spain might attempt to regain its lost colonies, which as independent states had become lucrative trading partners for Britain. Although a French army suppressed the Spanish revolt in the name of the congress, Metternich was never again able to muster a consensus for the principle of intervention.

South America and the Monroe Doctrine. The Spanish revolution of 1820 had begun as the crown organized an expeditionary force to suppress the independence movement in its American empire. After defeat of the revolution, the future status of Latin America was again open to question. Neither the United States nor Great Britain desired a reinstatement of Spanish authority, but their negotiations failed to produce a joint stand. As a result, President James Monroe announced the American position independently in his State of the Union address of 1823. The president's statement, later known as the Monroe Doctrine, rejected any future European interference in the affairs of the Western hemisphere. Although the British government did not endorse the American position, it was the Royal Navy that formed the buffer between Europe and the New World.

The Greek Revolution. Metternich also found it impossible to maintain the principle of legitimacy in eastern Europe. In March 1821 Greek nationalists led by Alexander Ypsilanti rose in revolt against the Turkish Empire. Western liberals took up the Greek cause, and even Alexander I, driven by Christian mysticism and dreams of Russian expansion, momentarily broke stride with Metternich. Metternich realized that the principle of legitimacy would collapse if exceptions were allowed. He supported the sultan's right to rule and suggested that the revolt be allowed to "burn itself out beyond the pale of civilization." Alexander halfheartedly returned to the fold at Troppau, but Britain and France lent aid and comfort to the Greeks. The Greek rebellion was bolstered in 1823 when Britain recognized its belligerent status, but suffered a sharp reversal when the sultan's Egyptian army counterattacked in the Morea (1825). The Greeks were saved by the intervention of the great powers. The Treaty of London (1827), signed by Britain, France, and Russia, demanded an armistice followed by Greek autonomy. When the sultan procrastinated, an Anglo-French squadron sank the Egyptian fleet at Navarino Bay (October 1827). Russia, whose policy had shifted with the accession of Nicholas I in 1825, declared war on Turkey in April 1828. The Turks soon capitulated, and Greece achieved its independence under terms of the London Protocol (February 1830). Metternich's policy, which had reached its zenith at Troppau, lay in ruins after the Greek war of independence. Although the conservative states continued to cooperate in the defense of the old order in Europe, the concrete apparatus of the Quintuple Alliance and the congress system was never revived.

21

Nineteenth-Century Intellectual Currents

Intellectual effervescence was one of the most striking aspects of postwar Europe. The majority of Europeans still found shelter under the traditional Christian value system, but the authority of divine revelation provided little solace for the intellectual community. The eighteenth-century philosophers believed that they would soon unlock the mysteries of human behavior in the same way that Newton had explained the mechanism of the universe. However, instead of achieving a rational and humane society based upon natural law, European civilization plunged headlong into a quarter century of ideological warfare. This disruption was compounded by the inexorable transformation wrought by industrialization. The nineteenth century is thus marked by a search for renewed certainty after a generation of disillusionment. This search produced three emergent political philosophies—conservatism, liberalism, and socialism—and two broad cultural movements—romanticism and nationalism. Although these movements will be examined separately, they are not mutually exclusive categories. Many combinations can be observed in the historical figures of the time; for example, romantic conservatism, Samuel Coleridge; romantic liberalism, Victor Hugo; and socialist nationalism, Louis Blanc.

Conservatism

Philosophical tracts defending the traditional political system and social organization began to appear after the outbreak of the French Revolution. Although nineteenth-century conservatives differed on many points, there are several congruent strains that run through their thought. Their essentially tragic outlook was derived from the belief that human behavior is dominated by man's baser instincts unchecked by the relatively weak power of human reason. The function of the state is to provide moral leadership and through its authority to maintain law and order against the degenerative pressure of human nature. This is not to say that society must be ruled from the executioner's block. Conservatives believed that people arrived at balanced social relationships through centuries of trial and error and that societies can reach high levels of achievement in such an atmosphere. Change is possible and sometimes necessary but must take place within the traditional framework. Conservatives argued that rationalist attempts to remake society completely would only lead to rootless anarchy. Finally, conservatives generally placed the safekeeping of society in the hands of an aristocracy, which set the moral and intellectual tone and in return for privileges was ethically bound to a life of community service (*noblesse oblige*).

England. Edmund Burke (1729–1797) is recognized as one of the most brilliant spokesmen for moderate conservatism. His conclusions were drawn from his experience as a workaday politician and his insights as a political theorist. His influence derives from his *Reflections on the French Revolution* (1790), in which he condemned even the generally nonviolent phase of the French Revolution. Burke defended the American revolutionaries because he felt they stood for traditional English liberties against despotic government. He condemned the French revolutionaries because they disregarded tradition in favor of untested social and political theories. He believed that the wholesale destruction of time-tested institutions was doomed to throw France into anarchy and threatened to drag down Western civilization with it.

Samuel Coleridge (1772–1834) is best remembered as a romantic poet, but his conservative political philosophy also had a significant impact on his contemporaries. Coleridge stressed the organic nature of society and thus rejected the atomistic individualism fostered by liberals. He viewed the state as a vital instrument in mobilizing the dynamic forces of society toward worthwhile goals. His position favoring state intervention in religious, social, and economic issues was in direct opposition to the liberal motto of laissez-faire.

France. Joseph de Maistre (1753–1821) and Joseph de Bonald (1754–1840) were the most influential spokesmen for French conservatism. While Burke was a pragmatist who supported English constitutionalism because it worked, Maistre and Bonald supported traditional French absolutism because they believed it to be divinely ordained. Both rejected the Enlightenment and the revolution that followed it as the work of prideful men who acted in the mistaken belief that human reason was competent to tamper with the wisdom of centuries. They were not blind to the deficiencies of the regime but argued that inefficiency and injustice were the natural outcome of human action and were in any case preferable to anarchy. While Bonald gave his attention to the absolute prerogatives of the crown, Maistre examined the theological basis of secular power. In his work *Concerning the Papacy* (1817), he concluded that the pope should preside as the supreme arbiter of affairs in Christendom, a position that was no longer maintained even by the papacy.

Germany. The chief spokesman of German conservation was Friedrich von Gentz, Metternich's secretary and confidant. After recovering from an initial infatuation with the French Revolution, Gentz devoted himself to the formulation and defense of Metternich's policies. His denunciation of nationalism in favor of international cooperation became a hallmark of German conservatism until the emergence of Bismarck in the 1860s. Gentz's translation of Burke's *Reflections on the French Revolution* had a profound effect on German political thought. Other leading German conservatives included Adam Müller, Karl von Haller, and Joseph von Radowitz. All were antirationalists who stressed the need for the mystical union of crown and altar as the foundation for all society.

Liberalism

The conservative restoration following the defeat of France in 1815 did not destroy the dream of freedom that had taken root in the European consciousness. In its broadest terms, this quest for freedom was known as *liberalism*. Liberalism, like conservatism, can best be described as a state of mind rather than a clearly delineated ideology. It is founded upon a belief in the moral worth and dignity of every human being. Its goal is to create an atmosphere in which the individual is able to pursue his own interests and fulfill his potential free from arbitrary restraints. The only legitimate limitations to be placed on the individual "pursuit of happiness" are the rights of others. Liberal confidence in the individual was derived from the conviction that human reason provided an adequate guide for personal action as well as a guarantee of society's continual progress.

When their outlook was reduced to specific goals, the liberals stressed the need for constitutional government based upon consent of the governed, which would protect the individuals rights of property, conscience, and expression. It must be stressed in this regard that most liberals were neither political democrats nor social egalitarians. Liberals feared the tyranny of the mob as much as the tyranny of crown or church. Equality before the law was regarded as a starting point from which each individual, through his own talent and effort, would rise in society. Inequality of attainment would be the natural result. Liberals further held that the propertied classes alone had a sufficient stake in society to warrant political rights and that only they had the leisure time to develop the necessary political skills. Thus the open sesame to political rights expressed by the French liberals of the 1830s was *enrichissez-vous* ("get rich"). Finally, it should be noted that, while individual rights were stressed by liberals in Britain and France, it was the right of the group, or nation, that became the rallying cry for liberals on the Continent in central and eastern Europe. National self-determination directed primarily against Austrian domination became the focus of liberal activity, often to the exclusion of individual rights, among the subject German, Italian, and Slavic peoples.

England. The dominant strain of English liberalism was called *utilitarianism* or *Benthamism*, appellations derived from Jeremy Bentham (1748–1832), the leading theorist of the movement. Bentham was a rationalist who believed that the pursuit of happiness (good) and the avoidance of pain (evil) were the sole motivations of human action. The *utility*, or capacity, of anything to produce good or avoid evil was therefore the sole test of its value. The goal of any institution or value was to produce the greatest good for the greatest number. Since Bentham believed that only the individual could judge pain and pleasure for himself, he was an extreme libertarian. He supported laissez-faire economics and championed democracy. With his associates James Mill and Francis Place, Bentham condemned all forms of special privilege as well as the hoary institutions cherished by Edmund Burke. Although the rising middle class and industrialists supported most utilitarian ideas, they were not prepared to accept the consequences of democracy. It remained for John Stuart Mill, in the next generation of liberal theorists, to reconcile for minority rights with majority rule and to give a social conscience to the concept of the "greatest good for the greatest number" by demonstrating liberalism taken to its extreme meant affluence for the few and misery for the multitude.

France. French liberals sought to find a middle way between the absolutism of the ancien régime and the egalitarianism of the Revolution. The center of the liberal movement was held by the so-called doctrinaires, whose most able spokesmen were Victor Cousin, François Guizot, and Pierre Royer-Collard. The doctrinaires were pragmatists who supported the concept of constitutional monarchy and bourgeois dominance. When the Charter of 1814 failed to protect their interests against the absolutism of Charles X, they helped overthrow the Bourbon dynasty and became the main ideological support of the July Monarchy (1830–1848).

To the left of the doctrinaires was Benjamin Constant, the most popular liberal theorist of the restoration period. Constant sought to put clear limits on the concept of popular sovereignty and government power, thus leaving the individual free to pursue his own interests. In this regard he stood firmly opposed to democracy. The most influential liberal economist of the day was Jean Baptiste Say, who attempted with only moderate success to displace the mercantilist outlook by popularizing the laissez-faire concepts of Adam Smith.

Alexis de Tocqueville broke free from the class-bound liberalism of the restoration. His *Democracy in America* (1835) is a classic exposition of the liberal dilemma of individual rights in the face of majority rule and marks him as the most profound French liberal of the nineteenth century. Tocqueville's travels in America brought him to realize the benefits of political democracy as well as the danger of mass culture. He was able to explain to his countrymen that democracy was a historical development to be welcomed not merely as majority rule but as a concept that when accompanied by balanced institutions and mutual respects for individual rights could promote both common interests and personal goals.

Germany. In some respect the German liberals were forced to live in a less hospitable intellectual climate than their English and French contemporaries. Germany's slow industrial growth and the continued dominance of the agricultural elite deprived them of both mass support and middle-class influence. It is, therefore, not surprising that liberalism in the first half of the century was best represented in the universities. In Hanover, where English influence had been strong throughout the eighteenth century, liberal scholars such as Friedrich Dahlmann stressed the significance of individual freedom within the context of deep-seated cultural traditions. In the Rhineland, where contacts with French intellectual currents were strong throughout the Enlightenment and the Revolution, the natural-rights theory predominated among such academicians as Karl von Rotteck and Karl Welcker. Although constitutionalism made some headway in western Germany, the liberal struggle for individual freedom was often sapped by the effort to obtain national unification.

Socialism

Despite the obvious benefits gained from industrialization, an undercurrent of intellectual discontent existed side by side with the optimism of laissez-faire liberals. These social critics recognized that while concepts of individualism and free enterprise produced vast new wealth for the relative few, at the same time they created economic catastrophe, social degradation, and psychological demoralization for the masses. Although the *utopians* produced widely divergent programs, they agreed on several fundamental points. They believed that men were essentially rational and good and that a change in basic values would lead to a change in the social environment capable of providing universal well-being. Central to their thinking was the dictum that unbridled individualist competition would lead only to class war and social anarchy. They were convinced that associative cooperation was the only path to human happiness. Of the five socialists listed here, Saint-Simon, Fourier, and Owen are usually classified as *utopian socialists*.

Saint-Simon. Claude Henri de Saint-Simon (1760–1825) combined the scientific rationalism of the philosophes with a critique of liberalism that reflected the opinions of his conservative contemporaries. He rejected democracy in favor of a highly stratified class system. At the apex of society would stand a caste of technocrats who would enforce a rejuvenated Christian orthodoxy, plan the economy, and direct society for the good of all.

Fourier. In contrast to Saint-Simon, François Fourier (1772–1837) was a romantic who longed to create a harmonious pastoral society instead of a gigantic social factory. His society would be built upon a series of autonomous self-sufficient communities called *phalanxes*. Life in these communities was to be regulated as rigorously as it was by the monastic rule, although the communal living arrangements hardly reflected the traditional Christian ethic. Although Fourier himself never created such a community, several Fourierist experiments were attempted. The famous Brook Farm community in Massachusetts foundered along with others for essentially the same reason. The inhabitants always contained disgruntled romantic intellectuals who played at the simple agrarian life but who lacked artisan skills and balked at the rigid rules the communities required.

Owen. Robert Owen (1771–1858) was a successful Scottish textile manufacturer who sought to demonstrate that human dignity and economic well-being for the working class would actually enhance productivity in the industrial system. He hoped that New Lanark, his model company town, would trigger a wholesale change of attitude among British industrialists, but his ideas failed to win wide acceptance, and his experimental community at New Harmony, Indiana, ended in dismal failure. Of longer lasting significance was his initiative in the creation of buyers' cooperatives.

Blanc. Louis Blanc (1811–1882) stands with Saint-Simon as the most influential pre-Marxist socialist. In his *Organization of Labor* (1840) he recognized the need for a reordering of the political and economic structure at its center rather than the reliance on utopian communities at the periphery. He believed that the masses could assure justice for themselves throught the democratic control of the state. From that vantage they could guarantee each man the right to earn a livelihood. National workshops that would provide the working class with the profits of their own labor were implemented only in caricature during the Second French Republic, but Blanc's conception formed the basis of later syndicalist thought.

Marx. Though destined to emerge as the most influential critic of capitalism and the prophet of communism, Karl Marx (1818–1883) and his associate Friedrich Engels (1820–1895) had little impact during the first half of the nineteenth century. Their *Communist Manifesto* (1847) was built around a philosophy that perceived history as a succession of clashes between a dominant class that held its position through control of the means of production and an oppressed mass that created the wealth of every society but was robbed of the fruits of its labor. Marx mocked the utopian panaceas. He called upon the working class to throw off its chains through revolution and create a communist society in which all productive capital would be held in common.

Romanticism

Romanticism dominated the realm of arts and letters during the first half of the nineteenth century. Although the work of a romantic writer, artist, or composer is readily identifiable, the movement was so diverse that it defies a precise definition. In many respects, Romanticism represented an escape from the intellectualism of the Enlightenment, from the political and social chaos engendered by the French Revolution, and from the pressure of the accelerating urban-industrial transformation. The romantics sensed that eighteenth-century intellectuals had overestimated the part played by the intellect in human activity and that the rationalists' facile theorems had done nothing to fathom the mysteries of life. In contrast, the romantics believed that the mysteries were infinite and that only the personal quest for reconciliation with these mysteries had any meaning. Thus, in place of reason, they exalted intuition and emotion. The Supreme Being of the deists gave way to the mystical Christianity of the medieval church or to a mystical worship of nature. The impulse of individual expression took precedence over the classical dictums of order and balance.

Poetry. By breaking away from the formalism of some classicists as Alexander Pope and John Dryden, the romantic poets were among the most expressive artists of the movement. In their *Lyrical Ballads* (1798), William Wordsworth and Samuel Coleridge collaborated to explore the mysteries of nature, the depths of the human soul, and the joys of pastoral life. The pattern was repeated in the work of John Keats, Percy Bysshe Shelley, Robert Burns, and Thomas Gray. The romanic penchant for the mysterious and exotic was displayed by George Gordon, Lord Byron, in *Childe Harold's Pilgrimage* and *Don Juan*. The greatest of the French romantics included Victor Hugo, Alfred de Musset, Alfred de Vigny, Alphonse de Lamartine, and, at the end of the era, Charles Baudelaire. In Germany the tragic life of Novalis (Friedrich von Hardenberg) typifies that of many romantics. After the death of his sweetheart, he sought solace in mystical Catholicism and expressed his melancholia in such works as *Hymns of Night*. The greatest of the German romantic poets was Heinrich Heine. Although he lived an often lonely and embittered life, his poems evoke the joys and hopes of youth and, as in *Die Lorelei*, the poignancy of unrequited love. Thousands of his poems were set to music by composers including Brahms, Liszt, Mendelssohn, Schubert, and Schumann. The romantic tide swept into Russia and found expression through the pens of Aleksander Pushkin, the country's most renowned poet, and Mikhail Lermontov.

Prose and Drama. The lifework and intellectual development of Jean Jacques Rousseau (1712–1778) and Johann Wolfgang von Goethe (1749–1832) serve as a warning against attempts to oversimplify intellectual movements or to exaggerate their dominance at any given period. Rousseau and Goethe are considered the founders of romanticism. Rousseau lived and worked within the Enlightenment and accepted the significance of reason in human development. At the same time, he rejected Voltaire's cynical rationalism. He called for the liberation of the human personality from the corrupting influence of society and a return to the humble virtues engendered by a rustic existence. In this vein *La Nouvelle Héloïse* (1761) stands as the first romantic novel. Goethe is among the greatest of the German classicists; yet his *Sorrows of the Young Werther* (1774) and *Faust* (1808) place him in the forefront of the romantic movement.

The romantic novel embodied mystery, love, and adventure and often pitted the protagonist in a hopeless struggle against the overpowering forces of nature, human institutions, or incarnate evil. The hero faced such adversity alone, often armed only with an irresistible and fatal impulse to fulfill his destiny. Those novels underscored the essential tragedy of human existence and yet emphasized that man was ennobled by his struggle. Among examples of this genre are Sir Walter Scott's *Ivanhoe*, Mary Shelley's *Frankenstein*, Victor Hugo's *Les Misérables* and *Notre Dame de Paris*, Aleksander Pushkin's *Evgeni Onegin*, and Mikhail Lermontov's *A Hero of Our Time*.

Romantic drama had its beginnings in the German *Sturm und Drang* ("storm and stress") movement of the 1770s and 80s. Among the most significant works of the period were Friedrich von Klinger's *Sturm und Drang*, Johann von Schiller's *The Robbers*, and Goethe's *Götz von Berlichingen*, a play modeled after Shakespeare's revived dramas. Other significant plays include Hugo's Shakespearean *Hernani*, which triggered a riot on opening night between traditionalists and romantics, and Pushkin's *Boris Godunov*.

Painting. The artists of the romantic persuasion found the rules of classical composition confining. They sought to express on canvas, not the witness of their eyes nor the mind's logic, but the vision of their souls. In England John Constable (1776–1837) forsook both aristocratic salons and urban contagion to portray the tranquility of the English countryside and the bliss of rustic life in such works as *The Hay Wain*. John M. W. Turner (1775–1851), also a gifted landscape painter, emerged as a precursor of impressionism. With swirling color and indistinct line, he evoked the essence of nature's power in leaping flames, heaving seas, lashing rain, and iridescent snow. William Blake transferred to canvas the terrors that stalk the soul in the long hours before dawn. On the Continent Frenchman Eugène Delacroix championed the causes of nationalism and social justice in such works as *Liberty Leading the People*. The romantic quest for adventure and exotic themes is nowhere better illustrated than in his Moroccan watercolors and the powerful *Death of Sardanapalus*. The melancholia and yearning that flow through romanticism is clearly expressed in the work of the German artist Kaspar David Friedrich (1774–1840), whose haunting, moonlit landscapes reflect the growing despair in his search for inner peace.

Music. Among all the arts, it might be music that most clearly expressed the message of romanticism. Romantic composers used every instrument and technique at their disposal to convey their deepest thoughts and a highly subjective view of the world around them. Through sound they sought to echo all the moods of nature, from the tranquil brook to the raging storm, and to conjure up in the listener the tenderness of love or the heat of battle. In this age of genius, only a few examples can be mentioned. Among the giants was

Ludwig van Beethoven (1770–1827). Though socially isolated by the embarrassment of his increasing deafness, Beethoven responded to the revolutionary age by throwing off the musical conventions of his time. His masterpieces include, among many others, his *Quartet in C Sharp Minor* opus 131, the opera *Fidelio*, and the *Ninth Symphony*, whose last movement is a setting of Schiller's *Ode to Joy*. The next generation provided such luminaries as Franz Schubert (1797–1828), Felix Mendelssohn (1809–1847), and Robert Schumann (1810–1856). It was during these decades that the piano and symphonic ensemble came of age. Frédéric Chopin (1810–1849) must rank among the greatest composers for the piano and Franz Liszt (1811–1886) as the outstanding piano virtuoso of the time. The romantic movement reached the peak of its development with the work of Richard Wagner (1813–1883), who combined all the arts to fashion his operatic masterpieces. Employing elaborate stage settings, Wagner put to words and music the heroic folk legends of Germanic mythology. His most powerful works include *Tristan und Isolde*, *Die Meistersinger*, and the epic *Der Ring des Nibelungen*, consisting of four interlocking operas.

Nationalism

Nationalism has been one of the most powerful cultural forces in Europe during the last two centuries. From its European seedbed, it has spread around the globe, and today it retains as great a potential for growth or destruction as any *ism*.

Concept of Nationalism. Nationalism marks a sharp break from Europe's universalist tradition. Both the Christian outlook and the secular ideology of reason view the individual as a distinct moral entity and conceive of humanity as bound together in a vast unifying system. Nationalists, on the other hand, feel that individual identity derives from membership in a social group—the nation. Thus, it is the nation rather than the individual or humankind that forms the ultimate social reality.

National consciousness developed as a result of many factors. Geographical homogeneity or isolation can play a part, as Shakespeare so eloquently pointed out when he described England as "this precious stone set in the silver sea, which serves it . . . as a moat defensive to a house." Though significant in English national development, the importance of natural frontiers has probably been exaggerated. The very lack of barriers between the Germans, Poles, and Russians probably heightened their nationalism and xenophobia. A more important fact in national development is cultural solidarity, which takes the form of a common language, religion, law, and historical tradition. Because these factors often exist in combination, they produce a sense of common destiny that extends from the mythical past into the unknown future.

The French Revolution had a decisive impact upon the development of a national consciousness in Europe. Although nationalism existed in England and to some degree in France preceding the Revolution, the dynastic state held sway in the remainder of Europe. In these countries class status was the most important consideration in social life, and the people were subjects rather than citizens. The territorial extent of such states was determined by war and marriage alliances, and people were transferred from one prince to another without compunction. During the French Revolution, the Bourbon claim to rule by divine right was cast aside for the concept of popular sovereignty that Rousseau had expounded in his *Social Contract* (1762). In it the state was conceived to exist above the monarch, and it became the political expression of the whole people. Western civilization has come to accept this concept of *nation-state*, a political unity embodying a national group, as the logical form of political organization.

Outside of France, the revolutionary promise of liberty, equality, and fraternity was first greeted with enthusiasm by the intelligentsia. It soon became evident, however, that instead of liberation the French were determined to enforce their imperial dream on the Continent. The emergence of a national sentiment and armed resistance in Spain, Germany, and Russia was clear evidence of the determination of subject peoples to protect themselves from French cultural and political dominance. Although it was longer in coming, a growing demand for cultural and then political freedom was also expressed by the national minorities within the Austrian Empire.

Cultural Nationalism. The most influential nationalist philosopher outside of France was Johann von Herder (1744–1803). In his masterpiece *Ideas on the Philosophy of the History of Mankind*, Herder developed his concept of a benign form of cultural nationalism. He believed that each nation had a personality or folk soul (*Volksgeist*) that had developed out of its unique history. This national culture was not superior to any other but allowed each people to develop its full potential, and the resulting cultural diversity gave a richness to civilization. In pursuit of these ideas, Herder made valuable contributions to comparative philology and German literature through the collection of folk legends. In this regard Jacob and Wilhelm Grimm should also be mentioned for their collection of German folktales (known in English as *Grimm's Fairy Tales*). This early form of nationalism was not parochial. Herder supported Slavic national aspirations and admired French achievements, although he did resist any notion of French cultural dominance.

Political Nationalism. During the apogee of the French Empire, German nationalists came to realize that political organization and military power were prerequisites for the development of purely German culture. Georg W. F. Hegel (1770–1831), one of the greatest German philosophers, developed his concept of the state as the highest expression of culture in *Philosophy of Right*. In the wake of the national humiliation resulting from Napoleon's victory at Jena, Johann Fichte (1762–1814) delivered his *Addresses to the German Nation* (1807–1808), calling for a regeneration of Germany so that it might fulfill its world destiny. His view that German culture was superior to any other was supported by some of his contemporaries, including Ernst Arndt (1769–1860). This form of ethnocentric and aggressive nationalism supplanted Herder's nonpolitical and cosmopolitan views and has become the dominant and most destructive form of nationalism in the twentieth century. It should not be assumed that the concept is exclusively German. The term *chauvinism*, used to denote extreme nationalism, is derived from Nicholas Chauvin, a soldier in Napoleon's army. It has found expression in the national consciousness of most modern states.

22

Reform and Revolution
1820-1848

The years immediately following the peace settlement of 1815 are known as the restoration era. However, it was impossible to restore the old regime. The revolutionary dreams of individual liberty, representative government, and national fulfillment had been momentarily defeated but not destroyed. Technology had begun the slow but accelerating alteration of economic activity that would in turn transform the social and political structure of Europe. Thus, from 1820 to 1848, the societies of western Europe faced the task of adapting to these new forces. Where history, culture, institutional framework, and intellectual acceptance permitted, the result was evolutionary change; where these factors stood in the way of adaptation, the result was revolution. Reform proved the exception to the rule of revolution in the decades from 1820 to 1848.

Reform in England, 1820–1850

Despite widespread discontent and sporadic outbursts of violence, the English political system weathered the crisis that followed peace in 1815. By 1820 the long-standing Tory establishment seemed solidly reentrenched. However, during the Napoleonic wars, England had begun a profound transformation into an urbanized industrial society. Major population shifts coincided with the emergence of an industrialized working class concentrated in the Midlands, an upper class of industrialists, and a middle class of managers. These groups challenged the old landed and commercial interests for a proportional share of power. The victory of reform instead of the outbreak of revolution can be credited in large measure to England's parliamentary tradition and the good sense of the ruling class.

The Tory Establishment. A new outlook was clearly evident among the Tories who continued to hold power after the accession of George

IV in 1820. The suicide of the able but detested foreign secretary Castlereagh led to a reorganization of the cabinet in 1822. The new ministers included Foreign Secretary George Canning, Home Secretary Robert Peel, and President of the Board of Trade William Huskisson. All sympathized with England's industrial interests and recognized the need to reform.

Huskisson labored to cut through the web of archaic tariff legislation. By moving toward free trade, he enhanced England's position as banker and mercantile carrier while at the same time stimulating the import of raw materials vital to England's burgeoning economy. The major stumbling blocks to these reforms were the great landowners, Whigs and Tories alike, who insisted on the maintenance of the Corn Laws. With the support of Peel, in 1824 Huskisson was able to carry through the abolition of the Combination Acts, passed in 1799 during the revolutionary scare, which had outlawed labor unions. Although unions were legalized, a rash of worker agitation brought crippling restrictions on their activity for the next decade.

Home Secretary Robert Peel worked to renovate the legal system. He upgraded the judicial process and was primarily responsible for abolishing capital punishment for over a hundred minor crimes. In this regard Peel is probably best remembered for the organization of the London police force, whose officers came to be known as Bobbies, after their founder.

This liberalized outlook was reflected in the foreign policy of George Canning, who withdrew England from Metternich's repressive congress system. Englishmen sympathized with the Greek patriots who fought for independence from Ottoman control, and it was clearly in the interests of mercantile England to support the movement toward independence in Central and South America.

However, Britain's liberal outlook should not be exaggerated. Close to home she maintained an iron grip upon Ireland, where nationalist demands were being renewed. The most renowned spokesman of Irish opinion at the time was Daniel O'Connell, who despite legal prohibitions stood for Parliament in 1828. Backed by his Catholic Association, O'Connell presented the Tories with the alternative of civil war or reform. Even Wellington shrank before the specter of domestic bloodshed. Guided by his grudging leadership, Parliament first repealed the Test Act (1828) and then voted full emancipation (1829), thus allowing Catholics the right to sit in Parliament and hold all but the highest offices of the realm.

Parliamentary Reform. The Tories, as part of the landed aristocracy, exercised their political control primarily through the House of Commons, which had emerged as the dominant legislative body during the constitutional struggles of the seventeenth century. The landed oligarchy, representing both Whigs and Tories, had managed to silence demands for legislative reform both immediately before and after the French Revolution. In 1830 agitation for reform began to crest again, and the rumbling was made more ominous by the wave of revolutions that inundated Europe in midsummer.

At the heart of the controversy was borough (town) representation. Every incorporated borough had the right to be represented in the Commons, but since no town charters had been issued in over three hundred years, the new urban population in the Midlands was unrepresented, while small villages, particularly in the south and southwest, held the majority of borough seats. The least populous of these were known as *rotten*, or *pocket*, boroughs because they contained so few voters that they were in the pocket of local magnates or wealthy *boroughmongers*. Leading the demand for reform were wealthy industrialists and the urban middle class, who in turn found support among the urban working classes.

The Whigs took up the banner of reform and carried it to victory in the general election of 1830. Lord John Russell, floor leader for the government of Prime Minister Earl Grey, introduced a parliamentary reform bill in March 1831. The action precipitated a constitutional crisis. For a year and a half, the struggle raged in Parliament and on several occasions spilled over into the streets. The confrontation reached a climax in March 1832, when Grey wrung from the king a pledge to pack the House of Lords with Whig peers if the recalcitrant Tories refused to accept reform. The Tories acquiesced, and the bill became law.

The Great Reform Bill is a milestone in modern British history. The struggle for its passage reconfirmed the supremacy of the Commons in the governmental structure. Further, it established the principle that population patterns should form the basis for representation in Commons. The rotten boroughs were for the most part abolished and the seats distributed primarily among the new cities of the north and the Midlands. This is not to say that the bill brought democracy. Only those in the boroughs dwelling in homes worth an annual rental of ten pounds sterling received the vote. Thus the middle class and the skilled artisans won the victory, while the unskilled of both town and county remained disfranchised. However, with the adoption of the principle, the democratic spirit slowly prevailed in the subsequent reform acts of 1867, 1884, 1918, and 1928.

The Wave of Whig Reform. The Whigs did not stop with parliamentary reform. In 1833, to the consternation of both the West Indian sugar magnates and South African farmers, the Parliament abolished slavery throughout the British Empire. Many people had also been stirred by the de facto slavery in English mills and mines. Under Lord Ashley's leadership, Parliament passed a Factory Act in 1833 regulating working conditions of women and children in textile mills. This act was also a milestone, although enforcement was often very lax. All the "reforms" were not so benevolent toward the under-privileged. The Poor Law of 1834 in effect made poverty a crime. To discourage idleness and to relieve the burden on parish taxpayers, the act established workhouses that were virtual prisons, with rules designed to make the impoverished inmates as miserable as possible. The pages of Dickens's *Oliver Twist* eloquently testify to their stark success. With a last burst of energy in 1835, the Whigs carried through the Municipal Corporations Act, which ended the govern-mental monopoly of a few families in each town and created a hierarchy of officials elected by the taxpayers and responsible for all municipal utilities and services. The beneficial results of this bill were much more quickly felt by the average Englishman than were those of the Great Reform Bill.

Queen Victoria and the Victorian Compromise. Queen Victoria ascended the throne in 1837 upon the death of her uncle William IV. Her reign, which lasted until 1901, marked a period of political and economic dominance in European and world affairs unprecedented since the time of Louis XIV. Victoria and her consort Prince Albert set the tone of industrious respectability that characterizes the age. During the first thirty years of her reign, Victoria presided over a political and social arrangement known as the Victorian Compromise. Under its unwritten terms, the old landed aristocracy accepted the industrial middle class as partners in government, and both agreed to block any demands by the lower classes for further reform. The regime stood for free enterprise, toleration, and law and order.

Chartism. The Victorian Compromise did not remain unchallenged for long. The Great Reform Bill did nothing for the working classes that had supported it. In their misery and disillusionment, they turned to political action on their own. William Lovett, Francis Place, and Feargus O'Connor were the most influential leaders of what came to be known as the Chartist movement. In 1836 Lovett founded the London Workingman's Association to rally the working class into a unified political action. In 1838 Francis Place drafted the People's Charter, which became the movement's basic program. Its six essen-tial demands were: (1) universal manhood suffrage, (2) the secret ballot, (3) equal electoral districts, (4) abolition of property qualifi-cation for members of Parliament, (5) pay for members of Parliament,

(6) annual election of Parliament. Although many Chartists had faith in the reformist tactics of Lovett and Place, Feargus O'Connor doubted that the ruling class would accept change without a fight. Through the columns of his paper, the *Northern Star*, he advocated the use of force if the Parliament failed to respond to persuasion. The Chartists held a national convention in 1838 and presented Parliament with the charter, supported by a petition bearing several hundred thousand signatures. The Commons received both but rejected the charter's specific planks. Division between the moral suasion and physical force factions robbed the movement of its momentum at this critical juncture. The charter was revived in 1842 and again in the revolutionary year of 1848 but to no avail. Soon afterwards the movement disintegrated.

Chartism was not a total failure. It had raised significant questions concerning representative government and provided a program of reforms. Although the Commons refused to accept the charter wholesale in 1839, it accepted its demands piecemeal. By 1918 Britain had adopted every plank of the charter except annual elections of Parliament.

Anti-Corn Law League. The demise of the Chartist movement may be ascribed in part to the success of the Anti-Corn Law League in diverting middle-class attention from the political issues raised by the Chartists to an economic issue much nearer their hearts.

In 1815 the Parliament had adopted a high wheat tariff to protect landowners from Continental grain imports. Although the law had been only moderately successful in protecting farmers, it was a source of grievance to the working poor. Free traders, including William Cobbett and John Bright, objected to it in principle as standing in the way of British industrial well-being.

The Anti-Corn Law League was organized in 1839 in the wake of a bad harvest and rising bread prices. The "hungry forties" in England were capped in 1845 by the Irish potato famine and the reality of widespread starvation. Conservative Prime Minister Robert Peel then rose above his partisan position and at the peril of his career pushed through a repeal of the Corn Laws in 1846. The repeal was a victory for the principle of free trade, which became a pillar supporting the Victorian Compromise, although subsequent good harvests had a greater immediate effect in reducing bread prices. The repeal eased social tension and demonstrated the ability of English conservatives to bend before the gale of popular outrage, a virtue often lacking among their Continental counterparts. Despite the failure of Chartism, the league had also demonstrated the power of

national organizations to influence parliamentary action. At midcentury a relatively affluent and stable Britain could view the European revolutionary upheavals as an interested but unscathed observer.

Revolutions of 1830

After 1789 it became a cliché of nineteenth-century politics that
"when France sneezes, Europe catches cold." In 1830 Metternich's
worst fears were confirmed when revolutionary contagion in France
spread to Belgium, Italy, Germany, and Poland.

France. Charles X's determination to resurrect the pre-1789 prerogatives of the Bourbon dynasty had by early 1830 brought him
into open confrontation with the proponents of constitutional monarchy. Having rejected retreat and compromise as suitable alternatives,
he planned a veritable coup d'etat that would silence the rising
criticism, disarm his opponents, and eviscerate the constitutional Charter of 1814. In the predawn hours of 26 July 1830, the government
issued a set of decrees (the July Ordinances) that dissolved the
newly elected legislature, which contained an opposition majority;
disfranchised a large segment of the middle-class electorate; and
abolished freedom of the press. More surprising than the repressive
decrees themselves was the government's total lack of psychological
or military preparation for the resistance that followed.

The liberal press, led by Adolphe Thiers, poured forth a torrent of
abuse against the king's usurpation. Small knots of angry men gathered on street corners, and by July 27 barricades barred the way to
government troops in the republican working-class districts. Despite
the lack of revolutionary organization or planning, the government
could not mount an effective counterattack. By July 29 the question
was no longer whether Charles would be deposed but whether he
would be replaced by a republic under the presidency of the aging
symbol of liberty, the marquis de Lafayette, or whether the constitutional monarchists could induce the duc d'Orléans (Louis Philippe),
leader of the junior branch of the royal family, to accept the throne
as constitutional monarch. Lafayette himself decided the issue on
August 2 when he appeared on the balcony of city hall with the duc
d'Orléans. After a futile attempt to pass the crown to his grandson,
Charles X, last of the Bourbons, quietly withdrew to English exile.
On August 7 the legislature bestowed the title King of the French
on Louis Philippe. The liberals congratulated themselves on their
easy victory, and Casimir Périer, the new premier, went so far as to
denounce those who thought that there had been a real revolution.
The republican working class kept a sullen silence as the Bourgeois

King inaugurated an eighteen-year regime that was known as the July Monarchy.

Belgium. Under the terms of the Peace of Vienna (1815), Belgium was united with the Netherlands for the purpose of forming a northern buffer against future French aggression. The predominantly French-speaking Catholic Belgians had hoped for local autonomy under Austrian rule and were outraged by the new constitutional arrangement that placed them under the control of King William I of Orange, who ruled the country for the benefit of the Dutch-speaking Protestant minority. William's refusal to make concessions to his opponents drove Belgian liberals and the Catholic hierarchy into alliance. While upper-class commercial interests merely demanded reform, radicals, heartened by the July Revolution in France, plotted for independence. Rioting broke out in Brussels on August 25. William's belated attempts at conciliation collapsed, and subsequent efforts to subdue Brussels by force failed after four days of street fighting that ended on September 26. The Belgians declared their independence and in February 1831 promulgated the most liberal constitution in Europe. It guaranteed representative government, supported by a broad suffrage and guided by a strong constitutional monarch.

Although the Dutch had momentarily withdrawn, the Belgians were still not the masters of their destiny. William was unreconciled to his loss, and the great powers had not yet spoken. Russia and Austria were hostile to revolution in principle but were preoccupied with revolts in their own domains. Britain and France, though generally favorable to Belgian independence, had confronted each other in the Low Countries for centuries. To preclude the possibility of a general war over the issue, the great powers met in London to work out a solution. Under the terms of the Twenty-four Articles (October 1831), the powers sanctioned Belgian independence, the new constitution, and the election of King Leopold I, and they guaranteed Belgium's neutrality.

Italy. The Italian dream of constitutional government and national reawakening had been subdued by Metternich in the early 1820s but not destroyed. It was nurtured in the circles of young professionals, journalists, and army officers who organized themselves in the clandestine Carbonari and other secret societies. Spurred by reports of the successful insurrection in Paris and encouraged by indications that the French might support their liberation movement, the Italian liberals rose in rebellion. They quickly overthrew the ducal governments of Parma and Modena and toppled the papal government in the Romagna, the Marches, and Umbria. However, these initial successes could not be consolidated or expanded. The revolutionaries had the support of only a minute fraction of the Italian people, and the new government of France was not interested in challenging the Austrian sphere of influence with force of arms. Backed by Prussian and Russian diplomatic support, the Austrians quickly crushed the insurgents and restored the legitimate rulers. Still the dream did not die. In exile Giuseppe Mazzini (1805–1872) founded Young Italy and thus began his lifelong crusade to end Austrian dominance, not through conspiracy but through the mass uprising of the Italian people.

Germany. The German revolutionaries suffered from the same weaknesses that destroyed the Italian movements. The revolutionaries were often drawn from the inexperienced ranks of young professionals and students. Their liberal, nationalist programs were vague and appealed to only a narrow segment of the population. The rebels seemed to believe that they could talk their way to power and made no provision for dealing with Metternich's statecraft or Austrian military power. The duke of Brunswick, the elector of Hesse-Cassel, and the king of Saxony were all driven from power, and new constitutions were extracted from their successors, but the revolutionaries were never able to carry forward the movement on a united front, nor could they rally the German people. Working through the Diet of the Germanic Confederation, Metternich managed to shore up the authority of existing governments and hound the troublemakers into prison or exile.

Poland. In Poland, as in Italy and Germany, news of the French Revolution stirred hopes of national liberation among young army officers and university students. Long antagonistic to Russian rule, they rebelled (November 1830) to block the possible intervention of Czar Nicholas I against the new regimes of Belgium and France. The nationalist appeals of such aristocrats as Prince Adam Czartoryski were of little interest to the Polish peasantry. After initial indecision that allowed the revolt to spread throughout Poland, Czar Nicholas crushed the rebellion (September 1831) and placed the country under martial law for the remainder of the century.

The July Monarchy in France

The July Monarchy was an experiment in nineteenth-century liberalism. The bourgeois establishment sought to maintain a *juste milieu* ("golden mean") between the arbitrary high-handedness of the former Bourbons and the democratic radicalism of what it considered the rabble. The Government of Bankers took special interest in the growing industrialism but had neither the interest nor the capacity to cope with the social problems that accompanied it. In the end the experiment failed to bridge the ideological gap between monarchism and republicanism that had divided France since 1793.

The King. King Louis Philippe (r. 1830–1848) was a descendant of Louis XIII through the Orléans branch of the Bourbon family. His father, Philippe-Égalité, had supported the Revolution in 1789 but had later been guillotined. Louis Philippe himself had supported the republican cause and fought at the battles of Valmy and Jemappes. Though driven into exile by the Terror, he took no part in émigré politics. He brought to the throne a willingness to accept the constitutional limitations of the revised Charter of 1814 and the symbolism attached to the revived tricolor flag. At the same time, he viewed his role as a ruling rather than simply as a reigning monarch. Despite his exemplary personal qualities, he became the target of those who held his regime in contempt. Honoré Daumier was the most renowned of the political cartoonists who caricatured Louis Philippe and his ministers to personify the materialistic, self-satisfied regime.

Political Factions. There were no well-organized political parties at this time. The factions usually reflected loosely defined ideologies that for practical purposes coalesced around dominant personalities.

LEGITIMISTS. The Bourbon aristocracy, from the great peers to the lowly provincial dignitaries, hated Louis Philippe as a usurper who had betrayed his own family to seize the throne. After an abortive attempt in 1832 to overthrow him and restore the Bourbons, they boycotted the regime politically and socially. Thus, they declined in influence and provided no support for the regime.

RIGHT-CENTER. Often referred to as the Party of Resistance, the Right-Center was the main political support of the regime. Led first by Casimir Périer and after 1836 by François Guizot, it represented the views of the new Orléanist aristocracy and the most conservative members of the *haute bourgeoisie* (the upper-class business community). They believed the king should exercise broad powers within the framework of the revised charter and that the select oligarchy of the rich, well-born, and able could successfully guide the destinies of France without further constitutional revision.

LEFT-CENTER. Often referred to as the Party of Movement, the Left-Center also represented men of property and education. However, they believed that political power should be vested in the entire middle class, and they saw the constitutional settlement of 1830 as the base on which to build a more liberal regime. Adolphe Thiers, their political leader, and Alexis de Tocqueville, their ideological spokesman, believed in a parliamentary system in which the king reigned but did not rule. The Left-Center remained in the political opposition throughout most of the reign.

REPUBLICANS. The rank and file of the republican movement came primarily from the urban working classes and its leadership from the middle class. These men felt betrayed by the events of July 1830 and never became reconciled to the regime. Their ideological hostility was compounded by increasing economic hardship and was reflected in a series of abortive insurrections between 1831 and 1834. The republican movement was momentarily weakened by the counterforce of the national guard and the police but retained its strong appeal throughout the period.

BONAPARTISTS. Bonapartism was one of the least organized and yet most persuasive political sentiments of the era. Napoleon Bonaparte himself had fostered the imperial legend from his lonely exile on Saint Helena, where he died in 1821. Nostalgia for imperial grandeur was nurtured by Napoleon's veterans and appealed to romantic writers, bored royalists, and civil servants. Despite its authoritarian cast, Bonapartism also had a strong strain of social paternalism that appealed to both urban and rural workers. Visible signs of Napoleonic sympathies began to appear in Paris after 1830. The government tried to associate itself with Napoleonic grandeur by completing the arc de Triomphe in 1836 and by returning the emperor's remains from Saint Helena to a final resting place beneath the dome of the Invalides in 1840. Louis Napoleon Bonaparte, the emperor's nephew, attempted to provide leadership for the movement. He led unsuccessful insurrections in 1836 and 1840 and despite the humiliating circumstances surrounding these failures was able to recoup his fortunes during the Revolution of 1848.

Political, Economic, and Social Trends. The political history of the July Monarchy can be roughly divided into three periods. The years from 1830 to 1836 were accented by sporadic outbreaks of violence against the regime, led by workers, royalists, and Bonapartists. The monarchy and its bourgeois allies fended off these attacks, consolidated their authority, and enjoyed a decade of undisturbed rule from 1836 to 1846. After 1846 an economic downturn and criticism of the regime's inflexible attitude combined to bring on the Revolution of 1848.

François Guizot (1787–1874) was the embodiment of the regime and directed its fortunes from 1840 until 1848. An eminent historian, he typified the academic community which, together with powerful bankers, merchants, and industrialists, provided the regime with its main support. In fact, the charge that the government was being run by and for the special interests of the upper-middle class is well founded. Guizot considered himself responsible only to the king and was contemptuous of those who had attained neither his intellectual achievements nor his social position. To those who complained that the regime failed to deal with the growing social stress and economic problems brought on by industrialization, he replied that every man in France was free to "get rich."

It is interesting to note that despite the materialistic values of the bourgeoisie, the Catholic church increasingly received its support during the 1830s and 40s. While the middle class had thoroughly absorbed the rationalist philosophy of the eighteenth century, it nevertheless came to regard the Church as a social bulwark against rising demands for reform by socialists and republicans.

Economically, France began to feel the full impact of industrialization during the July Monarchy. In the eighteenth century, France had possessed Europe's strongest economy. Her position had been based upon the largest population in Europe, a well-educated and innovative intellectual community, a skilled artisan class, and a highly productive agricultural sector. The government sought to enhance this position through a large-scale public-works program, particularly in the construction of roads, canals, and railroads. Nevertheless, the rate of French growth did not keep pace with that of its neighbors. The reasons for this relative decline are complex and interrelated. They include a declining birth rate; the high cost of raw materials, particularly coal; low wages, which mitigated against the use of machinery; high tariffs; and the conservative social and economic values that spanned the social spectrum from great bankers to peasants. The slow rate of growth gave France the opportunity to deal constructively with the social problems arising from industrialization (such as urbanization), but the government of Louis Philippe and Guizot was too class bound to see the needs of the working classes. The result was revolution.

Revolutions of 1848

In 1848 a revolutionary tide engulfed Europe from Paris to Budapest. To men like Metternich the coincidence of these outbreaks served as conclusive proof that a handful of international conspirators were determined to destroy the basic values and institutions of European society. It is clear, however, that the revolutionary upheaval was more than the work of a few radical malcontents. European civilization was in the midst of an industrial and intellectual transformation that the ruling classes were loath to accept and with which the established political institutions were unable to cope. Thus, in the absence of adequate evolutionary adjustment to new problems, a revolutionary explosion was inevitable.

There is a danger when considering the revolutions of 1848 to assume that since they erupted at virtually the same time, they must have sprung from the same cause. In fact, the mix of political, social, and economic factors was unique in each of the revolutionary societies. Nevertheless, there are several recurring themes. The demand for more representative government was widespread among the middle class, although the bourgeoisie stopped far short of the working-class demand for democracy. This division of opinion among the revolutionaries played a major role in the defeat of the revolutionary movement. Economic distress was an important factor in triggering the revolutions. Poor harvests of potatoes and wheat from 1845 to 1847 increased the misery of the working classes, who even in good times lived at bare subsistence in the unsanitary and overcrowded new industrial towns. National aspirations were also a major theme in all the revolutions except the French. Here again the revolutionaries weakened their position by demanding self-determination for themselves while showing little sympathy for the aspirations of their own national minorities.

France. By 1847 the bloom was off the July Monarchy. Agricultural and industrial depression gripped the country. In Paris tens of thousands of increasingly desperate proletarian families managed a bare subsistence amid small islands of affluence. On top of this substratum of real misery rested the discontent of the comfortable but politically powerless middle class. The focus of their hostility was François Guizot, the haughty and conservative prime minister, who was oblivious to any demands for reform.

THE FEBRUARY REVOLUTION. To circumvent the prohibition on political meetings, the reformers in 1847 organized a series of "banquets," at which after-dinner speakers called for change. Thousands thronged to these rallies to hear opinions ranging from constitutional monarchism to radical republicanism. The government underestimated the depth of hostility toward the regime, and when Guizot banned the climactic banquet in Paris on 22 February 1848, he was confident that the small Municipal Guard could easily handle a few recalcitrant rabble-rousers. When rock-throwing mobs proved too much for the Municipal Guard, the government called upon the National Guard, but the disaffected bourgeoisie who filled its ranks went over to the opposition. On February 24 after regular army troops had failed to breach the barricades that had sprung up throughout the capital, the king abandoned the struggle and fled to England. Amid the chaos a provisional government led by the poet Alphonse de Lamartine proclaimed the Second Republic.

The revolutionists soon perceived that they had been united only by their hatred of the July Monarchy. The bourgeoisie were appalled and frightened by the lawlessness of the rabble, while the working class, who had borne the brunt of the fighting, were determined to reap the benefits of revolution that had eluded them in 1830. In the euphoric weeks after the revolution, the leftists successfully pressed their demands for political and economic democracy. The provisional government decreed universal manhood suffrage, which, though theoretically favoring the left, in fact strengthened the hand of conservative rural France against the "red" capital. The moderates also accepted the concept of the "right to work" and grudgingly allowed socialist Louis Blanc to organize National Workshops. Within the framework of Blanc's theories, the workshops were designed to give the workers ownership of their factories. In practice they became vast relief projects that enrolled thousands of unemployed industrial workers and rural poor.

THE JUNE DAYS. The tide turned decisively against the Parisian radicals in the April elections for the Constituent Assembly when rural France returned a moderate-to-conservative majority. Seeing the revolution slipping from them and desperate to break free from the death grip of misery, the working class again took to the barricades. The struggle raged from June 23 to June 26, when guardsmen led by General Cavaignac subdued the last worker stronghold in the Faubourg Saint-Antoine.

SUBVERSION OF THE REPUBLIC. The republic did not survive the bloodbath for long. The sullen working class returned to the business of daily existence while the Constituent Assembly completed the constitution. Moderate and conservative republicans soon realized that they could expect no working-class support against the resurgence of the right. The presidential election in December produced a startling result. Louis Napoleon Bonaparte, neer-do-well nephew of the great emperor, brushed aside more prominent men in a landslide. In the spring of 1849, the republic's electorate returned a monarchist majority to the assembly. The destruction of the republic was completed by Louis Napoleon in a coup d'etat on 2 December 1851 when he extended his presidential term to ten years and curtailed the legislature's power. The day chosen was the anniversary of his uncle's great victory at Austerlitz, and exactly a year later, he proclaimed himself emperor.

Central Europe. The French Revolution of 1848 stirred the hopes of idealists and oppressed peoples throughout central Europe. The revolutions that swept the region from the early spring of 1848 until midsummer of 1849 reveal some significant similarities.

Liberalism was a catchword that encompassed demands for greater personal freedom and more representative government. In the early days of the insurrections, the liberals stood united against the Metternichian system that had dominated central Europe for forty years. But after their initial victories, constitutional monarchists, conservative republicans, and democratic socialists realized that they had little in common. Time and time again, differences of opinion and mutual distrust among the revolutionaries allowed the forces of conservatism to reorganize and successfully counterattack.

Nationalism was a second driving force of revolution. Idealists and political theorists among the Germans, Italians, Slavs, and Magyars strove to throw off Vienna's cultural and political dominance. The nationalist ideal is now so firmly embedded in our political consciousness that an effort must be made to remember that in the mid-nineteenth century, it was a minority view. In addition, while nationalists demanded self-determination for their own ethnic group, they were not sympathetic to the aspirations of the minorities around them. The Hungarian revolution in particular foundered because of Magyar refusal to permit equal status for the Slavs within their area of influence.

A third significant characteristic was the urban focus of revolution. The liberal nationalists were drawn primarily from middle-class intellectuals, professional men, the business community, and young army officers. Their aspirations hardly coincided with either the rural majority, who ultimately sided with the forces of tradition, or with the urban proletariat, who demanded sweeping social and economic changes.

For convenience the uprisings within the Austrian domains, Italy, and Germany can be examined in turn, but it must be remembered that events in these areas transpired simultaneously.

Austrian Empire. News of the Parisian revolt triggered outbursts in many of Austria's principal cities, including Budapest (March 3), Prague (March 12), Vienna (March 13), Venice (March 17), and Milan (March 18). In each case a few days of rioting demonstrated the government's inability to crush the movements. Even in Vienna Metternich realized the futility of resistance and fled to England. Emperor Ferdinand I appointed a liberal ministry and sanctioned the calling of a constituent assembly. Events followed a similar path in Budapest, where liberals led by Lajos Kossuth and Ferencz Déak formed a ministry dedicated to the creation of Magyar autonomy within the empire. The Hungarian Diet was transformed into a national parliament, which carried out reforms typical of the era. They included the creation of a national tricolor, formation of a national guard, freedom of press and speech, the abolition of feudalism, and increased political participation of the middle class. The Bohemian Diet followed a similar path, but Czech nationalists faced the hostility not only of the emperor but also of German and Magyar nationalists, who were determined to contest Slavic autonomy. To protect their interests, the Czechs called the Pan-Slavic Congress, which convened in Prague (June 1848).

In Austria's Italian provinces, the revolutionaries were not satisfied with mere reform or autonomy. Led by Daniele Manin, the Venetians expelled the Austrians and created the republic of San Marco. In Lombardy the Milanese drove Austrian troops from the capital after five days of hand-to-hand combat (March 18–22). Marshal Radetzky, the aged but able Austrian commander, withdrew his forces into the fortress cities (Peschiera, Mantua, Verona, and Legnago) known as the "quadrilateral" between Milan and Venice. There he reorganized and prepared for a counterstroke.

The imperial counterattack was not long in coming. In Prague the Pan-Slavic Congress adjourned on June 12 amid pronouncements of Slavic solidarity, but on the same day, student radicals and impoverished workers rose in revolt against the bourgeois government. Class interests took precedence over national affiliation. Field Marshal Windischgrätz, whose wife was killed in the rioting, soon had the city surrounded, bombarded it into submission, and installed martial law (June 1848). Radetzky likewise was able to restore the Austrian position in Italy by a decisive victory over the army of Charles Albert of Piedmont at Custoza (24 July 1848). The attempt by the Croats under Count Jelačić to suppress the Hungarian revolution led to renewed violence in Vienna that was overcome by Windischgrätz (October 1848). With order restored in Vienna and Prague and the tide turned in Italy, the imperial government moved to subdue Hungary; but the rebels hung on tenaciously. After suffering reverses, the Austrians appealed to the Russians, who subdued the rebellion (August 1849).

Italy. The first revolutionary outbursts of 1848 took place in the kingdom of the two Sicilies (Naples), where in January King Ferdinand II reluctantly sanctioned a liberal constitution. Further north Charles Albert, king of Piedmont-Sardinia, promulgated a liberal constitution known as the *Statuto* on 4 March 1848. This document is significant because it was one of only a few such instruments that remained in force after the defeat of the revolutionaries.

Despite the initial successes that forced Austrian retreat, the Italians were never able to consolidate their gains. Charles Albert aimed to incorporate Lombardy and Venetia to form a North Italian confederation. This policy caused antagonism between the king and those who hoped to unite Italy under papal guidance, as well as those who sought a totally united Italy rather than simply the aggrandizement of Piedmont-Sardinia. In addition, the middle class liberal nationalists that provided intellectual leadership were confronted with the demands of destitute peasants and urban workers. While the bourgeoisie were prepared to give constitutional sops to the lower classes, they were unwilling to allow the social or economic reforms that would have threatened their own position. Thus in Italy, as in Austria and Bohemia, the revolutionaries could not present a united front. Finally, the great powers all had a stake in the outcome of Italian events and were prepared to intervene to maintain the balance of power. Amid these crosscurrents, the divided Italians were no match for the Austrians. Charles Albert called for an armistice after his defeat at Custoza and when he resumed hostilities, he was soundly defeated at Novara (March 1849).

The last act of Italian insurgence was played out in Rome. Pius IX, long regarded as a liberal and supporter of Italian nationalism, could ill afford to take sides between Catholic Italians and Catholic Austrians. In addition, he became increasingly apprehensive about radical threats to the social order. Roman radicals were incensed over the pope's refusal to lend his assistance to Italian unification. After the assassination of his prime minister in November, Pius IX fled the city. In his place a Constituent Assembly declared independence from his temporal authority and called into existence the Roman Republic (February 1849). Amid these turbulent events, Giuseppe Mazzini (1805–1872) emerged as the intellectual leader of Italian unification. He was soon joined in Rome by Giuseppe Garibaldi (1807–1882), whose personal courage and flamboyant leadership helped boost morale in Rome as the city prepared for the expected Austrian onslaught. However, it was the French who, for domestic as well as international reasons, intervened to restore papal authority. The French expeditionary force landed at the mouth of the Tiber in April and after months of indecisive fighting were finally able to occupy the city in July. Mazzini and Garibaldi, who had hoped to reinforce the dreams of Italian unity by dying in the last ditch, in fact both survived to fight another day.

Germany. The revolutionary movement in Germany ran its course on two distinct levels. In major principalities, including Bavaria, Hanover, Hesse, Prussia, Saxony, and Württemberg, the conservative rulers were obliged to appoint liberal ministers and pledge sweeping reform. The Prussian revolution will be discussed here because of its significance for German affairs. On the national level, liberals convoked a parliament at Frankfurt to resolve the issue of German unification.

THE PRUSSIAN REVOLUTION. In 1848 Prussia reflected the tensions of many states on the threshold of industrialization. King Frederick William IV (r. 1840–1861), although he harbored a mystic nationalism and tended toward paternalistic liberalism, represented the traditional interests of an agrarian society and of the Junker class that controlled eastern Prussia. Rhenish Prussia, on the other hand, was becoming increasingly industrialized. The industrialists and middle class spawned by economic growth had become more and more offended by their exclusion from public affairs. At the lower end of the social ladder, skilled artisans were desperate to protect their livelihoods against the encroachment of machinery.

The news of the Paris revolution caused no immediate outbursts in Berlin. However, liberals had begun to gather in beer gardens to discuss needed reform, and the king called in troops to reinforce the large garrison. The military's contempt for civilians came down to the private soldier in the streets. Growing resentment triggered demonstrations and rock throwing, to which the troops responded with rifle butts and bayonets.

On March 13 news of the Vienna uprising ran through Berlin like an electric shock. The king, sensing the danger, agreed to consider a constitution and to work for German unification. However, what began as demonstrations of popular support on March 18 turned into a bloody riot when troops fired into the crowd that had gathered before the royal palace. Barricades went up all over the city, and though the royal troops soon gained the upper hand, it became obvious that wholesale bloodshed and destruction would be required to suppress the uprising. Unwilling to win at such a price, Frederick William ordered the garrison to withdraw from the city. From March 18 until November 2, the government of Prussia was in the hands of liberals. The newly elected Constituent Assembly became increasingly radical in its demands. The revolutionaries, however, were soon beset by internal divisions. The Junker aristocracy, gaining the support of peasants, skilled artisans, and the Lutheran clergy, were slowly able to isolate the bourgeois liberals and the industrial proletariat. After the restoration of the imperial government in Vienna, Frederick William felt safe to order troops back into the city. On November 2 he dissolved the assembly and declared martial law. The Constitution of 1850, as finally issued, reaffirmed the divine-right status of the monarchy and though maintaining universal suffrage, guaranteed a conservative regime through the use of indirect elections and a three-class voting system. The constitution remained in force until 1918.

THE FRANKFURT ASSEMBLY. The convocation of the all-German Constituent Assembly in Frankfurt on 18 May 1848 was the most ambitious undertaking of the revolutionary period. Its goal was nothing less than the unification of over forty sovereign states and free cities into a federal union. The assembly was the brainchild of a small group of liberals who had met in Heidelberg in March. They issued invitations to a preparliament (*Vorparlament*), which in turn drafted procedures for the election of a constituent assembly by universal suffrage.

The elected delegates who gathered in Saint Paul's Church on 18 March 1848 were drawn almost exclusively from the professions: university professors, lawyers, doctors, and university-educated civil servants. There was not a single urban worker or peasant delegate. Thus the assembly did not represent a broad social cross section, and though well-qualified to deal with the theoretical problems of constitution writing, it could not quickly come to grips with practical issues.

One of the most complex issues was whether the new state should be organized as a small Germany (*Kleindeutschland*), with only German peoples included, or a large Germany (*Grossdeutschland*), to include all peoples controlled by German dynasties. As a practical matter, this required a choice between the Hapsburgs and Hohenzollerns. The Hapsburgs were not prepared to abandon their non-Germanic possessions. The imperial crown was then offered to King Frederick William IV of Prussia in April 1849, but by then he had regained control in his own domain and refused to accept "a crown from the gutter." Abandoned by both Hohenzollerns and Hapsburgs, the only two dynasties that could command the respect of the lesser princes, the Frankfurt Assembly dissolved with a whimper. The radicals who continued to demand unification were dispersed by troops. By 1850 Austria had reasserted its dominance over the German confederation.

Conclusion. The revolutions of 1848 failed in their overall purpose of national unification and liberal reform. The assessment of many historians is that the revolution in Germany was talked to death by intellectuals who were out of their element in the arena of power politics. Within the Austrian Empire and in Italy, the revolutionaries came up against the reality of Austria's armed force. Finally, deep class antagonism surfaced in the French and German revolutions as a result of the very limited outlook of mid-nineteenth-century liberals. They had been willing to use the working class to fight street battles but were not willing to adopt reforms needed to maintain working-class support in the face of conservative reaction.

Bibliography

The following list is designed to provide the reader with a selection of readily available books to supplement the material covered in this book. Paperbound books are indicated by (PB) after the entry.

General Works

Artz, Frederick B. *From the Renaissance to Romanticism: Trends in Style in Art, Literature, and Music, 1300–1830.* Chicago: University of Chicago Press, 1962. (PB)

Brinton, Crane. *The Anatomy of Revolution.* New York: Random House, 1965. (PB)

Bronowski, J., and Mazlish, Bruce. *The Western Intellectual Tradition: From Leonardo to Hegel.* New York: Harper & Row, 1960. (PB)

Butterfield, Herbert. *The Origins of Modern Science, 1300–1800.* Rev. ed. New York: Macmillan, 1965. (PB)

Clough, S. B. and others. *Economic History of Europe.* New York: Walker, 1968.

Cobban, Alfred. *A History of Modern France.* 3 vols. Baltimore: Penguin, 1966. (PB)

Foster, Michael B. *Masters of Political Thought.* Vol. 1. Boston: Houghton Mifflin, 1941. (PB)

Heilbroner, Robert L. *The Worldly Philosophers.* New York: Simon and Schuster, 1972. (PB)

Holborn, Hajo. *A History of Modern Germany.* 3 vols. New York: Knopf, 1959.

Mason, Stephen. *A History of the Sciences.* New York: Macmillan, 1966. (PB)

Morton, Robert, ed. *Time-Life Library of Art.* 28 vols. New York: Time-Life Books, 1970.

Parry, J. H., ed. *The Establishment of the European Hegemony: 1415–1715.* New York: Harper & Row, 1961. (PB)

Riasanovsky, Nicholas. *History of Russia.* 2d ed. New York: Oxford University Press, 1969.

Willson, David H. *A History of England.* 2d ed. New York: Holt, Rinehart and Winston, 1972.

The Medieval Heritage

Cheyney, E. P. *The Dawn of a New Era, 1250–1453.* New York: Harper & Row, 1962. (PB)

Ferguson, W. *Europe in Transition, 1300–1520.* Boston: Houghton Mifflin, 1963.

Hay, Denys. *The Medieval Centuries.* New York: Harper & Row, 1964. (PB)

Huizinga, Johan. *The Waning of the Middle Ages.* Garden City, N. Y.: Doubleday, 1954. (PB)

Perroy, E. *The Hundred Years' War.* New York: Putnam, 1965. (PB)

The Renaissance

Elton, G. R. *Renaissance and Reformation.* New York: Macmillan, 1968. (PB)

Erasmus, Desiderius. *Praise of Folly.* Ann Arbor, Mich.: University of Michigan Press, 1958. (PB)

Ferguson, W. K. *The Renaissance in Historical Thought.* Boston: Houghton Mifflin, 1948.

————, ed. *The Renaissance: Six Essays.* New York: Harper & Row, 1962. (PB)

Gilmore, Myron P. *The World of Humanism, 1453–1517.* New York: Harper & Row, 1962. (PB)

Grey, Ian. *Ivan III and the Unification of Russia.* New York: Macmillan, 1967. (PB)

Hay, Denys. *Europe in the Fourteenth and Fifteenth Centuries.* New York: Holt, Rinehart and Winston, 1967. (PB)

————. *The Italian Renaissance in Its Historical Background.* New York: Cambridge University Press, 1961. (PB)

Machiavelli, Niccolo. *The Prince.* Baltimore: Penguin, 1961. (PB)

Potter, G. R., ed. *The Renaissance, 1493–1520.* New Cambridge Modern History series, vol. 1. New York: Cambridge University Press, 1964.

Reformation Era

Bainton, R. *Here I Stand: A Life of Luther.* New York: New American Library, 1950. (PB)

————. *The Reformation of the Sixteenth Century.* Boston: Beacon, 1956. (PB)

Bindoff, S. T. *Tudor England.* Baltimore: Penguin, 1950. (PB)

Chudoba, Bohdan. *Spain and the Empire, 1519–1643.* New ed. New York: Octagon, 1969.

Davies, R. Trevor. *The Golden Century of Spain, 1501–1621.* New York: Harper & Row, 1965. (PB)

Elton, G. R. *Reformation Europe, 1517–1559.* New York: Harper & Row, 1968. (PB)

————, ed. *The Reformation, 1520–1559.* New Cambridge Modern History series, vol. 2. New York: Cambridge University Press, 1958.

Erikson, Erik H. *Young Man Luther.* New York: Norton, 1962. (PB)

Geyl, Pieter. *The Revolt of the Netherlands, 1555–1609.* 2d. ed. New York: Barnes and Noble, 1966. (PB)

Haller, William. *The Rise of Puritanism.* Philadelphia: University of Pennsylvania Press, 1972. (PB)

Harbison, E. Harris. *The Age of Reformation.* Ithaca, N. Y.: Cornell University Press, 1955. (PB)

Koenigsberger, H. G., and Mosse, G. L. *Europe in the Sixteenth Century.* New York: Holt, Rinehart and Winston, 1969. (PB)

Mattingly, G. *The Armada.* Boston: Houghton Mifflin, 1959. (PB)

Wernham, R. B., ed. *The Counter-Reformation and Price Revolution, 1559–1610.* New Cambridge Modern History series, vol. 3. New York: Cambridge University Press, 1968.

Seventeenth Century

Ashley, Maurice P. *Oliver Cromwell and the Puritan Revolution.* New York: Macmillan, 1966. (PB)

Bazin, Germain. *Baroque and Rococo Art.* New York: Praeger, 1964. (PB)

Briggs, Robin. *The Scientific Revolution of the Seventeenth Century.* New York: Harper & Row, 1971. (PB)

Bromley, J. S., ed. *The Rise of Great Britain and Prussia.* New Cambridge Modern History series, vol. 6. New York: Cambridge University Press, 1970.

Carsten, F. L., ed. *The Ascendancy of France, 1648–1688.* New Cambridge Modern History series, vol. 5. New York: Cambridge University Press, 1961.

Cooper, J. P., ed. *The Decline of Spain and the Thirty Years' War, 1609–48/59.* New Cambridge Modern History series, vol. 4. New York: Cambridge University Press, 1970.

Descartes, René. *Discourse on Method and Other Writings*. Baltimore: Penguin, 1968. (PB)

Fay, S. B. *The Rise of Brandenburg-Prussia to 1786*. Rev. ed. New York: Holt, Rinehart and Winston, 1970.

Friedrich, C. J. *The Age of the Baroque, 1610–1660*. New York: Harper & Row, 1962. (PB)

Hill, Christopher. *Puritanism and Revolution*. New York: Schocken, 1964. (PB)

Kliuchevsky, V. O. *Course in Russian History: The Seventeenth Century*. New York: Quadrangle, 1968. (PB)

Lewis, W. H. *The Splendid Century*. New York: Morrow, 1971. (PB)

Locke, John. *Two Treatises of Civil Government*. Darien, Conn.: Hafner, 1947. (PB)

Lough, John. *An Introduction to Seventeenth-Century France*. 2d. ed. New York: McKay, 1969. (PB)

Nussbaum, F. L. *The Triumph of Science and Reason, 1660–1685*. New York: Harper & Row, 1962. (PB)

Ogg, David. *Europe in the Seventeenth Century*. New York: Macmillan, 1962. (PB)

Trevelyan, George M. *England under the Stuarts*. New York: Barnes and Noble, 1961. (PB)

Wedgwood, C. V. *A Coffin for King Charles*. New York: Macmillan, 1964. (PB)

———. *Richelieu and the French Monarchy*. New York: Macmillan, 1966. (PB)

———. *The Thirty Years' War*. Garden City, N. Y.: Doubleday, 1961. (PB)

Wolf, John B. *The Emergence of the Great Powers, 1685–1715*. New York: Harper & Row, 1962. (PB)

———. *Louis XIV*. New York: Norton, 1968. (PB)

Eighteenth Century

Becker, Carl. *The Heavenly City of the Eighteenth-Century Philosophers*. New Haven: Yale University Press, 1932. (PB)

Brinton, Crane. *A Decade of Revolution, 1789–1799*. New York: Harper & Row, 1963. (PB)

Bruun, Geoffrey. *Europe and the French Imperium, 1799–1814*. New York: Harper & Row, 1963. (PB)

Burke, Edmund. *Reflections on the Revolution in France*. New York: Holt, Rinehart and Winston, 1962. (PB)

Dorn, W. L. *Competition for Empire, 1740–1763.* New York: Harper & Row, 1963. (PB)

Gagliardo, John G. *Enlightened Despotism.* 2d. ed. New York: T. Y. Crowell, 1967. (PB)

Gay, Peter. *The Enlightenment: An Interpretation.* 2 vols. New York: Knopf, 1966, 1969.

Gooch, G. P. *Frederick the Great: The Ruler, the Writer, the Man.* Hamden, Conn.: Shoe String, 1962. (PB)

Goodwin, A., ed. *The American and French Revolutions.* New Cambridge Modern History series, vol. 8. New York: Cambridge University Press, 1965.

————. *The French Revolution.* New York: Harper & Row, 1962. (PB)

Lefebvre, Georges. *The Coming of the French Revolution.* Princeton, N. J.: Princeton University Press, 1947. (PB)

————. *The French Revolution, 1789–1799.* 2 vols. New York: Columbia University Press, 1962, 1964.

————. *Napoleon.* 2 vols. New York: Columbia University Press, 1969.

Lindsay, J. O., ed. *The Old Regime, 1713–1763.* New Cambridge Modern History series, vol. 7. New York: Cambridge University Press, 1957.

Malthus, T. R. *Population: The First Essay.* Ann Arbor, Mich.: University of Michigan Press, 1959. (PB)

Mantoux, Paul. *The Industrial Revolution in the Eighteenth Century.* Rev. ed. New York: Harper & Row, 1961. (PB)

Palmer, R. R. *The Age of Democratic Revolution.* 2 vols. Princeton, N. J.: Princeton University Press, 1969, 1970.

Plumb, J. H. *England in the Eighteenth Century: 1714–1815.* Baltimore: Penguin, 1950. (PB)

Rossiter, Clinton. *The First American Revolution.* New York: Harcourt Brace Jovanovich, 1956. (PB)

Sumner, Benedict H. *Peter the Great and the Emergence of Russia.* New York: Macmillan, 1962. (PB)

Tocqueville, Alexis de. *The Old Regime and the French Revolution.* Garden City, N. Y.: Doubleday, 1955. (PB)

Thomson, Gladys Scott. *Catherine the Great and the Expansion of Russia.* New York: Macmillan, 1962. (PB)

Voltaire. *Candide.* Rev. ed. Havens, G. R., ed. New York: Holt, Rinehart and Winston, 1969. (PB)

Nineteenth Century

Artz, Frederick B. *Reaction and Revolution: 1814–1832.* New York: Harper & Row, 1968. (PB)

Ashton, Thomas S. *The Industrial Revolution, 1760–1830.* New York: Oxford University Press, 1948. (PB)

Bury, J. P. T., ed. *The Zenith of European Power, 1830–1870.* New Cambridge Modern History series, vol. 10. New York: Cambridge University Press, 1964.

Crawley, C. W., ed. *War and Peace in an Age of Upheaval, 1793–1830.* New Cambridge Modern History series, vol. 9. New York: Cambridge University Press, 1965.

Kissinger, Henry A. *A World Restored: The Politics of Conservatism in a Revolutionary Age.* Boston: Houghton Mifflin, 1973. (PB)

Kohn, Hans. *The Idea of Nationalism.* New York: Macmillan, 1961. (PB)

Langer, William L., ed. *Political and Social Upheaval: 1832–1852.* New York: Harper & Row, 1969. (PB)

Namier, Lewis B. *Eighteen-Forty-Eight: Revolution of the Intellectuals.* Garden City, N. Y.: Doubleday, 1964. (PB)

Nicolson, Harold. *The Congress of Vienna.* New York: Harcourt Brace Jovanovich, 1970. (PB)

Ruggiero, Guido de. *The History of European Liberalism.* Boston: Beacon, 1959. (PB)

Schapiro, J. Salwyn. *Liberalism: Its Meaning and History.* New York: Van Nostrand Reinhold, 1958. (PB)

Shafer, Boyd. *Nationalism: Myth and Reality.* New York: Harcourt Brace Jovanovich, 1962. (PB)

Toynbee, Arnold. *The Industrial Revolution.* Boston: Beacon, 1956. (PB)

Woodward, E. L. *Three Studies in European Conservatism.* Garden City, N.Y.: Doubleday, 1963. (PB)

Index